W9-CBZ-018

AFTER THE WAR

AFTER THE WAR

*The Lives and Images of
Major Civil War Figures
After the Shooting Stopped*

DAVID HARDIN

CUMMINGS LIBRARY
THE PINE SCHOOL
HOBE SOUND, FLORIDA

Ivan R. Dee
CHICAGO 2010

AFTER THE WAR. Copyright © 2010 by David Hardin. All rights reserved, including the right to reproduce this book or portions thereof in any form. For information, address: Ivan R. Dee, Publisher, 1332 North Halsted Street, Chicago 60642, a member of the Rowman & Littlefield Publishing Group. Manufactured in the United States of America and printed on acid-free paper.

www.ivanrdee.com

Library of Congress Cataloging-in-Publication Data:
Hardin, David, 1940–
After the war : the lives and images of major Civil War
figures after the shooting stopped / David Hardin.
p. cm.
Includes bibliographical references and index.
ISBN 978-1-56663-859-3 (cloth : alk. paper)
1. United States—History—Civil War, 1861–1865—Biography.
2. United States—History—Civil War, 1861–1865—Influence. I. Title.
E467.H285 2010
973.7092'2—dc22
[B]   2010008819

To JONA
with love

CONTENTS

FOREWORD

FOR MANY of the principal figures of the American Civil War, the years afterward would tend toward the tragic even among the victors: a bankrupt former president; a mad presidential widow; a famous general with a family insanity streak. Those defeated would feel like earthquake survivors, trying to get their bearings in another world while caught between a beloved past and an incoherent future.

Whether Northerner or Southerner—or, as in the case of Union General George Thomas, a share of both—their lives were ended and begun anew by four years of war. Often they had to draw upon the courage that had got them through the war, but less to conquer than simply to endure. Inevitably, some would bring along the same defect that had made their wartime experience so memorable to history. A few would triumph—again, or finally—but would not live to see it. Their children would also have roles. The outcomes are a feast of irony.

My aim in this book is to tell some of these stories of the years beyond the war. None of them is secret; most, though, may be little known. Collectively they also serve up a portrait of cataclysmic change, of a divided nation that went to the extreme of war, of a defeated South uncertain of conciliation, of a hungry North turning west for its next feast. The antebellum period and the Gilded Age also make their appearances, inviting further knowledge of the family tree that has led to present times. If there is a lesson, it is that a democracy, a republic, can indeed be stood on its head from within, and having been so stood is capable of having it done again.

This book, though, is mostly about people. Even in their wildest dreams before the war, none could have foreseen themselves afterward. None could have anticipated the new world they would enter. It was as if they would walk through separate doors, one opening upon radiant sun, the other upon cavernous darkness, and yet their paths converging in a sort of grey light of fierce humility. Perhaps only Confederate General Joseph Johnston stayed defiant to the end—not on behalf of the old rebellion but by respectfully removing his hat on a wintry day for the passing casket of his foremost Yankee foe.

For this book, much is owed to the small corps of historians and biographers who have gone before. Many of their accounts were written before the internet offered access to archival sources—especially from newspapers—and these sources (with great care) have also been consulted. Every effort has been made to give credit where it's due, in source notes and a bibliography. Opinions not rendered by others are rendered by myself.

Among those I particularly thank (and hold blameless) are Ivan Dee, whose suggestions throughout were invaluable; Richard McMurry, expert on the Confederacy's Army of Tennessee, for offering suggestions regarding the Hood and Johnston chapters; Teresa Roane of the Museum of the Confederacy and Bonnie Coles of the Library of Congress for their help in chasing down letters of Winnie and Varina Davis; the Huntsville and Madison County (Alabama) Public Library for its complete collection of *Confederate Veteran* magazine and *Southern Historical Society Papers*; and my childhood buddy Bill Trebing, who fifty years later explored with me some of the more bygone passages of Nathan Bedford Forrest's Critter Company. I also thank various family members as well as the lost colony of newspaper book editors who over decades have freely bestowed so many copies of the works cited herein.

D. H.

Huntsville, Alabama
April 2010

AFTER THE WAR

· 1 ·

THE DAUGHTER OF
THE CONFEDERACY

Greatness seldom grants immunity from life's ordinary sorrows. They are a debt suddenly come due.

Confederate President Jefferson Davis, like his enemies Abraham Lincoln and General William Tecumseh Sherman, lost a favored son during the Civil War. Each boy had been too young to participate, but their premature deaths from accident or disease would be a payment demanded for what their fathers demanded of everyone else: the sacrifice of a son for an idea, hundreds of thousands of sons.

In these ordinary sorrows the modern observer finds kinship with the past. So much else of the war is fantastic to our times, whether in envisioning the evils of slavery or the courage of unquestioning men marching in resolute ranks head-on into bullet, ball, and grape. The great, the famous, are otherwise elusive, consigned to their bronze memorials and cement pedestals. But something like a child's death is a unifying sorrow in any age, and just for a moment there is a hush. Jeff Davis is within reach. The curtain has been briefly raised.

Joseph Davis had just turned five years old on the day he died in April 1864. He was playing in the executive mansion, the family's Richmond, Virginia, home, and fell from a high balcony onto a brick pavement below. The price of greatness, of power, of responsibility for a rebellious nation was never more evident as affairs pressed

3

upon the father regardless of this most personal blow. At last, to a request for more troops, Davis lamented, "I must have this day with my little child." He fled toward privacy and did not show himself.

The South Carolina diarist Mary Chesnut would complete this picture of unseen but evident grief. A friend of Davis's wife Varina, Mrs. Chesnut had a knack for often being in the wrong place at the right time. Upon the news of the child's death she had rushed to the house with Varina's hysterical sister Margaret (Maggie) Howell:

"As I sat in the drawing room, I could hear the tramp of Mr. Davis's step as he walked up and down the room above—not another sound. The whole house was as silent as death. . . .

"Poor little Joe, the good child of the family, so gentle and affectionate, he used to run in and say his prayers at his father's knee. Now he was laid out somewhere above us—crushed. . . .

"Before I left the house I saw him lying there, white and beautiful as an angel—covered with flowers.

"Catherine, his nurse, lying flat on the floor by his side, weeping and wailing as only an Irish woman can.

"As I walked home . . . I stopped to tell the Prestons. There I met Wade Hampton, who walked home with me. Even then! He told me again the story of his row with General Lee. I could see or hear nothing but little Joe and the brokenhearted mother and father. And Mr. Davis's step still sounded in my ear as he walked that floor the livelong night."

Jefferson and Varina Davis had six children, four of them boys. None of the boys outlived his parents, and of the two girls only the oldest, another Margaret, married and had children of her own. The second daughter and sixth child, named Varina Anne, was born in June 1864, less than two months after the death of Joe and less than a year before the war's end.

Joe, according to his mother, "was Mr. Davis's hope and greatest joy in life." In later years, however, Davis would turn to his youngest girl who served him in place of a son. Varina Anne was first "Piecake" to the family, then came to be called "Winnie." It was a nickname Davis had first bestowed upon his wife. The daughter was to explain that it derived from "an Indian name meaning bright, or sunny."

Jefferson Davis was a reluctant president. Given the choice, he would have much preferred to relive his frontier and Mexican War days and lead an army with his dear friend Albert Sidney Johnston. Nonetheless, and with his usual austere manner, he accepted the political cross laid upon him by his fellow members of the Cotton Kingdom. Davis would cling to the Cause of constitutional secession as tenaciously as he would stand by his friends and his mistakes— they often being the same. A postwar prison cell didn't modify his views in the slightest. Posterity would paint him as a stiff-necked man of forbidding presence, and even about his grief there was a grim if pacing stoicism. Yet there were things about Jeff Davis that might still surprise.

By early 1877, at age sixty-nine, Davis was staying in a cottage on the grounds of a Gulf Coast estate. This was Beauvoir, whose white, veranda-wrapped house near Biloxi overlooked the placid Mississippi Sound. There, as guest of the widowed Sarah Dorsey, Davis worked on his massive defense, *The Rise and Fall of the Confederate Government*. Mrs. Dorsey, herself a writer under the pen name Filia, served as Davis's amanuensis. This would seem to be a most convenient and even perfect arrangement except that wife Varina was in Europe when the informal partnership was decided. Varina, to say the least, was upset when newspaper stories reached her about her husband's helper.

Varina's attitude wasn't wholly without cause. A few years earlier, in 1871, the *Louisville* (Kentucky) *Commercial* had gleefully reported the efforts of a railroad conductor to dislodge Davis from the lower berth of a train's sleeping car during a run to Huntsville, Alabama. The berth was also occupied by an unidentified female. The story gained wider circulation in the *New York Times* and other papers. While publicly the lady remained nameless, gossip in Memphis, Tennessee—where the two were seen together and had boarded— alleged her to be Virginia Clay. Her still-alive husband, Clement Clay, was a former senator from Alabama who had shared Davis's jail at Fortress Monroe, Virginia. Varina and the children had been in Baltimore at the time, but she could hardly have missed the story.

Thus when Varina returned from Europe she chose not to live at Beauvoir but with her married daughter, Margaret Davis Hayes, in Memphis. Only in the following year did Varina relent to join her husband several hundred miles away.

In early 1879, Mrs. Dorsey sold Beauvoir to Davis for future payments totaling $5,500. She had kept secret that she was dying of cancer and had moved to nearby New Orleans, where she soon succumbed. The widow left her property, including Beauvoir, to Davis. This came despite the wishes of Dorsey family members who sued the ex-president, but unsuccessfully.

The Jefferson Davis who commanded not only the widow's loyalty but much of the postwar South's had, during the war, faced the burdens of a quarrelsome Confederacy, a relentless North, and an unsympathetic world. In the years following, the troubles had not let up. His bitterest enemies during the war had included generals in grey such as Joseph Johnston and P. G. T. Beauregard, and the rancor endured ever after. The deaths of children and the on-again, off-again sparring with Varina were blows that struck at the heart.

Like so many of the planter class, Davis had been left broke and in debt by the war. The cumbersome *Rise and Fall* failed to be a financial success. Prison had aggravated his personal constitution, which had seldom been healthy: fevers and an eye disease were longtime companions. He had worked at his writings though partly blind.

The gift of Beauvoir was a godsend for Davis. Imagining him walking along the beach just beyond and tossing sticks into the surf for his dogs to fetch humanizes the historical portrait. One animal, a part-Russian bulldog named Traveler, was a vicious brute trained as a bodyguard, and he and Davis were greatly attached. By one account, Traveler was originally acquired as a pup by Mrs. Dorsey and her husband while in Europe, and had saved her life from an attacker during a trip to the Middle East. The dog was similarly protective of Davis. On their beach walks Traveler would trot between Davis and the surf, tugging at his clothing if he strayed too close to a wave. Beauvoir's overnight guests had to pass muster with Traveler too, and his patrols on the encircling veranda made it possible to keep windows and doors unlocked.

For all his ferocity, Traveler was gentle with children—as was his owner. But like his owner, he also had his enemies. Traveler seems to have been poisoned.

There is also this portrait of pre-Varina Beauvoir as painted by Davis in 1877 in a letter to "My darling Baby" (Winnie), who had been enrolled in a school in Germany:

"The grounds are extensive and shaded by live oaks, magnolias, cedars, etc., etc. The sea is immediately in front, and an extensive orange orchard is near. Beyond that is one of those clear brooks, common to the pine woods, its banks lined with a tangled wood of sweet bay, wild olive, and vines.

"Then comes a vineyard, then a railroad, and then stretching far far away a forest of stately long-leaved pine. By night I hear the murmur of the sea rolling on the beach, by day a short walk brings one to where the winds sigh through the pines, a sad yet soothing sound. . . ."

"Sad yet soothing"—the Old South lingering and calling to its fallen leader, in mutual mourning but still proud. Could death be anything but near?

*

OF COURSE, plenty of people were still about who would not allow the antebellum South to expire under any circumstance. Although the Confederacy had been smashed, the South would endure. It might not rise again in the same form, but at least it could preserve certain attributes of the prewar society—in memory, if nothing else—as if they were precious heirlooms. That the South would become impossibly idealized would simply serve to immortalize it.

Just enough honor, beauty, hospitality, and gallantry had existed among Southerners before the war—whether recollected by diaries and maiden aunts or lavished upon the chivalric characters of Southern-admired novels—that these qualities now, in reflection, were more than generously distributed among the people as a whole.

In the shame of defeat and the squalor of Reconstruction, Southerners were again eager to fasten on to these cavalier notions. Mark

Twain in his *Life on the Mississippi* might jeer at the influence of Sir Walter Scott and his "Middle-Age sham civilization" for culturally misleading Southerners before the war. No matter. It was still how the South was often seen and remembered. It would later take William Faulkner and his Snopses and Sutpens and the revived Ku Klux Klan to begin altering that image. Until then, Southern doubters of the legend were as likely to put themselves at social risk for decades after the war, just as they would have for decades before.

Now, upon this rather makeshift stage with its musty-smelling costumes strode Winnie Davis. Glorified for her birthright, she was a symbol of old-guard expectations, not just for her own generation but of those to come, perhaps in countless series. God, in fact, might yet ordain a flawless bloodline were she to marry a Virginian heir of Robert E. Lee, or a reasonable (and wealthier) facsimile. Certainly it would have to be someone loyal to Jeff Davis. That left out even the farthest cousins of Joe Johnston or Beauregard or their fellow comrade-in-arms James Longstreet, now a turncoat Republican.

The Old South, the old dream, the Confederacy, states' rights, headlong courage, white male dominance, female virtue—the whole package, with the possible exception of the *code duello*—would be thrust as a bride's bouquet into young and slightly trembling hands for eternal preservation. Sometimes Southerners seemed to be in love with death.

Winnie had been a long time away, having spent seven years of her life in Europe. Most were at a boarding school in Karlsruhe. When fifteen she seemed a typical teenager, spoiled and full of herself. She wrote to her mother about her German school: "The new girls are all very fond of me but I am not so fond of them as I ought to be because I can not agree with their way of thinking. They are so high-church that they make objections to praying in an unconcecrated church and an awful fuss about things that are natural, for instance standing at prayers and sitting to sing."

When Winnie finally arrived at her new home on the Mississippi coast, it was 1881 and she was seventeen. Davis had been in his mid-fifties when she was born and so by this time must have appeared even more like a grandfather. Winnie, a precocious child, had been

Varina Anne "Winnie" Davis's famous father replied that "death would be preferable" before he would consent to her marrying the Yankee grandson of an abolitionist. Although Jefferson Davis eventually changed his mind, the South that had christened Winnie "Daughter of the Confederacy" never did. This photograph was taken in 1888, when she was in love with Alfred Wilkinson. *(Courtesy of the Museum of the Confederacy, Richmond, Virginia)*

schooled in the graces of her class—a class whittled considerably by war. She was acknowledged as competent in art, music, and literary composition. She also brought home a German accent, which she could never entirely shake.

It may be assumed that her appearance at this time approximated that recalled at her death, as possessing an olive complexion, "large, intellectual, bright eyes," and a tall body with small hands and feet— "the latter being particularly noticeable by the gracefully arched insteps, all characterizing her as a type of the Southern woman." In photographs she fortunately more favors her mother, though the grey eyes seem to have her father's resoluteness. In a later image, however, the impression is of a certain sadness, perhaps resignation. There would be reason for this.

But it could wait. Winnie was Davis's delight, and he was, to her, "My darling Father." Father and daughter would take long walks along the beach. Once she asked him what he would do if he could live his life over. The old West Pointer replied, "I would be a cavalry officer, and break squares."

They played backgammon and euchre at night, using buttons for gold. The gentleness came out in Davis. That most inflexible of men would unbend. Once he cautioned Winnie not to step on a bug: "Is there not room in the world, little daughter, for you and that harmless insect, too?" He had a room adjacent to his study converted into an art studio for her. She in turn would play Chopin and other of his favorites upon Beauvoir's piano.

Visitors to Beauvoir came from all over: friends and strangers, Northern as well as Southern war veterans, pesky journalists, professors, clerics—even Oscar Wilde. Hospitality must have taken a Traveler-like bite out of the family purse. Nonetheless Winnie helped with the throng, charming and gracious, an ideal woman for the South of the coming century. Winnie had a social life in New Orleans too, and was among the adored debs at Mardi Gras.

The daughter also accompanied Davis on his journeys. In 1886 she went with him on an arduous railroad trip to Alabama and Georgia to dedicate monuments and otherwise celebrate the Lost Cause with old Rebels. As one story goes, Davis was taken ill on his train just before the unveiling of a monument in Georgia. General John B. Gordon, a quick-thinking man, pushed Winnie to the back platform of the coach as a stand-in. It was there he introduced her as the "Daughter of the Confederacy." The veterans whooped, and the name stuck for life. An admiring postcard would be created with her profile within a heroine's wreath—above her head her name, below the wreath in script the magic *Daughter of the Confederacy*.

In a way, Winnie was a rather odd selection for the South. Varina's biographer Joan Cashin has noted that Winnie in "many respects . . . was scarcely an American. . . . In Karlsruhe she kept a scrapbook with numerous mementoes from such figures as Bismarck and Moltke, and a few images from her native country, including a Confederate flag. She was fluent in German and French, and her accent when she spoke English was mittel-European. Sometimes Winnie had to look up words such as *gingham* in the dictionary, and she made mistakes in usage, as if she were trying to translate German noun constructions into English."

It didn't matter. Nor did it matter that she had barely participated in the Confederacy's brief life, or that she had spent a good part of her existence outside its member states. She was Jeff Davis's child, the man who in the absence of the dead Lee most represented the Old South, the old dream, the old reassurance of states' rightness and the true reason for rebellion and war. The essence would be passed along with the torch.

If Winnie had any misgivings about this image, she seems not to have raised them publicly. Her often-ailing father also needed her help and companionship, which she readily gave. When illness curtailed his engagements, she filled in.

Her mother appears to have had for Winnie bigger dreams of family connections. Varina herself was later to play the role of Widow of the Confederacy, defending the truth of her husband's (and the South's) sacrifice. Still, there seems little appreciation by either parent at this time (much less by Winnie) for how such expectation and duty could also be an unremitting shackle, a sort of emotional slavery. Winnie had celebrity, Southern Victorian style, but celebrity's pitfalls could be as soul-depleting then as they are today.

In any case, obedient and loving daughter that she was, Winnie could scarcely renounce the connection or decline her service. Davis himself, rapidly nearing and then catching up with eighty years, counted heavily on her capable presence. She accompanied him on his trip to Montgomery, Alabama, and Atlanta without Varina. She laughingly pinned Confederate emblems on the lapels of Yankee reporters, and intervened (like the late guard dog) between the frail Davis and the grasping sea of hands that reached out to touch him.

In his public remarks Davis never urged another Fort Sumter. But his continued defense of states' rights, his particular reading of the Constitution, and his touchy comparison of the late rebellion to that of the glorified colonial revolution against the British were not the sorts of things Northerners wanted to hear.

Eleven years after the war Congress had voted a blanket amnesty to all the old Confederates except the die-hard Davis. Although he was often urged to seek a pardon, which would allow him to run for office, he refused. Other Southerners feared he might change his mind on his deathbed—an admission of error applicable to every Rebel. They needn't have worried. Davis remained true, and Congress did not restore his citizenship until 1978, almost ninety years after his death.

On the other hand, Davis openly advocated reconciliation. His last speech, made before a group of young men in Mississippi City in 1888, is notably eloquent:

". . . The faces I see before me are those of young men; had I not known this I would not have appeared before you. Men in whose hands the destinies of our Southland lie, for love of her I break my silence, to speak to you a few words of respectful admonition. The past is dead; let it bury its dead, its hopes and its aspirations; before you lies a future—a future full of golden promise; a future of expanding national glory, before which all the world shall stand amazed. Let me beseech you to lay aside all rancor, all bitter sectional feeling, and to make your places in the ranks of those who will bring about a consummation devoutly to be wished—a reunited country."

If Davis would have the South move on and reconcile with the North, he was soon to be put most sorely and personally to the test.

*

IN 1878, the same year Davis was trying to lure Varina to Beauvoir, a distant relative, Kate Davis, married the journalism dynamo Joseph Pulitzer. In 1883, Pulitzer bought the *New York World* from Jay Gould. A few years later Winnie was a guest of Kate and her husband. While in New York, a trip to visit family friends in upstate Syracuse put Winnie at a party. Apparently some of the Yankee locals were rude to the Daughter of the Confederacy. A young man present rose in defense of the Southern cause—and, incidentally, Winnie.

He was Alfred (Fred) Wilkinson, Jr., a Syracuse patent attorney then in his late twenties and grandson of Samuel May, a prominent abolitionist. He was also unattached. Winnie was in her early twenties and daughter of the man who had tried his best to break up the United States of America. It was love at first sight. Winnie, however, kept it from her parents back at Beauvoir. She and Wilkinson traded letters and met again during another of Winnie's visits to the Pulitzers.

At home, Winnie was also filling in at various veterans' gatherings and memorials for Davis, who had suffered a heart ailment in 1887. By now Winnie had been exposed to a sufficient number of unreconstructed Rebels to realize the delicacy of her situation. Kissing and making up was no more than metaphor when applied to the Confederacy's daughter. For a long time Winnie kept her secret, but the dilemma took its toll. Her health began to flag. Her father was baffled and distressed by the change. It is highly probable that concerns for *his* health also affected her's.

One day Wilkinson showed up at Beauvoir to ask Davis for Winnie's hand. It is said that when informed by Varina of Wilkinson's purpose, Davis replied, "Death would be preferable." He would never consent. Winnie, "white as death," declared she could never love another but would obey.

Then Davis began to find the young lawyer interesting. Wilkinson, it seems, was also a states' rights man. Davis invited him to stay longer. He even took him to a pier bathhouse one night where, under the light of flares, they watched the Gulf flounders—a guest's rare privilege. Wilkinson also went to work on Varina. Although his father, a banker, had lost most of the family fortune in a scandal, Wilkinson assured her he could make a home for Winnie. The son had bought the Wilkinson Syracuse mansion at auction, and family females lived within.

Consent, however, was still withheld. Davis not only had a daughter to please; he had the *South*.

Certainly better than Winnie, Jeff Davis knew the venom that was out there. He probably figured that many who had supported him against Joe Johnston and the like would never forgive this ultimate surrender—this yielding of sacred flesh—to Northern money changers with abolitionist blood ties. It would be worse even than accepting a federal pardon. Doors would be slammed shut—though more to his wife and daughter than to himself with such poor health.

On the other hand, there was Winnie's health. The miasma-like influence of thwarted romance might grow beyond repair. Davis also knew a little about young love and its loss. When he was Wilkinson's age, he had married Sarah Knox Taylor over the objections of her father, the future president Zachary Taylor. The bride had died of malaria three months later.

The flame for "Knoxie" had never quite gone out, and besides: perhaps a marriage of North and South might not be such a bad thing, particularly after his fine speeches. . . . Jeff Davis, the old ramrod horse soldier, had taken heat many times before. Finally, he gave his consent.

It was to be among his last executive decisions.

Accounts vary on when and how the news of Winnie's engagement got out. One says a radiant Winnie blabbed it to a neighbor. More likely, it wasn't generally known until announced in the newspapers in April 1890, four months after Davis's death.

The previous October, Winnie, probably due to stress, had gone to Europe with the Pulitzers for her health. In November 1889, Davis's own precarious health grew worse. Winnie, informed by letter from her mother that he had been sick but was better, was guilt-stricken. On December 5, 1889, she wrote to her father from Paris,

"My dearest, I know now that you were suffering all the time, and I cannot get reconciled to the idea of my having, no matter how unwittingly, left you while you were ill. . . ."

She concluded: "Dearest darling Father, when as now, I want to tell you how much I love you I grow bewildered; what words to choose which are able to express to you the devoted love and tenderness of which my heart is and always will be full for you, my darling Father. My pen is the mutest thing about me unfortunately and when I am away from you I can only think, and think, and love you for your goodness and tenderness, with which you covered me as with a cloak, all through my little childhood, screening my faults and answering my unreasonable questions with always an honest reply, the rarest thing given to a child in the world. And so, I will end by saying as I began 'My darling Father.' Good-night." She signed it "Your Winnanne."

The letter was too late to reach Davis an ocean away. He died on December 6.

*

PERHAPS had Davis hung on for a while longer, a marriage would have gone forward out of the man's sheer stubbornness. His consent had been that rarity of rarities: Jefferson Davis had changed his mind.

But there was no getting around the reaction when the engagement became known in the South. Condemnatory and threatening letters arrived at Beauvoir from veterans and strangers. Disapproval poured in from friends as well, including General Jubal Early, the self-appointed Watchdog of the Confederacy.

Varina wrote Early at least twice trying to smooth things over— that the groom-to-be was only a child during the war, was a states' rights Democrat and able to support Winnie. Early's replies don't survive, but Varina's letters suggest he apparently complained of being deceived, and he especially didn't like Wilkinson's abolitionist roots. In the collective view, Winnie belonged to the South. Giving her up to a Yankee was more despoilment of the past and worse than betrayal. It was . . . *without honor!*

In his last year Davis, with Varina's help, had completed *A Short History of the Confederate States* and begun dictating his memoirs. After his death, Varina took on the latter project. She had literary abilities and was up to the task. *Jefferson Davis, Ex-President of the Confederate States of America: A Memoir by His Wife* ran to two volumes. Scold and supporter, Varina had faithfully ridden fortune's roller coaster with her husband. She had also made clear that it wasn't always willingly. A year before the war she had commented presciently, "The South will secede if Lincoln is made president. They will make Mr. Davis president of the Southern side. And the whole thing is bound to be a failure."

As first lady, Varina could be brutally unpolitical. With war clouds looming, a woman of her own age once worried what she would do if made a widow. Varina's reply was merciless: "If ——— is the best you could do when you were fresh and young, what better chance could you hope for, old?" In the truest sense a survivor, Varina was more than a match for her daughter, and in her own way quite as remarkable as her husband.

Winnie, meanwhile, had also emerged as a writer. She had been drawn to the Irish rebel Robert Emmet, whose execution in 1803 had brought a swift end to a romance that was later the subject of poems by Thomas Moore and a story by Washington Irving. Winnie's biographic monograph, "An Irish Knight of the 19th Century," was privately published during the time she and Wilkinson were exchanging letters.

It is to wonder whether she saw any of herself and her young man in Emmet's futile love and tragic outcome, or whether it simply appealed to a sentimental Victorian heart. The title alone suggests Sir Walter was still not cold in his grave. Although his was an antebellum influence and technically before Winnie's time, time itself was strangely at odds throughout her life. Jefferson Davis could urge young men to forsake yesterday and look to tomorrow, but the Old South and the wartime past were all around his daughter too. Winnie was their prisoner.

In his will Davis left Beauvoir to Winnie, and she and her mother stayed there while Varina finished her memoirs. In the process Varina was attracted to New York, where Pulitzer's *World* offered her $1,200 a year for articles. In 1891 both women moved to the big city. In New York, Varina wrote various newspaper and magazine pieces.

Winnie tried journalism too but also would write two romantic novels. She was described as having "a clear style, a sprightly manner that was almost witty, and a remarkable flow of story telling power." She published under the name Varina Anne Jefferson Davis, while her mother—should there be no mistaking—had her own name changed to Varina Jefferson-Davis. Winnie's letters suggest an odd set of friends. Two from 1892 are filled with futile advice to the Marquis de Ruvigny, warning him against his own lost cause to restore the Stuarts to the British throne.

In the meantime, what of love and Fred Wilkinson?

For a while, matters seemed to calm down. In October 1890, however, reports came from New Orleans that the engagement with Winnie was no more. Wilkinson confirmed them to the Northern press. "Miss Davis's health," he explained, "has been poor for some time, and it was for the purpose of gaining strength that she went abroad. She returned in only a slightly improved condition, and but a few weeks ago she expressed the wish of both herself and her estimable mother that the engagement cease."

The press took the story a bit further. Shortly before the break-off, inquiries were made by a "prominent gentleman of Mississippi concerning Mr. Wilkinson's financial and social standing, his ability as a young attorney, and his prospects. That was soon after the burning of the old Wilkinson mansion in July. . . ." The inquiries tellingly included the family banking scandal and whether properties were transferred to dodge creditors. A recent conjecture even suggests that the mansion might have been torched by one of Winnie's unreconstructed admirers. Varina, though, was likely the greatest influence, or, as a newspaper put it: ". . . Miss Winnie having severed the engagement out of deference to her mother's wishes."

Varina had a lot of practice protecting Winnie, and a lot of reasons. One of them was the quiet disgrace of Margaret Howell, who bore the son of an unnamed father a year after the war. A romantic girl such as Winnie might grow up even more vulnerable than a wild one like Maggie, vulnerable not just to sex but to genteel poverty. So Varina's daughter was saved—yet for whom? Winnie, morally pure, never fully recovered her physical health. And having given her heart to Fred, she was to be no man's wife.

So was it health, or money, or was it yet the Old South's opprobrium that finally decided the matter? Southerners who counted showed little sign of reconciliation to the marriage. They looked to the great man's daughter as they had looked to the great man at the outset of the Confederacy, to shoulder the burden for the rest of them. They had struck Davis at his weakest spot: his formidable sense of duty. In a way, the same (if more ethereal) demand had been made of Winnie, the Daughter of the Confederacy.

Winnie's health, at any rate, seems not to have been an objection of Wilkinson, who also would stay unmarried. Who had been checking him out in Syracuse? Was it at Varina's instigation, or independently done—a "prominent gentleman of Mississippi" laying out the injurious evidence that Varina could not deny? This time the South had won. Maybe that was the reason New York City looked so good to two exhausted ladies.

Winnie Davis died in 1898 of "malarial gastritis" at the Rhode Island hotel where she and her mother were staying for the summer. The illness was brought about in another service to the South she had left. She had filled in for Varina at a veterans' gathering in Atlanta and returned sick to Rhode Island after riding in an open carriage in the rain. Winnie was only thirty-four. She had an enormous funeral—the blot of the engagement forgiven if not forgotten—and was buried next to her father in the Confederacy's last capital of Richmond, Virginia.

Her mother lived to be eighty and died of pneumonia in New York in 1906. Varina too was given a big sendoff (Teddy Roosevelt sent flowers). After Winnie's death, Varina had sold Beauvoir to the State of Mississippi to be used as an old soldiers' home and shrine to her husband. In 2005 the property and all within caught the full brunt of Hurricane Katrina.

*

IT WAS within the realm of chance that Winnie Davis might have had a happier life had she become the wife of Alfred Wilkinson, Jr. Somehow he might have reestablished the family fortune; good health might have magically returned; the South might yet have looked away. That none of this occurred presumes a tragedy.

And yet everything seems destined to have happened exactly as it did. Unless Jefferson Davis had left his daughter in Europe, which he could not have afforded to do even had he considered it, Winnie's participation in the salvaging of the Lost Cause was inevitable. There was never to be any "Son of the Confederacy" to divert attention, assuming that the mantle could be placed only upon the shoulders of its lone president's heirs. The parents' sole male child who lived to adulthood, Jeff Jr., wasn't especially promising (he had been expelled from Virginia Military Institute) and in 1878 had died in Memphis at age twenty-one of yellow fever.

But even were there male candidates, the preservation in public memory of the Old South and the war to save it became more the New Cause of the females left behind. They certainly outnumbered the veterans who had returned with diseased lungs, mangled limbs, and battlefield nightmares. The women, of course, had overseen the loss of fathers, husbands, sons, brothers, and sweethearts. They had suffered in their own way every bit as much as the family soldier, and had lost every bit as much, if not more. The Negro was now free in their midst; the chance for marriage and escape was diminished; and a secure white society, as it had been, was blown apart every bit as much as the armies at Shiloh and Gettysburg.

If the fallen Confederates were to be regarded as sacred—and they were—then so was the Cause for which they fought, for which the Southern male and female fought. And if the Cause were stainless and noble, what better representative than a virginal female, preferably young and perceptibly fertile? She thus would stand in for the future, the ultimate response to the North that the Southerner could not really be conquered.

Tiny Rebels would be spawned, not only to replace the dead but to preserve certain forms—good manners, for instance—that would segregate the South from Yankee vulgarity.

Within several years of Jefferson Davis's death, women of the South who were left to tend the graves and raise the monuments would organize as the United Daughters of the Confederacy. Winnie was not stripped of her singular title, by any means, and some UDC chapters would name themselves after her. Aspirants to the title following her death were smote down by General Gordon, who responded "Emphatically, no" to any suggestion that Winnie was replaceable. In 1899 a monument depicting a fallen angel—called the "Angel of Grief"—was unveiled at Winnie's grave site as part of the ceremonies having to do with the UDC's annual convention.

An ode by Dr. Henry Mazyck Clarkson was read to the convention in honor of the monument's dedication, which in part proclaimed:

Distinguished daughter of a race renowned, / In the full flush of faultless womanhood, / Before the world's admiring eyes she stood / A very queen, with every virtue crowned.

Mark Twain would have chortled, but it reflected the temper of the times in the new South—old times there not forgotten.

The United Daughters persist, but notice of Winnie gradually faded. The enigmatic Jefferson Davis and the vivacious Varina were more important and interesting to biographers and other manipulators of the past. A century after the angel monument's unveiling, Winnie artifacts exhibited at a New Orleans museum were being advertised as having belonged to the "Lost Princess of the South."

Like those who chose the opposite side from friends and family before the war, Winnie Davis was not the only person afterward to contend with scorn and abuse for a North-South attachment. It was just that, in her case, disapproval was something on the order of a public referendum. It is to wonder why few if any Southern suitors—as far as is known—did not seriously present themselves at some point. The arrangement would have allowed a secondary celebrity (Son-in-Law of the Confederacy?), and Winnie was by no means unattractive. She had been Queen of Comus at Mardi Gras. She had, among other charms, "gracefully arched insteps."

Still, the Davises had no fortune, and Varina as a mother-in-law might prove vexing. A Southern gallant of prominent family likely to win Varina's approval doubtless would prefer a role other than junior partner, and the Wilkinson affair was destabilizing. Gallantry does have its limits. In any event, the move to New York seemed to eliminate such scenarios.

After Wilkinson, Winnie in fact might have written off any further lover, North or South. Nor, with Davis dead, would she sully his name or that of the South. The dutiful daughter would scarcely have chosen someone he would not have approved of, and keeping watch on her every move were the ancient Rebels back home and their womenfolk. Indeed, she had sworn she could love no other but Wilkinson.

To the watchers, Winnie's disappointments may have symbolically honed her perfection as Daughter of the Confederacy. Her father might have talked of the future, but for a good many Southerners it was always the lost past that was uppermost. The future could never have its mythic grandeur. By this time only an eccentric Jacobite might have met their approval as a groom.

Winnie Davis could avoid in the North what must have become a sort of claustrophobia, even at Beauvoir with its long-leaved pines and murmurs of the sea. But she could not escape the South's sorrow, the pervasive melancholy. Jeff Davis's ghost was always nearby, staring out from every mirror, and so was the legacy of untold thousands of other dead.

How sad, for it meant she could not truly live, though she might mix with gaudy Northern society or throw herself into her work. Her time was not really of her own. It was that of someone else, who had belonged to a glorified but vanished state and civilization.

Winnie Davis, bright, attractive, with a bit of a German accent, joining her father on the sands before Beauvoir, would be among the casualties of a war she had only incomprehensibly witnessed.

· 2 ·

THE CONQUEROR'S
SON

For William Tecumseh Sherman, the lowest point in the Civil War would come in Kentucky during the conflict's first year. There Sherman was sent as a new brigadier to the assistance of Robert Anderson, the hero of Fort Sumter. Anderson and his men had crossed into the state after its neutrality was first violated by Confederate forces. The Confederates were attempting to forestall a Union march on the Mississippi River town of Columbus, and thus brought Kentucky into the war. Some sense of the confusion and consternation—if not outright panic—then present in the state was recollected years later by Sherman in his memoirs.

Step into Sherman's world at that perilous time in September 1861:

"The city [Louisville] was full of all sorts of rumors. The Legislature, moved by considerations of a purely political nature, had taken the step, whatever it was, that amounted to an adherence to the Union, instead of joining the already-seceded States. This was universally known to be a signal for action. For it we were utterly unprepared, whereas the rebels were fully prepared. General Albert Sidney Johnston immediately crossed into Kentucky, and advanced as far as Bowling Green, which he began to fortify, and thence dispatched General [Simon Bolivar] Buckner with a division forward toward Louisville; General [Felix] Zollicoffer, in like manner, entered the State and advanced as far as Somerset. On the day I reached Lou-isville the excitement ran high. It was known that Columbus, Ken-tucky, had been occupied, September 7th,* by a strong rebel force, under Generals [Gideon] Pillow and [Leonidas] Polk, and that Gen-eral [Ulysses] Grant had moved from Cairo [Illinois] and occupied Paducah in force on the 6th. Many of the rebel families expected Buckner to reach Louisville at any moment. That night, General Anderson sent for me, and I found with him Mr. [James] Guthrie, president of the Louisville & Nashville Railroad, who had in his hands a dispatch to the effect that the bridge across Rolling Fork of Salt Creek, less than thirty miles out, had been burned, and that Buckner's force, *en route* for Louisville, had been detained beyond Green River by a train thrown from the track. We learned afterward that a man named Bird had displaced a rail on purpose to throw the train off the track, and thereby give us time."

Matters, however, grew worse. Within weeks Anderson, say-ing he could no longer "stand the mental torture," resigned to be replaced by a reluctant Sherman. To Sherman, there would never be enough time in Kentucky: the army was too green, too few, too ill-equipped. Johnston, "who was a real general," could have united his forces and "walked into Louisville" had he so tried.

Sherman's doubts and worries began to snowball. During a meeting in Louisville with the short-term Secretary of War Simon Cameron, Sherman—who had a troop allotment of about 18,000— declared that he needed 60,000 troops for defense and 200,000 to march on Johnston. Cameron was aghast. "Great God! Where are they to come from?" he exclaimed to Sherman, throwing up his hands.

Soon a memo of their meeting began making the rounds in Washington, where Sherman's "insane" request for 200,000 men was published in the press. Sherman writes that he became aware of a widespread report that "I was 'crazy, insane, and mad.'" Rela-tions with his superiors deteriorated further as Sherman relayed his complaints and fears to Washington. "I again repeat that our force

*The Confederates occupied Columbus on September 4, 1861.

here is out of all proportion to the importance of the position," he said in one report, concluding: "Our defeat would be disastrous to the nation; and to expect of new men, who never bore arms, to do miracles, is not right."

Yet the big battle with Johnston's army still did not come.

By now Sherman himself was questioning his sanity. He ranted in a letter to his wife, Ellen: "Rumors and Reports pour in on me of the overwhelming force collected in front across Green River. . . . To advance would be madness and to stand still folly. . . . The idea of going down to History with a fame such as threatens me nearly makes me crazy. Indeed I may be so now, and the constant application for passes and little things absorbs all my time."

It didn't help when a plan to assist an uprising of Unionists in East Tennessee went awry. The scheme, at the behest of Tennessee senator Andrew Johnson and with President Lincoln's enthusiastic blessing, envisioned sending men under Sherman's subordinate, George H. Thomas, to work with partisans planning to destroy bridges on the vital East Tennessee–Virginia railway. Thomas had even set out, but Sherman, believing the force was about to be trapped, panicked and ordered him to pull back. Johnson, marching with Thomas, was livid. The partisans went ahead with the plan, but unprotected Unionists were rounded up and several hanged.

By this time Sherman had had enough of Kentucky, and his commander, George McClellan, had had enough of Sherman. He quickly granted Sherman's request to be relieved. While waiting for his relief, though, Sherman continued to send out warnings of imminent attack and the virtual doubling of Sidney Johnston's forces.

At this point Sherman's aide was sufficiently moved to telegraph the general's father-in-law in Ohio to "send Mrs. Sherman and her youngest boy to Louisville. There is nothing to alarm you but it is necessary to turn Genl Shermans Mind from responsibility now resting upon him."

Ellen Sherman, however, found reason to be alarmed after arrival. She wrote to Sherman's brother, John: "Knowing insanity to be in the family, and having seen Cump on the verge of it in California I assure you I was tortured by fears, which have been only in part

William Tecumseh Sherman greeted his son Tom's decision to become a Jesuit priest with anger and heartbreak. Later he would say of the Catholic church, "Why should they have taken my splendid boy? They could have brought over thirty priests from Italy in his place." *(Library of Congress)*

relieved since I got here. . . . Cump's mind has been wrought up to a marked state of anxiety which caused him to request McClellan to make the change. . . . I am puzzled to know what to advise or hope for & I am distressed by his melancholy forebodings. . . ." She added, ominously: "He thinks the whole country is gone irrevocably & ruin & desolation are at hand—For God's sake do what you can to cheer him & keep him in the position most advantageous to his mind & reputation. . . ."

Sherman, politically connected on both sides of his family, was packed off to St. Louis where Henry Halleck, an old friend from West Point and California days, was in command, then sent home to Ohio on leave. Meanwhile a Cincinnati newspaper, under the headline GENERAL WILLIAM T. SHERMAN INSANE, accused him of having tried to withdraw his army back across the Ohio River to escape the Confederates. Sherman's brother and father-in-law quickly rushed to Lincoln to contain the damage and save Sherman's career. A few weeks later the Kentucky crisis ended when the Confederates were rolled back all the way to Alabama by the combined if far-flung efforts of Thomas, Grant, and Sherman's successor, Don Carlos Buell.

Sherman would have to wait for the near disaster of Shiloh to renew his march to glory.

*

A SHERMAN BIOGRAPHER, Stanley Hirshson, records that the insanity mentioned by Ellen Sherman came through the maternal side of Sherman's family, the Hoyts. Sherman's grandmother, Mary Raymond Hoyt, was believed to have spent her last years in an asylum, and a maternal uncle, Charles Hoyt, was in and out of an asylum at the time of his death. One Sherman brother, Jim, died a drunk, and two others were plagued by dizzy spells. The aforementioned John Sherman, a congressman and senator from Ohio for whom the Sherman Anti-trust Act is named, died in 1900 after a mental breakdown and not long after resigning as secretary of state. Suspicions and accusations of insanity followed William Tecumseh Sherman from Kentucky onward. Madness would emerge again, in actuality and tragically, in yet another generation.

Although the mercurial Sherman would discover a latent zest for destruction as the war lengthened, his wife's passion had long been turned just as mightily toward religion. Ellen Sherman, as her husband would later say, was "absolutely more Catholic than the pope."

She was born Ellen Ewing and grew up as something of a sister to the young Cump, who was raised in the Ewing household after his father died when Sherman was nine. As man and wife they had eight children despite being separated for long periods by Sherman's various jobs. Ellen could never bear to be absent from other Ewings, particularly her father, Thomas, who had served in the U.S. Senate and as secretary of the Treasury and Interior departments. Two of the Shermans' four sons would die during the war, one as an infant. The other, called Willy or Willie, died at age nine in Memphis of typhoid after he and his mother had visited the general in Mississippi following the Vicksburg campaign.

Ellen's religion, and that of her five brothers and sisters, came from their mother, a Boyle, whose father had fled Ireland. Of his mother-in-law's Catholicism, Sherman would later say "that I am sure that though she loved her children better than herself, she would have seen them die with less pang, than to depart from the 'Faith.'" Ellen's politician father, born a Presbyterian, happily went along, though it was said that Thomas Ewing's real religion was federalism, and more of that rubbed off on the young Sherman than Catholicism. It did not, however, keep the rest of the Ewings, especially Ellen, from trying to convert him.

Priests were frequent visitors to the Ewing household in Lancaster, Ohio, and one was asked after Sherman's arrival to baptize him. Sherman's admiring father had named his son Tecumseh after the Shawnee chief—a name others shortened to "Cump"—and the priest was forced to halt the proceedings when told of it. He pointed out that to be baptized the boy must be named for a saint, not a savage. It being the feast day of Saint William, the baptism resumed for the redesignated *William* Tecumseh Sherman. The general would later insist it was his own father who had also given him the William, but then he never considered himself a Catholic, either.

W.T. (or "Cump") and Ellen Sherman had been married six years when their fourth child and second son, Thomas Ewing Sherman, was born in 1856. The first son, William Ewing or Willy and born two years before, seemed to hold the greatest hopes in Sherman's view and would be mourned by his father as his "Alter ego" after the child's death in 1863. The death would also heighten something of a schism in the household.

Ellen fastened early upon Tom. When less than a year old she informed Sherman that she intended to refer to the infant as Ewing. Before the boy had turned two, Ellen wrote her husband that her "great desire" was to see Ewing become "an eloquent Priest some day." To Sherman, the boy would stay Tom or Tommy, and the father was unequivocally opposed to his becoming a priest.

Ellen wrote of it again during Sherman's 1864–1865 march through Georgia and the Carolinas. In a letter she described the boy as "very backward for eight years old." Her plan was to enroll Tom in the same Catholic academy that his dead brother had attended, adding: "I am anxious that he should be a missionary Priest and join the Paulist Fathers. Of course he will decide for himself but I hope he may be called to that glorious life."

To this Sherman responded: "I will risk his being a Priest—Of course I should regret such a choice and ask that no influence be lent to produce that result—Let him have a fair manly education, and his own instincts will lead him right—I dont care how strict he may be in Religion, but dont want him a Priest, but he is too young for even the thought." Just in case, he also wrote young Tom, "I dont want you to be a Soldier or a Priest but a good useful man."

The pious Ellen seemed never to weary of trying to bring the general to the church. During this same destructive march that the South would condemn for generations—and that would take its own bizarre twist later with Tom Sherman—Ellen wrote her husband: "Why can you not make your great works meritorious by offering them to God and doing them in His honor? If you do this you will perhaps be rewarded with faith & receive for your labors an imperishable crown in the kingdom of God where our dear ones await us. . . . The members of the Sherman family would be glad to see you a

Even before Tom Sherman turned two, his mother Ellen Ewing Sherman hoped he would become "an eloquent Priest some day." The 1868 portrait by G. P. A. Healy shows the devout Ellen with a cross at her bosom. *(Smithsonian American Art Museum / Art Resource)*

Catholic because they fear to see you die without any faith. How you can live since Willy died, without the faith I cannot conceive & from my heart I pity you for my own sufferings since his death have been more than I could have borne without its consolations."

Sometimes Ellen Sherman's letters seemed to raise questions of her own stability, as she wrote when their sixth child, Rachel, was approaching her first birthday in 1862, a year before Willy's death: "She is too sweet to live here long & I pray from my heart that God may take her to Heaven in her loveliness & purity that her eternity may be secure & that we may have one at least of our little flock constantly interceding for us before the throne & in the presence of the Lamb that was slain for our redemption." (Rachel would survive into the next century.)

After Union Colonel Daniel McCook died of a wound received at Kennesaw Mountain, Georgia, in 1864, Ellen wrote to Sherman: "Poor Dan McCook is gone. I am very very sorry and feel truly sad about it, particularly as I fear whilst serving his country he forgot his God. . . . What is time & what is earthly glory to poor Dan McCook now? And our Willy—how differently he now views these things from his home in heaven. May his prayers be your shield & guard until we all join him to be separated no more."

And yet, while Ellen Sherman was writing with eyes uplifted, her husband was concentrating on a war that had intensified in its brutality.

Even before Georgia and South Carolina, the line had blurred between civilians and the military. Sherman's troops torched a Catholic church in Jackson, Mississippi, during the Vicksburg campaign. On the march through Columbia, South Carolina, soldiers drank whiskey from a Catholic communion chalice and burned an Ursuline convent and school—an incident that brought a defense from Ellen when, ten years later, a newspaper attacked Sherman over it. His army would shell noncombatants, and in Georgia Sherman ordered female factory workers and their children put aboard trains and sent north, to wander strange cities. In Columbia, white women were groped for valuables, and black women were raped by his troops.

When Sherman's deliberate profanity embarrassed the religious General Oliver O. Howard (later the namesake of Howard University) and prompted him to leave Sherman's presence, Sherman remarked to another general: "The Christian soldier business is all right in its place. But he [Howard] needn't put on airs when we are among ourselves."

Throughout his life Sherman fought off Ellen's pleas and prayers. Early, in the fifth year of their marriage, he wrote her of a visit while in San Francisco from a Father Gallagher, who had asked jokingly when "I proposed to come into the fold—I told him you had Catholicity enough for a very large family, and that my Catholicity was more catholic than his, as mine embraced all Creation, recognizing the Maker as its head and all religions past, present & future as simple tools in the Great accomplishment yet to be. A little too transcendental for Mr. Gallagher."

Clearly, Sherman and his wife were evenly matched, with neither giving ground. But it is also as if Ellen used their departed Willy to try to outflank her husband and somehow bring him around. Willy was Sherman's deepest grief. The boy's death brought perhaps the most excruciating pain to a man who both inflicted and witnessed so much of it.

*

IN HIS MEMOIRS, Sherman recalled that 1863 family visit to his camp outside Vicksburg: "Willie was then nine years old, was well advanced for his years, and took the most intense interest in the affairs of the army. He was a great favorite with the soldiers, and used to ride with me on horseback in the numerous drills and reviews of the time. He then had the promise of as long a life as any of my children, and displayed more interest in the war than any of them. He was called a 'sergeant' in the [Thirteenth] regular battalion, learned the manual of arms, and regularly attended the parade and guard-mounting of the Thirteenth, back of my camp."

When Sherman was ordered to move his men east by way of Memphis, he and Ellen, Willy, Tom, and the two oldest daughters took a Mississippi River steamboat together back to Tennessee. "When the boat was ready to start," Sherman continued, "Willie was missing. Mrs. Sherman supposed him to have been with me, whereas I supposed he was with her. An officer of the Thirteenth went up to General [James Birdseye] McPherson's house for him, and soon returned, with Captain Clift leading him, carrying in his hands a small double-barreled shot-gun; and I joked him about carrying away captured property. In a short time we got off. As we all stood on the guards to look at our old camps at Young's Point, I

remarked that Willie was not well, and he admitted that he was sick.
His mother put him to bed, and consulted Dr. [E. O. F.] Roler, of
the Fifty-fifth Illinois, who found symptoms of typhoid fever. The
river was low; we made slow progress till above Helena [Arkansas];
and, as we approached Memphis, Dr. Roler told me that Willie's
life was in danger, and he was extremely anxious to reach Memphis
for certain medicines and for consultation. We arrived at Memphis
on the 2d of October, carried Willie up to the Gayoso Hotel, and
got the most experienced physician there, who acted with Dr. Roler,
but he sank rapidly, and died the evening of the 3d of October. The
blow was a terrible one to us all, so sudden and so unexpected, that
I could not help reproaching myself for having consented to his
visit in that sickly region in the summer-time. Of all my children,
he seemed the most precious. Born in San Francisco, I had watched
with intense interest his development, and he seemed more than any
of the children to take an interest in my special profession. Mrs.
Sherman, Minnie, Lizzie, and Tom, were with him at the time, and
we all, helpless and overwhelmed, saw him die. Being in the very
midst of an important military enterprise, I had hardly time to pause
and think of my personal loss. . . ."

In a letter dated midnight, October 4, Sherman wrote to Captain
C. C. Smith of the Thirteenth to thank the battalion's men for their
kindness toward his son. His grief was scarcely contained: "Consis-
tent with a sense of duty to my profession and office, I could not leave
my post, and sent for the family to come to me in that fatal climate,
and in that sickly period of the year, and behold the result! The child
that bore my name, and in whose future I reposed with more confidence than I did in my own plan of life, now floats a mere corpse,
seeking a grave in a distant land, with a weeping mother, brother,
and sisters, clustered about him. For myself, I ask no sympathy. On,
on I must go, to meet a soldier's fate, or live to see our country rise
superior to all factions. . . . God only knows why he should die thus
young. He is dead, but will not be forgotten till those who knew him
in life have followed him to that same mysterious end."

He also soon wrote to Tom, now back home in Ohio: "You are
now our only Boy, and must take Poor Willy's place, to take care of

your sisters, and to fill my place when I too am gone. I have promised that whenever you meet a Soldier who knew Willy that you will give him half you have. Give him all if in want, and work hard to gain knowledge & health which will when you are a man, insure you all you need in this world."

A third son, Charles Celestine Sherman, born in June the following year and apparently conceived during the reunion at Vicksburg, lived only six months. Ellen told an aunt: "Mother's superstitions are generally regarded as idle but I always had a strong presentment that Charley would not live. I felt that Willy would pray to have him taken early to heaven." She also admitted in a letter to John Sherman that Willy's death overshadowed that of the infant, and that her husband had said "with Willy died in me all real ambition."

As victory neared and Sherman exulted in his popularity with Lincoln and Secretary of War Edwin Stanton (who soon would turn on Sherman over Confederate peace terms), he told Ellen: "Oh, that Willy could hear and see—his proud little heart would swell to overflowing."

Guilt was to remain thick for the trip to Vicksburg that cost the boy's life. Months after the war's end, and with Sherman as one of the North's great heroes, Ellen would defend her decision to travel there as being at her husband's request. "Poor Cump had no idea that he was inviting Willy to meet his death when he wrote for us to come there," she told a cousin.

Two years later, and shortly after the birth of their fourth son, Philemon Tecumseh Sherman, the general would say to a comrade about Mississippi: "It was Vicksburg that cost me my Willy. . . ."

Could Tom, the second son, ever fill the void left by the death of the first?

*

IF SHERMAN commanded thousands in the field, Ellen commanded at home. A niece of Ellen's recounted this scene while the family was living in Washington after the war:

"One day the General came in to dinner full of spirits, sparkling and happy.

"'I was talking to Grant today,' he said. 'He's going to send Fred to such and such a preparatory school and I'll have Tom go there, too; so Grant's boy and mine can be together. Later on, they can go to West Point together. That will be splendid.

"'And Senator Blank wants Ellie and Rachel to go to such and such a school with his little girls . . .'

"Aunt Ellen broke in—

"'Cump, tomorrow morning at 8 o'clock Tom's going to George-town to the Jesuit College and tomorrow morning the girls are going to the Sisters' school around the corner—or tomorrow morning at ten o'clock I'll take them all back to my father.'

"The General was terribly hurt, got up and left the table. He was mum for several days. But by the end of the week Aunt Ellen said he was reconciled to it and was helping Tom with his lessons as though nothing had happened. He was tremendously loving with his family, very close to them and affectionate."

When the war ended, and after the triumphant Grand Review of his army in Washington, Sherman and Tom had traveled to New York to see both the city and West Point, where Sherman had graduated in 1840. For the trip up the Hudson River, Tom had been outfitted in a corporal's uniform of Sherman's old Thirteenth Infantry—Wil-ly's battalion. In this and in his later remark regarding Grant's son, it would appear that Sherman had quite forgotten having said he did not want Tom to be either priest or soldier but "a good useful man." With Willy's death and the war concluded, the soldier's life—the "Alter ego"—seemed in the process of transfer. There is, however, a hint that Tom hadn't yet measured up to Willy. His corporal stripes were a rank lower than those of his late older brother; Willy was an honorary sergeant, and surely his father remembered. Still, Sherman had hopes for Tom . . . barring Ellen.

Although loving with wife and children, Sherman spent a large part of his life far away from them. His labors as both soldier and civilian before the war took him to such places as St. Louis; New Orleans; San Francisco; Leavenworth, Kansas; and Alexandria, Louisiana—places where Ellen either refused to follow him or soon abandoned, usually for Ewing nests in Ohio. The war naturally brought its separations, but even afterward Sherman was often occupied elsewhere by his fame or his duties (he would succeed to general of the army when Grant became president). Besides Washington, the family would again live in St. Louis, where Sherman moved his headquarters in 1874. One gets the impression of Sherman as a blustering—yet welcome—whirlwind when home, but Ellen was the daily omnipotent presence.

Despite distances, however, he always kept in touch. Perhaps Tom's entry into Georgetown quashed any military ambitions his father had for him, but Sherman didn't yield easily.

On a trip to Egypt in 1872 he wrote to Tom, now fifteen, to grouse that he was "not satisfied that Georgetown is a College with Professors skilled in teaching modern sciences that [in] spite of all opposition are remodeling the world, but your mama thinks Religion is so important that every thing else must give place to it, and now that you are big enough to think for yourself, you must direct your mind to the acquisition of one class of knowledge or the other. . . . Your Religion is good enough and I would not shake your Faith in it so long as you leave to others a free choice according to their moral sense, and their means of judgment. It may be that the Creator designed that all people should have the same general Faith, but somehow though his power & goodness are unlimited he has freely left all to choose."

This is Sherman, the man of the world, talking. Soon he was able to have Tom join him in Paris after another member of the party, Fred Grant, returned home. Two years later Tom was sent through a course at Yale's Sheffield Scientific School, then on to Washington University's School of Law in St. Louis. Sherman wrote optimistically from the city of Washington to Ellen in St. Louis in March 1877: "I am sure that if Tom goes on as now, he will in two years enter on a Career not only brilliant but successful in a business sense. My business friends there will be his, and they are among the best in the West. I know you are more concerned as to his Moral & Religious status—but the other is equally important."

That summer he took Tom along on a trip out West to inspect military outposts. In Montana they proceeded to the mouth of the

Little Bighorn River, near the scene of the previous summer's Indian massacre of George Custer and his cavalry. Sherman bragged in a letter to Ellen that the journey was something "that Tom will remember long after I am gone." He added proudly that "Tom can now eat hard bread & bacon, and thinks boiled cabbage a great luxury."

The contest for Tom—in Sherman's view, for his mind and body; in Ellen's, for his soul—continued. What must Sherman have talked about to his son in those long nights in the land of the Cheyenne and Sioux, beneath the stars? What must Tom have talked about?

For him, perhaps very little. Sherman was at his peak, bursting with impatience and self-confidence, unlike those dark days in Kentucky. He loved Dickens and the theater and was one of the great talkers of his time. Railroad lawyer and Republican politician Chauncey Depew, another noted after-dinner speaker, conceded that Sherman was "the readiest and most original talker in the United States." Depew recalled that once "I was with him from ten o'clock in the morning until six in the afternoon and he talked without cessation for the whole period. . . . He always ought to have been accompanied by a stenographer."

This is the Sherman who had more to say about war than "it is all hell," and who dismissed military fame as "to be killed on the field of battle and have our names spelled wrong in the newspapers." He also told one audience: "War is usually made by civilians bold and defiant in the beginning but when the storm comes they generally go below. Of the 500,000 brave fellows whose graves we strew with flowers, not one in a thousand had the remotest connection with the causes of the war which led them to their untimely death."

This was the opinionated Sherman who, though surrounded by a family thick with politicians, was contemptuous of politics, who time after time would spurn any suggestion for even the highest office. Perhaps by now Tom matched Willy in Sherman's affections, and Sherman thought himself immune to disappointment. Maybe Tom never had a chance to speak of his own future, or thought his reticence a kindness. Likely he remained in awe of the fearless and eloquent general, a little afraid of him. Besides, he knew well what the general would say.

*

TOM SHERMAN'S revelation to his father that he had decided to be a Jesuit priest came in the spring following their Western trip and a week after his graduation from law school. He broke the news in a letter. He explained that he had long desired to be a priest, but had he told Sherman earlier it would have been dismissed as being influenced by the Georgetown Jesuits. The years at Yale had only increased this desire.

"In justice to myself however," he wrote, "I must say just this one thing; that if you were a Catholic, instead of being chagrined, disappointed and pained at the step I am going to take, you would be proud, happy and contented in it."

Sherman's reaction was a mixture of outrage and heartbreak. Ellen was quick to say it wasn't her doing. She wrote to Sherman from St. Louis that "I have not dared to meddle with anything so sacred as between his soul & his God" and noted that "We would freely offer our son's life in battle for his country . . . and shall we thwart him or deprecate what he holds highest?"

A wrathful Sherman turned to his friends. He wrote to General John Schofield: "I have warned Bishop [Patrick J.] Ryan of St. Louis, that if the Catholic Church or papers boast of their achievements, of having captured the Son of General Sherman, that General Sherman will himself denounce them with all the vehemence of his nature, and with all the force of his personal & official character, for having perverted the nature of a noble son, not for his Eternal welfare but for their worldly purpose. Though they take him from me, they shall not carry with him my silent assent—but my open curse."

Sherman and Tom soon met in Washington where, Sherman lamented to another, "I tried coaxing, persuasion, threats, demands, every thing, almost abusing myself before my own son. . . . All he could answer is that it was a 'vocation' from Heaven—I thought in my heart it was a vocation from Hell." They did agree that Sherman would write a letter to John Cardinal McCloskey of New York, to be delivered by Tom, urging him to dissuade the young man. Yet, after hearing Tom out, the cardinal—the first American to hold that office—could not do it.

On the eve of his departure for a Jesuit seminary—in England— Tom wrote to a kinsman: "My father, as you know, is not a Catholic, and therefore the step I am taking seems as startling and as strange to him as, I have no doubt, it does to you. . . . I go without his approval, sanction or consent; in fact, in direct opposition to his best wishes in my behalf. For he had formed other plans for me, which are now defeated, and had other hopes and expectations in my regard, which are necessarily dashed to the ground. . . .

"Feeling painfully aware that I have grieved and disappointed my father, I beg my friends and his, one and all, of whatever religion they may be, to spare him inquiries or comments of any sort."

Tom's decision also caused a breach for Sherman with the family back in St. Louis. Sherman complained to a friend there who was himself a Catholic, "I am forced into the Ranks of those who regard the Catholic church as one of our public enemies. . . . I know that this alienates me from Saint Louis." He even made a new will and cut out Tom. It was a pity, said Ellen, "because Tom, dear fellow, would give his share to his sisters & he will never need it." Ellen chose to live in Baltimore for a few months before the family reassembled in Washington.

A lawyer friend tried to console Sherman by writing that Tom once confided he "was not in love with law studies. And I could see he was not cut out for a successful lawyer. He had no relish for a *contest*. He had little knowledge of business, and the crooked ways of mankind. And when he went to the courts, he saw lawyers wrangling over petty questions of form, and he felt himself incapable of entering into any such employment. And unless he loved the profession and could enter into it with spirit he would have proved a failure."

In time, all was forgiven between father and son. They began exchanging letters. When Tom returned from England and they met again, Sherman cried out and threw his arms about him.

All was forgiven between husband and wife too. A nephew would describe the scene when Ellen was in her final illness in 1888: "The General was seated in his office when the nurse came to the head of

Tom Sherman, probably as a seminarian. Tom was ordained in 1889, but his father skipped the ceremony. Father Tom, who as a priest would sport a beard like William T., "looked like nothing so much as a field commander addressing his troops" when speaking in public. *(University of Notre Dame Archives)*

the stairs and called to him that Mrs. Sherman was dying. Though he had known she was in danger, I think this was the first moment when he realized the imminence of her death. He ran upstairs calling out, 'Wait for me, Ellen, no one ever loved you as I love you'; if she was alive when he reached her bedside it was only for a moment."

But Sherman was never to forgive Rome. He avoided Tom's ordination in 1889, and bitterly commented in that same year: "I can't get over Tom. Why should they have taken my splendid boy? They could have brought over thirty priests from Italy in his place."

Nonetheless two years later when Sherman was on his deathbed, unconscious, two of his daughters—Tom was rushing home from England again—sent for a priest. The old baptism, long unmentioned by the crusty general, allowed the daughters to ask that he be given the last rites of the Catholic church, and the priest obliged. John Sherman would afterward reply to a newspaper that his brother was not Catholic but was "too good a Christian and too human a man to deny his children the consolation of their religion." The Catholic funeral service—defended by Tom who returned in time to officiate—must have surprised Sherman's friends, who had listened to his religious rantings. But all in all it pleased his children and undoubtedly would have been arranged by Ellen too.

*

THE LITERARY CRITIC Edmund Wilson suggests in *Patriotic Gore*, his classic study of Civil War–era writings, that Ellen Sherman's undiminished Catholic fervor after the war might have been a sort of expiation for "the horrors and griefs of Georgia." Tom's entry into the priesthood, Wilson continued, was "perhaps the price paid by his father for the reckless elation of his March to the Sea." Wilson also called attention to an 1868 portrait of Ellen by the artist G. P. A. Healy, where the observer's focus inevitably drifts to the cross that hangs at her bosom.

While such speculation is highly intriguing, it is not necessarily correct. Ellen Ewing Sherman, as related, had been a deeply devout Catholic since childhood, and her intensive efforts to bring Sherman to the church were on the order of a lifelong crusade. Moreover her hopes that Tom would be a cleric were first voiced when the second son was barely out of his crib.

Unlike her husband, Ellen Sherman never seemed to have had any particular fondness for the South, whereas Sherman spent years in various places there before the war and had (at least until secession) a number of Southern friends. In April 1865, about the time Sherman was being castigated by newspapers and Secretary Stanton for agreeing to a truce and offering generous surrender terms to General Joseph Johnston, Ellen would write: "You know me well enough to know that I never would agree in any such policy as that towards perjured traitors as many of them are being deserters from the Regular Army of the United States. . . . I know that you could not allow your army to be in the slightest degree imperilled by this armistice and however much I differ from you I honor and respect you for the heart that could prompt such terms to men who have cost us individually one keen great pang which death will alone assuage—the loss of Willy."

These are scarcely the words of an atoning nature.

As for Tom Sherman (and as his life would bear out), he took much pride in his famous father. Indeed, a case might be made that his choice of the Jesuits was a way of appeasing his parents' struggle. Murmurs of a vocation may have genuinely existed before his studies at Georgetown, but the Jesuit order itself had soldierly characteristics complete with a superior general who governed it. Moreover certain of its undertakings had been as hazardous to life and limb as most battlefields. To more fully realize this, one had only (perhaps as a student at Georgetown) to read Francis Parkman's 1867 account of the Jesuits in the wilderness of the New World. The French missionary priest Isaac Jogues, in particular, had suffered unspeakable tortures at the hands of the Iroquois, only to escape to return to martyrdom and sainthood. The Jesuits were tough and manly. With them, one was also a soldier—but for Christ.

Thus the Jesuits would hold the sort of natural attraction for a soldier's son that they would not, say, for a Voltaire, with whom they failed miserably. But then, Voltaire did not experience the religious tenacity of Ellen Sherman. This is not to suggest that Tom Sherman was incapable of deciding on his own or that he lacked a sincere spiritual commitment, a deep love of God and for his service. For him to become a priest required eleven years from the day of choosing to his ordination—certainly time enough to sort things out. But if any of this was as a penitent for his father's wartime acts, the Reverend Tom Sherman also would show no sign of it.

The similarity between Father Sherman and General Sherman was striking despite their divergent choices. In a 1959 biography of Tom, the Reverend Joseph T. Durkin, S.J., mentions a time soon after the general's death where the son's inherited speaking skills made him a popular orator and lecturer. Tom's appearance on a platform, as described by Durkin, "looked like nothing so much as a field commander addressing his troops. It was always noted that his spare, militarily erect figure of medium height, his snapping blue eyes, aggressive jaw, and decisive—almost impatient—gestures recalled his father's appearance. The lines of his pale face were clear-cut and refined. His voice had usually a metallic ring and great carrying power; but he had a trick of modulating it to a tense softness."

His public statements also were as forthright as those of Sherman the elder: "Socialism asks us to vote for the dishonor of our mothers"; and, "The man who shoots an anarchist at sight is a public benefactor."

The last, however, earned a rebuke and an order to discontinue his lectures from the Father Provincial of Missouri. This was followed by Father Sherman suffering a nervous breakdown. He served as a chaplain in Puerto Rico during the Spanish-American War and was able to wear a uniform. Afterward he again took on the role of speaker and writer, and was considered a leading apologist for the Catholic church in America. But in 1906 his name (and that of the other Sherman) suddenly broke upon the national scene in an unusual and humiliating way.

While attending the unveiling of a statue of the general in Washington, Father Sherman was invited by Theodore Roosevelt to accompany a small party of soldiers into Georgia to retrace part of General Sherman's war campaign. News of the expedition soon got out—expanded in the public mind to something of a triumphal tour of the infamous March to the Sea by the conqueror's son, and with a military bodyguard to protect him.

The uproar from Georgia politicians and newspapers soon reached the halls of Congress. One of the state's delegation, Representative Charles L. Bartlett, complained: "If Father Sherman had made his march to the sea any time up to ten years ago, he would not have needed a guide. He could have found his way by the ruined homes that marked his father's march. In the last decade we have removed those traces, and with their disappearance had gone all the hard feeling of those times with one exception—the memory of Sherman's causeless vandalism."

The War Department soon explained that the expedition was only a field trip to study Sherman's campaign from Chattanooga, Tennessee, to Atlanta—not the March—and, in any case, the party was called back after going about halfway.

Afterward an indignant Father Sherman blamed a complete misinterpretation of his motives by the people of Georgia. "My connection with the expedition," he told the press, "has never been understood. The military detachment was in the field by order of the War Department to study civil war manoeuvres. I was an invited guest because Gen. Sherman was my father. Nobody had any idea of affronting the Southern people. There was no such thing as a body guard. That word was invented by some Georgian who had the wrong idea of my purpose.

"I have no ill feeling toward Southern people, but I am disappointed that they should attribute purposes to me that I never entertained. It was more an outing for me. . . ."

Father Tom's years thereafter were increasingly marked by episodes of ravings, self-recriminations, relentless travels, and stays in sanitariums. Sometimes he lived an almost hermitlike existence. He warred with the Jesuits and wrestled with the state of his soul. In 1913 he desperately wrote: "Repeated confessions but no peace. No hope whatever of eternal salvation. Still my vows press on me and I will continue to obey blindly."

After fits of violent behavior he was brought at last by a relative to DePaul Sanitarium in New Orleans, a mental institution run by the Daughters of Charity. In his final moments, in 1933, he renewed his Jesuit vows. The son of the despoiler of Georgia lies in the Jesuit cemetery in Grand Coteau, Louisiana, next to the Jesuit grandnephew of Alexander Stephens, the Confederacy's vice president and a Georgian.

Although William Tecumseh Sherman would have a brush with the family insanity while in Kentucky, he would elude it and become a famous man. Not so the unfortunate priest. In the long run, neither the general nor Ellen Sherman could claim to have won the battle for Tom. Victory—on Earth at least, and of the cruelest sort—belonged to an ancestor named Hoyt, who had lived many years before in the darkest of worlds.

· 3 ·

THE GENERAL'S
LAST BATTLE

Ulysses Grant's life, with its astonishing ups and downs, is among the most extraordinary. Much of it is known from his four years of the Civil War, no less than from Grant's own, well-thumbed *Personal Memoirs*. But Grant did not go beyond the war in his book, and in a sense his admirers have only reluctantly taken the journey themselves. It has challenges, for Grant not only was a failure later; he was a puzzle throughout.

There is another thing troubling about Grant. His postwar life oversaw the forces his triumph unleashed. It was a time of sweep and scandal that awakened the world to the awkward giant across the ocean. Yet the crisis that had provoked a war was replaced by another provoked by peace. The future of the South's freed slaves remained uncertain; the South still bled. The healthier half of the nation—and Grant—might have done more to heal the wound, to absorb and reabsorb the bewildered and angry races quicker than history would finally have it. Instead its mind was on money, as was Grant's.

He could hardly help it. He had been poor and now he was a great man. People gave him stuff: medals, fancy dinners, houses, the presidency. His fall would be stunning. Yet from it Grant would stamp one last claim to greatness. It would be personal. He would find redemption.

*

LITTLE CAME EASY for Grant. His father, Jesse, was an ambitious and grasping man who dabbled in politics and ran a tannery in Georgetown, Ohio. His mother, Hannah, was cold and detached. He grew up loving horses and despising the tannery, though its gore and smell was inherent in the military career he would reluctantly turn to. Grant had none of Jesse's business savvy. In the *Memoirs* he relates a painful example from boyhood that still seethed years later:

"There was a Mr. Ralston living within a few miles of the village, who owned a colt which I very much wanted. My father had offered twenty dollars for it, but Ralston wanted twenty-five. I was so anxious to have the colt, that after the owner left, I begged to be allowed to take him at the price demanded. My father yielded, but said twenty dollars was all the horse was worth, and told me to offer that price; if it was not accepted I was to offer twenty-two and a half, and if that would not get him, to give the twenty-five. I at once mounted a horse and went for the colt. When I got to Mr. Ralston's house, I said to him: 'Papa says I may offer you twenty dollars for the colt, but if you won't take that, I am to offer twenty-two and a half, and if you won't take that, to give you twenty-five.' It would not require a Connecticut man to guess the price finally agreed upon. This story is nearly true. I certainly showed very plainly that I had come for the colt and meant to have him. I could not have been over eight years old at the time. This transaction caused me great heartburning. The story got out among the boys of the village, and it was a long time before I heard the last of it. Boys enjoy the misery of their companions . . . and in later life I have found that all adults are not free from the peculiarity."

Jesse wanted a college education for his boy—the cheaper the better—and in 1839 won for him a congressional appointment to the U.S. Military Academy before Grant knew anything about it. Grant, born as Hiram Ulysses, virtually had his name changed by act of Congress as Jesse's lawmaker hurriedly scribbled "Ulysses S.

Grant" on the application. Grant never bothered to change it back, and fellow cadets translated the "S" as "Sam."

Sherman, three classes ahead, would later say that "a more unpromising boy never entered the Military Academy." In fact, Grant at first kept a hopeful eye on an effort in Congress to shut down the school. He showed an aptitude for mathematics, map reading and broncobusting. He was an excellent artist. He also scoured the library for novels by Edward Bulwer-Lytton, James Fenimore Cooper, and Charles Lever. He was, however, an indifferent student, finishing twenty-first in a class of thirty-nine. His lasting accomplishment was with horses, where he set a West Point jump record. After the army he thought he might be a math professor. General Benjamin Butler, who served under Grant in Virginia, would describe him as "less like a West Pointer than any officer I ever knew," adding approvingly, "The less of West Point a man has the more successful he will be."

Assigned to St. Louis after graduation, Grant met a fellow West Pointer's sister, Julia Dent. Her father was a Southern caricature who liked his repose and was known as "Colonel." He also owned slaves. Later, during the Civil War, Julia Dent Grant would bring along a slave-servant—also named Julia—on her visits to Grant's Union headquarters. Writing of a journey where he had to cross a flooded creek to see Julia, Grant said of himself, "One of my superstitions had always been when I started to go any where, or to do anything, not to turn back, or stop until the thing intended was accomplished." This dogged persistence would be amply demonstrated.

Grant served as a quartermaster during the Mexican War. He often took it into his own hands to get into the fight. He was sympathetic to the Mexicans and impressed by the country's natural beauty. After his presidency he would be involved with the building of a railroad from Mexico City to the Rio Grande, but it would prove another of his business failures.

Grant and Julia were married soon after the Mexican War ended in 1848. James Longstreet, a West Point and Mexico comrade before he became a Confederate general, was a groomsman. The marriage was very much a love match, and Julia threw herself into making military life less dreary for Grant. In light of his later, notorious reputation for hitting the bottle, it is startling that he was president of a Sons of Temperance lodge while posted to Sackets Harbor, New York.

That reputation had its beginnings when Grant was assigned in 1852 to the Pacific Coast without Julia, who was pregnant in St. Louis with their second child. With time on his hands and gold rush fever not yet abated, he tried a number of schemes to make money so she could join him. They all failed. Floods wiped out his potato crop. Headwinds delayed a ship delivering ice and let his competitors beat him to market. His chickens died. Worst, he was cheated of his stake in a San Francisco store by a merchant he and Julia had known and trusted in Sackets Harbor.

In one of her letters Julia scathingly wrote that compared to Grant, "the Vicar of Wakefield's Moses was a financier." Although promoted from lieutenant to captain, Grant's commander was a martinet. Grant was drinking heavily and, under this cloud, in 1854 he resigned from the army. Fellow officers had to raise money for him to sail to New York.

How far he had fallen is indicated by his efforts to reach Julia. He borrowed from a providential West Point friend, Simon Bolivar Buckner, to pay his New York hotel bill and buy a train ticket to Sackets Harbor. Grant hoped to collect from the store owner who also had returned from California. Instead Grant was told the man had gone sailing on his new boat.

Grant farmed land given by his father-in-law, but his crops failed. He was forced to sell firewood around St. Louis. Just before Christmas 1857, he had to pawn his gold watch for $22. Ill health and poverty made him give up the farm and get a job collecting rents. Desperately he turned to his father. He was given a place in Jesse's leather goods store in Galena, Illinois. Two of Grant's younger brothers ran the store.

Secession saved Grant. Despite the circumstances of his resignation, his army background and an ability to train raw volunteers won him favor in Illinois and ultimately with a government desperate for veteran officers who had not gone south. For much of the first part of the war Grant was kept busy looking over his shoulder at his superior. This was the politically neurotic Henry Halleck, who seemed always on the verge of shipping Grant back to Galena. Two early victories brought Grant fame, if not favor with Halleck.

Fort Donelson, Tennessee, was Grant's first major triumph. It was a critical turning point that opened up the midsection of the Confederacy to Yankee invasion. Here the unfortunate but now Confederate Buckner was left to surrender an army of twelve thousand to fifteen thousand Southerners after being abandoned by Generals Gideon Pillow and John B. Floyd, who outranked him. Buckner, understandably, expected generous terms—the sort Grant later gave Lee at Appomattox—and suggested a meeting in a note passed along through Union General Charles F. Smith, a Grant subordinate. When he read the note, Grant turned to Smith for an opinion. Smith was a cranky West Point instructor of both Buckner and Grant. "No terms to the damned Rebels," Smith growled. Grant grinned. After acknowledging Buckner's note, he wrote a famous reply: "No terms except an unconditional and immediate surrender can be accepted. I propose to move immediately upon your works."

The North, still smarting from its loss at Manassas in Virginia seven months earlier, hailed the victory and especially its general. His initials were deciphered as "Unconditional Surrender" Grant. Cigars poured in when a reporter described Grant—an occasional pipe smoker—as a cigar-clenching general. But Fort Donelson was a near thing. The capture of so many of the enemy owed as much to the incompetence of Buckner's superiors as to Grant's aggressiveness.

Grant's next battle, at Shiloh in Tennessee, was an even closer victory. The Southerners, commanded by Albert Sidney Johnston, caught Grant's army by surprise and with its back to the Tennessee River. But Johnston died on the first day, and the arrival of a second Union army under Don Carlos Buell prevented the completion of a rout by the Confederates.

Thousands of Yankee soldiers were skulking under cover of a river bluff when Sherman, who was in the thick of Shiloh, sought out Grant to urge him to withdraw across the river under cover of the battle's rainy first night. Sherman colorfully recalled:

"Full of only this idea, I ploughed around in the mud until at last I found him standing backed up against a wet tree, his hat well slouched down and coat well pulled up around his ears, an old time lantern in his hand, the rain pelting on us both, and the inevitable cigar glowing between his teeth, having retired, evidently, for the night. Some wise and sudden instinct impelled me to a more cautious and less impulsive proposition than at first intended, and I opened up with, 'Well, Grant, we've had the devil's own day, haven't we?'

"'Yes,' he said, with a short, sharp puff of the cigar; 'lick 'em tomorrow, though.'"

Thus began the wartime legend of the U.S. Grant who "didn't scare worth a damn."

It isn't difficult to suggest that the Civil War was a personal war for Grant. It was a chance to rise above the humiliations of California and St. Louis and the tannery in Galena—the "Useless S." Grant to a taunting, peacetime world. The cigar was in the grip of a bulldog. Its glow provided a clue to the forcefulness Grant concealed behind an almost dull façade. Shiloh confirmed that with enough men, with enough determination and ruthless courage to go on the attack, to fight back from apparent defeat and keep thrusting forward, to not stop "until the thing intended was accomplished," he would prevail in the end. Lincoln would think so too. Eventually he would place Grant over the fussy Halleck to command the entire Union Army.

Shiloh also presaged the bloodbaths ahead. Of the 100,000 troops engaged from both sides, approximately one in four was either killed, captured, or wounded. The Union carnage to come in the Wilderness and at Spotsylvania and Cold Harbor in Virginia would bring taunts of "Butcher" Grant too. Still, the war was finally won as the Confederacy collapsed. Grant had broken the unbreakable Bobby Lee. The tanner's son, the drunken captain who had quit the army, the unremarkable Grant who had a talent for nothing other than riding a horse, was now—after Lincoln's assassination—the North's largest living hero. Who would've guessed it in Galena? Or at West Point?

Nothing could stop Grant now. Not even those cigars.

*

IT WAS a genuine rags-to-riches story, the kind America loves—given the exception that it came out of the destruction of a sizable portion of the country. Wealthy Philadelphians bought Grant a house. Grateful near-strangers bought him a second one in Galena. A third awaited him in the nation's capital. He went on tours. His advice was sought. Popular generals like Washington, Jackson, Harrison, and Taylor had enjoyed an almost open path to the presidency. Grant's path was greased further as the incumbent Andrew Johnson brawled with Congress.

Grant wasn't entirely a political babe in the woods. Washington politics as much as civil war had honed an instinct for both preservation and the main chance. He had moved nimbly just after Appomattox and Lincoln's death, when an out-of-control Edwin Stanton wanted the crowd-pleasing Sherman sacked for the surrender terms he had granted to Joseph Johnston. Sherman's generosity would have largely restored the seceded states and their leaders to their prewar status. War Secretary Stanton and congressional Radicals had something closer to lynch law in mind. But Grant avoided both Stanton's wrath and the removal of his friend. He calmly had the explosive Sherman renegotiate Johnston's surrender.

A less nimble exercise came three years later, in 1868, when President Johnson attempted to remove Stanton from his job. The Democrat Johnson had picked Grant (still general of the army) to serve as interim secretary of war while the Supreme Court took up the Republican Congress's Tenure of Office Act, which protected Stanton. Johnson would later insist that he had Grant's promise to keep the secretary's physical office out of Stanton's hands until the president could find a permanent replacement or the Court made its decision.

But when the Senate went ahead and restored Stanton, Grant became liable for a heavy fine under the act. Grant quietly yielded the office and left its keys for Stanton's triumphant repossession. Johnson was furious. At a cabinet meeting to discuss the crisis, the president also made his feelings clear to the general. Secretary of the

Navy Gideon Welles, who was present, described Grant as "humble, hesitating, and he evidently felt that his position was equivocal and not to his credit."

Welles—no friend of Grant's—continued with some glee: "There was, I think, an impression on the minds of all present (there certainly was on mine) a consciousness that he had acted with duplicity—not been faithful and true to the man who had confided in and trusted him. . . . The President, though disturbed and not wholly able to conceal his chagrin from those familiar with him, used no harsh expression, and committed nothing approaching incivility, yet Grant felt the few words put to him, and the cold and surprised disdain of the President in all their force."

Grant may have gone back on a promise, but he had dodged the bullets between Johnson and Congress, which soon would impeach the president. Johnson had minimal influence left. Meanwhile Grant had tried not to cross the ruling Republicans. In turn, many of them were eager to clutch his coattails in the 1868 election.

Although Grant had voted only once in a presidential election— in 1856, for Democrat James Buchanan—there is nothing to suggest he didn't have his eye on the job. The burning question, however, is why. Why would anyone of the most rudimentary common sense have wanted to be president during this ignominious and dangerous period?

The assassination of Lincoln could have been Grant's as well: the general and Julia had been invited to join the Lincolns on that fateful night at Ford's Theatre but had found better things to do. Lincoln's successor Johnson—who declined to attend Grant's inauguration—had more or less been run out of office by the same powerful men who had hailed Grant, and who were capable of doing the same to him should he prove other than malleable. In the South, a political civil war of Reconstruction was raging, often violently, over the role of the Negro in public life. The North, meanwhile, was full throttle into the Gilded Age with all its expansion, greed, and corruption. Eventually this would embroil even those closest to Grant. Out West the Indian tribes were being wedged into the corners of a once-limitless prairie. Ultimately, during Grant's last year in office, they would break out in one final, furious flurry at the Little Bighorn.

Perhaps Grant saw the presidency as merely his due, as the natural progression and reward for being savior of the republic, and more on the order of vengeance for those days of selling wood and collecting rents. The country owed him. Besides, as a general he would still be under the thumb of the next president—one Johnson-like rebuke was quite enough—and his own position could be weakened along with any future chance for the ultimate prize. He had come to like his comforts and cigars. Rich men were his chums. Hundreds of thousands of Union veterans would cherish more and more over the years their time with Grant, even had they lost a leg or a friend. He was already a great man, yet could be greater. What might he have in mind for the country? What sweeping visions would he promote as most fitting for the nation's new role on the world stage, or to sew up the wounds of a still bleeding South?

Called on at his Washington home to accept the Republican nomination, Grant ended a short speech by saying, "I shall have no policy of my own to interfere against the will of the people." Grant's biographer William S. McFeely has icily observed that the words came close to an admission he would have no policy at all. Even Grant's written acceptance, which included the slogan "Let us have peace," may have referred as much to the transient upheaval wrought by Johnson's narrow escape from ouster as to any long-term difficulty awaiting his successor.

At his inauguration, Grant blandly declared: "The office has come to me unsought; I commence its duties untrammeled." The speech was notable in only two respects: he called for ratification of the Fifteenth Amendment, which would give the vote nationally to adult black males, and he urged a study of the treatment received by "the original occupants of this land," the Indians.

His leadership, though, would rarely be vigorous. Grant was more inclined to live and let live (some would live very well indeed). In his first annual message to Congress, he mentioned appropriations for river and harbor improvements and for military fortifications, but lamely added: "Whatever amount Congress may deem appropriate for these purposes will be expended." Congress, Grant implied, could continue to do whatever it liked. And it did.

Surprisingly, whatever instincts he had used to get around Stanton and Johnson seemed blunted in high office. His first cabinet was chosen without any input from his party's leaders in the Senate—always a grave oversight. His selection for secretary of the treasury, a New York multimillionaire, was gone within a week when Senator Charles Sumner dredged up a 1789 law that prohibited business conflicts of interest.

Grant would always have trouble with appointments. In his two terms the seven cabinet posts were changed a total of twenty-four times. He also would have recurrent problems with Sumner, a cantankerous abolitionist from Massachusetts who before the war had been almost beaten to death by a cane-wielding congressman from South Carolina.

Widespread corruption ultimately would be the legacy of Grant's years in the White House. It was hardly confined to that one place or initiated by Grant, yet often it struck close enough:

* The Credit Mobilier swindle revolved around a construction company contracted to help build the first transcontinental railroad. Bribes flowed in Congress, and millions of dollars were needlessly appropriated. The scheme had its beginnings before Grant took office but blew up just as Grant was seeking a second term in 1872. Among others, Grant's vice president, Schuyler Colfax, was implicated.

* An effort to manipulate the gold market by speculators Jim Fisk and Jay Gould was nipped when Grant ordered the sale of $4 million in government reserves, which sent gold prices plunging. Thousands lost money in what became known on Wall Street as Black Friday. But Fisk and Gould had earlier gained access to Grant through one of his brothers-in-law, and Grant had figured out the scheme only shortly before acting. Julia Grant may have made a small profit from insider gold speculation.

* The Whiskey Ring siphoned off $3 million a year in federal taxes through bribes to U.S. Treasury employees, among others.

Dozens were convicted, but Grant's private secretary was acquitted only when Grant gave favorable testimony on his behalf.

* Toward the end of his second term, Grant's secretary of war, William Belknap, resigned over kickbacks involving Indian trading posts. Belknap was impeached anyway.

While Grant himself escaped voters' wrath for the scandals, the Republican party did not. In the midterm elections of 1874, Democrats took control of the House of Representatives for the first time since the war and gained four seats in the Senate. In the wake of the Belknap scandal, but applicable to all of them, Sherman would say of his friend: "All this time I am sorry for Grant, for while he supposed he was using others dexterously, they were using him. Barring his selfishness, I do not believe he would connive at wrong, yet here those who knew him best before the war make no comment & express the opinion that he has deliberately salted away a fortune. I almost hope so, for poverty will be terrible for him to struggle with again."

*

"LEE MASSED HEAVILY from his left flank on the broken point of his line. Five times during the day he assaulted furiously, but without dislodging our troops from their new position. His losses must have been fearful. Sometimes the belligerents would be separated by but a few feet. In one place a tree, eighteen inches in diameter, was cut entirely down by musket balls. All the trees between the lines were very much cut to pieces by artillery and musketry. It was three o'clock next morning before the fighting ceased. Some of our troops had then been twenty hours under fire. In this engagement we did not lose a single organization, not even a company. The enemy lost one division with its commander, one brigade and one regiment, with heavy losses elsewhere. Our losses were heavy, but, as stated, no whole company was captured. At night Lee took a position in rear of his former one, and by the following morning he was strongly intrenched in it."

Thus Grant in his postwar *Memoirs* would describe the fight near Spotsylvania Court House. The effect is like the pounding of guns, the sentences simple, controlled, precise. Nor is there mistaking that Grant is steady and in command. He knows where he wants to go. Although he writes while stricken with cancer and dosed on narcotics, he soldiers on to complete his pages. He is in his element. He is the man so seldom seen in those White House years. There his nimbleness is no match for men such as Sumner. Indeed, Grant is like a man with a bludgeon whereas everyone else wields a knife. The self-confidence seems a fraud. He appears lost. . . .

The Grant presidency has received a more sympathetic hearing in recent times, particularly for his standing by the South's emancipated blacks. Even here, though, it's a stretch—whatever his good intentions—for Grant to be considered an elder of the civil rights movement. His first secretary of the interior, Jacob Cox of Ohio, was a racist who had opposed black suffrage and advocated putting the freedmen on a reservation somewhere in the South. Cox hung around for a year and a half. Closer to home, the first black to be appointed to West Point, with Grant's blessing, was harassed out of the academy partly through actions of his fellow cadets who included none other than Grant's son Fred.

Grant's steps against Ku Klux Klan terror in the South were, at best, inconsistent. Congress overflowed with protective measures for blacks, but Grant was reluctant to give the army the sweeping powers to carry them out. When finally persuaded, Grant endorsed the move only because tax collections and the mail were endangered. The president did set a new and aggressive attorney general, Amos Akerman, on the trail of the Klan, but within months Grant fired him. Grant's secretary of state, the aristocrat Hamilton Fish, had counseled that the better way to ease Klan violence was to be more lenient. Besides, Akerman had also crossed Jay Gould and the railroads. Business would always take precedence in a Grant administration.

Grant's most personal initiative was the pursuit of U.S. annexation of Santo Domingo, the Dominican Republic. It is also one of the rare references to his presidency in the *Memoirs*, where he explains that "great numbers" of freed blacks could go there "so as to have independent states governed by their own race" but "still be States of the Union." The move, sympathetically intended either to win blacks (by their absence) better labor conditions back home or to escape the Klan, was not terribly distinct from Cox's segregation. In any case, the effort failed in the Senate, due largely to the enmity between Grant and Sumner.

Grant's calling for ratification of the Fifteenth Amendment during his inaugural speech at least put him on the side of history. The road to black voting rights had never been smooth, though the amendment's two immediate predecessors had staked out its logical direction. Even such ardent abolitionists as Sumner, Pennsylvania congressman Thaddeus Stevens, and the firebrand publisher William Lloyd Garrison had their doubts. Some sort of accompanying literacy test was often suggested before handing over the vote to a mostly unschooled black electorate. Politically more risky was that blacks in the South would be so influenced or intimidated by unreconstructed whites—read Democrats—that it would cost the Republicans their power.

One way around the latter problem (at least temporarily) was to disfranchise many white ex-Rebels while signing up freed slaves. Thus Congress in 1867 and over Johnson's veto handed to the occupying military the power to determine Southern voter eligibility. This step was not merely a desire of party radicals. The historian C. Vann Woodward has noted the interests of the no-holds-barred Northern business class that had hitched its wagon to the Republicans. By the time of the 1868 election, Woodward determined, more than 703,000 blacks were registered voters in the reconstructed states compared to 627,000 whites. The black electorate and their white allies were soon remaking the face of local government throughout the occupied South.

It is one of the curiosities—or hypocrisies—of the 1868 election that blacks voted in eight states of the former Confederacy and eight more outside (mostly in New England), but were not allowed to do so in twenty-one other so-called "free" states. This latter statistic, in fact, was a Northern application of the secession-spawning states' rights doctrine. Republicans managed to push the Fifteenth Amendment through enough legislatures for ratification in 1870, though it was left vulnerable to states to affix poll taxes and to gerrymander.

Passage of the amendment must be considered one of the few high points of the Grant administration, and the president hailed it to Congress as constituting "the most important event that has occurred since the nation came to life." Yet Hamilton Fish would write in his diary in the closing months of Grant's second term: "He [Grant] says he opposed the Fifteenth Amendment and thinks it was a mistake, that it had done the Negro no good, and had been a hindrance to the South, and by no means a political advantage to the North."

By this time much of the North had wearied of the Negro's struggle. Grant had become a fan of James Russell Lowell's "Hosea Biglow," a Yankee character who spoke in dialect and who at one point advises the South, "You take the Darkies, ez we've took the Paddies." The Irish gave New Englanders other things to be busy about. The nation's (white) attention span shifted elsewhere. A financial depression that began in Grant's second term and the usual political corruption were adequate distractions. One of Amos Akerman's successors, Edwards Pierrepont, replying to a request for troops to quell preelection troubles in Mississippi, sniffed that the nation "was tired of the autumnal outbursts in the South." The cause of black civil rights faded into the mists for nearly a century.

As to that other compelling matter that Grant briefly raised in his 1868 inaugural—the "proper treatment" of the Indians—he began by actually appointing an Indian, Ely Parker, as commissioner of Indian affairs. Grant's policy advocated reservations and a strong dose of education to bring Indians into the national mainstream. Missionaries were preferred for the low-paying agent jobs to discourage traditional trading-post graft. A private board was given oversight of these efforts.

Almost inevitably, though, quarrels between the board and Parker led to his resignation, the administration's own trading-post scandals were revealed, and, toward the end, Grant allowed the army to relax its efforts to keep white gold-seekers out of the Sioux's sacred Black Hills.

The disaster of Custer's last stand soon followed.

*

WHAT SORT OF MAN was Ulysses S. Grant? A very human one.

Henry Adams, in his *Education*, scathingly describes Grant as "inarticulate, uncertain, distrustful of himself, still more distrustful of others, and awed by money." To Adams, "the progress of evolution from President Washington to President Grant, was alone evidence to upset Darwin." Richard Taylor, a Confederate general and president's son who had known Grant for "thirty-odd years," wrote upon meeting him as president: "Of a nature kindly and modest, President Grant was assured by all about him that he was the delight of the Radicals, greatest captain of the age, and saviour of the nation's life. It was inevitable that he should begin by believing some of this, and end by believing it all."

Taylor is withering in his characterization of Reconstruction under Grant—a brother-in-law of Julia's was thick in Radical politics in Taylor's Louisiana—calling Grant as "ignorant of civil government as of the characters on the Moabitish stone." Having begun badly, "President Grant . . . went from bad to worse."

Grant's outer calm, one of his great strengths in war, could be viewed as cold and callous in peace. Shortly after the war when Grant was aboard a train, Theodore Bowers, an aide who had been with him through those days, slipped and fell while running to catch up and was horribly crushed. James Garfield, who in 1880 would be the Republican choice over Grant and James G. Blaine, would relate Blaine's account of Grant's reaction: "Grant did not rise from his seat but wrote a telegram, giving orders about the dispo[si]tion of the body, and let the train go on."

Of another occasion, after Grant quietly kept an appointment with a portrait artist while the Indian trading-post scandal was imploding around him, Garfield wondered in his diary: "His imperturbability is amazing. I am in doubt whether to call it greatness or stupidity."

Grant's ability to command loyalty from others seemed not to extend beyond old army buddies and his family, and even here he was ill-served. Orville Babcock, another aide from the war, was the private secretary Grant had to rescue with his testimony for Babcock's Whiskey Ring trial. Nonetheless Babcock was thick in the scandal, and Grant only reluctantly fired him—then found Babcock a job as a lighthouse inspector. Rumors circulated at the time that Grant's younger brother Orvil and Julia's brother Lewis, along with son Fred, had taken kickbacks from the whiskey fraud.

Orvil, earlier Grant's boss at the Galena store, appears as well to have been connected to a shady scheme involving "partnerships" in government surveyor contracts. Another of Julia's brothers, John, as well as the incorrigible Orvil, also held interests in Indian trading posts. This was the sort of dubious investment that Grant had once hoped to clean up.

Some of the morass might have been avoided had John Rawlins been around. The faithful Rawlins, a Galena attorney, followed Grant to war as another member of his staff and did what he could to intervene between Grant and the bottle. Afterward he was Grant's first appointed secretary of war, and was described by Jacob Cox as having a friendship for Grant of "so sacredly intimate a character that he [Rawlins] alone could break through the taciturnity into which Grant settled when he found himself in any way out of accord with the thoughts and opinions of those around him." Cox considered Rawlins as Grant's conscience.

Rawlins, however, had tuberculosis at the time of his appointment and died six months after Grant's inauguration. Instead of Rawlins for the long haul, Grant had the likes of Orville Babcock and William Belknap. Or a disloyal vice president, Henry Wilson, during the second term who in 1875 would tell Garfield that Grant "is the millstone around the neck of our party."

Sherman would say, as if in frustration: "Grant's whole character was a mystery even to himself—a combination of strength and weakness not paralleled by any of whom I have read in Ancient or Modern History. . . ."

And yet, small things make up a man as well. Grant loved his family for better or worse, and his life held humorous moments—charming intrusions—which also left their impressions. Grant and his then four-year-old son, Jesse, had a ritual when Grant would arrive home. The boy would challenge him to fight, and Grant would intone, "I do not feel like fighting, Jess, but I can't stand being hectored in this manner by a man of your size." Father and son would then commence to wrestling on the floor.

Grant, as he did in his memoirs, could also tell stories on himself. Once, after the war, when he was walking during a rainstorm to a reception in his honor, Grant offered to share his umbrella with a stranger. The stranger was going to the same reception and commented to him: "I have never seen Grant and I go merely to satisfy a personal curiosity. Between us I have always thought Grant was a very over-rated man."

"That's my view also," Grant replied. He would then recall that nothing gave him such quick delight as seeing the stranger's face while in the receiving line.

If Grant had a goal during the war, it was one of simply whipping the Rebels, whether to save the Union or, as he would later insist, to free the slaves. But as the Union's president he often seemed confused or detached. He had a habit of taking firm positions and then reversing himself, or appearing to assure callers of one thing and doing another (this was behind Taylor's scorn). He did not wish to look a fool, but he must have to those many who tried to bilk the government during his care, and to the few who actually tried to clean up the mess.

Remarkably, Grant in his final State of the Union message in December 1876 would apologize for his political ignorance, but only grudgingly did he accept responsibility for the results. "History shows that no Administration from the time of Washington to the present has been free from these mistakes," he said. While true, Grant most certainly did not raise the bar.

Out of office, he and Julia set off on a two-year global tour. In the commoner Grant, foreigners could take the measure of the upstart, postwar Union. He could take a little boy's pleasure in the sights and collect the adulation always necessary to a man out of power. He was greeted and feted by the likes of Queen Victoria, Germany's Prince Bismarck, and Japan's Emperor Mutsuhito—the latter two would shape their nations into rival world powers, which one day would confront Grant's Union—and was snubbed by Victor Hugo. Grant also had ample time to turn to the bottle. At a dinner in Bombay the host would recount how the general got "drunk as a fiddle" and began kissing and pinching the ladies. When he was escorted back to his ship, he hurled himself upon Julia and concluded the evening by throwing up.

That didn't make the papers back home, but questions began to arise about the financing of the trip as the Grants stayed on tour. Wise investments was one explanation put out. Still, the poorhouse never seemed far away. Seeing what a grateful British Empire had done for the Duke of Wellington, Julia—with the prospect of living in Galena ever hovering—wistfully sighed, "How would it have been if General Grant had been an Englishman—I wonder, I wonder?"

What was Grant to do with himself? Being president again would not be so bad. But his arrival back in the United States came nine months before the June 1880 Republican convention, too long to keep up appearances as a returning hero. Besides, there was something suggestively tawdry about it all. Joseph Keppler's *Puck*, for one, made sport with editorials and cartoons of Grant as "The Wandering Jew" and "The Hero of a Thousand Feeds." ("I will eat my way to the White House, if it takes another four years!" says the cartoon Grant.) The Grants returned to Galena to await the call from the convention in Chicago. Instead the party called for Garfield.

Ultimately the Grants would head to New York to live. Grant needed money—"General Grant was poor," Julia would say—and it was better to be back East and closer to the same rich men he knew as a victorious general and a pliant president. William Henry Vanderbilt, the commodore's wealthier son, would later explain that he had made a $150,000 loan to Grant because "He is one of us." Millionaires chipped in to buy Grant a brownstone house on East Sixty-sixth Street, near Central Park. A three-story "cottage" on the beach in nearby Long Branch, New Jersey, was another place to stay; the Grants had passed previous seasons there, courtesy of a Philadelphia publisher. A fund of $250,000 was invested for Grant to collect the interest ("I'd give $1,000,000 to have Grant as president again," said Jay Gould, who gave $25,000). Life was better back East.

The most promising opportunity came from a Grant son, Ulysses Jr., nicknamed Buck. Buck was friends with Ferdinand Ward, a minister's son, and together they started a brokerage firm, Grant & Ward. When Buck began to prosper, he invited his father in as a so-called silent partner. Grant borrowed $100,000 from family and friends and came along. So did acquaintances of Grant as well as old soldiers on pensions. Typically, both Grants sat back and let Ward run things. Return on investment seemed to quadruple. But Ward was running something on the order of a Ponzi scheme and borrowing heavily from a bank in collusion with him.

When the bank and Grant & Ward began to come apart, the general sought out Vanderbilt for the $150,000 that Ward had assured him would be enough to avert a crisis. It was merely a drop. Grant lost his investment, owed Vanderbilt, and, as a partner, was liable to other investors for their losses too. He was financially ruined; so were relatives who had followed him.

This was in May 1884. In June his life would grow worse. During dinner, Grant bit down on a peach. He leaped up from the table in pain. Julia thought he had been stung by an insect.

*

"I SAID I had been adding to my book and to my coffin. I presume every strain of the mind or body is one more nail in the coffin." Thus Grant, communicating only by note, spoke with the doctor treating his cancer in June of the following year.

Grant was remarkably free of self-pity. Lesser men might have wondered. It was as if he had been struck down from above. Why, and for what purpose? It was almost the same thing as saying that there was something tragically wrong with this renewed Union, that it had deviated from some sort of compact, some sort of understanding for betterment or spiritual growth in exchange for victory, and that its most notable living citizen, the embodiment of the rags-to-riches legend, was to be made the example of divine displeasure.

Hugh McCulloch, former treasury secretary to Lincoln, Johnson, and Chester Arthur, would say of Grant (if not the Union) in 1889: "For rich men he had great respect; for poor men, no matter how distinguished they might be by intellectual attainments, he had but little regard." Grant's greed, the "love of money [that] grew with the free use of it by himself, and by his observation of the influence which it commanded," had led him to the Grant & Ward disaster.

Success worshipers were given pause. Grant was baffling. Few if any knew the story of the boy and his colt, and how many were aware of California or St. Louis? Indeed, how could such a symbol of national glory, how could a leader of thousands in war and millions in peace, be such a . . . such a . . .

He was a dupe and a buffoon, his wartime achievements isolated and encircled by the dreaded "yes . . . but," his debts unpayable, and his honor in shreds. He was also to be condemned to a lengthy death and excruciating pain. And yet Grant, with all his failings and failures, for a final time drew upon the tenacity that had pulled him through poverty and the Civil War. He relit the light that Sherman had spied at Shiloh and that a desperate Lincoln would notice too. "Lick 'em tomorrow, though." Grant got off the floor.

But first the floor came calling. In the wake of the Grant & Ward collapse, Vanderbilt, leaving for Europe, sent his lawyer around to tell Grant he considered the $150,000 loan a debt of honor. Grant, he felt, would repay it when he could. But Grant was no longer "one of us," and it was no use pretending that he was. He transferred to Vanderbilt the houses in Philadelphia and Galena, many of his war mementos and honors from Congress, and loot from his travels (including elephant tusks from the king of Siam). Other than the real estate, it was all waiting in Vanderbilt's foyer when the millionaire arrived home from his trip. Vanderbilt attempted to return much of this, but Grant refused. Fearful he was perceived as squeezing Grant, Vanderbilt gained permission to make public their correspondence. At length, a settlement was reached.

The cancer was not immediately diagnosed. After the pain of the peach, Grant noticed a peculiar dryness in his throat. His doctor being abroad, and the Grants having retreated to the borrowed house in Long Branch, he asked another to examine him. The doctor wrote a prescription that seemed to help. Anyway, Grant shrugged it off. There was work to do.

In the summer of 1884 he began writing a series of articles about the war for *The Century* magazine. It was an ambitious project for the magazine, which had approached Grant in better days and had been put off. Grant had replied that Adam Badeau, his wartime secretary, had covered the same ground in Badeau's postwar, three-volume *Military History of General Grant*. Now Grant was again desperate for money. He would set out to write magazine articles, at $500 per, on Shiloh and Vicksburg, and he summoned Badeau to Long Branch to give him a hand. Grant confided to Badeau that he would begin writing his memoirs during the coming winter. The Century Company had expressed interest, but no contract was signed. Sherman had told Grant that his own memoirs, with a standard 10 percent royalty, had fetched between $20,000 and $30,000. That wouldn't clear Grant's debts, but it would help.

In October, Grant left Long Branch and returned to East Sixty-sixth Street. By this time he was having frequent coughing spells from congestion in the throat, and the pain would not subside. His doctor, returned from Europe, was sufficiently alarmed to send Grant to a specialist, Dr. John Douglas, who had known Grant during the war. What he found was at the root of Grant's tongue.

"Is it cancer?" asked Grant. Douglas hedged; he wasn't clinically sure. Muriate of cocaine was applied to the infected area, and Grant began to have twice-daily swabbings. These helped him sleep, but Grant at first kept the gravity of the illness private from even his family.

Douglas called in other specialists. One of them, Dr. George Frederick Shrady, was asked to confirm the biopsy of an unnamed patient. Shrady, who was both a microbiologist and a plastic surgeon, determined that the patient had cancer of the tongue. When told that the patient was General Grant, Shrady said: "Then General Grant is doomed." Because of the stage reached by the disease, even surgery was futile. The book would be a race against death.

Grant and Mark Twain were mutual admirers. Several years before Century and Grant talked, Twain had also tried to convince the general to put his memories on paper. Grant, however, doubted that he could write well and declined. The matter would not come up until the autumn of 1884. In November, as Twain would later tell it, he walked in on Grant as he was about to sign the contract with Century. Twain ridiculed its 10 percent royalty and expenses charged to the author. Grant could do better, he said, through Twain's own publishing company. Grant demurred, feeling disloyal to Century. But when Twain reminded Grant that "I came to you first . . . three years ago," Grant agreed. He accepted terms that would pay him 70 percent of the profits so that, he said, he could also assure Twain of some profit. Grant did not expect big sales.

He began the *Personal Memoirs of U.S. Grant* with this declaration: "My family is American, and has been for generations, in all its branches, direct and collateral." It was very much a summary of himself. In the library on the second floor of his house, Grant would dictate from notes to a stenographer provided by Twain. The stenographer would then hand the result to Fred Grant (who, at age twelve, had accompanied his father through the Vicksburg campaign) and Badeau. They in turn would fill in dates and fact-check against Grant's memory. Grant, in the meantime, would compose his notes for the next day's dictation.

Grant's meals were milk and cold soup, swallowed in one gulp because of pain. Pain and coughing kept him from sleep. Sleep, when it came, was disturbed by dreams of the war. Bouts of choking brought on panic attacks. Throughout, the loyal Dr. Shrady was near to do what he could, for both Grant and his stunned and helpless family. Grant's body became emaciated, but for visitors he would dress up and cover his lap with a shawl.

The old battles came back, to be put down on paper in Grant's direct and lucid style—the same as his headquarters orders or his surrender terms to Lee. When he struck a colorful phrase, he would call in Julia or a doctor and read it aloud with pride. The Wards of the world, the Radicals and Reconstruction-resistant Rebels, all the bedlam and bedevilment of the postwar years, could never subvert the glories of Grant as the nation's Supreme Instrument in its greatest need. There were those smaller political victories too, unlike his time as president:

"At this stage of the campaign against Vicksburg I was very much disturbed by newspaper rumors that General [John] McClernand was to have a separate and independent command within mine, to operate against Vicksburg by way of the Mississippi River. Two commanders on the same field are always one too many, and in this case I did not think the general selected had either the experience or the qualifications to fit him for so important a position. I feared for the safety of the troops intrusted to him, especially as he was to raise new levies, raw troops, to execute so important a trust. But on the 12th I received a dispatch from General Halleck saying that I had command of all the troops sent to my department and authorizing me to fight the enemy where I pleased."

By late winter 1885 the newspapers had found out about Grant's illness. A daily death watch involving reporters and admirers began collecting outside the New York house. In late March, Grant indeed nearly died after a choking fit, and the press braced for the announcement. Matters were so grave that Grant—never a religious man but certainly not as hostile as Sherman—had allowed Julia to summon the Reverend John Phillip Newman to baptize him. Newman, a Methodist, did so. Meanwhile Grant's doctors injected him with brandy, and the coughing this induced unclogged Grant's throat. Newman would say that Grant's recovery was due to the many prayers for his health. Dr. Shrady would credit the brandy.

Still, it was another of Grant's close calls, as much realized by Mark Twain as anyone. What if the general never finished the book? But Grant kept to the task. Joseph Pulitzer's invidious *World*, which had attacked Shrady's skills, now suggested that it was Badeau who

Ulysses Grant, with less than a month to live, works on his memoirs at a cottage on Mount McGregor, near Saratoga, New York, where the family relocated in June 1885. A shawl on the right side of his face and a scarf around his neck hide the swelling cancer in his throat. *(Library of Congress)*

was actually composing the book. Twain, comparing the *World* to "unmedicated closet paper," threatened a libel suit, Grant issued a denial, and other newspapers rose to his defense.

In June, Grant and his family fled the city's heat by moving to another large cottage outside a resort hotel on Mount McGregor, near Saratoga, guests of yet another rich man. Grant not only was writing but rewriting. Would he ever finish? The first of two volumes had gone to press, but that brought the story only to just after the Vicksburg campaign, the war's midpoint.

Twain waited anxiously.

Grant couldn't speak except with terrible pain. He would still dictate but communicated mostly through notes. Morphine eased the pain but interfered with his concentration to write his book, and write he must. Photographs show Grant on the porch of the mountain cottage seated in a wicker chair, scribbling while heavily covered to hide the egg-size swelling in his neck. Grant wrote on.

The triumph! The triumph! What of the little boy who couldn't trade horses? Or the disgraced captain, or the husband and father selling firewood on the streets of St. Louis? Halleck breathing down his back. Grant's drunk again. Johnson's chastisement. Humiliation, failure, and fraud; no new America in Santo Domingo; no third term, no wealth, no name, no honor—

His unconditional surrender was demanded. Grant would not make it easy. With his bulldog's grip he kept to his task hour on hour, bent to it as against Lee. The great Virginian had arrived at the McLean House in Appomattox thirty minutes before Grant and was waiting for him. Lee was escorted by the same Orville Babcock who later would both betray Grant and be saved from prison by him. Of his meeting with Lee, Grant had written:

"When I had left camp that morning I had not expected so soon the result that was then taking place, and consequently was in rough garb. I was without a sword, as I usually was when on horseback on the field, and wore a soldier's blouse for a coat, with the shoulder straps of my rank to indicate to the army who I was. When I went into the house I found General Lee. We greeted each other, and after shaking hands took our seats. I had my staff with me, a good portion of whom were in the room during the whole of the interview.

"What General Lee's feelings were I do not know. As he was a man of much dignity, with an impassible face, it was impossible to say whether he felt inwardly glad that the end had finally come, or felt sad over the result, and was too manly to show it. Whatever his feelings, they were entirely concealed from my observation; but my

own feelings, which had been quite jubilant on the receipt of his letter, were sad and depressed. I felt like anything rather than rejoicing
at the downfall of a foe who had fought so long and valiantly, and had
suffered so much for a cause, though that cause was, I believe, one
of the worst for which a people ever fought, and one for which there
was the least excuse. I do not question, however, the sincerity of the
great mass of those who were opposed to us."

And now here Grant was, desperately trying to achieve one last
earthly victory before he too should be overwhelmed by greater
numbers, by thousands upon thousands of marching faces who had
gone on before, by the inevitable Conqueror. Just like Lee. Just like
Lee!

*

"I FEAR the worst the day the General completes his book," one
of Grant's doctors said. And it was true. Sometime before July 20,
1885, Grant finished his book. On July 23, with family and doctors
gathered around, Ulysses Grant finally gave up.

The funeral parade in New York was massive. So would be his
tomb, made available twelve years later though never quite finished.
The *Personal Memoirs*—Grant's redemption—would be compared to
Caesar's *Commentaries*, would sell 300,000 copies in its first two years,
and would bring Grant's family $450,000. For a time the *Memoirs*
helped save Twain's publishing company too. Julia used $187,000 of
the profits to pay off Grant & Ward debts endorsed by the general.
She still had plenty of money, lived both in New York and Washington, traveled to Europe, and wrote her own memoirs (which were
not published until 1975).

Like Grant and Simon Bolivar Buckner, who was among Grant's
visitors in his last days, Julia would acquire her own ironic Southern
friend. Perhaps it was due to the occasional aspersions cast upon
their husbands' tenure of office, or the fact that both were also memoir writers, but she would grow close to another presidential widow,
Varina Davis. Julia and Varina would be like two aging school chums.
Or perhaps Julia was first touched by a comment of Jefferson Davis,

when he was contacted by the *Boston Globe* for a reaction during her husband's illness.

"General Grant is dying," said the gallant old enemy. "Instead of seeking to disturb the quiet of his closing hours, I would, if it were in my power, contribute to his peace of mind and the comfort of his body."

Grant, upon being told of this, had been pleased.

· 4 ·

THE DIARIST

O ne way of gaining some sense of defeat's impact upon the South is to measure the heights from which its white society fell. Among the very poor, past and present made little difference. For those of the highest class, such as the James Chesnuts of Camden, South Carolina, the plunge was a very great distance indeed. Mary Chesnut, whose remarks continue to enliven hundreds of Civil War studies, lived at the very heart of this higher society. Her keen, wartime observations of the Confederacy's famous and elite would leave the modern world with a vibrant and ultimately tragic picture of the Old South.

For a time, discoverers of Mrs. Chesnut's writings would think they were reading on-the-spot reports, due to the diary format in which they were presented. But much was written and shaped years after the war, amid circumstances far different from those she so meticulously portrayed and once enjoyed. Mrs. Chesnut, as lively a proper lady as one might hope to meet, wanted her past back. The present, though chaotic, almost bored her to tears.

*

WHAT, EXACTLY, was this aristocracy to which Mary and James Chesnut belonged? Although never a large class anywhere, it was peculiarly small in the South, even at the beginning of the war. In his remarkable 1941 polemic, *The Mind of the South*, W. J. Cash confidently hazarded "the guess that the total number of families in Virginia, South Carolina, Louisiana—in all the regions of the little aristocracies—who were rationally to be reckoned as proper aristocrats came to less than five hundred—and maybe not more than half that figure."

Edmund Wilson, in his study of Mary Chesnut's writings as well as those of another well-to-do journal-keeper, Sarah Morgan of Louisiana, was struck "by the recurrence of the same family names. Sarah Morgan in Baton Rouge is related to and knows the same families as the Chesnuts in Richmond a thousand miles away."

These aristocrats, clinging to or claiming the traditions of transplanted cavaliers, weren't always filthy rich, though. It took as much luck as skill to hang on to a fortune in an agricultural economy for more than a couple of generations, and the progeny of these planters were often outworked and outsharped when moving west into the newer parts of the Cotton Kingdom. The Yankee landscape architect Frederick Law Olmsted, who gave Manhattan its Central Park, was before then a journalist who traveled extensively through the South in the 1850s. He knew a little something about style and was particularly riled by the "vulgar rich" he met in Mississippi.

"Of course," he wrote, "there are men of refinement and cultivation among the rich planters of Mississippi, and many highly estimable and intelligent persons outside of the wealthy class, but the number of such is smaller in proportion to that of the immoral, vulgar, and ignorant newly-rich than in any other part of the United States."

But then, these flaws came with wresting wealth from a wilderness, while the ownership of slaves made its own contribution to the moral coarseness. The Northern threat to both class and further wealth, through opposition to extending Negro slavery farther west, was to be the major cause of secession. Here the elites were in the thick of the fray in Congress. Although public service was another characteristic of the Southern upper class—John C. Calhoun and Jefferson Davis being two examples of prewar national leadership—it was essentially a service to protect the baronages. Perhaps no different from the usual run of representation, here it served a consid-

South Carolina aristocrats James and Mary Chesnut, about the time of their 1840 marriage when Mary was seventeen. The Chesnuts were among those with the farthest to fall in defeat, though Mary's later "diary" portrait of the Confederacy's inner circles brought her posthumous fame. *(Granger Collection)*

erably smaller number of people. Eventually they would drag the masses along.

The men in charge of the South as landlords in obscure patches of its states—and later in Richmond where those states ended up— could be social gentlemen of the highest practice. The *code duello's* hair-trigger helped enforce or avenge behavior. But they were also slave masters and gamblers, spendthrifts when it came to public impressions, tightfisted when it was public need, and unusually tunnel-minded. They relied heavily on the goods of the North— too heavily, it would be charged—including their colleges. Yet even when planters' sons were sent away to school, they often retained the home biases. The lads had an attractive gloss when it served their purpose, though the veneer didn't always escape critical scratches.

Henry Adams, Harvard Class of 1858, had this to say of the South's young bucks when examining a fellow student, Virginian Fitzhugh "Rooney" Lee, son of Robert E.:

"Tall, largely built, handsome, genial, with liberal Virginian openness towards all he liked, he had also the Virginian habit of command and took leadership as his natural habit. No one cared to contest it. None of the New Englanders wanted command. For a year, at least, Lee was the most popular and prominent young man in his class, but then seemed slowly to drop into the background. The habit of command was not enough, and the Virginian had little else. He was simple beyond analysis; so simple that even the simple New England student could not realize him. No one knew enough to know how ignorant he was; how childlike; how helpless before the relative complexity of a school. . . .

"No doubt the self-esteem of the Yankee, which tended naturally to self-distrust, was flattered by gaining the slow conviction that the Southerner, with his slave-owning limitations, was as little fit to succeed in the struggle of modern life as though he were still a maker of stone axes, living in caves, and hunting the *bos primigenius*, and that every quality in which he was strong, made him weaker. . . ."

Still, such Ivy League primitives would make ferocious wartime heroes. Until then they could drink, wager, and take deadly umbrage at aspersions real or imagined. Sarah Morgan begins her diary in 1862 by recollecting the death some eight months before of her older brother Harry, a doctor. Harry had been killed in a duel by a man named Sparks. His death stemmed from a quarrel after Sparks's father was thought to have been insulted by the singing of "Annie Laurie."

This was the society Mrs. Chesnut was so much a part of and which she would describe in scintillating and sometimes uproarious detail.

*

MARY BOYKIN CHESNUT was born in 1823 in upcountry South Carolina. Her father, Stephen Decatur Miller, born in the same border-straddling settlement of Waxhaw as Andrew Jackson, had humble beginnings but, upwardly, became a lawyer, governor, and served in both houses of Congress. Mary's mother, the Boykin side, had deeper roots back to Virginia, was the daughter of a wealthy planter, and had been brought to South Carolina as a child. Mary grew up in and about Camden. It was a town not far from Columbia and scene of an American rout by Lord Cornwallis during the Revolution. She had scads of kinfolk on her mother's side. By all appearances, she enjoyed a pampered childhood.

Mary's biographer, Elisabeth Muhlenfeld, relates that in the 1830s Miller decided to uproot his family for the greater cotton promises of Mississippi and its former Indian lands. It was, as Olmsted implied, a trend being followed by swarms of Southerners from older planter empires where the soil had been exhausted. The young Mary spent much of this time at a female academy in Charleston but was in Mississippi long enough to get a taste of the wild frontier. She would later write of how wolves got under the family's cabin, "barking and howling, and roaring like a pack of hounds, knocking against everything and sniffing as if resolved to get in somewhere." Unfortunately, as with many others, the wilderness and its fevers soon killed Miller. The heavy debts left behind had to be rescued by Mary's Boykin uncles.

Back in South Carolina, Mary had met James Chesnut, Jr. He was wealthy, a Princeton graduate, a lawyer, and eight years older. Before leaving on a trip to Europe, he wrote her from Charleston: "Ah, dear girl, you know not how much I love you. If I could breathe my whole soul into a single word I would tell you." Whether he ever did, Mary married him just after her seventeenth birthday.

Chesnut was not intended to be his father's prime heir, but his older brother had recently died. James's father—the senior James and inevitably known as Colonel Chesnut—was the second generation of Carolina planters. By this time he was also one of the upcountry's richest. Among his possessions were Gilbert Stuart portraits of himself and his wife, along with that of George Washington. His various properties added up to about five square miles of land, and his slaves numbered around five hundred. A few of them—as the diarist would hint—likely were sired by himself. Expectations had been for the younger son to pursue some outlet for public service and family luster, and James Jr. was educated accordingly. Now, as the only son, James and Mary settled in on the massive Chesnut plantation, Mulberry, several miles outside Camden.

Colonel Chesnut, fifty years her senior, was described by Mary as kind and amiable but as "absolute a tyrant as the Czar of Russia, the Kahn of Tartary, or the Sultan of Turkey." Still, they became fond of each other. Mary's mother-in-law, who already had outlived ten of her fourteen children, was kind but irritating to the young bride (she would not allow ill to be spoken of anyone) and would seem to provoke outbursts. Two sisters-in-law also lived at Mulberry. Childless herself, Mary would come to love James's nephew, Johnny Chesnut, and to despise one of his nieces, whom she referred to as "Hecate."

Mary spent her days sewing clothes for the slave children at her mother-in-law's behest, holed up in her room with a good book (she was helpfully fluent in French and German) and otherwise trying to stave off boredom. "These people . . . were born and bred" to dullness, Mary complained of the continuing stream of Chesnut family visitors. It took eight years and a trip to London before she and James had their own place in town. The railroad had also come to Camden. Visits into Columbia or to Charleston were easier. Life at last was looking up.

In the several portraits and photographs of Mary Boykin Chesnut, her dark eyes and clear complexion are her best features. The period's costumes with their puffs and petticoats shielded the female figure to the extent that an uncovered foot could send male gallants into spasms of erotic delight. In any case, when she was young Mary

Chesnut must have been light; when old, she was stout. She was said to be about five feet tall.

Mary was gregarious—a reason for her boredom despite the luxuries of Mulberry—but could listen quite as well as she could talk. Extremely well. She was prudish but read Balzac, among many others, and loved a titillating story if tastefully titillated. She had a wicked sense of humor. She considered herself religious but attended no special church, preferring to shop around for a good sermon. She was popular in her own right, notably with younger women, and had a careful heart. She was especially close to a sister, Kate, and cherished Kate's five children.

Although she accepted its comforts, Mary hated slavery—but more for what it did to whites, particularly females, than to blacks. She also loathed abolitionists. She was a feminist for her time; but modern causes identified with feminism today, such as abortion rights and homosexual marriage, would have left her stunned. She was also a snob. Her husband was handsome, highly principled, and had a seldom exposed dry wit. James was a gentleman of impeccable manners. One might say he was also a stuffed shirt.

During the 1850s, James Chesnut moved up through the state's political ranks, serving in the legislature before being sent to the United States Senate in 1858. Mary, a politician's daughter, had also become a political wife. A larger house they had built in Camden was sold to meet anticipated Washington expenses. Despite plantation wealth, the colonel kept a good grip on it.

Mary eagerly leaped into the Washington scene. Her knack for languages helped greatly. Muhlenfeld writes that Mary once sat at a dinner between President Buchanan and a Spanish visitor, translating back and forth between the Spaniard's French and Buchanan's English. She employed a Frenchwoman as a cook. A "very plain but nice dinner" at the Chesnuts was described by a guest as consisting of "Julien soup[,] fish [,] tenderloin of beef and mushrooms & veal larded with vegetables & green peas & salad. Ice cream & champaign & Madiera as concomitants."

Mary made permanent friends with other Southern senators' wives, including Charlotte Wigfall of Texas, Virginia Clay of

Alabama, and Mississippi's Varina Davis. All would meet again in Richmond and in the pages of Mary's recollections. Later, of her experiences in the two capitals she would write, "I dare not look plantation and Camden life in the face. I am ruined for that by Washington and Richmond."

While in Washington, James had championed states' rights in the Senate and did his best to avoid the parties his wife so loved. When Lincoln was elected in 1860, Chesnut became the first of the Southern senators to resign in protest. Mary was away at the time, heading home after visiting sister Kate who had moved to Florida. She was crushed.

*

SHE CALLED her work a journal. It was a collection of diarylike notes and comments, and in its beginning she expressed regret for not having kept one during the Washington interlude. In any case, she knew enough of history to seize the moment of the Confederacy's beginnings. She was in Charleston, in fact, during the firing on Fort Sumter, and James had been sent to Major Robert Anderson to demand the fort's evacuation. But it wasn't until 1905 that her account of the war would see public light as *A Diary from Dixie*, a posthumous incarnation published by a friend who had Mary's various writings in her possession. It was reissued with alterations and expansions under the same title in 1949 by the writer Ben Ames Williams, who had first drawn on the material for a novel. Considerable liberties were taken with both versions of the journal, which—though lengthy—were scaled down from the hundreds of thousands of words assembled by its creator. The historian C. Vann Woodward took on the collection decades later and learned the truth of it.

Although Mary had kept her journal during parts of the war, she did not return to it as a literary project until the 1870s and 1880s. In effect she filled in the blanks from a perspective some years beyond the war—rewrote, expanded, suppressed, and began to give the vast story some shape. She had also taken an unsuccessful fling at writing novels and had learned enough by both this and her extensive reading to hone her memoir with a sense of plot and development. She retained the diary/journal form but had revised the project at least two times and still was not done when she died. Woodward reorganized all of it thoroughly. His assembled work, published as *Mary Chesnut's Civil War*, won for Woodward (and for Mary Chesnut too) the 1982 Pulitzer Prize for history.

Is it a true account, in that it really isn't the wartime diary it presents itself to be? It is true enough. It is such an astonishing book, guided by the very human (and opinionated) voice of its author, that it is probably truer to its times than official records could ever portray. Bible-thick, the book may also be dipped into throughout. Listen for a moment:

"At first Mrs. Joe Johnston called Mrs. Davis 'a western belle,' but when the quarrel between General Johnston and the president broke out, Mrs. Johnston took back the 'belle' and substituted 'woman.' . . ."

"Like the patriarchs of old our men live all in one house with their wives and their concubines, and the mulattoes one sees in every family exactly resemble the white children—and every lady tells you who is the father of all the mulatto children in everybody's household, but those in her own she seems to think drop from the clouds, or pretends so to think. . . ."

"My wildest imagination will not picture Mr. [James M.] Mason as a diplomat [to England]. He will say 'chaw' for 'chew,' and he will call himself 'Jeems,' and he will wear a dress coat to breakfast. Over here, whatever a Mason does . . . is above law. . . ."

"I do not believe Lamar [Lucius Quintus Cincinnatus Lamar, a Mississippi political and military figure, and later a justice of the U.S. Supreme Court]. With *Adam Bede* fresh in my mind, I cannot believe the woman who wrote it [George Eliot] 'is a fallen woman'—'living in a happy state of high intellectual intercourse and happy, contented immorality.' She could not be happy. Dinah and the retribution that overtook Hetty speak out that she knows good from evil. Lamar heard all this of some other of those literary ladies. . . ."

"Halcott Green came to see us. [General Braxton] Bragg is a stern disciplinarian, according to Halcott. He did not in the least understand citizen soldiers. In the retreat from Shiloh, he ordered that not a gun should be fired. A soldier shot a chicken. The soldier was shot. 'For a chicken!' said Halcott. 'A Confederate soldier for a chicken!'. . ."

"General Lee had tears in his eyes when he spoke of his daughter-in-law just dead—that lovely little Charlotte Wickham, Mrs. Rooney Lee. . . ."

Mary Chesnut's poignant book is the closest to an audio of the Civil War as can be found. It is, though, in a much deeper sense, a book of ghosts. To a Southerner accustomed to large family gatherings, with everyone talking at once and trying in their best way to be impressive, it is like passing through a room filled with ancestors. Except one is back in their time—they not in yours—and you can smell the lantern smoke and candle wax and touch the velvet and crinoline and look into marvelously bright eyes which look back and take no notice but proceed with whatever he or she was saying, gaily, grimly, forcefully.

However deep are the sins of the slaver, one is observing the exposure of a people at the abyss. Arrogance is still much a feature, but so is courage and love, cleverness and humor, and a wrenching, stifled hope. It is heartbreaking that the good is destroyed with the bad. Although the tale is told largely from the vantage point of twenty years, the hostess has taken her seat and invited your visit.

*

IN AN ENTRY for May 1865, Mary Chesnut recorded her first post-Sherman look at Mulberry. By this time her mother-in-law had died, but the old colonel was still much alive. Sherman had come in late February, and a Union detachment had moved through Camden, plundering stores and homes and spreading fires. The plantation, however, was spared through the fortitude of James's sister and one of the slaves, who convinced the soldiers that destroying the property would only hurt the Negroes. In April, though, another Union raid under Brigadier General Edward E. Potter did much more damage. Mary recalled:

"Mrs. Bartow drove with me to our house at Mulberry. On one side of the house every window was broken, every bell torn down, every piece of furniture destroyed, every door smashed in. The other side intact.

"Maria Whitaker and her mother, who had been left in charge, explained this odd state of things.

"'They were busy as beavers. They were working like regular carpenters, destroying everything, when the general came in. He said it was [a] shame, and he stopped them. Said it was a sin to destroy a fine old house like that whose owner was over ninety years old. He would not have had it done for the world. It was wanton mischief.' He told Maria soldiers at such times were so excited, so wild and unruly.

"They carried off sacks of our books. Unfortunately there were a pile of empty sacks lying in the garret. Our books, our papers, our letters, were strewed along the Charleston road. Somebody said they found some of them as far away as Vance's Ferry.

"This was Potter's raid. Sherman took only our horses. Potter's raid, which was after [Joseph] Johnston's surrender, ruined us finally, burning our mills and gins and a hundred bales of cotton. Indeed nothing is left now but the bare land and *debts* made for the support of these hundreds of negroes during the war."

Of these last, she concluded:

"The negroes would be a good riddance. A hired man is far cheaper than a man whose father and mother, his wife and his twelve children have to be fed, clothed, housed, nursed, taxes paid, and doctors' bills—all for his half-done, slovenly, lazy work. So for years we have thought—negroes a nuisance that did not pay.

"They pretend exuberant loyalty to us now. Only one man of Mr. C's left his plantation with the Yankees, and he was the boy who stole Mr. Davis's Arabian for them."

Besides the property damage, particularly the burning of the cotton, the colonel during the war had depleted his capital by converting his stocks and bonds into Confederate securities, now worthless. The following year, when he died at age ninety-three, his will left James, his heir, only heavy debt and the responsibility of supporting various relations. Mulberry also was James's for his lifetime only, not

Mary's. Actual money was scarce; Mary complained that she barely had enough for stamps and envelopes. She wrote to Virginia Clay:

"We live miles from any body. Some times do not see a white face for weeks—the coloured ones hang on like grim death. We will have to run a way from their persistent devotion—we are free to desert them now I hope. In point of fact their conduct to us has been beyond all praise."

She mournfully added, "[T]here are nights here with the moonlight, cold & ghastly. & the whippoorwills, & the screech owls alone disturbing the silence when I could tear my hair & cry aloud for all that is past & gone."

The Chesnuts were in no danger of starving; Mulberry would see to that. South Carolina, though, like most of the former Confederacy, was now a province of the North. On similar plantations in the upcountry, land improvements, livestock numbers, and property values continued to plunge. Payments for cotton were kept low to suit the production of Yankee mills. Meanwhile the punitive tax collector circled overhead. An upcountry planter named Renwick received this peremptory notice in 1869 from an unsigned assessor, which is probably typical:

"Dear Sir. I will be at Goshen Hill on tomorrow to assess Taxes. You will please attend at the time and place to make your return. Also the freedmen on your place above the age of 21 years, please inform them. All who fail to make their return will be liable to pay 50 percent of their tax."

The Klan was particularly fierce in the upcountry, so much so that a company of George Custer's Seventh Cavalry was ordered into York County in March 1871. By the following October President Grant, reacting to the findings of his attorney general, Amos Akerman, suspended the writ of habeas corpus in nine counties. Mass arrests and indictments followed—if not convictions. Camden's county, though neighboring, was not among the nine, and James would profess total ignorance of the Klan's workings to a congressional investigating committee. Nonetheless tension there remained rife throughout Reconstruction.

James had served Jefferson Davis as a military aide, and toward the end of the war Davis had promoted him to brigadier general in charge of South Carolina Reserves. That and his previous public service salvaged some of the old prominence in political circles. In 1867, James headed a state convention to protest federal military rule and the next year was a delegate to the Democratic National Convention. While neither effort led to much, he managed to stay active. He was also involved in a taxpayers' group looking into fraud by South Carolina's Radical government.

If James had expectations when Reconstruction tumultuously ended in 1877, they came to naught. He was again eligible to hold elected office, but gentlemanly James could never stoop to push himself on others. The door closed for good in 1882 when he was passed over for a job on the new Federal Tariff Commission. It had seemed like a sure thing, and the presidential appointment would have returned the Chesnuts to Washington and rescued Mary from oblivion. Perhaps by then she had given up on miracles. In her revised journal of the 1880s she had inserted: "Oh! Peace—and a lit[er]ary leisure for my old age—unbroken by care and anxiety!!"

After the war Mary had helped run Mulberry. She managed accounts and the several cottage industries involving clothing and food as well as a small butter and egg business. The freed slaves who now worked were paid on a barter system. Money continued to be scarce, though James had a small legacy from his mother. Mary, always the voracious reader, scrimped to buy books and even started a book club.

As the colonel's will left her in the cold upon James's death, they built a house on land in Camden using brick from a demolished kitchen at Mulberry. They moved there in 1873. Named Sarsfield, James had the property deeded to Mary so she wouldn't have to rely later on the slim charities of her in-laws. She would brag of her "splendid library," and Sarsfield would be their home until they died.

Their postwar lives were an ongoing financial struggle. James tried to sell the Stuart portraits but succeeded only with that of George Washington (which ended up in the Library of Congress). In 1875, Mary made out her will, leaving Sarsfield to a brother-in-law in case James survived her, so his creditors couldn't seize it. Years of crop failure in the 1880s also took their toll, and the old colonel's debts were relentless. At the time of her death, Mary's income was $140 a year from a Negro rental house and about $12 a month from her dairy cows.

As worrisome as finances was Mary's health. Her journal entries mention lengthy periods during the war when she had to take to her bed. Depression and fevers were blamed, but she was also diagnosed, later, with angina pectoris and seems to have had a lung disorder. She was prone to colds and flu and developed what a relative referred to as a "horrid cough." Opium was among the remedies for these protracted distresses.

The anxiety of the war years and its emotional excesses no doubt aggravated a nature that, behind its wit and good sense, was already high-strung. After the war, age and circumstance only added to Mary's disabilities. The early deaths of those close to her were savage blows to a childless woman: nephew Johnny Chesnut in 1868, sister Kate in 1876, and, five months later, Kate's oldest daughter, Serena, who was Mary's favorite niece. The last death made Mary so ill that her mother soon moved in at Sarsfield. Mary's health, never robust, could only weaken.

To Camdenites, her eccentricities seemed to flourish. Muhlenfeld comments that locals remembered her tending her garden while wearing a large shade hat and a pair of James's trousers, or seated in her library and chatting through the open window to a friend parked in a carriage in the yard. A tale would be told of her once greeting visitors in "an old western mackintosh and a funny old hat." Yet having invited them to dinner that night at Sarsfield, she presided in a velvet gown and fan, served "the most beautiful dinner," and carried on as if she were back in Richmond.

*

THE POSTWAR TRAVAILS of the Chesnuts differed only in detail from those of many others of their kind. The aged Mississippi planter Thomas Dabney, ruined by debt and having to borrow just to buy a postage stamp, bent to hard labor to grow food and cut wood throughout his seventies to provide for his family and to repay every cent. He would be remembered by one of his daughters as even doing the household wash, driven by a comment of Sherman's and vowing, "He shall never bring my daughters to the wash-tub."

More than a little can be gleaned of both circumstances and the marriage state between Mary's friend Virginia Clay and her ex-senator husband in Alabama, who complained of her frequent absences to Memphis and received her snappish reply: "I feel lonely & sad & poor, miserably enough to be sure, tho' I try to smile thro it all. When I see the luxurious homes of the Parkers & Bartletts & trousseaux from Paris, & think of my lot, my home & my one black silk dress,—I do not need in addition one word from you or any other one to realize my situation."

Sarah Morgan eventually found herself living in Charleston. The city was impoverished not only by war but by its aged, old-family leadership whose aristocratic distaste now included money. Sarah, in 1874, had married Francis Warrington Dawson, a newspaper editor who was among those urging on Charleston to better things. She seems to have done well enough until Dawson was shot in a quarrel with a local doctor and his killer acquitted. She ended her days as an exile in Paris, where her son had moved, and was recalled as "cold and reserved."

Mary Chesnut, in what spare time she could find, returned to writing. The question is why.

Again, a sense of history is offered for her reconstituted journal, but that came later. She also worked on three novels. Altogether these efforts suggest a bond she had with many other writers—that is, a reluctance to let go of the past. In Mary Chesnut's case—as with those same women who would rise up and lead the United Daughters of the Confederacy—the reluctance was very powerful indeed.

She always was a reader, and surely people who were not a target of her sarcasm enjoyed both her conversation and her letters. Praise that began when she was a precocious child undoubtedly continued and inspired her later on, as did the pitiable state she found herself in. She had, of course, seen much, and perhaps decided that fiction was a better way to convey her impressions and experience. Novelists were always a cut above—most of the time, anyway; they certainly were superior, in an artistic sense, to lowly journal-keepers.

But none of her novels saw publication until 2002, and only then because of the fame from her journal. She seems to have set them aside and possibly planned to try again one day. Or perhaps she heard the tiny, dreaded whisper of eternal failure.

She completed drafts of her novels in the mid-1870s. One effort, *The Captain and the Colonel,* was a tangled wartime romance that roped in the now-deceased Johnny Chesnut as a model. A second, *Two Years—or The Way We Lived Then,* drew heavily on her Charleston schoolgirl and Mississippi frontier experiences. Of the third novel, titled *Manassas* and also set during the war, only a few pages would survive.

She was obviously dissatisfied with each; likely she was bored with them. Sometimes books fail because the writer has nothing to say. Sometimes a writer has something to say and yet can't say it, not in the way it should really be said. Sometimes—many times—characters put to a page simply refuse to leap up and solve all problems of meaning and method. Things burn. Memories. Lives and deaths, joys and heartaches, the past, the old country—things that don't lend themselves to artificiality except in the hands of the most artistic liars. Her past, her war, her people, weren't really breaking through.

At some point Mary Chesnut discovered that her old wartime journal wasn't just history but autobiography. How much of it was available to her, though, is hard to say. Some appears to have been lost or destroyed, whether accidentally or deliberately. How much she actually wrote of her experiences at their time is also hard to say. Long gaps appear in the period covered, possibly due to busyness elsewhere or illness. However it was, she was highly protective of the journal, keeping its papers under lock and key and even away from James.

She returned to it for some months in 1875 and 1876, editing, deleting, finishing incomplete notes. Possibly the deaths of her sister and niece and a serious illness of her own contributed to her halting work on it. Moreover she had received some cautionary advice about it. She did not take up the journal again until 1881 when, in Woodward's words, "she was fifty-eight and in wretched health, plagued by a heart condition, lung trouble and minor ailments," and with daily responsibilities of "running a dairy farm and a household full of aging, ailing, and often demanding relatives."

Her novel writing, as unsatisfying as it had been, had improved her skills in shaping a story and sharpening dialogue. Details would be added in her last version of the journal to flesh out what would be memorable episodes. The old business was brought back to life. Some idea of what she put into it is gained from a letter to Varina Davis in 1883: "How I wish you could read over my journal. I have been two years overlooking it—copying—leaving myself out. You must see it—before it goes to print—but that may not be just now. I mean the printing—for I must overhaul it again—and again."

But then, she would never finish it. And it's quite possible that had she lived for many more years instead of just the three remaining to her, she still would not have finished it.

There was a serious problem with Mary Chesnut's journal-diary-history-autobiography.

The respected Robert Mercer Taliaferro Hunter, a former United States senator and Confederate congressman, at the time of the 1876 revision was asked by James on behalf of Mary to look at her journal. Hunter diplomatically replied that while anxious to read it "if published just now by a So Ca lady, such a work might make the world a little too hot to hold her. . . ." James also apparently thought it "a little too spicy." Hunter would say, humorously, "If so it would be better not to publish for as Grant said 'let us have peace.'"

Such a book, as feared, would be seen as a betrayal of the very class to which she belonged. Her candid and unconventional views, her allusions to miscegenation, her mockery and relentless recording of vanity and arrogance, her sometime puncturing accounts of the Confederate elite would have appalled that conventional society still bunched on Southern verandas and always given to overreact.

Moreover, as her book would later prove, there was no leaving herself out of it despite her assurances to Varina Davis. Never mind that her words were often harder on herself than anyone else. More important was that anyone else. No matter how she might disguise it, someone—and that someone's friends—would know quite well of what she was speaking.

It was all impossible. Fiction had been tried as a way of casting off some bits and pieces of the Great Experience, but again they were mere bits and pieces. She persisted in making her book a diary. That only added to the perception of how true it was. Her picture was also broadly stroked, of a Southern society from bottom to top, but never mind that, either. The upper crust—warts and all—might tolerate a rebel in its ranks who could still give a good dinner party, but it would be the kind of party far beyond the reach of the James Chesnuts of postwar South Carolina.

In a way, Mary Chesnut's dilemma prefigured that by a few years of Winnie Davis's. With her Yankee engagement Winnie had run afoul of the same sort of crowd that would have jumped on Mrs. Chesnut. Although Winnie's engagement came to nothing, Jeff Davis had come around to support it. This raises the question of just how supportive James Chesnut was of his wife's irreverent scribbling. In her journal Mary would praise R. M. T. Hunter as "the sanest, if not the wisest, man in our newborn Confederacy." Yet while his opinion seems always to have carried weight with her, his book advice suggests the influence of James's remark of it being "too spicy."

Moreover her writing was subject to continuous interruption by both James and her mother. She compared one intrusion to working in the presence of "the Czar of Russia," noting to herself that "I have been interrupted three times in trying to *accomplish* this sentence." Perhaps James was unimpressed. The only money known to have been earned by Mary Chesnut for her writing was for a wartime account titled "The Arrest of a Spy," taken from her journal and sold in 1884 to the *Charleston News and Courier.* Francis Warrington Dawson sent her $10.

Perhaps, in 1882, Mary saw James's opportunity in Washington as a literary chance for herself as well. The city was certainly a safer location from which to lob her Civil War grenades—if she could ever complete her book. James also would have part of his reputation back, which would be a sort of imprimatur. But President Chester Arthur killed their hopes. With them went any semblance that James

Chesnut counted for anything outside Camden. And with that went whatever social armor plate remained to protect his wife. Still, for a little longer, she pressed on with her project.

There had always been plenty to rework or delete, to attempt to finesse or simply to strike through. In other words, much still remained where she could play it smart and scribble it out. And that was just it: How bland could she be? No, no, no! Mary Boykin Chesnut had never been boring in her life. She refused to be boring now. No! But on the other hand . . . The book stayed unfinished and the dilemma unresolved: to publish or not. Mary Chesnut would be the South's Emily Dickinson.

*

JAMES and her mother died eight days apart in 1885. On the first anniversary of his death, Mary wrote in a letter to a relative:

". . . I have been so ill—and am still so feeble. And these awful anniversaries take the little life out of me that is left—Last night Mothers clock sounded every hour—and when I dozed—it was 'Yes Master! I am coming Sir'—as I heard Moze tearing thru the passage—& Mr Chesnuts impatient calls. Strange to say—at first Mother was here most—now she seems to have gone to her rest in Heaven—I never see or hear her—But Mr Chesnut—I have to sit with my back to the door not to see him come in. It is all bodily weakness I know."

James's illness that preceded his death seems to have interrupted, perhaps permanently, any further work on the journal, just as the circumstances he left behind discouraged its resumption. Mary had no portion of the Mulberry property and retained only Sarsfield. James's debts were estimated as "between 35 & 40 thousand dollars." She complained in a letter that "one by one the things my husband thought he left me have been taken away from my [sic] by these Camden lawyers—by a cruel spirit of a pen—The Insurance money then my dower lands—as soon as I showed them where they were—*legally* they seized them for a *bad* debt of Old Mr C to Dr Deas. So I am stripped naked—but the hundred a year for the negro

house rents—and what I can make by the Jerseys . . . still I can laugh
& gird at the world as of Yore."

Her yearly income now was said to equal the cost of one of the
lace capes she had bought when living in Washington. She was distressed by sick cattle and the death of a bull, and blamed herself for
the animals not being insured. She wrote one of Kate's sons that "I
am awfully tempted to sell out to some rich Yankee for cash—and
run away—but I am too old—and too ill."

Mary Chesnut died on November 22, 1886, probably of a combination of ailments. She was sixty-three. She left Sarsfield to a
nephew but instructed him to hold it in trust for his wife. She asked
to be buried beside James and under a marble slab in a family cemetery near Camden. At one point toward the end of the war she
was describing, she had written: "Stop, Mrs. C. At best, Camden for
life—that is worse than the galleys for you." And now it was Camden
for eternity.

She had placed her unfinished journal and her hopes for it in
the hands of a friend, Isabella Martin, a schoolteacher in Columbia, but nothing was done with the material until 1905. Miss Martin
faced the same dilemma—Confederate legends having become even
more sacred in the meanwhile, and some of the horrors of slavery set
aside—and felt free to alter or excise any embarrassing passages from
an already scaled-down work.

No one had the slightest appreciation of what they actually had.
Memoirs of wartime belles were big at the time, and the Chesnut
extravaganza was just more cashing in on the trend. In that same
1905 Virginia Clay published her own memoirs. So did Louise
(Louly) Wigfall Wright, daughter of Charlotte Wigfall. Louise
would remember Mary as "one of the most brilliant women of her
time." Virginia remembered that "childless, property-less, our well-
loved Mrs. Chestnut [sic] suffered a terrible eclipse after her brilliant
youth and middle age."

So much for *their* memories, but who would remember *them*
were it not for some mention from Mrs. Chesnut's storehouse? Of
Virginia Clay as told by Mary (page 451):

"We came near having a compliment today, but a further development of Dr. Rufus's taste deprived it of all value.

"'Mrs. Davis, Mrs. Clay, and you—I do declare, you are the cleverest ladies in the Confederacy. Mrs. Clay, now—you know I proclaim her supreme for wit and beauty as well as refinement.'"

And of the young Miss Wigfall (page 506):

"Louly Wigfall snubbed Mrs. Preston.

"Mary P[reston], lifting her hands to heaven in protest: 'Not even to see three stars on John Darby's coat collar could I bear to have mama's feelings hurt.'

"We could see no connection between the two things, but Mary's heart is always right."

And so was Mary Chesnut's. Her old friends might have hated the book openly and secretly delighted in it. However their feelings, Mrs. Chesnut would do for them the one thing they couldn't do for themselves, whatever their sensibilities, whatever their worth in gold or Confederate bonds. She restored them to life, where they're likely to stick around for a good many more years. She had, in fact, done the fellow members of her class the best (or worst) of favors: she had handed them back their mirrors.

· 5 ·

THE CRIPPLED KNIGHT

John Bell Hood was determined. His plan to take the Confederacy's Army of Tennessee and march north—leaving Georgia to General Sherman—had always been a risk. Yet the rewards, if successful, were almost limitless: the capture of the Union-occupied city of Nashville; the advance to the Ohio River and on to Cincinnati; or perhaps a swing east to rescue Robert E. Lee in Virginia, where combined Rebel armies could then whip Grant and turn on Sherman. Before any of that could happen, however, his army had to get through or around the Yankees he was chasing. They had stopped at the little town of Franklin, Tennessee, and had dug in.

It was the last day of November 1864, and the bitter, freezing weather that for weeks had accompanied Hood's men had turned unseasonably warm and sunny. That did not make the entrenchments, the guns, on the outskirts of the town any less grim. The Confederates had been in pursuit of the enemy all day. During the previous night, the federal troops—some twenty thousand of them—had slipped right by Hood, who thought he had them trapped. Hood had angrily awakened to that fact. Now, before Franklin, he called a council of war. He wanted a frontal assault across a two-mile open plain.

Hood's generals were stunned. Two of them, Patrick Cleburne and Frank Cheatham, spoke of the formidable strength of the enemy's position. Another, the great cavalry leader Nathan Bedford Forrest, insisted that his men instead could flank the Yankees out of their works. Hood was unmoved. The attacking columns were to "go over the main works at all hazards."

The Battle of Franklin was nothing short of a slaughter. The late-afternoon charge across the plain and without one of the army's three corps, which had not entirely caught up, engaged fewer than 16,000 Confederate infantry. Yet Rebel casualties were more than 6,200. Dead stacked up seven-deep in front of the Union entrenchments. The 1,750 Confederates killed were more than the Union battle deaths at Fredericksburg, Chickamauga, Chancellorsville, Shiloh, or Stones River. The Confederate carnage was worse than the more famous "Pickett's Charge" at Gettysburg.

Cleburne, the army's best division commander, had despondently remarked to a subordinate before the attack that "if we are to die, let us die like men." He was among the six slain Rebel generals. He and three others were laid out stiff on the veranda of nearby Carnton plantation while surgeons inside sawed into the wounded and piles of discarded limbs grew higher in the yard. Nonetheless because the federal forces pulled out that night for nearby Nashville, Hood declared a success. Then he issued marching orders in the same direction, past—according to a Confederate captain—the "sickening, blood-curdling, fear-kindling sight" of unburied dead.

*

HOOD WAS the youngest of the Confederacy's eight full generals during the war. They included Lee, his idol, whose aggressive tactics Hood tried to emulate. But Hood was no Lee. Given the Army of Tennessee at Atlanta after Jefferson Davis fired the ever-retreating Joseph Johnston, Hood lost four battles in Georgia. In Tennessee, after Franklin, he was routed at Nashville. The army remnant surrendered four months later to Sherman in North Carolina, without Hood.

Hood would be so identified with Texans as to be considered one, due to his successful leadership of them during the first half of the war. He was, however, a native of Kentucky, born in 1831 near Lexington. His father was a doctor who prospered by selling trusses. The young Hood grew to be six feet two inches tall with broad shoulders and a deceptively shy manner. Friends called him Sam. He was attracted to women and they to him. Like Grant, he also took to horses. Unlike Grant, Hood wanted to be a soldier and entered West Point in 1849.

He was no genius. Hood finished forty-fourth out of fifty-two in his class, including a last in ethics. He is known to have checked out just two books from the school's massive library: Jane Porter's *Scottish Chiefs* and Walter Scott's *Rob Roy*. Lee, the academy's new superintendent, busted Hood from cadet lieutenant to private for a rules infraction. His classmates included John Schofield, the Union commander at Franklin, and James Birdseye McPherson, killed by Hood's men at Atlanta. George Thomas, who would complete the defeat of Hood's army at Nashville, was his cavalry and artillery instructor. After leaving West Point, Lieutenant Hood chased Comanches with Lee in Texas and later followed him to war against the army they both had served.

John Bell Hood was a curious but lethal mixture of ingredients. Variously described as gallant and knightly, he was one of the most courageous leaders of troops in the war. He paid a high price personally, losing the use of an arm at Gettysburg and a leg at Chickamauga. His soldiers, of whom he expected equal bravery, also paid dearly. Hood was a man of action; he was not—to a fatal degree—a detail person, yet he made his way up through the ranks to full command. He was one of those Southerners whom Henry Adams would have found "simple beyond analysis." Mary Chesnut found him "the simplest, most transparent soul I have met."

He was certainly not without ambition. Mrs. Chesnut once scolded him as an awkward flatterer, that he should praise her husband to someone else rather than to her. Unlike Lee, who accepted the blame for his army's defeat at Gettysburg, Hood had a habit of blaming others. While his later defeats had help, once away from his Texans Hood was an object of warm hostility from fellow generals and lowly privates. He and Joseph Johnston came to hate each other, which only brought Hood still closer to Johnston's archenemy, Jefferson Davis.

John Bell Hood, described by an admiring belle as "superbly handsome, with beautiful blue eyes, golden hair and flowing beard—broad shouldered, tall and erect," during the war would lose the use of his left arm at Gettysburg and have his right leg amputated at Chickamauga. *(Chicago History Museum)*

Yet Hood may also be viewed with sympathy. Perhaps it was his eyes. Said to light up in battle, they were otherwise cast in a soul-reflecting sadness. There was a sort of clumsy nobility about him, even were he not hobbled by battle wounds, by his crutch and wooden leg. He reached, but he always overreached. His self-confidence was constantly betrayed. He was like one of those planter sons who goes off to Mississippi to make a fortune in cotton and miserably fails.

What sorrow he brought was returned to him. What victories he could claim on or off the battlefield were clouded by his defeats. He was called chivalrous and no doubt was viewed as another creature of romance come alive. Other than battle, though—and that while under the command of someone like Lee, where he could be watched—life seemed to be a mystery to him.

What use had peace for a knight? Maybe he had given some thought to that. Maybe that was in the back of his mind as he scanned the Richmond belles who so wanted to be near the hero-general in the war's early days, when his star shone bright with his Texas Brigade at Gaines' Mill and Second Manassas and Antietam—while he was still physically whole. Other than his battle experiences, Hood's adventures in Confederate society were the most interesting period of his life.

Louly Wigfall was one of the belles who had a crush on Hood. Her father, Louis, was at this time a Confederate senator and a power back home in Texas. Louly, not quite eighteen, would later remember her knight: "A braver man, a purer patriot, a more gallant soldier never breathed than General Hood. . . . He was a man of singular simplicity of character and charm of manner—boyish in his enthusiasm—superbly handsome, with beautiful blue eyes, golden hair and flowing beard—broad shouldered, tall and erect—a noble man of undaunted courage and blameless life."

Unfortunately for Louly—or perhaps not—Hood had eyes for another.

She was Sarah Buchanan "Buck" Campbell Preston, a daughter of John Preston, a wealthy South Carolinian who owned Louisiana sugar plantations and spent a lot of time in Europe. The Prestons were also friends of Mary and James Chesnut, and Mary's shoulder and wit were often sought by Buck and her sisters. Buck had a French education, blue eyes, long lashes, and was a self-centered flirt. Hood became interested in 1863 when John Darby, his army physician who was in love with Buck's sister Mary Cantey Preston, introduced them in Richmond. Gettysburg had not yet occurred. Buck was twenty. Hood was not yet thirty-two.

Buck, according to Mrs. Chesnut, attracted men with ease. "But then," she wrote, "there seemed a spell upon her lovers—so many were killed or died of the effects of wounds. Ransom Calhoun, Braddy Warwick, Claude Gibson, the Notts." Hood was drawn to Buck and she to him. The arrogance of South Carolina aristocrats toward all but their Virginia betters made patriotic allowance for outsider knights in wartime. Hood was allowed into the circle.

He would inform Mrs. Chesnut that he had proposed marriage to Buck before he went to Georgia and Chickamauga, but she had not accepted, and after losing his leg there "I gave it up." The flame was rekindled after returning to Richmond to recuperate during the winter of 1863–1864.

In the capital Hood was an observer not only of Buck but also of an almost frenzied party scene. At the time the city's poorer citizens were suffering food shortages and surging inflation. The *Richmond Daily Whig* had chastised the upper-class revelers while "mothers, wives, and children of the gallant defenders of our country's rights are . . . starving, or dying from broken hearts." No matter. Distracting charades and amateur theatricals such as *The Rivals* were lustily performed even as doom edged ever closer. Other theater also began.

As Mary Chesnut would famously tell it, though Buck seemed no longer to care about Hood, she couldn't resist flirting with him. Matters soon turned serious once more. When Hood received orders to return to Georgia and lead a corps under Joe Johnston, he again proposed to her—perhaps several times. One night, Mrs. Chesnut recalled, Buck brought notice to herself by protecting Hood on his crutch from a crowd rushing by. Impressed, General John Breckinridge had asked Mrs. Chesnut if Buck was going to wed Hood.

Mrs. Chesnut soon scolded Buck: "Now, Buck! You know you are not childish, that you have more strong, good common sense than anyone in that house except your mother. Why are you playing with him in that way? I told General Breckinridge that you had been engaged before and probably would be engaged again. . . . You are so unhappy about so many of those men who cared for you having been killed. It was odd, you say, that Hood was always lucky till he fell in love with you, that you were ever so sorry for him, and so many farewells nowadays (with the chances never to meet again softening a girl's heart) ended in 'engagements.'"

But the romance continued. One day, when Buck yawned at Hood, he offered his hand. Reluctantly, she took it. "Heavens, what a change came over his face," Buck told Mrs. Chesnut. "I pulled my hand away by main strength. The practical wretch, he said at once: 'Now I will speak to your father. I want his consent to marry you at once.' Did you ever know so foolish a fellow?"

News of an engagement soon leaked. Buck complained: "Look here! My engagement is announced in the *Charleston Mercury*. Mama blames me. How could I keep it?" James Chesnut also had criticized Buck for letting Hood kiss her hands in public.

The coolness of Buck's parents to the engagement puzzled Hood. He told Mrs. Chesnut: "Parents' ways are incomprehensible to me. I can't see through it all. They let me ride with her, drive with her, come and go unmolested. They asked me to dinner, to breakfast, to tea. When I became engaged to their daughter, I expected to have the run of the house. No—far from it. I never see them at all. I am never asked there. When I call, or when I go to spend the evening there, I see her only in the drawing room, where there are always a parcel of giggling girls listening, watching, and that Brewster [Henry Percy Brewster, a Hood friend from Texas] setting them on. But I'll kill him." Mrs. Preston was also reported as annoyed when the story of Buck protecting Hood from the crowd got back to her.

Obviously, to the Prestons, Hood had pushed his luck too far. With his wounds and headlong reputation, he must have seemed a likely candidate to join Buck's stream of dead admirers. Mostly, though, they thought him not good enough. Maggie Howell, Varina

Davis's catty sister, gave some hint of this in her own opinion, which might have mirrored or influenced the Prestons', though Maggie's motives could also have included jealousy. According to the diarist: "Maggie said people who knew General Hood before the war said there was nothing in him. As for losing his property by the war—he never had any. West Point was a pauper's school, after all. It was only military glory—and all that he had gained since the war began."

In Georgia, despite bracing for the oncoming Sherman, Hood wrote Buck daily, including a thirty-page letter. It also may have been to impress Buck (or at her urging) that Hood was baptized by the Episcopal bishop-turned-general Leonidas Polk. Still, even the love-smitten Hood had little time for letters once the fighting resumed in May 1864.

Buck was back home in Columbia, South Carolina, when two months later Hood was named to take over the army from Johnston. Her bitter reaction was a surprise.

"Things are so bad out there," wrote Mrs. Chesnut, quoting Buck. "They cannot be worse, you know. And so they have saved Johnston from the responsibility of his own blunders—and put Sam in. Poor Sam!"

"Why? Buck, I thought you would be proud of it," said Mary, Buck's sister.

"No—I have prayed God as I have never prayed him before since I heard this. And I went to the convent and asked the nuns to pray for him, too."

Soon after Hood's promotion, the Preston family was devastated by the death of Buck's brother Willie, an artillery officer killed during one of Hood's Atlanta battles. A silence seemed to fall. Two months later, Mary Cantey Preston married John Darby. She and Darby had turned bitterly against Buck and Hood's engagement.

In December, apparently after the disastrous losses in Tennessee, Buck received two letters from Hood—"and he is coming in January to be *married*."

But their wedding would never take place. In January 1865, Hood was relieved of command of the Army of Tennessee. In February, now returned, Hood was described to Mrs. Chesnut by Jack Preston, another brother of Buck's, as staring into a fire while "that agony in his face comes again and again. . . . It is pretty trying to anyone who has to look on. . . . I get up and come out, as I did just now."

In March, Mrs. Chesnut declared: "The Hood melodrama is over, though the curtain has not fallen on the last scene." There was a parting in April as Confederates fled Richmond through the Carolinas, and in May there was this startling confession from Buck to Mary Chesnut:

"I think it began with those beautiful, beautiful silk stockings that fit so nicely. I have been afraid to warm my feet on the fender ever since. You ought to hear him rave about my foot and ankle. Before that he was so respectful. He kissed my hand, to be sure, but that is nothing. Sometimes when he kissed my hand he said I was his queen and what a grateful fellow he was that I liked him, and I was proud of that very respectful style he adopted.

"But as I stood by the fender, warming my feet, he seized me round the waist and kissed my throat—to my horror—and when he saw how shocked I was, he was frightened in a minute and so humble and so full of apologies. Said it was so soft and white, that throat of mine, he could not help it. It was all so sudden. I drew back and told him I would go away, that I was offended. In a moment I felt a strong arm so tight around my waist I could not move. He said I should stay until I forgave his rash presumption, and he held me fast.

"I pretended to be in a rage. He said, after all, I had promised to marry him—and that made all the difference in the world. But I did not see it. So I wear boots, and I never warm my feet, and I wear a stiff handkerchief close up around my throat. . . .

"You see, I never meant to be so outrageously treated again," she continued. "It was a shame. Now, would you believe it, a sickening, almost an insane, longing comes over [me], just to see him once more, and I know I never will. He is gone forever. If he had been persistent, if he had not given way under Mamie's [sister Mary] violent refusal to listen to us, if he had asked *me*. When you refused to let anybody be married in your house—well, I would have gone down on the sidewalk. I would have married him on the pavement, if the parson could be found to do it. I was ready to leave all the world for him. . . . Does that sound like me? It was true that day.

"Now let us talk of something else. Fancy we have been translating from the French."

Buck eventually would marry Rawlins Lowndes, another character who flits in and out of Mrs. Chesnut's recollections. Lowndes, of an old Charleston family, had risen to colonel on General Wade Hampton's staff. In one of the more humorous episodes, Lowndes had gone to his tailor and selected a fine piece of grey cloth for a new uniform, only to be told that Hood had reserved the cloth for his own wedding. Still, Lowndes' presence is hardly a shadow until the end. The Prestons would flee to Paris after the war. They were so cash-poor that John Preston would ask the equally hard-pressed James Chesnut for payment on a small debt of Mary's.

Hood's war ended when he surrendered with two of his aides in Natchez, Mississippi, while trying to reach Texas. He would continue on by train. For part of the way he rode with the Wigfalls. This had a certain combustible potential. Louis Wigfall was a booster of Joe Johnston and a Jeff Davis–hater—all contrary to Hood's tastes. Louly had been dropped for Buck. In the end she had the triumph, though, as did so many over Hood.

Free with her praise earlier, she would unsparingly recall the burnt-out Hood as sitting "with calm, sad eyes. . . . The cause he loved was lost—he was overwhelmed with humiliation at the utter failure of his leadership—his pride was wounded to the quick by his removal from command. . . . In the face of his misery, which was greater than our own, we sat silent—there seemed no comfort anywhere."

*

IN HER original journal, Mary Chesnut had written: "Buck, my poor darling, as far as I see, they did you cruel wrong when they did not let you marry and share the fate of your poor wounded hero and patriot, the only true man I have seen in your train yet."

Thus Hood, the knight. Except for a few moments of provoca-
tion by cold feet and warm throats, he had been knightly toward
Buck too—and incredibly patient. The streak of romanticism that
ran in these rather lofty circles of Southern society had been fed
for years not just by Walter Scott but by a number of home-grown
types extolling the fictions of colonial life and cavaliers. The critic
Edmund Wilson points out that the chivalrous ideal became popular
enough even to be satirized in its time, in the 1830s, by the Maryland
writer John Pendelton Kennedy. Whether Hood ever read beyond
his two novels at West Point is not known; but he didn't have to read
to be aware of the prevailing conventions. Moreover bravery and
gallantry were etched on his soldierly being.

Yet Hood was a lonely knight in peace. So many knights had been
struck down: the cavalier Jeb Stuart; Buck's list of unlucky beaus;
the Irish immigrant Cleburne, more suited than Robert Emmet for
Winnie Davis's monographic admiration. Others would survive, like
Rawlins Lowndes. He had ridden with Wade Hampton the elder and
had fainted at the sight of the young Wade's wounds. But he had also
challenged the Yankee Judson Kilpatrick to a duel of sabers—Hampton's thousand men against Kilpatrick's fifteen hundred. Lowndes'
family had tucked away its wealth in England at the war's outset.
Knights aren't supposed to lose the fair maiden, but when two are in
contention, money will always decide.

So many Southrons had been schooled to take over the plantation at some point, or the law firm, or a congressional seat, or
simply to enjoy whatever leisure or credit was available. But now
their land and their future had been laid waste. Some, like Hood,
were schooled only for war. One of Sarah Morgan's brothers, James
Morris Morgan, an Annapolis midshipman, spent much of his war
running the Union blockade and afterward married the daughter
of George Trenholm, the Confederacy's treasury secretary. But her
death from fever in 1866 broke all ties and left young Morgan aimless. He enlisted in the Egyptian army and later failed as a cotton
planter and silver prospector. He drifted until rescued with a government job in 1885. He was not unlike others.

Hood, with his wooden leg and the use of only one hand, wouldn't be riding any camels across deserts. And if by some miracle he had returned to the service of American arms, he would not have been trusted to lead any group of men above division level. That is what Hood had been: a good division commander, just like poor Pat Cleburne.

Knights were meant to follow into battle kings and princes like Robert E. Lee or, even for a brief time, Joseph Johnston. With luck they would die in battle and become immortalized for their courage and tragic end. They would not be forced to survive and survey the charred landscape they had been helpless to prevent. They would be deaf to the laughter at their dreams. They would not be left to stare into flames.

Other Texans were kinder than Louly. They remembered Hood's Texas Brigade and the victories in Virginia and at Chickamauga; they had nothing to do with Atlanta and Franklin and Nashville. Hood was cheered in Houston and San Antonio, and the *Dallas Herald* rang out: "Long may he live to enjoy the gratitude of his countrymen." Hood's spirits perked up.

After several months, however, he left Texas for Washington, ostensibly to visit the imprisoned Jeff Davis. Along the way he talked to a newspaper reporter, explaining Atlanta and the rest as being the result of dispirited men and the failure of officers at crucial times. It would be his explanation to the end. The visit to his friend Davis was likely to help bolster Hood's account, should he ever put it into memoirs. Unfortunately no friends were allowed to see Davis just then.

What was Hood to do with himself? He returned to his native Kentucky where his mother still lived. There he found friends enough to loan him $250 each—a total of $10,000—so that he could enter the cotton business in New Orleans. It was a city that would provide him with plenty of soldierly company from the war, harboring within or nearby former generals P. G. T. Beauregard, Braxton Bragg, James Longstreet, Jubal Early, Joe Wheeler, Dick Taylor, and the inimitable Simon Bolivar Buckner. Hood also had a chance to go elsewhere. Texas friends in San Antonio had begun raising money to provide him with "a suitable homestead and competency." Having made up his mind for New Orleans, Hood politely declined the gift.

It would look like another of his bad decisions. In February 1866, with two partners, he established the firm of J. B. Hood and Company, cotton factors and commission merchants. The city on the Mississippi had long been a major cotton center, and there seemed little reason for it not to continue. The extent of Hood's cotton expertise is unknown. Perhaps his partners knew all about pricing and speculating and shipping and the like. Perhaps Hood's role was to call on as many of the former movers and shakers and old soldiers he could find from the glory days, those who were now trying to scratch out a living, and appeal for cotton—if they had any. For instance, he immediately wrote to Stephen Dill Lee, the general whose men had brought up the rear and had mostly missed the charge at Franklin:

". . . as commission merchants need Cotton And that Cotton must come from friends and As I take you to be one of my best, I without any reserve ask that you will thro' your many friends in Miss[issippi] & elsewhere turn in the direction of this house all the Cotton you can. We are poor but claim to be honest and promise to do the best we can for those who trust us."

Within three months newspapers were reporting that the cotton crop in nine Southern states was seriously impaired by cold, rains, and bad seed, and that not more than a third of it would be realized. Just upstream from New Orleans disastrous flooding along the Red River, where the levees gave way, destroyed so much of the crop that it was likened to only one-third that of 1861. The same conditions that hampered upcountry planters in South Carolina would hamper Hood. And increased shipments of cotton north by railroad had taken the shine off New Orleans' prominence as a necessary seaport.

Within several years, Hood's cotton business was no more. It may never have been very much to start with.

A separate opportunity, meanwhile, had come Hood's way. It might be said to have fallen into his lap.

Pete Longstreet in Virginia and at Chickamauga had been, as a corps commander, Hood's immediate superior in the armies of Lee and Bragg. Now in postwar New Orleans Longstreet was president of the Texas and Louisiana offices of the Life Association of America, an insurance company. When the Radical Republican Congress established martial law in ten states of the old Confederacy and pressed for black suffrage, the *New Orleans Times* in 1867 editorially sought the counsel of the Rebel generals as to the wisest course to follow.

Longstreet was the only one to step forward in print. Basically, he said, the South had lost the war, it was pointless to resist, and the only way to regain full rights was to go along with Congress and its laws. Speaking to the South, he said: "The views that we hold cease to be principles because they are opposed to law. It is therefore our duty to abandon ideas that are obsolete and conform to the requirements of law." Put another way, might makes right. Longstreet also embraced the Republican party.

The South was aghast. Longstreet's insurance business slumped, friends shunned him, and he was branded a scalawag—a Southern carpetbagger. Fellow general D. H. Hill wondered if the Republican endorsement was a joke.

Longstreet turned to the venerable Robert E. Lee in Virginia for support. Months later, Lee at last replied that he "avoided all discussions of political questions." President Grant, whose brother-in-law was New Orleans' collector of customs, ultimately saved Longstreet—his old wedding groomsman—with a job as port surveyor. Pete had broken ranks.

Hood's action during this scuffle was to take no public role at all. Longstreet would recall: "General Hood met me and we talked about the editorial. He said in effect that it aimed at a condition that we all devoutly hoped for, but he added: 'If you declare yourself on those lines the Southern press and the Southern people will vilify and abuse you. It may be very patriotic and all that, but it will be very foolish.'. . . However much General Hood may have shared my sentiments he never trusted himself to public expression of them." Still, Hood would be "the only one of my old comrades who occasionally visited me."

Hood also, in Longstreet's words, "thought that he could save the insurance business, and in a few weeks I found myself at leisure." Hood would take it over in 1869. As president his salary was a welcome $5,000 a year. Insurance would be his business until he died.

Hood was in fact the beneficiary of a friend's misfortunes brought on by stubborn honesty. If Hood did share any of Longstreet's sentiments, it raises the question of whether he should have stood more firmly alongside his old commander in public, just as he had in battle during the war. Of course, if one's cotton business was doing poorly, why risk the same sort of costly wrath? For once in his life Hood played it safe, and while not especially knightly it was the smart move. Moreover he was in position to take over the insurance company once Longstreet was gone for good.

There is no evidence of anything untoward. Still, a less attractive aspect of Hood's character was his calculation or ambition, and it is only natural to ask. He had gained the command of Joe Johnston's army in part by falsely magnifying to Richmond his differences with Johnston in Georgia and by besmirching a senior rival, General William J. Hardee. He had gambled on Buck Preston—or, perhaps more precisely, on John Preston's brandy and cigars. But perhaps the insurance company was no more than being just enough of a friend to Old Pete. Perhaps.

*

THE WAR would never quite end for Hood. It would be there for him every morning when he dressed. With his maimed limbs, though, he became active in efforts to help other crippled soldiers. After a time he began appearing at military reunions, particularly in Texas and Louisiana. A touching moment occurred in early 1866 when Hood was in Louisville and heard that George Thomas was in town. Hobbling on his crutch, Hood was embraced by Thomas, and they talked for more than an hour in Thomas's hotel room—student and instructor, both at West Point and Nashville. Afterward Hood said of Thomas, a Virginian: "Thomas is a grand man; he should have remained with us, where he would have been appreciated and loved."

And yet, could Hood guarantee appreciation and love even for himself? It seems likely that for all the glory among Texans and the fellowship of New Orleans' cadre of generals, Hood would always be kept aware of those fatal days in Georgia and Tennessee. Not that he was eager to forget; just eager to explain. He could not have felt welcome everywhere. He had not the widespread worship of Lee and Davis. Reunions to attend would have to be chosen carefully. There was just so much sorrow, and no doubt something of hate as well.

Pat Cleburne had a sweetheart in Alabama named Sue Tarleton. She was prostrate with grief at his death, wore mourning for a year, then married another and died shortly thereafter, in 1868. Frank Cheatham, a Tennessean and one of the generals Hood blamed for letting the enemy slip by in the night, thus leading to Franklin, couldn't bring himself to visit the battlefield until the 1880s. Sam Watkins, another Tennessean and the Confederacy's most famous private, would write several years after Hood's death: "As a soldier, he was brave, good, noble, and gallant . . . but as a general he was a failure in every particular."

Whether known or unknown, whether said or unsaid, the dark cloud that was shaped by these and thousands of other experiences and memories awaited Hood in large parts of the South. Nor was it just those in the Army of Tennessee who might hold a grudge. Vast numbers of civilians deeper into Georgia and through the center of the Carolinas must have wondered of different outcomes had not Hood's march north allowed Sherman's virtually unopposed mayhem.

By late 1865, Hood had begun making plans to write his memoirs. Well into the next year he reached out to former comrades for information. This effort came while he was starting his cotton business, at what would be a financially demanding time. It smacks of the same impulsiveness as his thirty-page letter to Buck Preston

while preparing for Sherman. In any event, the book Hood intended
evidently had nothing to do with atonement. Hood wanted justice.

A letter to Stephen Lee in Mississippi came right out with it,
though it was probably not the first time Lee had heard the performance. "The war is over," Hood wrote, "and the time has come for
facts to take the place of falsehood. . . . I expect to die more proud
of my defense of Atlanta & my Tenn Campaign than all my career as
a Soldier. Considering the Small & dispirited Capital I had to work
with. Injustice has been done me but that is Easy work for a 'Mob'
when led by . . . bad men. I have never feared but I would get justice,
but expect it to be tardy."

Stephen Lee replied that "prejudice was then too hight [sic] for
him to have an impartial hearing." Hood appeared to agree. "The
injustice done me by my countrymen," he grandly replied, "has
ceased to trouble me. How beautiful it is to have a God to look to
in all of our afflictions." Nonetheless he was soon asking elsewhere
for wartime information until, apparently, business affairs overtook
these efforts.

And Hood had found a woman who would marry him.

She was Anna Marie Hennen, daughter of the late Duncan Hennen who had been a member of the New Orleans bar, and granddaughter of a Louisiana Supreme Court justice. She was thirty-one—
five and a half years younger than Hood—and, like Buck, had been
educated in Paris. She was therefore charming. A portrait shows her
as an attractive brunette with fair skin and dark eyes.

Despite the war, Marie Hennen and her mother remained com-
fortably off. They owned a plantation near the town of Hammond as
well as an apartment in New Orleans. The Hennens were Catholic,
so a dispensation was required for marriage with the Episcopalian
Hood.

Of many things not known about John Bell Hood, at least to his
biographers, is whether at any point in his postwar life he spoke to
anyone about Buck Preston. There seems to have been no communication with Mary Chesnut in these later years; though she would
note Hood's death in one of her daybooks, she otherwise saved her

memories for her journal. Hood himself was no love-smitten boy and had plenty to keep him busy. And yet . . .

Something a little tantalizing suggests that, like his other defeats, the romance was never quite behind him. Buck and Rawlins Lowndes married on March 10, 1868, in Columbia. A little more than a month later, Hood married too. Had he heard it was coming and therefore proposed? Did he scan the newspapers each day for old names? Did a friend of a friend of a friend pass the word in a letter or anonymously slip a telling clipping into an envelope?

It had been fewer than three years since he had seen her. Love and humiliation deal the heart equal blows. Was marriage another example of the impulsive Hood? Or was it calculation and ambition, a not-so-successful cotton factor finding providence through a respectable New Orleans name with a little money? Beauty and romance are attractions to any knight worth his salt. But this was a knight back from the Crusade, who had seen the gore and left the field to Saladin.

On the other hand, maybe it was a love match after all. Hood and Marie married at the Church of the Immaculate Conception— ex-General Buckner stood in as best man—and Hood, wife, and mother-in-law moved into a high-ceilinged house in the Garden District. "Conception" would certainly summarize the marriage. Although Marie Hennen was getting a late start on motherhood and Hood had his disabilities, eleven children—including three sets of twins—were born to the couple over the next decade. On the family's summer trips north, hotel help would humorously call out, "Here comes Hood's Brigade."

Marie was a welcome break from the oppressive past. What could she really know of the dead piled in the ditch at Franklin? She didn't laugh at him behind his back as the belles in Richmond had done, or spread malice. She put her faith in his prospects. For Marie Hennen, it must have been love.

Life, in fact, finally was looking better for Hood. Insurance was an improvement over the cotton business, and even some of the bitterness from the war could be set aside. As with so many generals, a Rebel and a Yankee made up. Hood and Sherman had not only battled in Georgia in 1864 but at the time had carried on a famous and rancorous correspondence over Sherman's banishment of the entire population of Atlanta. Now, in 1871, they became friends after a Sherman visit to New Orleans. A few years later Sherman called on Hood at his hotel during a visit to St. Louis and invited him to dine with his family. Hood would be remembered by another visitor as "tall, full bearded and handsome with a sad face." Sherman would tell a West Point friend that the bitterness in the South was not "manifested . . . by the active combatants" but by "women & boys grown up since the War."

Hood also proved an exception by refusing a position with the notorious Louisiana Lottery, a private company begun by two Northern-born partners. The lottery raked in millions, paid out a lot less, and was the rage not only in Louisiana but also in other states where it operated. In Louisiana, Generals Beauregard and Early were hired by the lottery to oversee its prize drawings and lend it respectability. The same sort of job was offered to Hood. Hood declined, though Beauregard and Early were each earning $10,000 a year to just show up, and a Hennen relation was one of the lottery's chief promoters. Perhaps Hood was sensitive for business reasons: many others (even in fast and loose New Orleans) disapproved of the lottery. Or maybe he had too much honor.

He was comfortable enough to make a speech in Charleston at the 1875 meeting of the Survivors' Association of South Carolina. He kept it general as to the causes and results of the war and set aside his personal grievances. Interestingly, though, he regretted that the Confederacy had not made better use of nearly four million black slaves during the course of the war—that is, in large part added them to the military ranks in exchange for freedom.

The survivors' reaction to this isn't known. Of course, any Southern dismantling of the slave system to continue a war ran head-on into the question of why the South had already spent so many lives defending it. That had been a crucial question years earlier when the idea was proposed. It was, in fact, proposed in Georgia by General Pat Cleburne in early 1864, after the ascendancy of Johnston to lead the Army of Tennessee. It fell like a Yankee bomb and likely cost Cleburne promotion. He would command no Confederate corps as Hood did a short time later when he joined Johnston. Nor would he be in a position to take over the Army of Tennessee when Johnston was removed. Cleburne's had been a lonely voice. Where had been Hood's when it mattered?

No one appears to have asked. Everyone no doubt wished to get on with their lives. Hood's flowed smoothly except for the wailing of infants and the chaos of Louisiana's Reconstruction. He could have been kept busy enough with speeches and insurance, might have put a lot of things to rest, might have enjoyed life more—except for Joseph Johnston.

According to Hood's biographer Richard McMurry, Hood apparently discovered that Johnston's own memoirs were near publication and, expecting less than favorable treatment, took up the task that he had set aside seven years earlier. The day after Christmas 1873, Hood wrote to Sherman. This time he solicited his former enemy's Confederate casualty figures during the Atlanta campaign.

Johnston's book, laboriously titled *Narrative of Military Operations Directed During the Late War Between the States* and published in 1874, attacked Jefferson Davis, defended his own retreat to Atlanta, and portrayed Hood as a bungler. Of Hood's campaign in Tennessee, Johnston made such references as "useless butchery at Franklin" and "the disastrous expedition against Nashville."

Hood got busier on his rebuttal. Then the next year Sherman published *his* memoirs, which once more refought Atlanta. Hood, over the next several years, fell to expanding his response. He blamed Johnston for leaving him a demoralized army that wouldn't fight well; he blamed Hardee and Cheatham for actions—rather, inactions—that also contributed to defeat. He made no mention of Forrest's objections to his plan at Franklin, and had this odd remembrance of Pat Cleburne shortly before the fatal assault:

"About that time Cleburne returned, and, expressing himself with an enthusiasm which he had never before betrayed in our intercourse, said, 'General, I am ready, and have more hope in the final success of our cause than I have had at any time since the first gun was fired.' I replied, 'God grant it!' . . . These last words, spoken to me by this brave and distinguished soldier, I have often recalled; they can never leave my memory, as within forty minutes after he had uttered them, he lay lifeless upon or near the breastworks of the foe."

It's entirely possible that Cleburne, though he had glumly remarked on doom about the same time, should try to put on the best face for his troops and his commander. It's also entirely possible that the account is a self-serving fiction by Hood. As written, the tragic hero of the attack has taken Hood off the hook for the suicidal nature of his orders. In his memoirs, Hood is battling not just Yankees but often his comrades too. Sometimes when reading them, it's not hard to think of Captain Queeg in *The Caine Mutiny*.

Hood would continue to labor on his book, interrupted by business, family, reunions, and celebrations of Reconstruction's end in Louisiana. Years after Appomattox, the clash of war memoirs would sound through the land, but with more confusion as to infidels and shiny knights. These battles seemed likely to continue as long as the principals lived.

*

IN LATE SPRING 1878, two ships from Cuba arrived in New Orleans. Both brought yellow fever. The families of the officers of one ship then contracted it. In July a four-year-old girl became the first recorded fatality. Soon the city would see an exodus of roughly one-fifth its population. Up the Mississippi River went the outbreak. A towboat crew helped spread it to Vicksburg later that month. In August it reached Memphis.

The toll was staggering. The Mississippi Valley experienced 120,000 cases of yellow fever, of which approximately 20,000 were fatal. By the end of the year the pandemic had killed more than 5,000 people in Memphis. The toll was at least 4,600 in New Orleans.

Among the dead were Gideon Pillow, the Tennessee political general who had abandoned Buckner to Grant at Fort Donelson. Reduced to near poverty, Pillow had fled Memphis for safety in

Arkansas, only to be pursued. The fever claimed Jefferson Davis, Jr., too. Memphis was bankrupted. New Orleans was almost as destitute. The Hoods had been able to leave the city during the summer, thus the family was spared. Hood's livelihood, however, quickly deteriorated.

The disaster had closed the New Orleans cotton exchange and had multiplied demands upon the insurance companies. Only two such companies seem to have survived, and Hood's was dissolved late in the following year. To raise money he tried to sell his Civil War papers to the War Department. He again solicited Sherman's help, haphazardly leaving the papers behind with Sherman's daughter, Lizzie. Nothing came of it.

In the spring of 1879 he spoke before a group of Louisiana veterans—perhaps he was paid for it—and declared: "They charge me with having made Franklin a slaughter-pen but, as I understand it, war means fight and fight means kill."

The headlong Hood was more in evidence, prodded by Johnston, hemmed in by money problems. It must be assumed that whatever money Marie Hennen brought to the marriage had been spent or invested and placed out of reach, possibly lost with all the rest. This time Hood and his family did not leave New Orleans when summer—yellow fever season—returned.

Presumably Hood couldn't afford to leave. Still, questions endure about the children's safety. Perhaps the Hammond plantation, a possible refuge, had been sold. Perhaps Marie was not up to taking the children elsewhere; one report indicates that their last and eleventh child, another girl who would be named Anna, had only recently been born. Perhaps Mrs. Hennen was by this time too old or frail to take them away by herself. Indeed, how many individuals of perfect health can attend to a brigade of children, the eldest of whom is only ten?

Yet it seems incomprehensible that Hood's friends or Hennen relations could not be (or were not) turned to or called upon, or did not step forward. Epidemics that occur in one year can create a temporary immunity, but New Orleans had a history of such plagues.

The impression can't be helped that Hood decided to risk it, as he had taken risks at Atlanta, Franklin, and Nashville.

On July 24, 1879, a newspaper reported that not a single case of yellow fever had occurred in New Orleans so far that summer. Four weeks later there was a case. It was across the street from Hood's house.

Hood's family physician grew concerned. He was T. G. Richardson, the doctor who, in the absence of John Darby, had amputated Hood's right leg at Chickamauga. Now he urged Hood to take his family out of the city. Hood did not. Surely it was the most personally reckless of all Hood's decisions. Or else he was in the most personally desperate circumstances.

The next day, August 21, Hood's wife was stricken. Three days later she was dead. On August 26 the oldest child, Lydia Marie, became sick. Two days before she died, on the 29th, Hood was taken ill. Dr. S. M. Bemiss was called to the home and diagnosed Hood's illness as a virulent case of yellow fever. Hood became delirious and once called out, "I want those stores taken from my own commissary"—the old war raging with the fever. Toward the end he regained consciousness and talked with friends. He wanted his beloved Texas Brigade from Virginia days to care for his orphans. Then he died. The date was August 30, 1879.

Hood was forty-eight. Death had been chasing him since Gaines' Mill and had almost caught him at Gettysburg and Chickamauga. Only six people were to die of yellow fever in New Orleans that summer; three were in the Hood household. The general's luck always had a tendency to turn bad in the end for those in his care.

Hood's ten orphans did not wind up with the Texas Brigade. They did, however, become wards of the South. Offers to care for them poured in. The children were split up (the twins were kept together) and scattered among homes in five states, including New York, instead of being placed in a proposed group home in Texas. All but the two oldest, raised by a New Orleans uncle, would be adopted by their new families. A fund was also set up, and Hood's posthumous memoir, *Advance and Retreat: Personal Experiences in the United States and Confederate Armies*, was published in 1880 with Beauregard's help by the Hood Orphan Memorial. The fund would grow to $30,000, to be divided among the children when they reached twenty-one.

In 1898 one of the sets of twins, Odile M. and Ida Richardson Hood, was present at the reunion of old Rebels held that year in Atlanta. Odile had been named a sponsor of the Louisiana Division of attending veterans. The Texas Division, however, had no sponsor, and so Ida was recruited. "With maidenly modesty and becoming womanly dignity, she accepted the position," wrote the enthralled correspondent for *Confederate Veteran* magazine. In the receiving line, "battle-scarred, silver-haired men who followed the knightly Hood tenderly caught up and kissed the gentle hands of these fair daughters and wept over them, saying such as, 'I was in your father's brigade, and loved him. God bless you!'. . . Tears were seen to trickle down the bronzed cheeks of the veterans, and the young ladies became visibly affected. A more touching, pathetic scene did not occur during all the days of that reunion, and will never be forgotten by those who witnessed it."

It was about this time that news of the death of Winnie Davis was circulating among keepers of the Southern flame. Ida Hood likely would have been the nominee of the Texans as the next Daughter of the Confederacy had John B. Gordon been more flexible toward pretenders. Something of Winnie, though, does seem applicable to Ida: another loyal champion of one of the war's most controversial figures; another daughter whose life was bound up in the past; another child with sad, wistful eyes.

Like Winnie, Ida also had a literary if florid touch. In 1904 the *New Orleans Picayune* printed a lengthy biographical tribute that Ida had written of her father, a paragraph of which said: "To mere slander he replied with the silence of contempt. And to the unjust strictures derogatory to his fair name and character, which were passed on him by his former comrade on the field"—Ida apparently had taken up the cause against the now-dead Joe Johnston—"and echoed by many to whose honor it would have redounded more had they held their peace [sic], General Hood replied towards the end of his life in a book, singularly temperate and liberal in tone, and free from all bitterness."

Never mind that Hood's book has been faulted in more recent times for being "bitter and sarcastic, as well as inaccurate." A daughter's support is universally expected. How could she understand that Hood's great flaw was his great courage? She was also very likely spared the gossip of the Richmond and South Carolina parlors, and why should it have mattered any more, anyway? Hood didn't marry that *woman*, in any case, and she never loved him, or thought she didn't; at least most of the time. . . .

Buck died in 1880, a year after Hood. She was the mother of two girls and a boy. John Darby, who had turned against Hood and married Buck's sister, died the same year as Hood. Mary Chesnut, of course, died seven years later in the obscurity of Camden. Rawlins Lowndes lived on in Charleston until New Year's Eve 1919.

And then there were the other dead, the other knights who didn't even make it to Appomattox. Hundreds of defiant monuments would spring up on the squares and at the crossroads of hundreds of Southern towns and villages. One of them, in tiny Mulberry, Tennessee, is typical with its lone soldier standing tall above its inscription: "In grateful remembrance of the 300 Confederate unconquered soldiers who went out from Mulberry." They were at Cheat Mountain and Stones River, and possibly some of the originals were still alive with their regiment, the Eighth Tennessee, when it charged at Franklin. There the regiment's general, John C. Carter, was among the mortally wounded. It was all a waste, a terrible waste. What is the value of knighthood and chivalry and gallantry and courage when it is all stacked seven deep in a ditch, or laid out stiff on a porch, or left to scrounge for pennies from insurance policies?

· 6 ·

THAT DEVIL FORREST

In the person of the cavalry general Nathan Bedford Forrest,
the Confederate leadership moved about as far as possible from
the dashing cavalier and chivalrous knight. Violent, headstrong,
ruthless, unschooled, and yet a success before the war, Forrest would
also come closest to military genius of any general on either side.
Asked to name his choice as the war's greatest soldier, Robert E. Lee
was quoted as replying, "A man I have never seen, sir. His name is
Forrest." Joseph Johnston thought the same thing, adding that had
Forrest been educated, he would have been the war's "great central
figure."

Years after the war in late 1873, when the United States was
going through one of its periodic misunderstandings with Spain
over Cuba, the fifty-two-year-old Forrest wrote to Sherman, offering his services in case of trouble. Forrest thought he could bring
"1,000 to 1,500" of his old troopers with him. Sherman cautiously
replied that he expected no war but had forwarded Forrest's letter
to the War Department with his own comments. These included:
"I believe now he would fight against our national enemies as vehemently as he did against us, and that is saying enough."

It was Forrest who refused to surrender to Grant at Fort Donelson and led his command through freezing waters to escape. It was
Forrest's rearguard action that protected Hood's beaten army from
being wiped out during its retreat from Tennessee. In the time
between, Forrest and his "winged infantry" caused havoc throughout

the Confederacy's Western theater. It was Sherman who complained to Grant in 1864 about "that devil Forrest." Utterly fearless and always in the thick of the fight, he was wounded several times. He claimed—without contradiction—to have lost twenty-nine horses and to have personally killed thirty men.

Forrest (and a biographer) would call his life a "battle from the start." Born in 1821 in the frontier hamlet of Chapel Hill, Tennessee, his family later moved to vacated Indian lands in Mississippi. His father died before he was sixteen. To Forrest and his widowed mother fell the task of raising nine other children. Unlike Mary Chesnut's family, there was no turning back. Forrest farmed and split rails—like Lincoln. When he was still a teenager, a panther attacked his mother. The angry Forrest tracked the cat to its perch in a tree, waited just below the growling animal throughout the night, then shot it at first light. He returned home with its scalp and ears.

At age twenty-three, given a job in an uncle's livery stable in Hernando, Mississippi, he interceded when four men threatened the uncle. Gunfire soon erupted between the parties. Wounded himself, Forrest shot two of the men. Out of ammunition, he then chased off the remaining two with a Bowie knife. Later that same year, 1845, he married Mary Ann Montgomery after scaring away rival suitors. In 1851 the couple moved to Memphis. Forrest became a dealer in black slaves and bought large amounts of land in Mississippi. When the war arrived he was a millionaire planter. He was the sort of man who would have chewed up any misplaced aristocrat in the Mississippi Delta.

Richard Taylor, one of his military bosses, thought him a "tender-hearted, kindly man" but also said, "I doubt if any commander since the days of lion-hearted Richard has killed as many enemies with his own hand as Forrest." Sherman would claim to have barely escaped Forrest's hand at Shiloh. A general whose service under Forrest would include Hood's disastrous campaign, James R. Chalmers of Mississippi, would say of Forrest fifteen years afterward: "He was restrained by no knowledge of law or constitution. He was embarrassed by no preconceived ideas of military science. His favorite maxim [and Hood's] was, 'War means fighting, and fighting means killing.' Without the slightest knowledge of them, he seemed by instinct to adopt the tactics of the great masters of the military art, if there be any such art."

Forrest was anything but orthodox. Among the names admirers bestowed upon him was "Wizard of the Saddle." His young artillery captain, John W. Morton, would write in 1909: "General Forrest, as a commander was, in many respects, the negative of a West Pointer. He regarded evolution, maneuvers and exhaustive cavalry drill an unnecessary tax upon men and horses. He cared nothing for tactics further than the movement by twos or fours in column, and from column right or left into line, dismounting, charging, and fighting. As attested by his unparalleled successes, these simple movements proved sufficient."

Forrest thought cavalry sabers worthless and armed his men with pistols and carbines. He was equally contemptuous that a West Point education made for better leaders, saying, according to Morton, "Whenever I met one of them fellers that fit [fight] by note, I generally whipped h-ll out of him before he got his tune pitched."

As might be surmised, Forrest was eminently quotable and startlingly to the point. "Git thar fustest with the mostest men," or "first with the most," has come down from his time as his colorful self-explanation of battle success, though in fact he usually had the fewer soldiers. "Charge them both ways!" he ordered when he was uncharacteristically surprised from the rear during an assault on Union forces at Parker's Crossroads in Tennessee. Perhaps ruefully regarding his lack of education, he also remarked, "I never see a pen but what I think of a snake."

With pen in hand, though, he was just as direct. When a soldier dared to ask a third time for a furlough, Forrest scribbled on the back of the application, "I told you twist [twice] Goddammit know." To a fellow lodge member in Memphis, he wrote from Corinth, Mississippi, in 1862: "I had a small brush with the Enamy on yesterday I Suceded in gaining thir rear and got in to thir entrenchments 8 miles from ham burg and 5 behind farmington and Burned a portion of thir camp at that place they wair not looking for me I taken them

by Suprise they run like Suns of Biches. . . ." Examples left behind of
formal speech were the translations of others.

Nor was Forrest adverse to taking on his fellow generals. During
Hood's retreat from Nashville, Forrest clashed with Frank Cheatham
over whose men were entitled to first ford the Duck River after they
had arrived simultaneously. Forrest drew his pistol. "If you are a better man than I am, General Cheatham," he said, "your troops can
cross ahead of mine." A third general, Stephen D. Lee, intervened
to restore the comparative peace.

When his commander Braxton Bragg ordered him to turn over
his veteran cavalry to General Joe Wheeler after Chickamauga, Forrest marched to headquarters to call an astonished Bragg a "damned
scoundrel" and "a coward." He also warned Bragg: "You have threatened to arrest me for not obeying your orders promptly. I dare you
to do it, and I say to you that if you ever again try to interfere with
me or cross my path, it will be at the peril of your life."

The tenderhearted Forrest witnessed by Taylor was seldom in
evidence in war or peace. The number of his Union enemies personally slain or wounded might be no more than the Confederates
he shot at or thrashed for desertion or alleged cowardice in battle.
One of his war wounds came in a quarrel with an artillery lieutenant who had lost two of Forrest's cannons during a counterattack.
When Forrest called his conduct less than praiseworthy, the officer
answered by shooting Forrest above the hip with a pistol, and in
turn was stabbed by the enraged general who then chased the mortally wounded man. Forrest's size (he was just under six-feet-two and
weighed 180 pounds) made his murderous temper that much more
convincing.

Chalmers would later praise Forrest for keeping "able and reli-
able scouts all around him," but they learned quickly. During the
pursuit of Union cavalryman Abel Streight, when a Rebel scout
passed on a citizen's report of having seen Yankees but was unable to
confirm it himself, Forrest jerked the poor man from his saddle and
beat his head against a tree. "Now, God-damn you," he said, "if ever
you come to me again with a pack of lies, you won't get off so easy."

Certainly his men knew he meant business. One sees a comparison between Forrest and another hot-tempered cavalryman of a later time, General George S. Patton, whose veterans were proud of their service but more feared their leader than loved him. "The dog's dead," moaned one trooper on his transfer to Forrest's cavalry. "'The Wizzard' now commands us."

This then, is the outrageously colorful and courageous Nathan Bedford Forrest. Although his cavalry battles were comparatively small scale, often he distracted and diverted Union forces that otherwise might have ended the war much sooner in the West. When major battles loomed, he was usually misused, as at Fort Donelson and Franklin, or sent away from the main action, as at Nashville and just before Stones River. Other than Thomas "Stonewall" Jackson, Forrest had more success than any other Confederate general, and Jackson was killed midway through the war.

Yet Forrest's reputation and performance have never been given the bookshelf-bending notice and praise of Lee or Jackson, or threatened the plumed-hat mythology of another trooper, Jeb Stuart. Not being of the Virginia-centric school of Civil War studies—or of any school other than the hardscrabble frontier—Forrest's work has often seemed (when noticed) a sideshow in a Confederate backwater. His reputation has fared even worse among modern sensibilities, whose appraisals too often give short shrift to the context of the times in which he lived. It is the paradox of Forrest that the qualities that made him a superb Rebel general are the same that have made him a lightning rod for those who view the Confederacy as a racist rebellion worthy only of shame, and whose flags and statuary should be torn or toppled—beginning with those of Forrest.

*

THREE EPISODES of Forrest's life are the basis for this last, and likely permanent, view. The first is his prewar time as a slave dealer. A man who had known the severest poverty, Forrest was on the make. In Hernando the slave trade was only one of his interests; the others included a stage line to Memphis and a brickyard. Moving to Memphis, he expanded his slave business. A biographer, Jack Hurst, mentions a Forrest advertisement from these times:

> FIVE HUNDRED NEGROES WANTED—WE will pay the highest cash price for all good Negroes offered. We invite all those having Negroes for sale, to call on us, at our Mart, opposite Hill's old stand, on Adams Street. We will have a lot of Virginia Negroes on hand, for sale, in the fall. Negroes bought and sold on commission. Hill & Forrest.

Lafcadio Hearn, the wandering writer, would report that at his death Forrest was said to have been "kind to his negroes; that he never separated members of a family, and that he always told his slaves to go out in the city and choose their own masters." Yet it is doubtful Forrest could always avoid not splitting families, and toward his slaves he was also said to have "taught them to fear him exceedingly"—as he would later do his troops. Of course this may suggest intimidation as a preference to physical abuse; it would make no sense to damage the "merchandise." Forrest was obviously good at his work amid stiff competition. His fortunes rose, he became a member of the Memphis City Council, and he began dabbling in real estate. By 1860 he owned more than three thousand acres of cotton land and no longer dealt slaves. He had risen to planter heights.

If there was a lasting stigma among Southerners to being a slave trader—who was basically a middleman and no more culpable than a buyer or seller—it didn't attach itself to Forrest in Memphis. When the war came, he was a civic leader widely connected and wealthy. What got him there—a talent to organize, command, and exploit— would be used to the fullest as a leader of troops. These same inherent qualities also had pointed him toward the slave trade.

The second episode so damaging to his reputation occurred during the war, along a bluff overlooking the Mississippi River.

Fort Pillow, about forty miles north of Memphis, had been built by the Confederates early in the war and then abandoned to federal troops. Much of West Tennessee had become one of those dead zones where neither side exerted control. A great deal of partisan

The ferocious Nathan Bedford Forrest, physically intimidating before and during the war, found his fortunes and health rapidly deteriorating in the years afterward, and died in 1877 at only age fifty-six. While he turned to religion toward the end, his violent temper continued to flare. *(Confederate Veteran)*

warfare, murder, and soldierly plunder went on. The casualties were often civilians.

The primary purpose of Forrest's April 1864 raid into the region, including Western Kentucky, was to inflict the usual havoc upon Union supply lines and to round up Rebel deserters and reluctant draftees. But the raid was also a chance to pay back so-called "home-made Yankees"—Tennesseans who fought for the Union. Some 295 white Yankees were at the fort, including deserters from Forrest. They were joined by 262 black soldiers sent from Memphis in expectation of a Rebel attack. Forrest had also probably considered that the fort's capture would "show up" the black soldiers as ineffectual. From several accounts, the battle proceeded this way:

On the morning of April 12, an attack under Chalmers was launched. Soon the federal garrison found itself pushed from its entrenchments and into the fort. The Confederate force was about fifteen hundred men. Sharpshooters not only kept the Yankees pinned down but unknowingly killed the fort's commander. That afternoon, Forrest sent a note to the fort demanding surrender.

Such notes, concluding that "I cannot be responsible for the fate of your command" if not obeyed, were a familiar ploy of Forrest's. Tellingly, he also promised the garrison treatment as prisoners of war, an important concession when considering the special enmity toward those inside. An aide to Chalmers who relayed the note would remember both Forrest and Chalmers agreeing that the terms would extend to black soldiers as well as white. Nevertheless the fort did not surrender, and Forrest ordered the attack resumed.

What followed was horrendous. The Confederates soon overwhelmed the fort, the garrison fled down the bluff to the river, and many were shot in the water. Others were killed at very close range. Witnesses on both sides told bloodcurdling tales. "The poor deluded negros," wrote one Tennessee Confederate, "would run up to our men, fall upon their knees and with uplifted hands scream for mercy but they were ordered to their feet and then shot down. The white men fared but little better. . . ." This same soldier blamed Forrest for ordering "them shot down like dogs." Mutilations, the murder of wounded, and the burning of bodies would also be charged. Others, however, would credit Forrest and his officers with finally intervening and stopping the slaughter.

One reckoning of Fort Pillow's toll put Union deaths in the high 40 percent range, with nearly two-thirds of them black soldiers. Another accounting noted that of the 262 blacks, only 58 were able to be marched off as prisoners, compared with 168 of the 295 whites. Forrest's casualties were just 14 dead and 86 wounded. The final attack lasted twenty minutes.

What had happened? It was never proved that Forrest had ordered what became known as the "Fort Pillow massacre." After the war, in a letter to President Andrew Johnson, he even offered to "waive all immunity from investigation into my conduct at Fort Pillow." Further, a number of Union officers inside the fort who might have prevented the garrison's panic had also drawn the lethal attention of Rebel sharpshooters. The officer left in charge, Major William Bradford, who led the "homemade Yankees," was regarded as "entirely inexperienced in these matters." It was Bradford, signing his predecessor's name, who refused to surrender. Reports would emerge of heavy drinking by the garrison and the exchange of taunts. Also, Union gunboats on the Mississippi River seemed to hold out hope of rescue or reinforcement of the fort, thus bolstering its defiance and feeding Rebel impatience and anger.

Nonetheless in this 1864 election year an investigation by Congress promptly followed. For Republican abolitionists it was a handy tool in smacking appeasing Democrats. It was even handier when the Southern general had been a loathsome dealer in slaves. Fort Pillow was branded as the "atrocity of the war."

Forrest, as in his letter to Johnson (doubtless written by a friend), regarded Fort Pillow accusations as "widely believed and injurious calumnies." In his own words he told a Northern interviewer after the war that the fort was filled with "niggers and deserters from our army" who "were all drunk" and "kept . . . firing" as they ran with their flag "still flying" above the fort.

General Tyree Bell, who led part of the assault, would write thirty years later that there was "promiscuous shooting for some time at different places, whenever they [other Confederate soldiers]

saw a negro or a white man running. This was contrary to the commands of the commanding officer." But Bell would also maintain
that the "drunken condition of the garrison and the failure of Colonel [sic] Bradford to surrender . . . were the causes of the fatality" and
that Forrest had ordered the firing to stop. As for the "homemade
Yankee" Bradford, he was shot and killed—that is, executed—while
being marched south with the other prisoners. Forrest would say he
did not learn of it for more than a week afterward.

Forrest's men were among the most hardened and disciplined of
any. They had to be, to take on the similarly steeled Midwestern-
ers under Sherman and Grant. For that discipline to suddenly come
apart must also be viewed in the context of its times. The black soldiers they faced had been subservient men in bondage only a short
time before. Their white Union comrades included homemade
"renegades." Forrest didn't have to give an order to kill them; on
the other hand, the temper that always drove his troops wasn't used
immediately to restrain them, either. For only briefly—but long
enough—the general who often raised the threat of no quarter as a
bluff saw it carried out.

*

FORT PILLOW would stalk Forrest to the grave. Horace Greeley's
New York Tribune, which wondered why Forrest wasn't placed on
trial, referred to him as "the hero of the Massacre of Fort Pillow."
Other Northern papers said much worse while Southern editors
defended him.

In 1868, when Forrest was aboard a train to New York to attend
the Democratic presidential convention, a town bully entered his
coach, shouting, "Where's that damned butcher Forrest? I want
him." But when Forrest stood up, stepped forward, and gave him
one of his battlefield scowls, the man "darted into and down the
street with quarterhorse speed." Later in New York, supposedly, a
woman with a Bible and umbrella barged into Forrest's hotel room.
She demanded to know if the reports of Fort Pillow were true. She
fled when he answered: "Yes, madam. I killed the men and women
for my soldiers' dinner and ate the babies myself for breakfast."

In the annals of wartime atrocities, Fort Pillow was hardly singular. It was all a matter of degree. The fratricide in West Tennessee was comparable to that on the Kansas-Missouri border. In fact the Fort Pillow attack was not far removed from the homicidal sacking of Lawrence, Kansas, a year earlier by Rebel guerrillas under William Quantrill. In Alabama, the town of Athens was turned over by a Russian-born colonel to his three Union regiments, whereupon Yankee soldiers rushed to a Cossack-style orgy of civilian robbery and "every outrage," including rape. Atrocity begat atrocity. Mississippians, Georgians, and South Carolinians could make similar claims of Sherman's ravages. On the same day Lee surrendered to Grant, black soldiers gave no quarter to some of the surrendering whites at Fort Blakeley near Mobile, Alabama.

For sheer numbers, though, both sides stand condemned for the merciless horrors of their prison camps: 30,000 Union dead of its 194,000 POWs; 26,000 dead of 214,000 Confederates. Medicine and sanitation may still have been in the Dark Ages, and disease in close quarters may have accounted for most deaths; on the other hand, sheer neglect can be an atrocity too. It is worthwhile to ask—though there is no answer—how many other captive soldiers were killed *before* prison camp, as at Fort Pillow, for the scattered instances that were recorded also suggest a high number. Many crimes were unspeakable in a society where even the pretense of chivalry had died. What was glorified of the war is probably a tenth of what was kept hidden or nudged toward obscurity.

At war's end in 1865, more was on Forrest's mind than Fort Pillow. He would tell a congressional committee six years later that "I went into the army worth a million and a half dollars, and came out a beggar."

Sherman had feared that men like Forrest would turn to crime. Instead he went to work with typical energy and quickly tried to prove himself reconciled to Union victory. He returned to his large Mississippi plantation below Memphis to plant crops. He also applied for a presidential pardon. He smartly took on some Northern partners, or, as Forrest would tell it, "I carried seven Federal officers home with me, after the war was over, and I rented them plantations, some of my own lands, and some of my neighbors." He also credited his partners for helping him contract for freed black laborers. Some of them were his old slaves. He wrote optimistically to Stephen Lee shortly after his return: "I have Setled for the present at my plantation in Coahoma Co Miss have gone to hard work have a fine crop of corn if the Seasons hit wil make a fine crop Mrs F is making Buter & Rasing chickens[.]" Despite his efforts, accumulated debt on the land as well as new debt hounded him, and he began selling off his holdings.

In April 1866 he was startlingly in the news again.

The tension of the altered relationship between old masters and recent freedmen was vividly displayed when Forrest struck and killed one of his black workers. The man, Thomas Edwards, was said to be a wife beater and had attacked Forrest when he had interfered. The death had inflamed the other workers. They gathered outside Forrest's home, threatening revenge. Eventually he was rescued by the midnight arrival of a deputy sheriff sent to arrest him. The next day Forrest and the deputy left on a riverboat. Aboard was a party of Yankee soldiers. The trip took a comic turn when the soldiers became so enamored of Forrest that they offered to throw the deputy overboard. Months later a jury decided the killing of the worker was self-defense, acquitting Forrest of manslaughter. Before the war, however, the case would never have seen a courtroom.

As Forrest yielded his plantation lands and hopes, he searched for other ways to rebuild his fortunes. In 1867 he was a partner in a paving firm that took on the onerous task of Memphis's muddy streets. Being paid, though, with unsalable City of Memphis bonds, the firm was forced to give up its contract with only a third of the work completed. That same year—like ex-generals Hood and Longstreet—Forrest was drawn to the insurance business, becoming president of a Memphis fire and life insurance company. But by the following year it too would prove unsuccessful.

Forrest filed for bankruptcy in February 1868. Shortly thereafter he had a discussion with a couple of old army comrades, including General Thomas Benton Smith. The desperate Forrest had been looking at Mexico, then in chaos from its French and Maximilian experience. To his small audience he outlined a grand plan of conquest, requiring only six months and with an army of 30,000 men. Along the way Forrest would confiscate Mexico's mines and church property, and open immigration to "at least 200,000 people from the southern states." Norman Farrell, the other ex-Confederate present, was unimpressed. He wrote his fiancée that Forrest would "take possession of all the offices for himself and his men, among which, of course, N.B. would get the lion's share with the title of King or President; while the private would get his in bullets. . . ."

This scheme got no farther than any of the others. Soon, though, a group of Mississippi businessmen invited Forrest to head their own grand plan for a railroad. From late 1868 into 1874, he was busy as president of this project across Mississippi to connect Memphis with Selma, Alabama. It would also involve a constant search for financing in the face of unanticipated obstacles. Among them were the business repercussions of the Franco-Prussian War and the increasing disrepute of railroads in general. A Grant depression would add to the load.

Even Nathan Bedford Forrest could not go on, and resigned. He and his wife moved into a log dwelling on President's Island in the Mississippi River opposite Memphis. There he leased land worked by convict labor. He would also finish his days there. His plight wasn't much different from that of other Rebel generals, particularly those who would die broke like Hood or Dick Taylor or Braxton Bragg, or that namesake of Fort Pillow, Gideon Pillow.

If this were all there was to Forrest's postwar life, even Fort Pillow would likely recede, a regrettable lapse in an overall battle record of military genius. A third episode, however, would keep Fort Pillow alive, while it—along with memories of the slave trade—would feed the repercussions of this last stain. A little context, however, is helpful.

*

IN LATE 1865 or early 1866, six bored ex-Confederates sitting around a law office in Pulaski, Tennessee, decided to form a secret social club "just for fun." In a mockery of college Greek-letter fraternities, a corruption of the word *kuklos*, or circle, was settled on to establish the Ku Klux Klan. Its establishment was not especially ominous, considering other groups. Radicals in cooperation with the Freedmen's Bureau had organized Loyal Leagues—quasi-military in nature—to press for Negro rights. White supremacists had organized as Pale Faces.

Soon, however, Ku Klux parading through Pulaski and galloping about at night in ghostly bedsheets were proving particularly frightening to the freed slaves. What began as anonymous pranks turned into a realization of intimidating power. This would spread the Klan throughout much of the South.

It may be proposed that the "South" actually did not exist until *after* the Civil War. Robert E. Lee did not go to war for the South but for his state, and how many more thought the same way? But the Confederacy and the joined experience transferred local loyalties onto a broader canvas, one now tattered but with a blue St. Andrew's cross. If anything, four years of war had brought home the deep divide that had existed with the North, and that had become deeper still despite a reconciliation at gunpoint.

As W. J. Cash has written of the ex-Rebel white Southerners at this moment, "four years of measuring themselves against the Yankee" had left them "far more aware of their differences and of the line which divided what was Southern from what was not. And upon that line all their intensified patriotism and love, all their high pride in the knowledge that they had fought a good fight and had yielded only to irresistible force, was concentrated, to issue in a determination, immensely more potent than in the past, to hold fast to their own, to maintain their divergences, to remain what they had been and were."

Fanning the flames as the postwar period wore on was the lack of political power of too many non-Unionist whites, and the scant hope of regaining it anytime soon. Lincoln had suggested quick and benevolent reunion; Johnson, a "War Democrat" who had joined Lincoln's ticket, had been briefly harsh but had moderated. It was soon clear, though, that Johnson's own power was secondary to a

Republican Congress. And Congress's version of Reconstruction only stoked the suspicions of former Rebels that a sort of reverse servitude was to be their lot.

One could expect an American of today, used to a government of random generosity and a populace unconsciously compatible, to have trouble imagining a South in this postwar period—that is, a South as seen through the eyes of defeated whites amid free Negroes, federal soldiers, revengeful Southern Unionists, and descending Northern opportunists. Yet something of a similarity might be gleaned from an account closer to the present by the American diplomat George Kennan, after returning to a destroyed Germany following World War II.

"I had been twice in Germany," Kennan wrote in his *Memoirs*, "since the termination of hostilities. Each time I had come away with a sense of sheer horror at the spectacle of this horde of my compatriots and their dependents camping in luxury amid the ruins of a shattered national community, ignorant of the past, oblivious to the abundant evidences of present tragedy all around them, inhabiting the very same sequestered villas that the Gestapo and SS had just abandoned, and enjoying the same privileges, flaunting their silly supermarket luxuries in the face of a veritable ocean of deprivation, hunger, and wretchedness, setting an example of empty materialism and cultural poverty before a people desperately in need of spiritual and intellectual guidance, taking for granted—as though it were their natural due—a disparity in privilege and comfort between themselves and their German neighbors no smaller than those that had once divided lord and peasant in that feudal Germany which it had been our declared purpose in two world wars to destroy. That many Germans merited punishment was clear; but their delinquency was not the proof of our virtue. Nor was all that had gone down in the wreckage of Germany valueless or evil. Much—sickeningly much—that was innocent and precious had gone down with the rest. This was, however one viewed it, a tragedy of appalling dimensions. . . ."

In May 1866, several weeks after Forrest had killed the worker Edwards, a confrontation in Memphis between white police and recently discharged black soldiers flared into a race riot. Other racial clashes would occur that same year in New Orleans, Charleston, and Norfolk, Virginia. In Tennessee the frail and vindictive Radical governor, William G. "Parson" Brownlow, used the Memphis riot to assume state control of local police.

Growing congressional pressure for black suffrage in the South (to enhance the Republican vote), and these further displays of black assertion (or self-defense), undoubtedly added to the Klan's allure for many ex-Rebels. In March 1867, Congress passed—over Johnson's veto—the first of several Reconstruction Acts. It divided all the former Confederacy—except Tennessee, which had gained readmission into the Union the preceding summer—into five military districts and disfranchised many ex-Confederates. In April the Klan held a reorganization meeting at Nashville's Maxwell House hotel. All indications are that, as a result, Forrest was selected as the Klan's first Grand Wizard.

On the eve of his inauguration as president of the new Confederate States, Jefferson Davis had been hailed with an unforgettable phrase from the old fire-eater William L. Yancey: "The man and the hour have met." The same could much be said of Forrest on this occasion. This was the general who would later float his Mexico conquest scheme and volunteer himself and some of his old troopers if war came with Spain. A business failure in the postwar years, a soldier without an army, an ego that had known its greatest glory as a warrior—the Klan's appeal must have been enormous to him. Some old comrades such as Captain Morton were right beside him too.

As time has gone on, Forrest's role in the Klan has been ascribed to racism or to a hatred of blacks. Forrest was certainly a racist; judging by the white-only election laws in the North and the required bayonets to open voting in the South, so was most of the United States. As far as hatred, however, Forrest later would accommodate himself to black freedom and come to condemn the rampant violence. In 1874, when blacks were killed by a band of masked men in Trenton, Tennessee, a Memphis newspaper quoted Forrest that were he "entrusted with proper authority he would capture and exterminate the white marauders who disgrace their race by this cowardly murder of negroes." Business reasons—racial violence chased away critical outside investment in the South—may have had as much or more to do with his stance at the time, but it doesn't substantiate any sort of incurable hatred that Forrest allegedly carried in his bloodstream.

Political motives came into play as well in his embrace of the Klan. The Democratic South wanted its power back. It could not regain it under the current conditions of Republican Reconstruction. Forrest, who had served as an alderman before the war, afterward probably knew every Democratic politician in Tennessee and Mississippi. He also saw the Klan as a necessary tool to blunt black (Republican) political power. Yet again, politics was just part of it.

Forrest was an underemployed leader of men. All the qualities that had shaped him as the South's greatest soldier were under unbearable restraint. This would continue throughout his life as he alternated between business and yearning for another war to fight. The talents that made him such a natural to wage battle had now made peace almost unendurable. It would play hell with his reputation a century later, but he likely leaped at the opportunity offered by the Klan. The Wizardry put him back in the saddle.

Of course, it was an appalling organization. By 1871, when Congress investigated the Klan and passed a strong act aimed at its activities, some thirteen thick volumes had been gathered of testimony detailing or denying a vast sweep of beatings and murders of blacks and their white Republican allies throughout the South. Looked at in another way, however, the Klan wasn't simply a terrorist club. It was very much a Democratic party instrument too.

Forrest was thick with some Northern as well as Southern Democrats. These included Francis Blair of Missouri, whose brother, Montgomery, had been Lincoln's postmaster general. Frank Blair would try to intercede for Forrest through his brother on behalf of Johnson's tardy presidential pardon. In September 1866, Blair wrote of Forrest, "His noble bearing since the war in accepting without complaint the result and using his powerful influence to make others accept it in the same spirit, have inspired me with a respect and admiration I have not felt for any other man."

This was seven months before Grand Wizardry, but it nonetheless required some risk to stand up for the villain of Fort Pillow. Later, in 1868, the Blair connection would become even more valuable. The now-secret Klan leader attending the Democrats' convention witnessed his admirer win the nomination for vice president. A short time later and three years after making application, Forrest's presidential pardon finally arrived.

The connection between Democratic politics and the Klan were a given in the South, if something of an embarrassment elsewhere. Forrest's biographer Hurst has observed that the postwar Democratic clubs that began to appear "often were virtually indistinguishable from the Klan in many Southern towns." In Memphis, though, the Klan apparently stood aside and looked on approvingly when one Democratic Club was organized by sixty-five "right-thinking" blacks! However odd that might be, the freedmen were likely acting out of self-preservation. But then, so were the ex-Confederates.

By this time the Klan attacks were spreading throughout the South. In the summer of 1868—the year of presidential conventions—blacks were whipped, shot, or killed by the Klan in South Carolina, Alabama, Texas, and Tennessee. In Tennessee the crime was the lynching of a black accused of rape in Pulaski, the Klan's birthplace fewer than three years earlier as a harmless social club. The alert Governor Brownlow called for the reassembling of the hated state militia, and a small war loomed with Rebel Klansmen. At length and to most everyone's relief, the governor settled for federal troops instead of Republican posses.

In the midst of this hostility, on August 28, 1868, Forrest gave an interview to a reporter from the *Cincinnati Commercial*. This was the same newspaper that in 1861 had headlined, GENERAL WILLIAM T. SHERMAN INSANE. The formalized interview showed that Forrest had a good deal of inside knowledge about the Klan while, as might be expected, denying any official connection. Asked what would happen if Brownlow called out the militia, Forrest replied, in part, "If the militia are called out, we cannot but look upon it as a declaration of war, because Mr. Brownlow has already issued his proclamation directing them to shoot down the Ku-Klux wherever they find them, and he calls all Southern men Ku-Klux."

"Why, general," said the reporter, "we people up north have regarded the Ku-Klux as an organization which existed only in the frightened imagination of a few politicians."

"Well, sir," said Forrest, "there is such an organization, not only in Tennessee, but all over the South, and its numbers have not been exaggerated."

"What are its numbers, general?"

"In Tennessee there are over 40,000; in all the Southern states they number about 550,000 men."

"What is the character of the organization; may I inquire?"

"Yes, sir. It is a protective political military organization. I am willing to show any man the constitution of the society. The members are sworn to recognize the government of the United States. It does not say anything at all about the government of Tennessee. Its objects originally were protection against Loyal Leagues and the Grand Army of the Republic; but after it became general it was found that political matters and interests could best be promoted within it, and it was then made a political organization, giving its support, of course, to the democratic party."

"But is the organization connected throughout the State?"

"Yes, it is. In each voting precinct there is a captain, who, in addition to his other duties, is required to make out a list of names of men in his precinct, giving all the radicals and all the democrats who are positively known, and showing also the doubtful on both sides and of both colors. This list of names is forwarded to the grand commander of the State, who is thus enabled to know who are our friends and who are not."

"Can you, or are you at liberty to give me the name of the commanding officer of this State?"

"No; it would be impolitic."

Later Forrest was asked: "Are you a member of the Ku-Klux, general?"

"I am not, but am in sympathy and will co-operate with them. . . ."

More about this article would be heard on June 27, 1871, when Forrest appeared before the Joint Select Committee of Congress that was investigating the Klan. Forrest had issued rather weak denials just after publication of the *Commercial* interview—that he was misrepresented—and he did so again when it came up before the committee. As to other testimony, Forrest's information was mostly piecemeal, vague, prone to forgetfulness, and rife with admissions of being on the fringes of the Klan—though any knowledge was secondhand. Nonetheless Forrest, noting in detail that Southerners had much to complain of, now insisted that he had been active in having the Klan disbanded "in the latter part of 1868, I reckon."

"Were you trying to suppress the organization, or the outrages you speak of?" a committee member asked. Forrest replied: "I was trying to suppress the outrages."

"Outrages committed by colored men?"

"By all people; my object was to keep peace."

"Did you want to suppress that organization?"

"Yes, sir; I did suppress it."

"How?"

"Had it broken up and disbanded." This, he explained, was by talking with and writing letters to different people, and because "I had the confidence of the Southern people, I think."

Any crimes committed since disbandment, Forrest added, were not by Ku Klux but by other "wild young men and bad men" and "parties who are not responsible to anybody." In other words, *this* Klan wasn't *that* Klan.

Forrest's claims aside, Congress saw no need to reverse its passage of two months earlier of a tough Ku Klux Klan Act to ensure black voting rights. Yet apparently the Klan that Forrest was associated with *did* begin to disband after the presidential vote of 1868. The Klan had failed to defeat Grant's election, but several considerations argued for a change.

In Tennessee the battle between the governor and the Klan had subsided once more when Brownlow departed for the U.S. Senate in early 1869. His short-term Republican successor, facing a tight race within his own party, won election by opening the vote to thousands of former Rebels and current Democrats. This cleared the way for the Democrats' eventual return as the state's party in power, the objective of the Klan. An anti-black poll tax followed in 1870.

As a whole the South also was desperate for capital—Northern or foreign—and Klan violence and political upheaval closed the door to long-term investment. Forrest likely discovered this firsthand when he became a railroad president in late 1868, as did other influential Southerners who earlier had supported the Klan.

Another reason for disbandment was simply that the Klan had grown beyond the control of its Grand Wizard. With its disguises and deadly secrecy, it was quite easy to spawn Klan imitators with their own localized hostilities. It was like dozens or hundreds of little Fort Pillows.

A Klansman would say in an interview some sixty years later that orders went out from Forrest to disband and destroy all records and regalia shortly after the new governor's election in Tennessee. Another would put it months earlier. A third—John Morton, who was also, allegedly, a Grand Cyclops—would place it later, after "the white race had redeemed six Southern states from negro rule in 1870."

Hurst estimates that after 1868 the Klan passed virtually out of existence in Texas, Arkansas, and Louisiana, and would be abandoned by more prudent Democrats in Tennessee and Georgia, though "it would continue periodically vicious activities in both states." It would remain potent in Alabama, Mississippi, and the Carolinas as Reconstruction played out. Regardless, by the end of the 1870s the Klan or its imitators had served the purpose of entrenching Democratic and (white) Southern power. It would reawaken nationally forty years later with a revised and even broader list of hates and fears.

*

TODAY Forrest often is mistakenly believed to be the founder of the Klan and its Grand Wizard until he died. This added blow to his reputation is, of course, his own fault. It's difficult to think of any other prominent Confederate general who would have stepped forward or answered the call of the Klan, including the ensemble of generals in New Orleans. Lotteries were more to their taste.

The various talents useful in leading the Klan seem unique to Forrest. He was both warrior and detail person to a degree unlike his peers, as well as politically savvy. He could talk to rich and poor alike, and could well hold his own among the prominent and still influential. His fame alone offset his lack of proper schooling. He remained a striking figure, always careful to dress neatly, and his spoken English was called "very correct" (one might yearn, though, for an exchange of letters with Mary Chesnut). Forrest also possessed a persuasive nature that could swing to murderous extremes—a useful rage perfect to lead desperate men in desperate times.

But there is little reason to doubt his dissociation from the Klan. This is first indicated by several actions during 1869 as he labored to raise money for his railroad. In another newspaper interview he daringly advocated repopulating the Southern wasteland with Northerners and blacks, the latter to be brought in "from Africa." Several months later he offered to hire a thousand Asian workers if they were available. Forrest also began courting Republican county leaders along the railroad route, and greeted visitors from Massachusetts and Connecticut at a barbecue in Alabama. A Memphis newspaper put Forrest among those former Rebels who now supported black voting rights!

When scolded in print by an Alabama editor (and Klansman) for his Republican associations, Forrest replied that had his critic "striven as hard in his paper to bring peace and prosperity to the country as he does to keep up strife and discord, it would have been more to his credit and better for the people of the State." Surely Forrest had left the Klan.

If Forrest appeared to mellow, there remained enough flashes of the past to advise caution. One contemporary would recall that during the last few years of Forrest's life the famous temper "was just as ungovernable as ever." While running his railroad, Forrest nearly provoked a duel with a contractor. In a separate quarrel with an ex-employee, he had driven the man's wife to arm herself to kill Forrest should he assault her husband. Forrest eventually gained control of himself and apologized to both men.

Near the end of 1875, Forrest found religion. Accompanying Mary Ann to services at a Cumberland Presbyterian Church in Memphis, he became so moved by the sermon that afterward he grasped the pastor's arm and tearfully confessed, "Sir, your sermon has removed the last prop from under me. I am the fool that built on sand; I am a poor miserable sinner."

That is how the minister would describe it. Still, it's arguable whether religion had any immediate influence on Forrest's behavior. About this time he also threatened a tailor over a ruined suit of clothes and waved a pistol at him, despite the tailor's eagerness to make the matter right. "Why, General, you would not shoot me for such a trifle as that!" protested the tailor. "God damn you, yes!" answered Forrest. "I'd shoot you like a rat."

The next day Forrest apologized.

Yet, toward the end of his life a different Forrest was also in evidence. He accepted an invitation to a cemetery ceremony to decorate the graves of Union dead. And in a gesture of racial harmony in Memphis, he attended the barbecue of a black organization designed to bring "peace, joy, and union." Forrest's remarks were especially interesting in light of his past: ". . . I came here with the jeers of some white people, who think that I am doing wrong. I believe I can exert some influence, and do much to assist the people in strengthening fraternal relations, and shall do all in my power to elevate every man—to depress none. I want to elevate you to take positions in law offices, in stores, on farms, and wherever you are capable of going. . . . You have a right to elect whom you please; vote for the man you think best, and I think, when that is done, you and I are freemen. . . . We have but one flag, one country; let us stand together."

Racial tranquility and trust still had a ways to go, however. It was said that when having his throat shaved by one of the city's black barbers, Forrest would avoid conspiracies by never using the same barber twice in a row.

Forrest once commented that he had "not been in good health since the war." He seems to have been afflicted with chronic diarrhea. No doubt the river island with its malarial threats added to the decline. Some references also say he may have been diabetic. In 1877 he turned to the healing waters of several Southern spas. His wife had noticed an "unnatural appetite" and stayed near to make sure he ate correctly. Joe Wheeler, his former cavalry boss, saw Forrest during one of these stays and commented on the startling change. Forrest's "pale, thin face," said Wheeler, "seemed to bring out in bolder relief than I had ever observed before the magnificent forehead and head . . . suggestion[s] of harshness had disappeared and he seemed to possess . . . the gentleness of expression, the voice and manner of a woman."

The year 1877 would prove a memorable one, a historic year. For the white South, including those who now disowned the Klan and those who didn't, it marked the ascendancy of the Democratic party throughout the old Confederacy. This was done, ironically, by helping a Republican, Rutherford B. Hayes, become president. Hayes had agreed to pull federal troops out of the South at last, thus effectively ending Reconstruction. For the black South it would mean for most who stayed only a segregated, bare-bones freedom well into the next century.

Some observers might say that, except for slavery, all was as before the war. That wasn't entirely true. The era remembered as that of the antebellum South was never so dark for those who would avert their glance from the squalor and the chains. Many had done so. Yet who, after four years of war and more of Reconstruction, could escape the darkness of *that* experience, the peering into the human well until one pulled back in horror? It had been impossible to avoid looking. The lash had striped the backs of black and white alike. No, this South would be somehow different, though in what way was not yet clear, and the white man was indisputably on top again. The antebellum South was dust and beyond reassembly, legend to the contrary. It was as dead as some of its enemies—Parson Brownlow conveniently died in 1877—and some of its heroes, such as Lee or, soon, Nathan Bedford Forrest.

Toward the last, the general would tell his legal adviser: "My life has been a battle from the start. It was a fight to achieve a livelihood for those dependent upon me in my younger days, and independence for myself when I grew up to manhood, as well as in the terrible turmoil of the Civil War." He would add: "I have seen too much of violence and I want to close my days at peace with all the world, as I am now at peace with my Maker."

Forrest died on October 29, 1877, exhausted at age fifty-six. His last words were "Call my wife." Mary Ann Forrest lived on until 1893. Their only adult child, William, himself wounded three times during the war, died in 1908. A grandson would be involved in the twentieth-century Klan. A great-grandson would die a World War II brigadier general in a bombing run over Germany.

At Forrest's funeral, Jefferson Davis was one of the pallbearers. It is said that during the procession to the cemetery the former Confederate president admitted that Richmond had never fully appreciated Forrest's military skills or taken true advantage of them. North of Memphis, in New York, the *Times* recalled Fort Pillow and predicted that Forrest would be remembered for it too. And, of course, as time went along, there was also the slave trade. And the Klan . . .

There is simply no escaping the linkage. To the arguments and denouncements, one can only suggest the perspective of the times, and that Forrest could no more resist what he was or what he became than most anyone else. But there was a little glow at the end, and once in a while there's a glimmer of humane progress. Take the Klan and its Pulaski birthplace.

Through good times and bad the Klan would pick on the Tennessee town to parade itself, usually outnumbered by naysayers and police. The law office off the square where the Klan was first organized has a plaque that once proclaimed this fact to the world. There's no getting rid of history, as uncomfortable as it might be, and the plaque is still there, on the wall where it was bolted years ago. Except its lettering is now turned toward the wall instead of to the street, and there is nothing at all to read and nothing to indicate anything special about the building unless one already knows about it. Presumably that would have to be either a longtime resident of Pulaski or a pilgrim Klansman. It's the sort of solution that might have pleased the wily old cavalryman blamed for it all.

· 7 ·

THE MAD WOMAN

In the last weeks of the war, President Lincoln accepted Ulysses Grant's invitation to visit him and Julia Grant at the general's headquarters in City Point, Virginia. Lincoln brought along his wife, Mary, and their son, Tad. On the first day a misunderstanding that the wife of General Charles Griffin had seen the president privately put Mrs. Lincoln in a snit. The next day, while riding with Mrs. Grant in an ambulance struggling through mud to attend a review of troops, a bump slammed Mrs. Lincoln's head against the roof and gave her a migraine.

Mrs. Lincoln began to berate everyone nearby, including Julia Grant. The situation was not helped when Mrs. Lincoln discovered another general's wife, the decorative Mary Ord, riding alongside the president on horseback. In no mood for being usurped by lesser army wives, the first lady gave full vent to her famous temper. The unfortunate Mrs. Ord is said to have broken into tears. That night at dinner and before guests, Mrs. Lincoln lit into the president too.

Julia Grant saw all.

After Lee's surrender, Grant joined Lincoln at the White House, every bit the man of the hour as the president. Perhaps this helped Julia Grant when she answered a note from her husband wondering if they were free that evening. Lincoln, wanting to celebrate the Union victory, had asked the Grants to go with him and Mrs. Lincoln to see a play. Julia's answer was an unequivocal "no." So Grant told Lincoln that he and Julia were having to leave on an afternoon train to visit their children.

Like other of this war's many might-have-beens, it is intriguing to consider the consequences if Grant had been sitting alongside Abraham Lincoln at Ford's Theatre. Had the general been an even more inviting target for the assassin's one-shot derringer, or had suddenly intervened in time (and it's easy to envision Grant springing to action), the postwar period for the defeated South—and perhaps for the emancipated Negro—could have been fundamentally altered.

But Julia Grant did not like Mary Todd Lincoln. And Julia Grant was not alone.

*

MARY ANN TODD was born in 1818 in Lexington, Kentucky, the third daughter of Robert and Eliza Parker Todd, who were second cousins. The Todds and Parkers were Presbyterian pioneer families of some prominence whose members served in the Revolution and the War of 1812. Mary soon would have to surrender her "Ann" when the name was chosen for a younger sister, to better honor a family aunt. By all accounts she seems to have had a comfortable if not luxurious upbringing in a steadily growing household of sisters and brothers. Before Mary was seven, however, Eliza Todd died after another session of childbirth.

Robert Todd was soon (*too* soon, according to some) courting Elizabeth Humphreys, niece of two United States senators and of an upper-crust family in nearby Frankfort. "Betsey" Humphreys came late to the eventual marriage. She was in her mid- to upper twenties and sensitive as to age, even declining to have it noted on her tombstone. By both necessity and temperament, Betsey took a stern and direct approach to the six children she inherited from Todd as well as eight more of their own who would survive. She had a habit of referring to any stepchild who crossed her as a "limb of Satan," and Mary was frequently so accused.

Mary began attending school at a local academy at the age of eight, studying such subjects as reading, writing, grammar, arithmetic, history, geography, natural science, French, and religion. Robert Todd's strong belief in education for females, coupled with the loathing that both stepmother and stepdaughter had acquired for each other, would install Mary when she was fourteen in a boarding school fewer than two miles from home. In all, she had about nine years of schooling, or roughly double that for most girls of leading families at the time.

The young Mary Todd possessed "clear blue eyes, long lashes, light brown hair with a glint of bronze and a lovely complexion." She tended toward the plump, though someone recalled her figure "as beautiful and no master ever modelled a more perfect arm and hand." She was more outgoing and personable than her two older sisters. She was also a wicked mimic and would later admit that during these youthful years "friends were few."

Mary showed an early interest in politics at age nine when she refused to attend a Lexington appearance by Andrew Jackson. She favored her father's Whiggish views and fervently supported Commonwealth hero Henry Clay. The two older sisters, like much of Kentucky, would migrate to Illinois. When the second married, Mary, at age twenty, moved to join both sisters and their husbands in the recent state capital of Springfield. A lawyer named Lincoln was already there as a legislator in the state Assembly. He and Mary met at a party at the home of one of the sisters.

Undoubtedly they made an odd couple. Lincoln was a gawky six-feet-four whose clothes didn't fit. Mary loved a good dress but considered herself a short "ruddy pine knot" with "periodic exuberances of flesh." The second sister thought Lincoln "the plainest man" in Springfield. The eldest, Elizabeth Edwards, thought him socially backward. Nonetheless for two such unattached people not getting any younger, and with mutual Whig affections exerting a gravitational pull, Mary and Abe survived a series of ups and downs. They married in 1842.

Her gold band was inscribed "Love is Eternal." She was passionate, he was dour. She was afraid of lightning, dogs, and imaginary robbers. He wasn't afraid of anything but had terrible nightmares. Both were prideful and ambitious; a sister would say that as a girl

Mary contended that "she was destined to marry a President." They were more opposite than alike.

But there was something. Mary delivered her first of four sons, Robert Todd Lincoln, almost a perfect nine months after their vows. She called her husband Mr. Lincoln; he called her Molly before their marriage and Mother after Robert's birth. He also called her "little woman." He was often away on legal or political business. She ran a household with a succession of hired women who didn't stay very long. Her tongue-lashings—also inflicted on her husband—were famous in Springfield. When Lincoln once ignored her to continue reading a book, she hit him in the nose with a piece of firewood.

Yet she was always loyal, his constant champion, and some remarks suggest that she missed Lincoln not only sorely but sexually whenever he was away. When someone compared Lincoln to his rival Stephen Douglas, who had also been one of her beaus, the little woman vigorously replied: "Mr. Lincoln may not be as handsome a figure . . . but the people are perhaps not aware that his heart is as large as his arms are long." Both parents were indulgent with their children (the best Lincoln's law partner and future biographer William Herndon had to say was to call them "brats"). After Robert came Eddie (1846), Willie (1850), and Thomas, or Tad (1853). Eddie would die of tuberculosis ten months before the birth of Willie—the first in a family that would evaporate before Mary's eyes.

While Lincoln served several terms as a state legislator, he held—and only briefly—just one national office before his 1860 election to the presidency. That was a single term in Congress, and his Whig opposition to James K. Polk's popular Mexican War led to the rival Democrats claiming the seat in the following election. For the next twelve years Lincoln rebuilt his law practice and immersed himself in Illinois politics. He successfully made the transition from the dying Whigs to the new Republican party, formed largely in opposition to the westward expansion of slavery. But further election victory eluded him when tempted.

Throughout this uncertain period his wife is seen as helping lift Lincoln's spirits or, as Herndon put it, acting "like a toothache, keeping her husband awake to politics day and night." As a couple they were unusual for their era in that, as a wife, Mary took an active interest in politics and Lincoln, as a husband, allowed it. Perhaps he couldn't prevent it. Mary Lincoln, though, did not share his civility toward opponents or their wives. Her no-compromise attitude and grudge-bearing kept her circle of friends thin and impermanent. But her faith in her spouse seems equal to his, if not more so.

Lincoln would contend that "I do not think myself fit for the Presidency," and maybe he was tempted to believe it. He was said to have paled when he got the news back in Springfield that the 1860 Republican convention in Chicago had nominated him. The Democrats' split over guarantees for slavery enabled Lincoln a few months later to win an electoral majority, if only 40 percent of the popular vote (most of the future Confederate states had left him off their ballots). Again, Lincoln received the news in Springfield. The next president reportedly rushed home from the telegraph office, calling out, "Mary, Mary, *we* are elected!"

How much influence Mary Lincoln had on her husband's reaching the White House cannot be measured. A lot is simply not known. For all the colorful, down-home anecdotes about him, Lincoln was far from being plain old Abe. According to Herndon, he was aloof and private and didn't really care much for anyone except his wife and children. He had plenty of ambition in his own right by the time he met Mary Todd. He had risen above his backwoods beginnings and had strength and brains enough to be looked to as a leader on the rough frontier.

He was also a careful man, given to calculation. Herndon would call Lincoln's perceptions "slow, cold, clear and exact." John Hay, one of his secretaries as president, said that it was "absurd" to call Lincoln "a modest man" and that his "intellectual arrogance and unconscious assumption of superiority" was what political rivals could not forgive.

Lincoln seems the sort of brilliant but occasionally self-doubting man who could not have gone as far if alone, who profited from another's comfort and prodding—even haranguing. Whether he would have succeeded with someone other than Mary Todd is impossible to know. But it seems nearer the truth that he became president more *because* of her than *despite* her.

*

THAT THE United States was in its greatest crisis since its infancy would be little apparent if judging by Mary Lincoln's behavior during the Civil War's first year, though for a time a squad of protective Zouaves moved into the White House East Room. The mansion was described as resembling "an old and unsuccessful hotel." The new first lady jumped right in to beautifying the place with rugs, wallpaper (from France), paint, furniture, and china. To do so she made regular trips to Philadelphia and New York. She soon outspent the entire four-year, $20,000 budget for upkeep. When creditors made themselves known, she cut the White House staff, pocketed the steward's salary, hired freed blacks, and had the gardener sell manure from the stables. About the White House she acquired the names of "Hell-Cat" and "her Satanic Majesty."

She was, in fact, a shopaholic. Her purchases afar amused neither Washington merchants nor a public just awakening to the human and financial cost of the war. She spent lavishly on White House receptions as well as herself. She looked more to France's Eugenie for fashion than to the Albert-mourning and black-draped Victoria. Despite this, Libbie Custer, for one, would find Mrs. Lincoln "short, squatty, and plain." Unlike Honest Abe, she accepted most gifts, including diamonds. In turn, she lobbied hard for the jobs and favors their givers expected.

Like the Grants later, she did not neglect her relations back home. The financially strapped husbands of the sisters who had sneered at Lincoln were rescued by him with government jobs. And, like the Grants, Mary Lincoln would savor the seaside pleasantries of Long Branch, New Jersey. She was there during that first frenetic summer of the war. Abe stayed home.

Like the First Family of the Confederacy and the Shermans, the Lincolns also would lose a young son during the war. At the White House in early 1862, Willie and Tad—Robert was away at Harvard—were stricken with typhoid fever. The sickness was rampant, brought on by the tripling of Washington's wartime population and the subsequent pollution of the city's Potomac River water supply. Willie, at eleven the older of the two youngsters, was given a better chance of survival but died after great pain.

Lincoln stoically bore the loss in public and wept alone in a private room. He also turned to a Presbyterian minister for assurances of God and heaven. Although he wasn't "churched," Lincoln would later say that he underwent "a process of crystallization" in his religious beliefs during this time. His wife found less comfort from the clergyman. Nor did she have the singular faith of Ellen Sherman, who almost happily would have sent a child unto the angels. Mary Lincoln took to her bed and grieved for weeks. Then she took to mediums and séances.

Jean H. Baker, one of Mrs. Lincoln's biographers to whom much of this account is indebted, has noted the prominence of spiritualism in Boston and New York in the 1850s. William Dean Howells was said to have estimated, perhaps jokingly, that every other house in Boston had a medium standing ready. By 1854, says Baker, spiritualists outnumbered abolitionists. Congress was even called on to investigate the authenticity of postmortem contact—the matter being humorously deferred by whether it belonged before the Foreign Relations Committee or that of the Post Office. Spiritualism most certainly gained in popularity as Northern war casualties mounted.

So Mary Lincoln talked to Willie and Eddie, her two dead boys, through a medium. When they were indisposed she looked for messages from slain Union officers to pass on to the president. As many as eight such séances might have been held in the White House and many more elsewhere. Lincoln himself attended one of them and read some of the books and letters sent by spiritualists, but it's likely that any interest on his part was simply to buy a measure of domestic peace. The practice at high levels was not that unusual. In Europe, Eugenie and Victoria were also in the clutches of sorcerers. After a time, though, Mary Lincoln learned to induce her own visions.

The White House years were largely strange and alienating for Mrs. Lincoln. Try what she would—accompanying her husband on reviews of troops, visiting the wounded in hospitals, raising money for clothing and shelter for the Negro "contraband" flooding into

Mary Todd Lincoln ran up huge bills on furnishings and fashions as first lady, then spent her years after her husband's assassination in mourning, self-exile abroad, and feuding with her only remaining son Robert, who would have her briefly committed to a mental institution. *(Library of Congress)*

Washington—her efforts were often negated by suspicion and dislike. Of the fourteen adult children of her father, Robert Todd, eight had favored the South and six the North. Three of her half-brothers were Rebel soldiers who died in battle. The unbridled *Cincinnati Commercial* called her "a fool—the laughing stock of the town, her vulgarity only the more conspicuous in consequence of her fine carriage and horses and servants in livery and fine dresses, and her damnable airs."

She surrounded herself with gossips and favor seekers, yet it's not difficult to appreciate her sense of loneliness during this time. Lincoln himself had the loneliest job in the world. Even grief for a son could not bring them together now. There were fields full of dead sons. The ever-increasing burdens of the war removed him further from whatever insights or consolations she could offer. Although she witnessed his troubles, just as often she drew attention to her own. Her comforts and tantrums were all of a mix. Who had time when McClellan wouldn't budge and Grant had vanished and George Meade had missed a chance to trap Lee and end the awful war?

And then there was Mary Ord on her horse, and at last the box at Ford's. Secretary of War Stanton and his wife, like the Grants, turned down an invitation too (Ellen Stanton also couldn't stand the first lady). So did two governors, another general, a postmaster, and a major. At last a senator's daughter, Clara Harris, and her fiancé were found to go along. In the course of the play and seated side by side, Mary Lincoln was nestled coyly against her husband.

"What will Miss Harris think of my hanging on to you so?" she whispered to him. Lincoln, enjoying that rare peace after four years, smiled and replied: "She won't think anything about it."

The assassin's moment was at hand.

*

THE POSTWAR SCRUTINY of Mary Lincoln continues to this day. While it has not been a cottage industry like books about her husband, it seems to have fostered its own little but vigorous engagement between two contentious sides. New documentation—that is, letters involving the main parties or those otherwise prominent in her life—also keeps turning up. For instance, a bundle of papers tied with a pink ribbon and labeled "MTL Insanity File" was found at Robert Lincoln's summer home, Hildene, in Manchester, Vermont, in 1975, nearly fifty years after his death. More letters of Mary Lincoln's have since been discovered as well as those of others close to the stark event that would so scar her later life: her commitment to a private sanitarium for the mentally ill.

One school would have Mrs. Lincoln as an eccentric but stubbornly independent woman, trying to make a widow's way in a Victorian world that treated women as children. Here the main villain of the piece (among many) is Robert Lincoln, cold and aloof and a lawyer on the make in the Gilded Age. The other school might be said to view Robert as the dutiful but unfortunate son and proper gentleman, regrettably acting in his insane mother's best interest with little hope of ever winning thanks for it. Thus the contest. Both views might find a middle ground in that Mary Todd Lincoln, insane or not, had an almost unmatched capacity for driving other people toward the brink.

The relationship between Mrs. Lincoln and her eldest son appears to have been an edgy one from the Civil War on. Having buried two boys, she had wanted to keep Robert in Harvard and out of harm's way, fending off the military-minded (and her husband) by replying that "an educated man can serve his country with more intelligent purpose than an ignoramus."

Shy and stiff and unlike either parent, Robert no doubt was keenly aware of his mother's buying binges and other criticisms. He likely stayed in a state of embarrassed apprehension. Once, when Mrs. Lincoln threw a White House party for the Barnum dwarf known as General Tom Thumb and his new bride, Robert refused to participate in what he considered an undignified sideshow. "My notions of duty, perhaps, are somewhat different from yours," Robert told her.

After Harvard and with his father's help, Robert was taken onto Grant's staff as a captain in the last months of the war. Still, that would have also placed him at City Point, where he could not help but be aware of his mother's behavior. Later in life Robert would loyally support Grant for a third term as president. In this he was indifferent to one of Mary Lincoln's wartime complaints to her husband. Grant, she had said, was "a butcher who is unfit to be at the head of an army."

Willie, not Robert or Tad, had been the favorite of both parents, and Mary Lincoln's grief in 1862 at the boy's death was inconsolable, even by Lincoln. Her seamstress, Elizabeth Keckley, would write after the war that in "one of her paroxysms of grief the President kindly bent over his wife, took her by the arm, and gently led her to a window. With a stately, solemn gesture, he pointed to the lunatic asylum. 'Mother, do you see that large white building on the hill yonder? Try and control your grief, or it will drive you mad, and we may have to send you there.'"

Her mourning over Lincoln's assassination was even more pronounced. For nearly six weeks she refused to leave the White House, consigning Andrew Johnson to a small room in the Treasury Department. Meanwhile servants and visitors made off with the mansion's silver and china. She roused herself infrequently. Once it was to fight a civic effort back in Illinois to plant Lincoln—alone—beneath a monument in the center of Springfield. She successfully launched a letter campaign to keep all the Lincolns together in a cemetery outside the town.

When she finally departed Washington, with Robert and Tad, she took along twenty trunks and some fifty boxes filled mostly with old clothes. Keckley would quote Robert as grousing: "I wish to heaven the car would take fire in which you place these boxes for transportation to Chicago, and burn all of your old plunder up." If true, he did have a point. The frills and colors were yesterday, for Mary Lincoln would wear nothing but widow's black for the rest of her life.

The family settled in Chicago. Abe Lincoln, the lawyer, typically had died without a will. Robert selected Supreme Court Justice David Davis, a Lincoln friend and appointee from Illinois, as estate administrator. It would take two years to sort things out, during which Mary, Robert, and Tad were each entitled to $1,500 annually while they waited.

To Mrs. Lincoln, they were staring at starvation. Moreover merchants seeking their return on about $10,000 in charges from White House days came calling. Mrs. Lincoln gave back much of her jewelry, sold off an expensive dress, and took out a high-interest loan from the banker Jay Cooke. She also hired an agent/lobbyist to negotiate settlements and solicit contributions to her newly created Mary Lincoln Fund, a subscription-like approach to raise money. Mrs. Lincoln herself kept busy writing letters—what Robert called "Mother's begging letters"—to rich Republicans. She reminded them of how easily they could prevent a future "spent without a home, forever a wanderer on the face of the earth."

She also nagged Congress for Lincoln's full, second-term salary of $100,000, less the several weeks of service paid before his death. Precedent existed for presidential widows to receive the remainder of the first year of such salaries (in Lincoln's case, $25,000), but she wanted more.

In one of her oddly punctuated letters, to congressman and Lincoln friend Elihu Washburne, she urged him "in view, of the necessities of your case [to] *insist* upon the *four years salary* & have the tax removed from it—The $10,000—off—the 4 years salary, would be a great deal to us, who have a home to obtain, furniture & need the interest to live on—It will be small enough & I shall have to exercise much economy with *that*—If a *grateful* American people—only give us the $25,000—our portion, is a boarding house forever—a *fitting* place, for the wife & sons, of the man—who served his country so well & lost his life in consequence."

But Congress went with precedent and voted her only a year's salary which, after deductions, came to $22,025. To Mary Jane Welles, the wife of Lincoln's navy secretary, she complained, "What a *future* before us—The wife & sons, of the Martyr President, *compelled* to be inmates of boarding houses, all their lives." Nevertheless she put most of her windfall into a new house, only to find that she couldn't afford the upkeep. She was forced to rent it out the following year.

In 1867, still waiting on Justice Davis to wrap up her husband's estate, Mary Lincoln concocted a scheme to sell off her first-lady finery in New York. She called upon the loyal Lizzie Keckley to meet and assist her. Mrs. Lincoln had taken an alias, Mrs. Clarke of Chicago, which did not last very long when she handed over for appraisal a diamond ring with her name inscribed. Having found brokers and commissioned a private sale, she sat back to await the horde of buyers—who never came. Compelled to stage a public showing, the newspapers stopped by and jeered. *Frank Leslie's Illustrated Weekly* called it "Mrs. Lincoln's Second-hand Clothing Sale," and reporters described the clothes as soiled and perspiration-stained. Back in Illinois, the newspapers called her deranged.

Robert wrote to Mary Eunice Harlan, whom he would marry: "The simple truth, which I cannot tell anyone not personally interested, is that my mother is on one subject not mentally responsible. I have supposed this for some time from various indications and now have no doubt of it. . . . You could hardly believe it possible, but my mother protests to me that she is in actual want and nothing I can do or say will convince her to the contrary. Do you see that I am likely to have a good deal of trouble in the future, do what I can to prevent it."

At last, though, the estate was settled. The three heirs divided $110,295 equally, or $36,765 apiece. Put in bonds at 6 percent interest, Mrs. Lincoln was guaranteed an annual income of less than $2,500—better off than before but never enough. The faithful Keckley, who understandably was expecting *something* from the New York adventure, was stiffed, so wrote her 1868 exposé. The public could savor Abe's lunatic-asylum warning, Robert's mention of plunder, and the "butcher" Grant remark.

Mrs. Lincoln concluded during the same year as Keckley's mischief that it would be best to live abroad. Robert was now a Chicago lawyer, and Mary Harlan was a senator's daughter. After their autumn wedding the elder Mary Lincoln sailed to Germany with Tad. He would go to school there, just as Winnie Davis would do. His mother, draped in widow's black and with many trunks, would seek an expatriate's solitude. They settled in Frankfurt, which she always spelled as Frankfort—as in Kentucky.

A great deal of Mrs. Lincoln's next two years in Europe would be spent writing letters and, of course, shopping. These diversions were often packaged together as gifts and advice shipped off to Chicago and the daughter-in-law. From Frankfurt went dresses, pillowcases, bonnets, and needlework along with gushes of wisdom when a granddaughter was announced. "Do not allow the baby to walk too soon or she will become bowlegged," warned Mary Lincoln. The child, with the same name as mother and grandmother, would be necessarily referred to as "Mamie."

The widow also read a lot, favoring bleak novels by Edward Bulwer-Lytton, Wilkie Collins, and Elizabeth Stuart Phelps. She took trips to spas. Her ailments included weak nerves, joint and muscle pains, migraines, incontinence, and insomnia. With Tad out of school, she managed a summer journey to Scotland as guest of another of Lincoln's rescued Springfield appointees.

As shopping and saving were contradictory impulses, money cravings were ever about. Soon after her arrival in Frankfurt, the widow decided to lobby Congress for an unprecedented annual pension. Mrs. Lincoln's outpourings again reminded lawmakers of her husband's service and death. She then complained that her income was inadequate to live "in a style becoming to the widow of the chief magistrate of a great nation." In this view of a permanent national indebtedness, she was not unlike Julia Grant. She also pleaded her health. A figure of $3,000 to $5,000 a year was suggested. The latter was the same as a congressman's salary.

Understandably, the request was hardly popular, and perceived friends both in and out of Congress—including Grant's vice president—were solicited to campaign heavily for its passage. Justice Davis was appealed to thusly: ". . . [Congressman] *Thad Stevens is gone* & they speak of increasing [President] Grant's salary to $100,000- a year. My husband, was Commander in Chief & directed every move Grant ever made—Surely, surely with ill health upon me & physicians bills, that often *Appall* me—*I will be remembered. You can do much*, dear Judge, in influencing public opinion, will you not use, that great influence?"

After a year-and-a-half barrage, and with the powerful Senator Charles Sumner coming to the rescue, finally Congress approved a $3,000-a-year pension bill. In July 1870, Grant signed it.

What of Tad? Willie was the most loved, but Tad was something of a pet to his parents, and both boys (as Herndon would have it) ran amuck in Lincoln's law office and later in the White House. Tad lisped and may have been mildly retarded. Although tutored in the White House, he didn't go to school until age twelve in Chicago. He was barely literate, if that. Shown the word "ape" in a primer and given many hints, he identified it as "monkey." Yet Tad was always a comfort to his mother and was said, after the assassination, to be the only one who could persuade her to cease weeping. They remained close and consoling in Germany, where he would bring her food and nurse her when sick. He also seems to have made educational progress under Teutonic discipline. In any event, it was Tad's home-sickness—and likely that of his mother too—that convinced Mary Lincoln to return to Chicago after almost two years in Germany.

Not right away, though. Another half-year was spent in Eng-land, first to take the waters at Leamington, then to mix with other exiles and pass the time in London. The pension from Congress had doubled Mary Lincoln's annual income, and so she also journeyed to Italy and left Tad with a tutor. Her relentless shopping now focused on gifts for Mamie, and she wrote Robert's wife begging the couple to bring the baby to England (they didn't).

The trip home in May 1871 ended Mrs. Lincoln's self-imposed exile. It would seem to have been an uneventful crossing and a happy return. But Tad had caught a cold, and his mother soon moved them out of Robert's small Chicago house and into a hotel. Tad's illness worsened. He had pleurisy, his lungs filling with fluid. Tad Lincoln died on July 15 at only age eighteen. His mother took to her bed again. The unnerved Robert went for a month's rest in the Rockies.

*

IT WAS during this period that a permanent breach occurred with the daughter-in-law. Mary Lincoln had always been generous toward Robert and the second Mary, and even more so when the third Mary arrived. In fact Robert had protested that he and his wife were "frightened" by the excessiveness of some of the baby clothes sent from Europe. Tad's death made Mrs. Lincoln no easier to live with when a houseguest. Given her imperious temperament, clashes were inevitable; for one, the elder Mrs. Lincoln would fire the servants of the younger Mrs. Lincoln.

Robert's wife would, in his words, "break up housekeeping," which meant she would go home to her own mother until Robert's went elsewhere. These separations in turn reduced the widow's access to the granddaughter and two other grandchildren to come. The two Mrs. Lincolns would seem to despise each other to the end.

Although she was entitled by law to two-thirds of Tad's $35,750 estate, Mary Lincoln split it evenly with Robert. Her worth had risen to more than $75,000 and her annual income to $8,000, but she was also more adrift. She spent part of the next few years traveling to spas and visiting mediums. One of her séances yielded the face of Tad. Most famously, during a trip a Boston spiritualist and photographer, William Mumler, having been recently acquitted of fraud, made a portrait picture of the widow Lincoln. In it, Abe's ghostly image stands benignly behind her, white hands protectively upon the shoulders of her black dress.

In February 1875 she fled a Chicago winter for the sulfur springs of Florida, accompanied by a nurse. In March, unaccountably, she took it into her head that Robert was dying. She sent a telegram from Jacksonville to his law partner asking of Robert's health and saying she was taking the train home right away. Soon she sent a second telegram to Robert: "My dearly beloved son Robert T. Lincoln rouse yourself and live for my sake all I have is yours from this hour. I am praying every moment for your life to be spared to your mother."

A puzzled Robert wired the telegraph office manager about his mother and was told she had appeared "nervous and somewhat excited" and that the nurse believed she should return to Chicago immediately. A third telegram from Mary soon came, assuring Robert: "Start for Chicago this evening hope you are better today you will have money on my arrival." Upon arrival, she was, of course, relieved to find her son perfectly healthy, if very worried for herself.

She also confided that a man had poisoned her coffee on the train.

What had happened? Theories abound. It was the time of year when Willie and Eddie had died, which always seemed to encourage morbid and lengthy bouts of self-pity. The approaching tenth anniversary of her husband's assassination may also have induced a special dread. According to later testimony, Mrs. Lincoln had believed she would die on September 6, 1874—a date that came and went— and that Robert would follow during this anniversary period. She was also taking chloral hydrate, a sedative, for her insomnia. Chloral hydrate was a favorite Victorian depressant that if used with similar drugs or alcohol could produce psychotic episodes.

Whatever the cause, her bizarre behavior continued, and Robert was forced to act. Mrs. Lincoln's conduct had gone beyond the bounds of mere eccentricity. A world largely given to already thinking her mad (when it thought of her at all) would scarcely be surprised that a team of doctors and lawyers called in by Robert had concurred—as now did Robert.

Here Robert Todd Lincoln becomes the focal point of both the Mary defenders and those who still hold to the nineteenth century's original verdict. On the one hand, Robert Lincoln has been accused of rushing to put away his mother for reasons of money or political ambition. On the other, he is accepted as the devoted and harassed son fearful that Mary Lincoln could no longer control either her money or her life. Certainly he was aware that her notoriety compromised the family prestige left him by his father; if anything, the fatal wound delivered on a Good Friday had made Abraham Lincoln that much more a Christlike figure to Republicans and freedmen. In any case, Robert acted. Convention expected it, and he did his duty. Lingering if exhausted love may or may not have had something to do with it too.

The Illinois law regarding the institutionalizing of the mentally ill was rare among the states. It required a jury trial with the accused present. This reform had grown out of a scandal when a Calvinist preacher had had his disobedient and spiritualist wife forcibly committed, and she later led a crusade to make the law less of a weapon for thwarted husbands. Although this was a fortunate circumstance for Mary Lincoln, the trial itself—on May 19, 1875—was a humiliating ordeal.

She knew nothing of her trial until the lawyer hired by Robert to press the case for commitment showed up at her hotel room an hour before its start, to escort her (forcibly, if necessary) to court. The judge was honest, the jury respectable, and Mary Lincoln was provided with counsel. But her lawyer, another Abraham Lincoln friend, only reluctantly took on the task and was virtually silent throughout. Nor did he call Mrs. Lincoln to rebut the witnesses who paraded with details of her erratic behavior.

Employees of the Chicago hotel where she lived spoke of her unreasoned fears of fire and strange men. One saw her mix several kinds of medicine together. Merchants testified about her purchases since returning from Florida. These included forty pairs of lace curtains and three expensive watches and other jewelry, none of which—having no home and no longer wearing jewelry—she had a use for (Robert had sent some of it back). Five doctors were called. Dr. Willis Danforth, who had treated her since 1873, told of observing "nervous derangement" and of having Mary tell him of her 1874 death date. She had been assured of it by table taps from the departed president.

At last Robert was called. He spoke of his mother's restless behavior in the hotel after her return from Florida and how he had stayed in an adjoining room. Once he found her half dressed and attempting to go down the elevator. When he tried to lead her gently back to her room, she had screamed, "You are going to murder me!" He testified about the purchases. He told of her fear of a Chicago fire like the famous one of 1871, and that she had shipped eleven of her trunks to safety in Milwaukee. She had also shown him her petticoat, where she had sewn $57,000 in securities just in case she had to run from a fire. When he left the hotel he had hired Pinkerton agents to keep watch on her. Newspapers would call Robert teary-eyed. At the last he said: "I have no doubt my mother is insane. She has long been a source of great anxiety to me. . . ."

Eighteen witnesses were called to testify against her, none for her. The jury took ten minutes. During that brief interval, Robert approached his mother. "O Robert," she exclaimed, "to think that my son would ever have done this!" The *Chicago Times* headlined its story that she had been adjudged insane A SAD REVELATION, with an addendum below: "At Last The Strange Freaks Of The Past Ten Years Are Understood."

Back in her hotel room to prepare for her train ride to the sanitarium, Mary Lincoln briefly managed to slip away from her keepers. She futilely sought to buy from a pharmacist enough laudanum and camphor to kill herself. By the time she was put on the train, however, she was said to be reconciled and even cheerful.

*

MODERN MARY-APOLOGISTS have come to view the sanity proceedings as a male-ordered kangaroo court. In essence, they say, she had a right to spend her money any way she wanted to. Other activities viewed as aberrant were induced by unfortunate events, and she was more in need of compassion than doctors (if one, like Robert, had compassion). Some behavior also may have been medicinally induced, and as for the spiritualism and table-thumping . . . well, a good many Americans and foreigners believed in that sort of thing and still believe in ghosts. Even the suicide attempt, though well reported, might not be true, and if it were it would be even more understandable as the reaction of someone left abandoned in a cruel world than as the act of an unstable mind.

Anyway, Mary Lincoln had always been a little odd—but that did not mean crazy. She was narcissistic, but in that she was ahead of her time. Actually she was little different in personality and habit from the much younger woman Abraham Lincoln had married, and wasn't Lincoln's judgment always impeccable? Or nearly so? Robert wanted her money for his real estate speculations. Many who took Robert's side did so only superficially. They hoped the embarrassment would wreck any political ambitions and enhance their own. . . .

And so the arguments go.

The public reaction at the time to Mary Lincoln's circumstances was, for once, widely sympathetic. Her misfortune was largely blamed on the assassination. Robert received some of this kindness too, and the court named him as conservator of her estate. There was another heartrending scene when, back at the hotel, the lawyers made her surrender the petticoat bonds.

"And you are not satisfied," Mary said, weeping, "with locking me up in an insane asylum, but now you are going to rob me of all I have on earth. My husband is dead, and my children are dead and these bonds I have saved for my necessities in my old age; now you are going to rob me of them." Still, she took five trunks with her, with more to follow. She also took—to Robert's puzzlement—a number of carpetbags filled with footstools she had bought.

Bellevue Place Sanitarium was in Batavia, Illinois, about thirty-five miles west of Chicago. It was a neat and peaceful hospital on a large campus with gardens, walkways, and clean rooms catering to a small and upscale clientele. Carriage rides were available. It was also a place for mental patients of wide degrees of competency. Mrs. Lincoln, of course, was something of a celebrity. Robert visited each week and brought granddaughter Mamie along.

The owner of Bellevue, Dr. Robert Patterson, diagnosed Mary Lincoln's case as monomania, a deceptive condition that made the patient appear perfectly normal in some behaviors but irrational in others. Modernists have suggested bipolar disorder. Patterson's approach to patients was "rest, diet, baths, fresh air, occupation, diversion, change of scene, an orderly life and no more medicine than necessary." The unruly, however, might find themselves heavily dosed with opium, morphine, whiskey-laced eggnog, or the increasingly popular chloral hydrate. Mrs. Lincoln gave little trouble.

On July 15, 1875, the anniversary of Tad's death and after nearly two months as a patient, Mary Lincoln unexpectedly announced to Patterson that she wished to go live with her oldest sister, Elizabeth Edwards, and her husband back in Springfield. The sisters had been estranged for years, but when Mary mentioned it to Robert he favorably suggested that at least a visit might be a good thing and for her

to write to her sister. This she set down to do. The letter she personally mailed, however, was to a formidable lawyer couple, Judge James
and Myra Bradwell. It was, in effect, an SOS. She begged them to
come to her immediately and to bring powerful friends.

What followed has, by necessity, received considerable attention.
One of the most riveting and recent accounts is in Jason Emerson's
The Madness of Mary Lincoln, which makes use of a cache of twenty-
five letters discovered in 2005 that are mostly Mrs. Lincoln's from
this period.

To summarize, the Bradwells in their initial visit expressed to Dr.
Patterson that while Mrs. Lincoln was "not quite right," she should
be allowed home care. Myra Bradwell was one of the country's first
female attorneys, though Illinois would not let her practice. Among
her many friends was Susan B. Anthony. Mary Lincoln became Mrs.
Bradwell's latest cause. She sneaked in a newspaper reporter from
the *Chicago Times* during one visit when Patterson was absent. Meanwhile letters of complaint and instruction from Mrs. Lincoln flowed
out. In one she also asked Myra to bring her some black alpaca clothing material.

It was Myra who wrote Elizabeth Edwards. Mrs. Edwards, having health problems of her own, waxed back and forth, telling the
Bradwells she agreed that while Mary wasn't sane, she herself would
not have taken the same step as Robert. To Robert, however, she
expressed her reluctance to be either host or keeper. By this time
Robert was beginning to feel defensive about the Bradwells' interest
while his mother complained of him to Myra that "I rather think he
would prefer *my* remaining *here* in his heart." Robert wrote the lawyer that the increased excitement seemed to be reversing whatever
progress his mother had been making, and to limit the visits.

This request only made the redoubtable Myra more determined.
She traveled to Springfield to see Mrs. Edwards, who soon wrote to
Robert that she would be "perfectly willing" to welcome "the experi-
ment" of his mother's visit. Robert now ordered that the Bradwells'
contact with the patient be cut off. The Bradwells then leaked to a
newspaper that Mrs. Lincoln was better, would visit her sister, and
might not even return to the sanitarium. Judge Bradwell also gave an

interview alleging that the widow never should have been locked up and was "no more insane today than you and I are."

Finally the earlier interview with Mary Lincoln—two and a half weeks after its occurrence—was published by the *Chicago Times* and under a happier headline than in May: REASON RESTORED, the reporter had concluded. Myra had also been interviewed and blamed the hapless Patterson. The immediate fallout from newspapers belatedly following the *Times*, and from those *they* interviewed, was to blame the Bradwells as meddling "busybodies." But it was all too much for Robert. His mother was agitated, and her health might also decline if denied her visit. Patterson was understandably agreeable. On September 10, 1875, after fewer than four months in Bellevue, Mary Lincoln left for Springfield, never to return.

A visit was all that had been agreed to, but Mrs. Lincoln was cheerful and on her best behavior. She remained with the Edwardses. She was, however, increasingly hostile toward Robert. Most of all, she wanted her property returned—especially the bonds from her petticoat.

This was not easy for Robert to do, even had he wanted to. As court-appointed conservator, he was locked into his thankless service until the following summer, unless he could find someone else to take it on (no one would). Moreover he had been required to post surety bonds of $150,000 to protect his mother in case he spent all of her estate. In fact, if *she* should run through her estate before the conservatorship expired, he would be liable to repay that bond to her. It occurred to Robert that his mother was quite capable of doing just that to spite him.

After all, he still thought her mad.

At length, though, Robert turned over everything to her except the petticoat bonds, and even here she began to receive the monthly income they earned. Mrs. Lincoln wasn't appeased. She also had a pistol. Elizabeth Edwards's husband, Ninian, wrote to Robert: "She says she will never again allow you to come into her presence." Robert was also hearing from friends in Springfield that his mother was back shopping and running up bills. Mary in turn began to demand he send back everything she owned that was in the possession of the

Robert Lincolns, including the mountain of gifts she had given them through the years.

Robert hinted that he might have her sent back to Bellevue. Instead he turned for advice to Justice Davis, who counseled simply to get out from under and "trust to the chances of time."

In June 1876, Robert returned to court and asked another jury to remove him as conservator and declare his mother fit to control all her property, including the precious bonds. Her estate had grown $8,000 richer under his control. Although the jury was not called on to decide Mary Lincoln's sanity, in returning her property rights its verdict also declared her as "restored to reason." Ninian Edwards, who testified, would write Robert afterward that Mrs. Lincoln—who never believed she had lost her reason—disliked the wording of the verdict, but at last it was done. Robert personally carried the bonds to Springfield. His mother accused him of bringing false charges and said that if he ever got to "the other world" he wouldn't be allowed to approach the rest of the family.

In October, Mary Lincoln decided to try Europe again, without telling her son. She did tell her sister, though, "I go an exile, and alone!"

*

HER REFUGE was the French Pyrenean city of Pau, and here she stayed for four years. Its calm weather and nearby mineral springs were said to work wonders, and Americans such as William Cullen Bryant had praised it as a place of silence and slumber (word having spread, Pau had become a little less sleepy). The city was also attractive to Mrs. Lincoln because she had been fluent in French since a girl. Still, she would write in 1877, "I live, very much alone and do not identify myself with the [French]—have a few friends and prefer to remain secluded—My *Gethsemane* is ever with me." When she got away it was to take a rare trip to Italy or to Marseilles and Avignon.

Amazingly, the Ulysses Grants passed through Pau on the ex-president's world tour, and of course were toasted and banqueted. But they paid no call on Mrs. Lincoln. Robert remained unforgiven (his mother referred to him as R. T. Lincoln in a letter), but she still sent presents to Mamie. Her interest in Robert perked up briefly when she read of him being mentioned as a presidential prospect for 1880. She could also pity another first lady in exile, Empress Eugenie, when during this same time Eugenie's only son was killed by Zulus.

Despite the waters, Mrs. Lincoln's health declined. She also suffered a series of injuries in several falls. In 1880 she sailed for the United States. She was sixty-two and weighed a frail one hundred pounds. A fellow passenger was Sarah Bernhardt, who had grabbed Mary before she could tumble down a staircase during a rough passage. The actress in her memoirs would recall, "I had just done this unhappy woman the only service I ought not to have done her—I had saved her from death."

Mrs. Lincoln returned to her sister's in Springfield, preferring to remain in a darkened bedroom and exasperating Mrs. Edwards. She also brought with her sixty-four trunks of clothing and would spend much of each day unpacking and repacking.

She and Robert finally reconciled in May 1881, probably through Mrs. Edwards or Mamie, but little is known about the meeting. Robert, having become a successful Chicago lawyer, was President Garfield's new secretary of war. The appointment terrified Mrs. Lincoln, who cried out that "he'll be shot for sure! That's always the way in war!" Instead of Robert, it was Garfield who was shot.

Her delusions of imminent poverty returned, and she successfully lobbied Congress to raise her pension to $5,000 a year to equal the widow Garfield's. She also went back and forth between Springfield and New York for medical baths and other treatments. By March 1882, however, her deteriorating health confined her to the Edwards home. There she died on July 16 of an apparent stroke, having collapsed the previous day in what has been suggested as a diabetic coma. Her collapse had occurred on another anniversary of Tad's death.

It had been an exhausting life, and Mary Lincoln had been exhausting. The death she had so pined for now, presumably, reunited her with Eddie, Willie, Tad, and Abraham—all together in a massive tomb in Springfield's Oak Ridge Cemetery, which she had insisted on. The reconciliation with Robert had gone so far that he planned for himself and his own family to join them when their time came. It came tragically early for his only son, Abraham II, called Jack, who died of blood poisoning as a teenager while Robert was serving as U.S. ambassador to Britain. With Jack went the Lincoln name.

Robert was incredibly successful in a somewhat narrow way. That is, he worked hard as a lawyer and on the political fringes. Opportunities were obviously provided by the Lincoln legacy—that part detached from Mary—and by wealthy Republicans who owed it. From time to time Robert Todd Lincoln was also mentioned as presidential timber. But he had no liking or longing for the job, and history was never thrust upon him as it had been upon his father. As a matter of fact, aside from George Washington no American had ever had it so severely thrust. Robert, in the 1890s, would end up a railroad baron as head of the Pullman Palace Car Company. The position came a few years after one of the nation's worst labor strikes directed at the company, and after the death of founder and client George Pullman.

Robert also ended up with his mother's quite healthy financial estate. It included the sixty-four trunks filled with old clothes carefully packed, and other plunder. The latter must have thrilled Mary Harlan Lincoln, who did not attend her mother-in-law's funeral. In any case, Robert became not only rich but another of those captains of industry who would leave behind more impressive monuments than most presidents. For Robert it was Hildene, a regal mansion and gardens in rural Vermont, whose name was a combination of hill and the Gaelic *dene* for valley. Mamie would marry and live nearby. From Hildene and a home in Washington, Robert ran his railroad company and kept a lawyer's grip on the Lincoln story.

Lord knows, he had good reason. Herndon's efforts introduced questions of Abe's true love—a woman named Ann Rutledge—and his belief in God. Another writer suggested Lincoln was illegitimate. As guardian of his father's papers, Robert granted access only to former secretaries Hay and John Nicolay for their ten-volume biography. Robert edited every line.

But it was the Mary story he was most concerned about, the dark shadow over the Lincoln mystique. Before his death in 1926, Robert agreed to a controlled biography of his mother—the first one—to be written by a cousin. Work on it continued after his death but received a brusque interruption when Robert's widow was told of a rival project. This one would focus on Mrs. Lincoln's insanity based on letters between the subject and the author's grandparents, the pesky Judge and Myra Bradwell. Ultimately the project was bought off with a check, yet it was another aggravation for Mary Harlan Lincoln.

The latest Widow Lincoln had a marked decisiveness as well as an unforgiving memory. Robert had wanted to be placed in the family tomb in Illinois, which now contained his parents, brothers, and son. Mary Harlan had been expected to be alongside in due time. It seems, though, she had had her fill of the Lincolns, or at least of her mother-in-law. Perhaps she thought Robert had accomplished enough on his own to stand (or lie) apart from the rest. Perhaps she just didn't like the thought of eternity in Illinois. In any case, Robert's brief service on Grant's staff and his term as war secretary were qualifications for Arlington National Cemetery. And there Robert went. Son Jack was disentombed and joined him. The break, it might be said, was restored and made permanent.

Mary Todd Lincoln cannot be pleased by the separation. She and Robert certainly had their differences but, after all, families should stay together; Mister Lincoln would insist upon it—in his own joking and indirect way, of course. Besides, separation would mean victory by another woman, an ungrateful woman.

But it's difficult for the dead nowadays to get their point across. So many people are so self-absorbed, rather like Mary Lincoln, in fact, that hardly anyone has time or energy to call up the spectral faces or listen for their table thumps.

· 8 ·

THE GOOD HATER

In a passage written during the South's post-Chickamauga euphoria, Mary Chesnut passed along these observations:

"J.C. [her husband, James] said he told Mr. Davis that every honest man he saw out west thought well of Joe Johnston. He knows that the president detests Joe Johnston for all the trouble he has given him. And General Joe returns the compliment with compound interest. His hatred of Jeff Davis amounts to a religion. With him it colors all things.

"Joe Johnston advancing, or retreating, I may say with more truth, is magnetic. He does draw the goodwill of those by whom he is surrounded. Being such a good hater, it is a pity he had not elected to hate somebody else than the president of our country. He hates not wisely but too well."

She wrote a bit later of this same Joe Johnston being so considerate of his military aides that he sent them far away when fighting came. One of them, Wade Hampton the younger, had complained, saying: "No man exposes himself more recklessly to danger than General Johnston, and no one strives harder to keep others out of it. But the business of this war is to save the country. And a commander must risk his men's lives to do it." The irrepressible diarist added: "French saying, can't make an omelet unless you are willing to break the eggs."

This, then, would be history's complaint against one of the soldiers who, like Robert E. Lee, General Winfield Scott tried desperately to keep in Union blue as the great war threatened, and who responded instead to the call of his native Virginia. Overcautious, truculent, cool yet hot-tempered, a defeatist, a perfectionist, a peacock, spiteful, politically unskilled and unguarded, a man more magnanimous toward the enemy than toward his own—all would be impressions and judgments of Johnston both during the conflict and after.

He was a man of whom much had been expected and who delivered much less. Unlike John Bell Hood, he had an eye for detail but lacked Hood's fire. Indeed, there was just enough good military material between the two of them to make one Nathan Bedford Forrest.

Thus Joseph Johnston (his preference) has been dismissed and disparaged. Although his role was often prominent, his accomplishments were few. With Johnston there is seldom suspense as to the outcome of battle and little for Rebels to celebrate. Memorials to him barely exist. Yet Northern opponents such as Sherman and Grant and George McClellan respected him, and his Southern critics were not without glass houses of their own. His grievances against Jefferson Davis would continue long after the war while their feud during it did nothing to advance the Cause they both defended. It may have done much to make it Lost.

Joe Johnston is an interesting man if for no other reason than his enemies, the greatest of whom was himself.

*

JOSEPH EGGLESTON JOHNSTON was the seventh son of nine surviving children. He was born in 1807 near Farmville, a village not far from Appomattox. The family soon moved to Abingdon in the southwest corner of Virginia and not long removed from the frontier of Daniel Boone and the Wilderness Road. Here in the mountains, Joseph grew up with Sir Walter's novels and showed early signs of soldierly courage. Once, after a horse threw the young Johnston and broke his leg so that the bone showed itself, the youth had to be carried a considerable distance on the shoulders of his companions. Not for one moment, goes the story, did he complain.

West Point was a natural fit for Johnston, who entered in 1825. A demerit-prone Jeff Davis was a class ahead. Classmates included Lee while the pride of the corps was Albert Sidney Johnston (no relation). An undying rumor is of a fistfight between Joseph Johnston and Davis while both were cadets. It would explain a lot later, if true, but seems highly doubtful. Johnston was a studious sort who would graduate thirteenth of forty-six and have the kind of conduct record that chaplains point to. The near perfect Bobby Lee, however, would leave West Point with an even higher place. Except for two prewar promotions, Lee's edge would parallel both men's lives and reputations. They would alternate as friends and rivals.

Johnston's physical appearance also was not the equal of the Byronically handsome Lee. He stood five-feet-seven, with direct brown eyes but impaired nighttime vision, and a broad forehead with a retreating hairline. Still, the images left to us are of a dignified, serious, and spotlessly dressed army officer whether in Union blue or Rebel grey—gentlemanly if stiff and hinting of prickliness. His West Point classmates tried to puncture some of this when they nicknamed young Johnston "The Colonel."

A Johnston biographer, Craig L. Symonds, has provided a full picture of the man who, like Lee, often unbends in his letters with a playful humor and a romantic heart. When his beloved nephew Preston Johnston repeated a sister's tale of Johnston being jilted by a woman who then married someone else, he wrote back: "Tell Lizzie that nobody has yet been furnished with an opportunity to commit what she esteems the folly of rejecting me." To his wife, Lydia, fifteen years his junior, he invariably signed his letters, "Good night my love, my life, my soul."

Preston Johnston's death in the Mexican War—coming at the time of a successful American attack in which Joseph Johnston himself had played a key role—was a sorrow he felt deeply ever after, as he and Lydia would remain childless.

In peacetime he chafed at incompetent officers, the army's resistance to change, and the slowness of promotion. He wrote of "build-

ing castles in the air" to his close friend McClellan, who had left the
army to command the Illinois Central Railroad. Johnston longed
for action, to lead men, to do something spectacularly. Instead his
battles were unseemly ones over rank.

In the U.S. Army, brevet promotions were a way to reward officers with a higher honorary rank, though usually without corresponding pay or authority. They were testaments to valor in lieu of
medals. Brevets flowed like water during wars, and Johnston's record
was a breveted mess. It included a dubious brevet to captain for bravery in 1838 against the Seminoles in Florida. It was dubious because
Johnston had temporarily left the army and was serving as a *civilian*
engineer during his act of heroism. More honors came in Mexico
when he was breveted to colonel—at least Johnston thought so—but
the War Department ruled otherwise.

Over the years Johnston stubbornly but unsuccessfully appealed
his claim of a colonelcy brevet to two consecutive secretaries of war.
One of them was Jefferson Davis. Davis, however, did give Johnston a
regular army lieutenant colonelcy as second-in-command of the new
First U.S. Cavalry regiment. Although it was permanent and more
meaningful, the promotion didn't end the argument. The righteous
Johnston continued his brevet claim with Davis's successor.

He was John B. Floyd, a distant Johnston kinsman by marriage.
In 1860, Floyd agreeably ruled that his predecessors had been wrong.
Johnston at last was satisfied. Influence-sensitive officers such as Lee
were not. A few months later, the death of the army's quartermaster
general left an opening and a brigadier's star. General Scott recommended Johnston and three others, including Lee and Albert Sidney
Johnston. Again Secretary Floyd decided for family.

During this time the Johnstons had become implanted in Washington, and Lydia and Varina Davis were fast and thick. This held
career potential when the nation split apart and Davis became the
Confederate president. Winfield Scott urged Lydia to get her husband to stay on. Instead Union General Johnston—answering his
state's siren song—became a Confederate general. Among his first
acts was to abandon the indefensible armory at Harpers Ferry, Virginia. A month later his timely arrival with Jeb Stuart and Stonewall

Jackson at First Manassas saved the day for P. G. T. Beauregard and the Confederacy. At last he would be appreciated. . . .

Then Jefferson Davis made known the top five generals of the new Old South.

The Confederate Congress had stipulated the positions be filled on the basis of relative rank during prewar service in the U.S. Army. As Johnston read it, and having been a brigadier general, he should have been first in seniority of those Davis named, the rest of whom had ranked no higher than colonel. But the law also made a distinction between staff and line promotions—that is, between paper shufflers and combat officers.

Johnston's brigadier star was in a staff role. As a regular army line officer in the cavalry, he had ranked no higher than lieutenant colonel. Now, recast as a Confederate line officer, he had slipped a couple of notches in seniority. As to Davis's list, the new adjutant general, Samuel Cooper, had remained a staff officer and was ranked first, followed by line officers Albert Sidney Johnston and Lee. Joseph Johnston, who had gone from line to staff and back, was now ranked fourth. Beauregard, previously a major, brought up the rear.

Johnston was stunned. He unwisely wrote Davis a blistering letter. He could never be reconciled to what he considered a professional injustice and a blow to his honor. The equally prickly Davis could never be reconciled to Johnston's "unbecoming" insinuations.

At least one historian has suggested that, legal interpretations aside, Davis made his selections solely on the basis of friendship. He would display this damaging peculiarity throughout the war—especially in his tolerance of Braxton Bragg—so it is not out of the question. In any case, the relationship between Davis and Johnston spiraled downward. Predictably, the friendship between Varina and Lydia went with it.

Johnston's suspicion and distrust of Richmond authority would deepen. It did not help that Davis began relying more on Lee for advice. Both began to go behind Johnston to deal with other parts of, technically, Johnston's command.

In March 1862, George McClellan's Union hordes arrived in Virginia and disembarked upon the peninsula between the James and York rivers, about eighty miles downstream from Richmond. Johnston fell back, purportedly waiting for an opening to strike. Davis grew anxious. By May, Johnston had retreated to the city's outskirts. Yankees could hear its clock bells chime.

When McClellan split his forces on both banks of the flooded Chickahominy River, Johnston struck at a crossroads called Seven Pines. It was a well-conceived but utterly uncoordinated and unsupervised attack. Pete Longstreet's men took the wrong road, and control of the battle was soon beyond Johnston's grasp. Probably to evade Davis who had dropped by his headquarters, Johnston rode off to the front lines late in the day and was wounded by shrapnel. He was out of action for six months and never regained his Virginia command. Davis gave it to Lee.

The rest is history.

*

THE ENMITY between Johnston and Davis would only worsen throughout the war, and bears some (if brief) retelling.

While recuperating from his wounds, Johnston fell in with Davis's political enemies who were equally drawn to him. Louis Wigfall was among their leaders. This was the same Wigfall who rode with his family on the sad return with Hood to Texas. Through the rest of the war Johnston would be futilely promoted as a Southern savior. Lydia Johnston, who had retracted (as Mrs. Chesnut also recorded) her compliment of Varina Davis as a "western belle," fell in with Wigfall's wife. Charlotte Wigfall couldn't stand Varina. The Johnstons had tumbled into a nest of vipers, but a nest neither tried to escape.

There was, however, one shining moment when Johnston stood tall. At a champagne breakfast, Davis-hater William Lowndes Yancey—that same Yancey who had once extolled Davis's ascendancy as a meeting between "the man and the hour"—hoisted a toast to Johnston as "the only man who can save the Confederacy." In response, Johnston gravely rose to his feet.

"Mr. Yancey," he demurred, "the man you describe is now in the field, in the person of General Robert E. Lee. I will drink to *his* health."

Lee, however, had his army, and Virginia was no longer big enough for both Johnston and Davis. Johnston was sent over the mountains to command the Department of the West, a vast region stretching from the Appalachians to the Mississippi. His job was to oversee the armies of Bragg in Tennessee and John C. Pemberton in Mississippi. It was Davis's idea to offset the superior federal numbers by shuttling troops between the two armies. Johnston thought the idea unrealistic, given the distance and the dismal state of Southern railroads. Davis had Bragg and Pemberton send their reports directly to him, thus circumventing Johnston who soon felt useless.

Still, after Bragg's blunders at Stones River, Johnston turned down an offer from the Confederate War Department to command Bragg's Army of Tennessee. He thought acceptance would look like he had conspired against a brother officer. It was an odd excuse, considering Bragg's incompetence, the fate of the army, and his own willingness to listen to anti-Davis plotters. Bragg stayed on and was soon rolled back to Georgia.

Sent next to Mississippi to help Pemberton at Vicksburg against Grant, and greatly outnumbered, Johnston could do little else than urge Pemberton to evacuate the city. Instead Pemberton dug in deeper. The siege of Vicksburg was a catastrophe for Southern soldiers and civilians alike. Confederate Sergeant Willie Tunnard described the gruesome scene from within: "Dogs howled through the streets at night; cats screamed forth their hideous cries; an army of rats, seeking food, would scamper around your very feet and across the streets and over the pavements. Lice and filth covered the bodies of the soldiers. Delicate women and little children, with pale, careworn and hunger-pinched features, peered at the passer-by with wistful eyes from the caves in the hillsides. . . ."

On the Fourth of July 1863, Pemberton surrendered an army of some thirty thousand. Vicksburg would shun the holiday well into the twentieth century. Pemberton would always blame Johnston. So would Jeff Davis. When someone observed that Vicksburg had fallen for lack of provisions, Davis had snapped, "Yes, from want of provisions inside, and a general outside who wouldn't fight."

Yet, six months later, after the failed Confederate siege of Chattanooga, Johnston had Bragg's job. Davis had little choice. Among comparable generals, Lee didn't want it, and Beauregard was even more distasteful to Davis. Meanwhile Wigfall & Company in the Confederate Congress pressed Johnston to accept. The new commander—always popular with those below and a trial to those above—issued furloughs and back pay, improved the food and clothing, and restored morale. When Johnston returned the Tennessee regiments to Frank Cheatham's division that Bragg had spitefully removed, Cheatham—perhaps on the sauce—marched the entire unit to Johnston's headquarters, threw his arm around the dignified general, and patted his balding head.

"Boys, this is old Joe!" Cheatham announced to a crescendo of cheers.

What ensued well into 1864 was wrangling between Johnston and Richmond. Sherman was in Chattanooga. Davis wanted Johnston's army in North Georgia to launch an offensive deep into Tennessee to draw the Yankees away. Johnston argued that he needed more men and that the move would leave Atlanta to the south exposed. Hood was sent to help. Sherman settled the debate in May by attacking Johnston. Instead of heading north, the Army of Tennessee retreated south, grudgingly but monotonously yielding ground until outside Atlanta. In July, Davis fired Johnston for Hood.

Johnston and what was left of the army would be briefly reunited in North Carolina and again against Sherman in the war's last weeks. He would surrender the army—twice—to his Georgia nemesis. His other nemesis, Jefferson Davis, now a fugitive, wanted Johnston to let any mounted Confederates escape to Texas, which Davis was trying to reach. Instead Joe Johnston, humanely and maliciously, told the ragtags to go home.

*

THE MAIN PROBLEM was that both were prideful men. Johnston and Davis were cut from the same cloth as so many Southern gentlemen. Among this quarrelsome class, outlandish honor laced with explosive self-esteem created occasional face-offs with a smoothbore pistol or unforgiven hates. Especially here the result proved disastrous. The reluctance of a head of state and a leading general to compromise and cooperate was worth a legion to an advancing enemy. Lee got around the touchy Davis by keeping him informed and building on trust. Joseph Johnston never got that far. It was another battle—winning Davis's trust—he retreated from. After all, with the promotion dispute and so much else, how could *he* ever trust *Davis*?

The retreats didn't help. No need to complain of being outnumbered. Lee was always outnumbered yet would attack ferociously and often win. So would that cavalryman Forrest. But both were willing to risk all to procure Southern peace and independence, by shedding blood and cultivating Northern fear. It wasn't that Johnston's retreats were planned in advance. It's just that . . . things happened.

In Georgia, for instance, plans for a counterblow always seemed to be thwarted, if not by an unexpected flanking move of Sherman's then by Hood's failure to attack at the right time, or by Joe Wheeler's inadequate cavalry. It was always something. Heavy rain. A lost federal brigade popping up in the wrong place. Objections from Hood or another corps commander, the bishop-general Leonidas Polk, who was a much better bishop than a general. Circumstances never appeared exactly right for the bold stroke.

Or perhaps there was something more basic to Johnston's problem. As usual, Mary Chesnut may have put her finger on it in a conversation only eight months into the war: "'Now,' says Mr. Hamilton Boykin, 'we all knew [Algernon] Sid Johnston, the general's brother. Never in his life could he make up his mind that everything was so exactly right, that the time to act had come. There was always something to fit that would not fit. Joe Johnston is that way, too. Wade Hampton brought him here to hunt—he is Mrs. Hampton's cousin. We all liked him—but as to hunting, there he made a dead failure. He was a capital shot, better than Wade or I, and we are not so bad—that you'll allow. But then with Colonel Johnston—I think he was colonel then—the bird flew too high or too low—the dogs were too far or too near—things never did suit exactly. He was too fussy, too hard to please, too cautious, too much afraid to miss and risk his fine reputation for a crack shot. Wade and I bulged through the mud and water briars and bushes and came home with a heavy bag. We shot right and left—happy-go-lucky. Joe Johnston did not shoot at all. The exactly right time and place never came. . . .'"

Looking back twenty years later, Rebel Private Sam Watkins, who at the time had cheered Johnston's takeover from Bragg, would say that "I can see where General Joseph E. Johnston made many blunders in not attacking Sherman's line at some point. He was better on the defensive than the aggressive, and hence, *bis peccare in bello non licet* [one must not blunder twice in war]."

It wasn't that Jefferson Davis and the Confederacy itself were free of responsibility for the military mess. The states' rights that was the South's constitutional argument for leaving the Union often as not worked against it throughout the war. Governors wrangled with Richmond over men and supplies. Politician generals in the first part of the war brought on such disasters as Fort Donelson (though Davis may have enjoyed firing one of the generals responsible: former war secretary John B. Floyd). Meanwhile favoritism kept such West Point mediocrities as Bragg and Polk in their jobs. The political unity needed to fight an established Union splintered into jealous and hotheaded factions. Efforts at wartime cohesiveness were mocked as the reason for leaving the Union in the first place. For these feeble efforts, Davis was called a would-be dictator.

Jeff Davis was anything but. His exchanges with Johnston— besides showing a mutual pettiness—were too often suggestions rather than orders, while the legalistic Johnston was eternally seeking clarification. Each man seemed determined to avoid responsibility for whatever emergency was at hand. Both were stiff-necked and shortsighted. In fact, both were a great deal alike.

Davis was never so skillful a politician as to be a conciliator *or* a dictator. As Johnston could not meet him halfway, Davis could never bring himself to win a modicum of trust from the general he had put in charge of the crucial West. Davis could never divorce himself from "friends" such as the obtuse and vengeful Bragg. Johnston could never distance himself from Wigfall.

The Confederacy waited and prayed for the powers of Europe to welcome it into the fold of nations. It would remain a rebellion in the eyes of all but the Southerner.

When the brawl ended after four years, history would begin its search for answers. There was for the South the especially vexing point about God who, toward the last couple of years, had chosen to lean North. The suggested moral answer—slavery—was not easily consumed; indeed, preference was to have God stay impartial and assign the outcome to that old Northern superiority of numbers— more factories and more foreigners in the ranks. Not to mention, of course, certain military mischances along the way.

The excuses would arrive by the droves from eager generals and political figures ready to jump in with their memoirs. Fortunately for this refighting among one's own kind, the process was temporarily restrained by lack of access. Most Confederate records were in the possession of the victors' government. That and the fact that ex-Rebels were looking starvation in the face deferred the urgency to put the past to paper. Some, like General Lee, never published. Some, like Hood, might not have had others, like Johnston, been less unkind.

The impression exists that the challenge to publish was much like the strategy for a battle: Did one strike with his memoirs before a foe's attack, or wait and repel the attack with withering argument? As he published before both Hood and Davis got around to it, Johnston's book was one of the few times he ever struck first.

*

LIKE MOST Confederates after the war, ex-General Johnston's immediate priority was to find a job. After a couple of failures with an express company and a railroad, he became agent and Southern manager for a British-based insurance company as well as for New York Life. His headquarters were in Sherman-spared Savannah, Georgia. This was in late 1868. Four years later he was prospering with 120 agents throughout three states.

If a breach had existed with Lee, this had healed too.

His biographer Symonds notes Johnston's jealousy of Lee's success. Johnston also had held a suspicion that Lee's closeness with Davis made him part of a Richmond cabal always intriguing against him. A Johnston aide was recorded by Mary Chesnut as abusing Lee and Davis "with equal virulence. Lee was a solemn hypocrite. He used the garb of religion to mask his sins, but his iniquities were

Joseph Eggleston Johnston, at left, and Robert Edward Lee, rivals and friends both before and during the war, meet for the last time in 1870 in Savannah, Georgia, where Johnston's insurance company had offices. Lee, president of Washington College, had only six months to live. *(Library of Congress)*

known." Yet it was Lee, near the end in 1865, who had pressed the resistant Davis to restore Johnston to command and who had faith in him.

When informed at the time by the omniscient Wigfall, Johnston had melted: "In youth and early manhood [he wrote of Lee to Wigfall] I loved and admired him more than any man in the world. Since then we have had little intercourse and have become formal in our personal intercourse. . . . I have long thought that he had forgotten our early friendship."

Johnston, all chivalry, then vowed: "Be assured that Knight of old never fought under his King more loyally than I'll serve under Gen. Lee."

In 1870 they met again, in Savannah. Lee since the war had been president of Washington College in Lexington, Virginia. The great commander was on his way to visit the grave of his disgraced father, on Cumberland Island, Georgia. Lee was also a dying man. What Lee and Johnston spoke of is not known. In any case, there was more than the old days to discuss. The South remained devastated. Just in Georgia, average farm income had recently dropped below one hundred dollars a year. Crime was rampant along with massive poverty, yet the poor had turned out to cheer their grey, grim General Lee.

Together Johnston and Lee allowed their pictures to be taken while seated almost knee to knee at a parlor table. Both posed in their dark, civilian suits, thin, trim, dignified. In one photograph Lee holds a pen in his hand and looks down at the paper it is poised above. Johnston stares at Lee and waits, as if Lee is writing an order to be carried out. Lee commands. Lee always commands.

The same sort of reunion—pleasant or otherwise—did not occur between Johnston and Davis.

The Confederate president's interlude just after the war was far worse than that of his two generals. Captured in Georgia and accused of being involved in the Lincoln assassination, he was imprisoned in Fortress Monroe, Virginia. His jailer was a young Nelson A. Miles. Miles would go on to marry Sherman's niece, chase Sitting Bull into Canada, capture Geronimo, break up the Pullman strike, and become general of the army. At this point in his career, however, he was simply the sadistic army officer who had Davis immediately clapped in leg irons.

The public outcry soon unlocked his shackles. Nonetheless Davis was kept isolated and subject to Miles's taunting, his health suffering all the while. Eventually, and under a different keeper, Davis's situation improved. Varina was allowed regular visits. The so-called Lincoln evidence was discredited. But he was held inside the fort for almost two years, looking forward to his day in court to take on a charge of treason. That day never came. The federal government quietly put its case aside and rested the contentious issue. The field was left to Davis to make his defense in his memoirs.

Davis's suffering (or atonement) secured his affection among many Southerners and added the office of living martyr to his earlier positions. Even such equally steeled political enemies as his former vice president, Alexander Stephens of Georgia, had given him their sympathy. Stephens, who also was imprisoned though briefly, commented to his diary on Davis's jailing: "Widely as I differed from him on public policy before and after secession, ruinous to our cause as I have thought his aims and objects, much as I attribute the condition of our country to his errors, yet I do now most deeply pity him and comisserate his condition."

Joseph Johnston never joined in. Davis was forever the unforgiven, and Johnston's truth would out. He was not a failure. He was not! The politically savvy Wade Hampton the elder tried to discourage Johnston from going public with the old feud. "I feel sure," Hampton wrote Johnston in 1870, "no good could come in any way by any publication by you raising an issue on the point. Any controversy between Mr. Davis & yourself would jar upon the feelings of thousands who are friendly to both of you & would tend to throw discredit on our cause."

The advice rolled off. Johnston continued to solicit records and press the memories of those around him during the war. He even encouraged them to tailor their recollections to bolster his own decided opinions. Sometimes, though, Johnston seemed to realize he had gone too far. Try as he might, his invective against Davis would break through, leading to second thoughts (or retreats).

After one such exchange with an old comrade, he wrote a quick letter of apology: "I wish very much that I could make you forget our
conversation in relation to Mr. Davis. It is very pleasant to think
well of people, and much the reverse to think unfavorably of them.
Therefore there was something very like malice on my part in saying anything calculated to shake your belief in the good qualities of
our late President. Selfishness made me, in love of my own opinion,
forget you."

It was, of course, a courteous gesture. Or perhaps he was trying
to keep a lid on the direction of his memoirs. Still, to anyone who
knew him, it shouldn't have been a secret.

When, in 1874, Johnston's numbing *Narrative of Military Operations Directed During the Late War Between the States* appeared, all
the old battles (or missed battles) were replayed. Seven Pines was a
clear victory up to the point when Johnston was wounded. Davis had
withheld from him sufficient strength to avoid the Vicksburg catastrophe and the Georgia retreat. Much of one chapter took up Davis's
denial of Johnston's seniority in the first year of the war—thirteen
years in the past. Hood and Bragg were also targets. Beauregard's
feathers were ruffled in passing.

General Johnston had stated his unarguable case. He had salvaged the pride that had never abandoned him. He had corrected
history, or at least what history might perceive, given his enemies.
Ironically, all his prominent enemies were Southerners. Grant and
Sherman—neither of whom he ever defeated—regarded him quite
favorably.

*

THE FALLING OUT between Jefferson Davis and Louis Wigfall
likely began over a series of slights, real and imagined. One of them
was that old bugaboo, military promotion. During a very brief army
career Wigfall had wanted to be a brigadier general. Instead Davis
made him a lieutenant colonel. Although later corrected, it ensured
Wigfall's sympathy for Johnston's seniority complaint. The enmity
between Varina Davis and Charlotte Wigfall—Charlotte had called

Varina "a coarse western woman"—threw oil on the fire. By early 1862, Wigfall had moved to the Confederate Senate. From there he attacked Davis for the rest of the war.

It was Johnston's political naiveté and desperation for ego-stroking that snared him in the web of Wigfall and other of Davis's Richmond enemies. These enemies, observed Davis's former brother-in-law Richard Taylor, gathered behind Johnston's shield "and shot arrows" at the president. Naturally, the gulf deepened. Despite his several opportunities to command, Johnston could never shake the suspicion that Davis was out to get him—to induce failure and thus bring him down. It could be easy to conclude from all this that Johnston saw the Civil War as something waged less against the Yankees and more between himself and Jefferson Davis.

If Johnston's memoirs were intended to continue that war, Southerners either didn't want to read about it or were too poor to buy in. Book sales were flat. Davis harrumphed to Varina that "Johnston has more effectively than another could shown his selfishness and his malignity." Even Wigfall wasn't around to enjoy Johnston's moment. He had died in Texas at age fifty-seven, two months before the book's appearance. With him, of course, went a leading voice in support of all of Johnston's claims.

The feud with Davis would abate for a few years as Johnston turned to the politics for which he was so ill-suited. In 1876 he agreed to stand as a Georgia delegate to the Democratic National Convention, which would choose Samuel J. Tilden of New York to challenge Republican Rutherford B. Hayes of Ohio. Johnston, though, kept himself aloof from the glad-handing necessary for the seat and, unsurprisingly, failed to be selected. It was a result he accepted, but not without grumbling about a "few Managers" making the decisions who "are not generally of the best class."

Still, he was almost dragged into public service. A few months later the new President Hayes floated Johnston's name for a cabinet post. Hayes wanted a Southerner, and Johnston, like James Chesnut, had been restored to his full political rights in early 1877. Hayes apparently considered Johnston for secretary of war, but that would have put Johnston over Sherman, the general in chief. Sherman protectively reminded Hayes that an ex-Confederate general would be "distasteful to the ex-soldiers of the Union Army and to the public." Hayes turned elsewhere.

Johnston moved back to Virginia and set his sights on a seat in the U.S. House. This time, in 1878, he actively entered the fray against six rivals who "resorted to the lowest tricks to defeat me." Politics in the Gilded Age was especially no place for a gentleman. Lydia would also express her husband's distaste in a comment to supporters: "It's shameful a man of his age and reputation going around to your cross roads like a common member of Congress."

When campaign money ran low, the general's supporters went to Lydia for it. They feared that asking the highly principled Johnston for a large sum would imply that the seat was for sale, and he would resign the race. Lydia quietly found the money.

Johnston's good friend, General Dabney Maury, would recall: "Of all the men in the world he was the least fitted for the work of canvassing a Virginia district, and he never went upon the hustings that his friends did not fear that he would give offence to somebody. . . ." According to Maury, Johnston could never overcome his embarrassment to make a speech *extempore*, and "found it impossible to commit to memory what he had written himself." Luckily for Johnston, none of this mattered. Mere name recognition in a crowded field carried him to victory.

The Congress that Johnston entered (the Forty-sixth) was the first to be elected after the last federal troops were withdrawn from the former Confederacy. It had been a long struggle back toward power for the South and the Democrats. From the ten states (excepting Tennessee) placed in five military districts for Reconstruction, 251 men were sent to Congress between June 1868 and March 1879. In the first session during this period, the Fortieth Congress, Republicans outnumbered Democrats in the U.S. Senate and House by 42 to 3 in the six states then allowed representation. By the time of the Forty-fifth Congress and all ten states being eligible, the Democrats were in the ascendancy by 74 to 14.

Nationally, however, the Democratic household was not a close-knit, postwar family. When the electorally short Hayes-Tilden race was left to a Republican-majority commission to decide, Southern Democrats looked away when Hayes was named president. As a reward for their complacency, Hayes quickly followed through on ending Reconstruction.

Hayes had visions of rebuilding the Republican party in the South. Unfortunately, ending Reconstruction couldn't compensate most white Southerners for their time under previous Republican rule, including the sending of carpetbaggers and freedmen to Congress (in all, sixteen blacks had served). Of Johnston's Reconstruction-free Southern class that followed, no Republican senators were selected, and of the four Republicans sent to the House only two would serve full terms. Aside from future presidential elections, the Republican party would be an irrelevancy in the great part of the South for the next hundred years.

A typical freshman legislator, Johnston mostly kept still and voted the party line. He was not the first Civil War general to win a place in Congress, though he was its highest-ranking Rebel officer. Wade Hampton and John B. Gordon (coiner of "Daughter of the Confederacy") were then in the Senate. In the House with Johnston were Fort Pillow's James Chalmers and two former Confederate cabinet members, Vice President Stephens and Postmaster General John Reagan. Johnston served only one term and left voluntarily. While he seems to have liked being a congressman, the office could never be worth another demeaning campaign among the Rebel rabble.

It wasn't long before he was back to his life's preoccupation with Jeff Davis.

In the same year—1881—that Johnston left Congress, Davis published his own memoirs. *The Rise and Fall of the Confederate Government* was about as negative toward Johnston as might be expected. In December, Johnston struck back.

During a lengthy conversation with a Philadelphia reporter, when he was asked whatever became of the Confederacy's missing gold reserves, Johnston had carelessly replied, "Mr. Davis has never given any satisfactory account of it. . . ." The resulting newspaper headline was sensational: CONFEDERATE GOLD MISSING—GENERAL JOHNSTON CALLS JEFFERSON DAVIS TO ACCOUNT FOR OVER $2,000,000 IN SPECIE.

The uproar had many rallying to the honorable and scarcely prosperous Davis while the Memphis *Appeal* called it a "mean and dastardly assault." Others blamed the reporter, Frank A. Burr. Dabney Maury, somehow friend to both Johnston and Davis, wrote to Davis: "The pestilent interviewer F.A.B. has unintentionally done you a kindness by showing you how warmly you are treasured by true Confederates. If our enemies really desire to split the 'solid south' they have adopted the wrong means—for this vile slander has rallied us to you very warmly."

Johnston himself was forced to retreat, suggesting to the *New York World* that he had been "beguiled" into making his statement. But he went no further.

Reporter Burr, meanwhile, wrote Davis to reassure him that Johnston had been quoted correctly, and that Burr had offered him a chance to revise a copy of their conversation. Johnston had declined, he said, and replied that "no man ought to make a statement to a journalist that he was not willing to stand by."

Senator Ben Hill of Georgia wrote Burr: "I am sorry for Genl Johnston. He has always had a respectable party of admirers in the South. He will have none now. His reputation and his character are both ruined. . . ."

It wasn't quite that bad. A lot of his old soldiers in the Army of Tennessee still remembered him fondly, particularly when recalling their treatment under Bragg and Hood. Yet if certain important parties in the South no longer welcomed Johnston, he had elsewhere he could turn.

*

ONE OF the more enduring discoveries from this postwar period is how military leaders of both sides often found more comfort among their former enemies than their former comrades. Hood with Thomas and Sherman. Longstreet with Grant. Buckner with nearly everyone. Sherman with nearly everyone: he was even kind to Bragg, recommending him for a staff job with Egypt's khedive. Joe Johnston stayed friends with his "castles in the air" pen pal and Peninsula foe McClellan, and made new ones of Grant and Sherman.

Johnston had many more kind words for them than for Jefferson Davis. He answered a young inquirer that McClellan was "the best organizer in the Federal army" and Grant "the best fighter" but that Sherman "was the genius of the Federal army." Generously he then added, "But young man, never forget that Robert E. Lee was their superior in any capacity."

McClellan's death in 1885, just a few months after Grant's, was a blow. Johnston, who was a pallbearer, wrote a mutual friend: "This death has been to me like the loss of my brother. That of no other man could have been so afflicting to me.... He will appear in history as an exemplary Christian, noble gentleman, valiant soldier and wise leader." Actually, McClellan—short, extra cautious, and proud—was closer to a *twin* brother. Had Johnston, though, hung on against Sherman at Atlanta in 1864, McClellan—the Democrats' nominee against Lincoln—might have won that year's election and let the South finally go its own way.

One of Congressman Johnston's few legislative actions had as its intended recipient none other than Grant. Grant's biographer Richard Goldhurst mentions that Johnston in 1880 introduced a bill to reinstate the pensionless former president as an army lieutenant general. This may have been a Democratic device to keep the Republican Grant from seeking the White House again. In any event, Grant's friends arranged to kill the bill and then watched the Republicans select James Garfield.

As an exercise in political deviousness, Johnston's bill was entirely out of character for him. His proposal may have been sincerely intended, or else he was naively used. Johnston did have reason to be appreciative. Grant was quoted as saying during the war that when he heard of Johnston's removal from command in Georgia, "I was as happy as if I had reinforced Sherman with a large army corps." At Grant's death, Johnston would be among the honorary pallbearers named by President Grover Cleveland—at Julia Grant's request.

Johnston, though, was thickest with Sherman. The two men had hit it off during their extended surrender negotiations in North Carolina, where they met face-to-face for the first time. The negotiations had not been easy, coming in the hysteria following Lincoln's assassination. The initial surrender ran into Edwin Stanton's hostility and rejection of Sherman's lenient terms. The second attempt more closely reflected the terms to which Grant and Lee had agreed. Sherman allowed Johnston the honor of signing first and issued ten days' rations to the surrendered Confederates. He wrote to Johnston: "Now that the war is over, I am as willing to risk my person and reputation as heretofore to heal the wounds made by the past war, and I think my feeling is shared by the whole army."

A grateful Johnston replied: "The enlarged patriotism exhibited in your orders reconciles me to what I have previously regarded as the misfortune of my life, that of having you to encounter in the field. The enlightened and humane policy you have adopted will certainly be accepted." Sherman had made another conquest.

Throughout the years the two would stay in touch. Sherman, in his own *Memoirs*, would be kinder to Johnston than to Hood. They exchanged letters and visits, and Sherman sent Johnston government publications on the war. The Johnstons often dropped in on the Shermans while in Washington, to the extent that Lydia told Sherman: "Well, General, during the war I spent all my time running away from you; but now it seems that I am spending all my time running after you."

Sherman also made amends for sabotaging Johnston's war secretary job with Hayes. After the Democrat Cleveland was elected president in 1884, Sherman helped Johnston gain appointment as U.S. railroad commissioner. Four years later, though, the job was in jeopardy after Cleveland was defeated by Republican Benjamin Harrison. Seminarian Tom Sherman asked his father in a letter: "Did you succeed in keeping for Gen. Joe Johnston the office that you obtained for him? He is so little of a politician either way that he might well be left without having his head cut off." Nevertheless the politically harmless Johnston lost his job.

None of this had any effect on the old feud. In 1885 he responded to Davis's remarks in *The Rise and Fall* by writing his own account of First Manassas for *The Century* magazine, a piece that quickly expanded to include other grudges. Soon Johnston was also bickering with *Century* editors over corrections and maps. In defending his reputation, Johnston seemed unaware of placing it more at risk, something he had resolutely tried to avoid all his life.

Even Lee's memory had not brought a reconciliation. At the 1883 unveiling of the tomb statue of a recumbent Lee at the college in Lexington, Johnston excused himself from attending the ceremonies for reasons of illness, though he was president of the Lee Memorial Association. The illness more likely was Davis, who had been invited to be among the speakers. But then Davis—for similarly obvious reasons—was "prevented by circumstances" from also attending. Instead Winnie Davis sent two bay wreaths, one for Lee's tomb and one for Stonewall Jackson's, also in Lexington.

Dabney Maury would comment in a letter to a fellow general, Richard Ewell, after Johnston's death, "If Genl. Johnston had never written any thing . . . how much better it would have been!"

*

LYDIA JOHNSTON died in 1887 at the age of sixty-five. She had suffered poor health for most of her life, and after the war much of her time was spent at spas. Her ailment was diagnosed as neuralgia—something shared with Jefferson Davis—a name then randomly given to various discomforts, including headaches. Doubtless the times contributed, and Johnston was not easy to live with.

Yet they were devoted to each other, and Lydia had been the most loyal of all. During one lengthy stay at White Sulphur Springs, West Virginia, Maury would remember Johnston as nursing her "with the tender care of a mother." Even when she improved he "would never go far from their cottage door, but sat upon a fallen tree on the lawn in sight and sound of it. . . ."

Johnston was one of those Southern gentlemen who were like coiled springs. Maury saw him as "genial and confiding" to the "friends he knew and trusted," but quick to resent and challenge any slight or unwelcome liberty. Only to Lydia did Johnston yield. It was she who could laugh at him and defuse tense moments.

Maury would write of a dinner party where all present were sitting around drinking "great hail-storm juleps." A young woman outside began to shriek. The source of her disturbance was a turkey gobbler that had confronted her, and she stood frozen in place and screamed each time the turkey charged. Johnston, "deep in some narrative," kept being interrupted. Maury recalled: "Fierce as Mars, he looked down upon the screamer and said: 'Why don't you run away? Why don't you run away?' I suggested, 'Well, that's fine advice for a great general to give.' Turning savagely upon me he said, 'If she will not fight, sir, is not the best thing for her to do to run away, sir?' Mrs. Johnston, with a burst of her hearty laugh, said, 'That used to be your plan always, I know, sir.' This relieved us all, and we burst into a laugh in which he joined as heartily as any."

After Lydia's death, Johnston could not bear to write or speak her name. When he lost his railroad job in 1889, he retired to his Washington home. Jefferson Davis died in December that year, so Johnston no longer had to be careful about attending Confederate functions. One was in Atlanta in April 1890, where hundreds of old soldiers crowded around, unhitched his carriage horses, and cheerily pulled him the length of the planned parade. The next month he helped unveil yet another Lee memorial. Little was left to do but await death.

It called next for Sherman in the winter of 1891. Johnston again was an honorary pallbearer at the New York funeral. While six sergeants bore the coffin on a bitterly cold day, the eighty-four-year-old Johnston stood bareheaded in tribute. Someone said, "General, please put on your hat; you might get sick."

Johnston turned. "If I were in his place and he were standing here in mine, he would not put on his hat."

Stubborn to the end, it would be Joseph Johnston's final fatal decision. A month later, on March 21, 1891, he would be dead of pneumonia. The general's great pride and sense of honor had played him one last, mean trick.

He had become so embittered at his treatment by Davis and so reconciled with Northerners that it could be wondered whether Johnston regretted going south in 1861. Perhaps he should have listened to old Winfield Scott? But no, he could never have taken up his sword against Virginia; no, of course not. No more than Lee.

Still, in the old army he had outranked Lee. And in the old army, except for a single episode, he had avoided Jefferson Davis and his evil machinations. If Virginia could have been left out of it, and Lincoln had given him the same huge army as McClellan and Grant had enjoyed . . .

He was a better general than either. Grant had killed so many of his own, and Johnston had whipped McClellan at Seven Pines, would have destroyed him if not for his wounds! Why—why, Grant had even become president, though a very bad one. And McClellan *almost* became president. Would have, except that Lincoln was elected because Hood had yielded Atlanta to Sherman. And that was because Davis had taken away the army from Johnston and had given it to Hood. . . .

Davis. *Davis!*

No matter where he might look, Jefferson Davis was there somewhere, always assailing Joseph Johnston's castles in the air.

· 9 ·

THE LEGEND

As he rode into Richmond on a dreary Easter Saturday in 1865, Robert Edward Lee hadn't the slightest idea of the remarkable place he would rise to in the sight of a reunited nation. Richmond was in ashes and so was Lee's life. The previous Sunday he had surrendered the brave remnants of the Army of Northern Virginia to Ulysses Grant. Lee had rejected taking his men and slipping into the Appalachian mists to prolong the war. He had come home to his invalid wife and old-maid daughters. Matthew Brady, a prewar acquaintance and the first of the paparazzi, soon showed up. Lee was persuaded to pose for posterity in uniform with two of his wartime aides, including his son Custis. In the photograph the aides appear almost to be restraining the white-haired but still formidable general from lunging from his chair.

For the coming weeks Lee would live in someone else's house on East Franklin Street. Visitors sought him out, and they came from all over. Some were Yankees. One of them was a Union sergeant who had served under Lieutenant Colonel Lee in Texas before the war. He was Irish and had with him a Negro carrying a basket of food.

"I've come to see me old Colonel," he explained at the door. "He'll know me from the days with the Second Cavalry. They tell me he's without food, and I've brought some." When Lee appeared, the sergeant stiffened and saluted. "Colonel, Sir—" he said, then broke into tears. Lee thanked him but told him the food was more needed at a hospital. The sergeant threw his arms around Lee. "Goodbye,

Colonel!" he said. "God bless ye! If I could have got over in time, I would have been with ye!"

*

WHAT SORT of man was the Yankee sergeant's old colonel? Generations of writers have taken a stab at describing Lee from others' memoirs, Lee's own letters, and family accounts. He was a combination of so many qualities that to summarize him routinely as stoic and heroic is, in effect, to lessen him. He was, true enough, austere and stern, but much more so with an overpowering sense of duty, an almost appalling respect for authority, and an off-putting (even oppressive) dignity. He had the same sort of Virginia aristocrat's remoteness as did George Washington and George Marshall. He also had a savage temper which he struggled to check, moods of depression and self-pity, and yet a capacity to weep over a parson's sermon or the death of military friends.

He loved horses and children and let the latter ride his faithful Traveller. Lee also loved to kiss young ladies. Although devoted to his crippled wife, he was in fact an outrageous flirt who for years carried on a teasing correspondence with other women. He had a wry wit. When a spiritualist wrote him after the war asking his opinion on some military question, Lee begged off and suggested that any of the better-qualified but dead captains of the past be consulted instead.

He longed for his family during their lengthy separations yet rigidly ran his children's lives from both home and afar. He was deeply religious and accepted his life as one long test from God. He was magnanimous and honorable. Indeed, his moral force and character were such that his burdens and travails begat an image almost Christlike in Southern imaginations.

He was a splendid general, a fearless killer. Nonetheless he pictured himself as running a farm and remarked on separate occasions in old age, "The great mistake of my life was taking a military education," and that "I . . . find too late that I have wasted the best years of my life."

Other than Abraham Lincoln, Lee is the preeminent figure of America's bloodiest war. The irony is greatest in a country that worships success, for Lee was a failure. As in the instances of Grant and Sherman, the war would rescue him from oblivion. Unlike them, it would leave him worse off. "How can I sit for a photograph with the eyes of the world upon me as they are today," he is said to have asked Brady. Failure was in the family, in the blood.

To try to understand Lee is first to regard him as human, as Lee understood himself, not as the almost mythical hero whom Lee would never have understood. No one would have been more astounded than Lee to find himself in the company not only of Lincoln but of Washington, his own hero. Of those who made their mark in the Civil War, death hardly ended Lee's life at all. The sad actuality of existence was glorified in his absence. This would serve the purposes not merely of a few who had military reputations to protect but of an entire region searching for answers in defeat. His beloved commonwealth especially would hold tighter to his lengthened coattails.

Lee's life was perhaps the saddest of all, and even in death the burdens placed upon him would not cease. They had begun almost from birth.

His father, Henry "Light-Horse Harry" Lee, was a brilliant cavalry leader under Washington in the Revolution. He also served as Virginia's governor and as a member of the first U.S. Congress. Henry Lee was a widower when he married Robert's mother, black-eyed Ann Hill Carter, daughter of a Tidewater oligarch. He was also a charmer and a speculator who, after Robert's birth in 1807, went to jail for debt and later cleared out for the West Indies. A half-brother of Robert's, another Henry, further stained the family name when he seduced his young sister-in-law and ward, thus becoming "Black-Horse Harry" Lee.

Ann Lee's lifetime struggles included frail health. By the time Robert was twelve he was her nurse and household manager. Mother and son were extremely close, and Lee's female tastes would run ever after to dark-eyed brunettes. When Lee went away to West Point in 1825—despite her other children—Ann had mourned: "How can I live without Robert? He is both son and daughter to me." The

Ex-General Lee poses uncomfortably for Matthew Brady on April 17, 1865—
eight days after Appomattox—on the porch of Lee's temporary home in Richmond, Virginia. Lee is flanked by two aides, son Custis, left, and Walter Taylor.
(Library of Congress)

shame of the two Harrys and his mother's instruction and integrity
influenced his character. Lee was near perfect at West Point.*

*Lee narrowly finished behind classmate Charles Mason of New York who, like
Lee, graduated in 1829 without a demerit. Mason soon left the army and eventually became a federal judge. He would confide to his diary in 1864 that as he
had once excelled Lee and might have been his equal had he stayed a soldier, "I
sometimes regard his fame as a reproach to myself. . . ."

In 1831, two years after his mother's death, Lee married Mary Anne Randolph Custis. She was the only child of George Washington Parke Custis, Washington's adopted son who touted himself as "the child of Mount Vernon." She was also heiress of Arlington, the family plantation where Lee, a distant cousin, had been a playmate. While Lee could understand Mary Custis's attachment to Arlington, filled with its Washington relics, it was often impossible to pry her away during his nomadic career as a U.S. Army officer. She was a daddy's girl and spoiled, careless of her looks, somber and anti-social. Her health diminished after the birth of their second child. She also may have developed rheumatoid arthritis. By the 1860s, Lee's wife was an invalid.

It is assumed that love entered into their marriage. They had seven children. It would also seem to be as much a marriage of class and convenience. Lee had the looks and the deadly family charm. Mary Custis had the prestigious Washington connection and money. Lee was a sociable, even gregarious sort, romantic and attracted to ladies. Through the mails he carried on a teasing banter with various female correspondents, married or not. This continued even during the war. To Mrs. Roger A. Pryor, described by another as a "beautiful *brune*," he wrote: "Last night when I reached my head-quarters, I found a card on my table with a hyacinth pinned to it. The card read, 'For General Lee, with a kiss.' I have my hyacinth and my card—*and I mean to find my kiss!*"

All sources seem to agree that Lee remained physically faithful as a husband. Still, these exchanges must have been a sort of emotional release from the often bleak circumstances of his life that came with both marriage and the army. With Lee one catches the loneliness of distant outposts during long family separations, the dismay and frustration (as with Joe Johnston) over the slim chances for promotion despite feats of heroism during the Mexican War, and the relentless call of duty which peculiarly and tragically with his wife's declining health repeated the experience of Lee as his mother's nurse, her "son and daughter."

Helpless to be a companion, he also tried to be a parent despite his postings. "You must endeavor to learn," he lectured one child in a letter in 1845, "in order to compensate me for the pain I suffer in being separated." Surely he must have seen himself as his own eternally absent father. When home, though, he was no less stern, demanding progress reports and making notes to himself on child rearing. With his children, Lee—so conscious of blood—seems always on the alert for weakness to reappear.

Lee's loneliness is gradually realized in any reading of his adult years before the Civil War, a time truly of wandering in the wilderness. A certain hardness or coldness seems to grow as part of the man who could tease his female correspondents. Family scandal and his early responsibilities to his mother had strengthened him, and there was always George Washington and his struggles to shine as an example. Also, religion had begun to play an increasingly important part in his life. And yet the years as husband and father and United States soldier weighed heavily. While much would be made of Lee's attachment to Virginia and the legacy of Lees and all the intertwined families, there persists the impression that, though he has married well, he is alone and somehow on the outside looking in.

Throughout his life, recalled his youngest daughter, Mildred, Lee was "always wanting something." Whatever it was, no one could say beyond a guess. Perhaps Lee himself could not explain this mystery.

Being a Virginian, though, if even on the outside, was at least a fact fixed in the cosmos, no matter where he might be. It couldn't be helped. As Congressman John Randolph of Roanoke expressed it: "When I speak of my country, I mean the commonwealth of Virginia." Well into the twentieth century, Virginia writers would wax rhapsodically over its republican legacy and cavalier mythology. Lee would be their anchor.

But even in Lee's day Virginia had slipped a few notches. In the South the commonwealth was still no slouch. Its railroads were first-rate, and of the eleven states to form a Confederacy, Virginia produced roughly one-third of the total manufactured goods. On the other hand, the value of those goods in *all* the Confederate states combined, including Virginia, in 1860 was roughly half that of Massachusetts alone in 1855.

Once a land of visionary politicians and constitutional genius, Virginia's string of distinguished presidents ran out with the accidental John Tyler in the 1840s. In the Civil War, Virginia's presence would be on the battlefields, not in political leadership and governance.

Then there was slavery. In the 1830s the Nat Turner slave-rebellion scare and an end-to-slavery proposal by Thomas Jefferson's grandson offered a chance to make history. A freedom-through-deportation scheme was bandied about by legislators. Its flaws were many, not the least its cruelty and deception. Its virtue was that it reignited debate over eventual abolition. Great reforms have small beginnings, but unfortunately this one went no further. Opportunity was squandered for Virginia to set the example for a headstrong South and avoid a future war.

When push came to shove, the Old Dominion understandably preferred the company of Dixie sycophants, not New England scolds and Midwestern foreigners. The Confederacy would pay due homage by moving its capital from backwoods Alabama to (comparatively) bustling Richmond. The argument for Virginia by Virginians was always an emotional one, and Lee was not immune. Even when chasing Texas Comanches, he was tethered to the old country by blood.

Lee was appalled by the prelude to war. In 1860, as the national crisis heightened, he wrote home from San Antonio of his disapproval of secession ("nothing but revolution"). And yet "a Union that can only be maintained by swords and bayonets, and in which strife and civil war are to take the place of brotherly love and kindness, has no charm for me." Were the Union dissolved, Lee declared, "I shall return to my native State, and share the miseries of my people, and save in defense will draw my sword on none."

Winfield Scott, himself a Virginian, did all he could to persuade Lee to stay on with the Union. After Texas seceded in early 1861 and Lee returned to his Arlington home, he was summoned to Washington and given a quick promotion to full colonel and command of the First U.S. Cavalry. For a time anti-secession sentiment in Virginia as well as in Tennessee, North Carolina, and Arkansas kept those states neutral. But the Confederate firing on Fort Sumter on April

12, and Lincoln's call three days later for 75,000 volunteers to "suppress the combination," changed everything. In particular, Virginia and her three reluctant sisters were expected to furnish their share of the volunteers. On April 16, Virginians in convention began a secret debate on secession.

The next day Lee received two messages at Arlington. One called him to General Scott's office on the 18th. The other asked him first to drop by and see Francis Blair the elder, yet another Virginian, Republican party founder, and Lincoln intimate. Blair offered Lee command of the new army intended to suppress the combination. Lee politely declined, responding that he "could take no part in an invasion of the Southern states."

When Lee passed this on to Scott in their later meeting, Scott famously replied, "Lee, you have made the greatest mistake of your life. But, I feared it would be so." Less remembered, but as good advice for the ages, Scott also observed: "No one should remain in government employ without being actively employed."

Lee took the hint, returned to Arlington but hesitated until, on the 19th, newspapers confirmed the rumors of the convention's prosecession vote. Then Colonel Lee wrote Scott his letter of resignation from an army he had served loyally, courageously, and, most of all, dutifully for thirty years. His wife wrote a friend: "My husband has wept tears of blood over this terrible war, but as a man of honor and as a Virginian, he must follow the destiny of his State."

Lee's decision today is generally regarded as tragic and heroic. It would require a bit of time, however, for the North to see it that way.

In 1868, three years after the war's end, a debate broke out in the U.S. Senate over Lee's 1861 resignation. Senator Simon Cameron, who had been Lincoln's secretary of war at the outset, alleged that Lee had accepted Union command and gone home to Virginia to settle his business affairs before he returned—which he had not done. "He deserted under false pretenses," Cameron charged. In postwar life Lee normally avoided confrontations. In this case he shot back a letter explaining the circumstances and denying Cameron's slander. Nevertheless a good many Northerners through Reconstruction and beyond regarded Lee, Johnston, and other West Pointers who went South as untried traitors.

Lee would prove more upsetting than any of the rest. On the other hand, had the war lasted no more than a year, the North might not have noticed. On the eve of the Seven Days battles in June 1862, George McClellan would give his estimate of the man who now stepped in for the wounded Joseph Johnston, and who General McClellan eagerly awaited. "I prefer Lee to Johnston," McClellan wrote. "The former is too cautious and weak under grave responsibility. Personally brave and energetic to a fault, he yet is wanting in moral firmness when pressed by heavy responsibility, and is likely to be timid and irresolute in action."

The morally shaky and irresolute Lee would give the Yankees fits for the next three years.

*

NOW LEE had finally failed, and so had the Confederacy. Nor was Richmond to be his home. He wrote to one of his former military staff: "I am looking for some quiet little house in the woods where I can procure shelter, and my daily bread . . . and get Mrs. Lee out of the city as soon as possible." Not only were visitors and curiosity seekers a nuisance but the scenes of defeat were all about: aimless crowds of freed Negroes, swarms of carpetbaggers and missionaries, battalions of hapless Confederates and away-from-home Federals— hundreds, thousands amid the backdrop of charred ruins. Civilization was done; where was home?

Union soldiers had crossed the Potomac and taken over Arlington in 1861. By the next year they were burying their war dead on the grounds. Mary Custis Lee lost the house to taxes in 1863 and remained embittered forever after. Once, asked what she would do with the Northern graves if Arlington were regained, she was said to have replied: "My dear, I would smooth them off and plant my flowers."

During the summer of 1865 the Lees accepted the hospitality of a cottage on the grounds of an estate west of Richmond. The general was able to ride Traveller in the quiet countryside. He also began to consider writing a wartime history that would tell the world "what my poor boys . . . succeeded in accomplishing"; several publishers had approached him. First, though, Lee had to support a family—three daughters and a wife in a wheelchair. In the end he could never find or make time for a book. After his death a scribes' army would spring up to perform the task many times over, eagerly and profitably.

In this same summer, Lee's daughter Mary had mentioned casually to someone, "The Southern people are willing and ready to give Father everything he needs—except the chance of earning a living for himself and his family." This comment apparently reached the trustees of Washington College in Lexington, Virginia, who were looking for a president. Lee was happily acclaimed. Unfortunately the school was nearly bankrupt, and the member chosen to approach Lee had to borrow a suit and money for the trip. Lee was offered $1,500 annually and a house.

Lee gave the offer much thought. The college was not unknown to anyone with a George Washington connection, but it was a challenge. At this time it had only four teachers and forty students. During the previous summer of war it had been sacked by Yankee soldiers who also had burned its neighboring college, the Virginia Military Institute. Lexington, across the Blue Ridge, might just as well have been on the other side of the world from the Tidewater.

Two other concerns, however, were more troublesome to Lee, which he mentioned in a letter responding to the board. One was the workload, where he felt he could not regularly teach classes while trying to administer the college. If anything, Lee was no academic, and he knew it. And he was probably feeling his age (a very tired fifty-eight).

The second was Lee's standing with the federal government after leading a Confederate army. He had been required to apply directly to Andrew Johnson for a pardon, had done so, but had heard nothing. Thus he was a noncitizen. This limbo was further aggravated by the views of other Southerners who thought such applications were dishonorable admissions of wrongdoing. Lee pointed out that his placement "might draw upon the college a feeling of hostility." Eloquently, the most prominent Rebel made himself known as the most reconciled: "I think it is the duty of every citizen, in the present condition of the country, to do all in his power to aid in the restoration of peace and harmony, and in no way to oppose the policy of the State or general government directed to that object. It is particularly incumbent on those charged with the instruction of the young to set them an example of submission to authority. . . ."

If the board had no qualms with these reflections, Lee concluded, he would accept its offer. The surprised trustees, of course, were overjoyed.

Lee arrived in September 1865. The mountain town as much as the college was happy to see him, and the Rebel yells that greeted him—with all their subversive suggestion to the North—soon prompted him to slip out of town to a nearby spa. Lee wanted for himself a low profile. The plight not only of the college but of the South, as well as his own character, recommended a dignified reticence. When school began in October, the student body leaped to fifty. "It is supposed that many more will be coming during the month," Lee wrote. "The scarcity of money everywhere embarrasses all proceedings."

More students would come. By 1868 more than four hundred were registered. Letters came addressed to "General Lee's College." Whereas before the war it had been virtually a Virginian-only school, two-thirds of the student body were now drawn from outside the commonwealth. Money too began to arrive from elsewhere. The inventor Cyrus McCormick, a local native, endowed a chair in experimental philosophy and practical mechanics.

The college remains today as in Lee's time a pretty assemblage of Greek Revival buildings. Before the Civil War its four professors taught six subjects: mental and moral philosophy, political economy, Latin, Greek, mathematics, and physical sciences. Although nondenominational, it had not lost touch with its Presbyterian roots, and both morning and evening chapel were required of the students. Educated as a military engineer, Lee became enthusiastic about school plans to add new departments emphasizing chemistry, metallurgy, astronomy, and engineering as well as modern language, history, and literature. A connection was established with a local law school. A journalism school took rough but premature shape.

"We must look to the rising generation for the restoration of the country," Lee said in 1868, reflecting in spirit the views of his first letter to the college's trustees.

As gentlemen now had to labor, he encouraged agricultural and technical training. "The great object of the whole plan," Lee wrote, "is to provide the facilities required by the large class of our young men, who looking forward to an early entrance into the practical pursuits of life, need a more direct training to this end than the usual literary courses."

Lee's female family had joined him in December 1865. They were something of an odd lot, though perhaps not for Victorian or male-depleted postwar times. Of Lee's four daughters, Annie had died during the war. The others—Mary, Agnes, and Mildred—would remain unwed. One of Lee's three sons, Rob, would recall his father as constantly urging him and his brothers "to take to themselves wives. With his daughters he was less pressing. Though apparently willing to have another daughter, he did not seem to long for any more sons."

A biographer, Marshall Fishwick, has suggested that pride as a Lee also might have been involved in the daughters' inaction, in that their father had instructed: "Never marry unless you can do so into a family which will enable your children to feel proud of both sides of the house." Reasonable advice, to be sure, yet who could measure up to the Lees? Consequence of place was to find its equivalent elsewhere. After all, if the fondest fancy of the unreconstructed South was to have Jefferson Davis's unwed daughter betrothed to a son or grandson of the great General Lee, what could be done with the general's daughters if all the Davis sons were dead?

Not a lot, apparently. A young instructor at the college remarked of the Lee girls that they "don't seem to like Lexington much—think the people stiff and formal, which is very much the case. The seeming haughtiness of Agnes . . . offends the Lexingtonians."

At the same time Lee was no easy person to live with or be around. He had seen too much, had been weighed down too much. He could be quite sour, as when he wrote of Mildred: "She rules her brother and my nephews with an iron rod, and scatters her advice broadcast among the young men of the College. . . . The young mothers of Lexington ought to be extremely grateful to her for her suggestions to them as to the proper mode of rearing their children."

How much of this was mere show? Lee's heart could also be pierced. During the war when news of Annie's death arrived in the mail, an aide would recall Lee silently reading through his letters and then calmly dispatching his orders. When the aide suddenly returned to Lee's tent, he was "startled and shocked" to see Lee overcome by grief. "His army demanded his first thought and care . . .," the aide wrote. "Only then could he surrender to his private, personal affliction."

While Lee was always thoughtful of his wife, Mary Custis Lee scarcely lightened any lives. Perhaps worse than the crippling pain of her illness was the loss of Arlington and the anger and self-pity it induced. Now, as further punishment, came confinement in isolated Lexington. "Life is waning away," she wrote in 1868, "and with the exception of my own immediate family, I am entirely cut off from all that I have ever known and loved in my youth. My dear old Arlington—I cannot bear to think of that used by the enemy and so little hope of my ever getting there again."

The college built an expensive new residence, "the president's house," complete with a spacious veranda and first-floor bedroom to accommodate Mrs. Lee's wheelchair. Despite this, nothing could ever replace her spiritual home. She sadly visited Arlington in 1873 and died several months later. In 1882 the U.S. Supreme Court returned the property to son Custis, who then sold it to the government.

For more than twenty-five years Lee carried on a correspondence with Martha Custis Williams, known as Markie. She was another dark-eyed beauty some twenty years younger, and his wife's cousin. In 1851, after not writing her for several months, Lee would explain in a letter: "But oh, what lengthy epistles have I indited to you in my mind! Had I any means to send them, you would see how constantly

I think of you. I have followed you in your pleasures and your duties, in the house and in the streets, and accompanied you in your walks to Arlington, and in your search after flowers. Did you not feel your cheeks *pale* when I was so near you?. . ."

In his last years he wrote Markie that "there is nothing . . . that I want, except to see you, and nothing you can do for me, except to think of and love me." In such letters is the mystery of Lee, the romantic who could send thousands to their death, the seeking man who, in a household of women, must reach out through letters to that thing not yet found—the Lee so described by daughter Mildred as "always wanting something."

*

LEE WOULD KEEP a low profile when looking north, counseling conciliation and offering encouragement when informed of how "my poor boys" were struggling to make a peacetime life. He worried and warned. "I fear the South," he wrote one old comrade, "has yet to suffer many evils, and it will require time, patience, and fortitude, to heal her affliction." To a local minister reporting on a speech, he cautioned: "I would suggest that you leave out all the bitter expressions against the North and the United States government. They will do us no good under our present circumstances, and I think such expressions undignified and unbecoming." He held a long and private discussion with a British visitor about the war. But when the visitor sent Lee a written account, wishing to publish it and asking permission, the careful Lee withheld consent.

Being careful of public attention was one thing; being protective of his military reputation was quite another. Thomas "Stonewall" Jackson, his great lieutenant and "right arm" who had been killed during the war, was buried in Lexington where he had once been an instructor at VMI. The death of Jackson was a saber slash across the Confederacy's breast. Newspapers called him "the idol of the people" and anxiously asked, "Who will rise to fill his place?" Mary Chesnut would moan to her diary, when hearing of Johnston's retreats in Georgia, "Oh! for an hour of Stonewall!" A rush of admiring biographies had followed his death, and for a time his fame equaled and possibly eclipsed that of Lee.

There is no evidence of jealousy on Lee's part, but he didn't hesitate to set the record straight when he thought Jackson's admirers went too far. Some of Lee's corrections were made when Jackson's widow brought him a biographical manuscript written by Stonewall's chief of staff. One especially galling error to Lee was the credit given to Jackson for devising the daring flank attack at Chancellorsville, perhaps Lee's most perfectly planned victory.

The Jackson issue would continue to pester, but there is no reason to believe any sort of rift ever existed between the South's two most famous generals. Any hint of one—during or after the war— would have bordered on sacrilege, as a number of Southerners worshiped a popular lithograph by A. J. Volck entitled, "Lee Kneeling at the Grave of Jackson." Still, Lee said little and wrote nothing about Stonewall. Moreover while Jackson's grave was just a short walk, no record mentions a Lee visit, nocturnal or otherwise. That fact, of course, could be just another of Lee's cautionary attempts to keep a lid on Rebel yells.

For Lee was hardly forgotten by the North. In Congress the Radical Republicans were beginning to run roughshod over the Southern-born and thus suspect Andrew Johnson. In early 1866, Lee was summoned to testify before the congressional Joint Committee on Reconstruction. The committee was chaired by Thaddeus Stevens, one of Johnson's implacable foes.

Committee witnesses already had recited a litany of Southern atrocities, including the murder of blacks. For two hours Lee maneuvered as congressmen probed for Southern attitudes toward the government, taxes to repay the federal war debt, the treatment of Union prisoners of war, and the enfranchising of the former slaves. Lee refused to be trapped by speculations. In a typical exchange, Michigan senator Jacob Howard—with Maximilian and the French in Mexico on his mind—had asked Lee:

"In the event of a war between the United States and any foreign power, if the recently rebel states were given a fair prospect of gaining their independence and shaking off the government of the

United States, is it, or is it not, your opinion that they would avail themselves of the opportunity?"

Lee replied: "I have nothing whatever to base an opinion upon. So far as I know, they contemplate nothing of the kind now. What may happen in the future I cannot say."

"Do you not frequently hear in your intercourse with secessionists expressions of a hope that such a war may break out?"

"I cannot say that I have. On the contrary, I have heard persons express a hope that the country may *not* be led into a war."

"If war came, would the people whom I call secessionists join the common enemy?"

"It is possible. It depends upon the feelings of the individual."

"What, in such an event, might be your own choice?"

"I have no disposition now to do it, and I never have had."

"And can you foresee that such would be your inclination in such an event?"

"No. I can only judge by the past. I cannot pretend to foresee events."

Lee's forbearance notwithstanding, the full weight of Reconstruction was yet to be realized by the former Confederacy. Within a few weeks Congress passed over Johnson's veto a civil rights bill extending equal protection of the laws to the ex-slaves, and in June sent the Fourteenth Amendment to the states to ratify. The Ku Klux Klan would spread in reaction.

Some chroniclers of Nathan Bedford Forrest have raised the possibility that Lee may have been offered the Klan's Grand Wizardry before Forrest. This is based on Klan claims that a committee of Klansmen traveled to Virginia to wait on Lee. Purportedly the general declined the offer, citing health reasons. Lee allegedly wrote a letter of support instead, but stressed that his approval must be "invisible." At the mention of Forrest for the job, Lee is said to have replied: "There is no man in the South who can handle so large a body of men so successfully. Will you pay my respects to the General and tell him I hope he will accept."

Other than this bit of lore, there is no evidence or "smoking gun" of either a Klan offer to Lee or—a later claim—that Lee's reply inspired the Klan to call itself the "Invisible Empire." It's arguable that the ultra-cautious Lee would have put anything in writing, or that his private opinions—even if in agreement—would be so entrusted. Regardless, Lee's blessing, true or not, became part of the Klan's history. Doubtless it helped recruiting.

Actually the commonwealth would prove touchy about the Klan, which seemed to lack the presence it demonstrated in the Cotton South and Tennessee. A modern writer has quoted a Virginia girl of the times as feeling "defrauded of my rights" because she never saw a Klansman. Some credit is given to Lee's postwar "reconciliatory position." A more recent biographer, however, has noted that judging from racial tensions in Lexington after the war, it appears that some of Lee's own students had formed a Klan chapter at Washington College!

*

DESPITE THE AFFECTION Southerners had for Lee and the respect with which they usually treated his views of reconciliation, something always smoldered beneath the surface: Gettysburg.

More than Appomattox or any other encounter where Lee was defeated or checkmated, Gettysburg was the great what-if, the high-water mark of Confederate hopes, the point where God at last declared himself. Years afterward the South was still in shock, frozen in that Faulknerian moment where time stood still just before Pickett's Charge. No matter that Lee had plenty of help in losing—not the least, the valor of the Union Army—the result remained incomprehensible. Of Lee, Southerners did not dare ask but only wondered.

Except for one public occasion. When Lee traveled to Washington to testify, crowds had pressed to see the famous Rebel at his hotel. An ex-Confederate soldier was so persistent in wanting to shake Lee's hand that he was finally allowed to approach. He then shocked Lee's entourage with the unspeakable.

"General," he said, "I have always thought that if I ever had the honor of meeting you face to face, and there was an opportunity allowed me, I would like to ask you a question which nobody but you can answer. I seem to have that opportunity now. This is what I want to know: What was the reason that you failed to gain the victory at the battle of Gettysburg?"

Lee's handlers fumed, but the old general stepped forward and spoke quietly, nimbly.

"My dear sir," he replied, "that would be a long story, and would require more time than you see I can possibly command at present; so we will have to defer the matter to another occasion."

The subject indirectly intruded again in Lee's last year during a stop in Richmond while on his way to Georgia. John Singleton Mosby, the famed Confederate ranger, had encountered the general in a hotel and returned to Lee's room for a long chat about nonwar things. Leaving the hotel, Mosby ran into George Pickett—he of the disastrous charge.

Pickett agreed to call on Lee, but only if Mosby went with him. There was bad blood between Pickett and Lee, and not only for Gettysburg. Shortly before Appomattox, Pickett had been ordered relieved of command after another calamity at Five Forks, but failed to get the word. Seeing him riding along, Lee had remarked with surprise, "I thought that man was no longer with the army." Mosby would recall that the hotel room meeting between Pickett and Lee was short and frosty. Once outside, Pickett railed to Mosby against "that old man who had my division massacred at Gettysburg." Remarkably, Pickett would be among Lee's honorary pallbearers.

Lee's "long story" would never be written by himself, but the many versions by others that would follow his death would sow enough division and strife as to regard Lee's silence as yet another failure.

*

LEE WOULD WRITE to Markie Williams as early as April 1866, "I am easily wearied now, and look forward with joy to the time, which is fast approaching, that I can lay down and rest."

A life's inner discipline kept him going—the relentless call to duty first made by his mother, then by generals and Jeff Davis, then by God. He demanded the same discipline of his students, many of whom were war veterans. Lee's rules of behavior were known on campus as "general orders." He once banished a student from his office for chewing tobacco when appearing before him. After the student returned, still chewing, Lee quietly wrote out a note of expulsion "for disrespect to the President" and handed it to him. He added calmly that the note would be posted on a bulletin board in ten minutes.

Lee knew each of his students by name and would write their parents an annual letter about their conduct. Once he lectured a student on bad grades, wondering aloud how sad the young man's parents would be when the report was made known. It was a quandary for Lee, too, who knew the parents. "I don't know what to do," Lee said, then tore up the report. Another student recalled: "I wished he had whipped me but he talked to me about my mother and the sacrifices she is making to send me to college . . . the first thing I knew I was blubbering like a baby."

When Lee counseled a lagging sophomore that if he did not improve "you will fail your work," the student retorted: "But General, *you* were a failure."

"Yes," said Lee, restraining himself. "But let us hope you will be more fortunate than I."

Restraint was not always possible, and Lee's explosive temper kept staff, students, and faculty on their guard. Many, though, regarded him as kind. He invited new students to his home where Mildred served "cold tea"—cobbler laced with enough sherry to send visitors reeling. Alumni would proudly refer to themselves long afterward as "General Lee's boys"—some of them having been "my poor boys" from the Army of Northern Virginia.

The memories were poignant too. John B. Collyar, a former student, recalled: "I never saw a sadder expression than General Lee carried during the entire time I was at Washington College. It looked as if the sorrow of a whole nation had collected in his countenance, and as if he was bearing the grief of his whole people."

One of Lee's earlier acts was his insistence on building a new college chapel. He followed the construction closely and located his office in its basement. It was where he would go after morning services to take on the day's paperwork and problems. He was delighted when students converted. After a revival in 1869 where more than one hundred young men made professions of faith, Lee called it "the best news I have heard since I have been in Lexington."

He practiced as a Low Church Episcopalian, and all accounts note his religiosity. But he wasn't confirmed until 1853, when he was forty-six. He was greatly influenced by the charity and cheer of his devout mother-in-law, Mary Fitzhugh Custis, and deeply grieved by her death. It was only a few months afterward that Lee finally took the step of confirmation.

The Civil War put Lee's faith to its gravest test, yet he never seemed to waver. During the post-Gettysburg winter of 1863, he had mused: "We do not know what is best for us. I believe a kind God has ordered all things for our good." Revivals, prayers, and conversions were particularly thick among Confederate ranks after Gettysburg, and Lee urged both troops and populace to hew to righteousness.

Yet no amount of prayer could stave off defeat. Lee took it personally. During the siege of Petersburg he lamented, "How thankless and sinful I have been." It was as if he were again back at Gettysburg, trying to reassure his columns, "Don't be discouraged. It was all my fault this time. . . ." One could do nothing but trust God. Unworthiness and sin had brought his wrath at last upon the South, and yet it might still be for a worthy purpose later on. "God's will be done," Lee often said. And: "I know affliction has been sent me by a merciful God for my good."

He had failed in his duty to the United States when General Scott had called him. He had failed in his duty to Virginia and the Confederacy. Perhaps, Lee may have come to think, these failures were in fact a way of performing a greater duty to God as his instrument for some unknowable purpose. It was therefore Lee's duty to accept the outcome.

The old soldier had lived past his time. His world was like Arlington. As he had watched the Union dissolve, he had commented: "It has been evident for years that the country was doomed to run the full length of democracy."

Lee had suffered an "inflammation of the heart-sac" during the war, and aches and pains immediately following. After 1867 he became more susceptible to colds. Friends could not help but notice his rapid decline. He told them he was having trouble "about the heart" and experiencing frequent pains while walking. Doctors apparently thought that his 1870 trip to the Georgia coast would do him good, though Lee was dubious. "Doctors do not know everything," he wrote daughter Mildred, "and yet I have often had to do what I was told, without any benefit to myself, and I shall have to do it again."

What the doctors had blamed on rheumatism was angina pectoris and, likely, hardening of the arteries. Stopping in Richmond on his return from Georgia, Lee was measured for a bust by the sculptor E. V. Valentine, who told Lee he would have to do the modeling in Lexington.

"You had best make the visit at once," Lee replied.

On an autumn afternoon in 1870, Lee had walked in the rain to a meeting at his Episcopal church and returned home sick. When he bowed to say his blessing at tea, words wouldn't come. Confined to bed, he spoke with effort or with weary gestures. Toward the end, after two weeks, his pain intensified. On October 12 the great general died. He was buried in a vault below the college chapel. A statue sculpted by Valentine of the "recumbent Lee," depicting the general asleep on a camp bed and with the torso modeled by Lee's son Rob, lies some feet above the family crypt. Traveller's grave is just outside the chapel.

The papers necessary for Lee's federal absolution were found a century later in a box in the National Archives. In 1975, General Lee finally regained full American citizenship.

*

THE ASCENDANCY of Lee to a figure larger than life, from Southern hero to the national pantheon with Lincoln and Washington, began immediately at his death. The college added his name to what is today's Washington and Lee University, and friends quickly organized as the Lee Memorial Association to create a campus monument. Shortly, a rival Lee Monument Association began plans for the principal memorial to be erected in Richmond. Both memorial factions would compete for money and even for Lee's body. By these gestures the seeds were planted to immortalize and indeed perfect the admirable but very human Lee.

In the 1970s the historian Thomas Lawrence Connelly produced his remarkable study *The Marble Man: Robert E. Lee and His Image in American Society*. Connelly retraced and detailed these efforts that not only achieved their aims regarding Lee; they also gathered what Southern glories could be found in the war and lavished them on the beloved Commonwealth of Virginia.

It is not the purpose here to reproduce Connelly's account of the antics of what he called the Lee cult, but some summarizing is necessary to help explain Lee's subsequent elevation to legend.

Other than his widow and children, Lee's most diligent champion after his death was another Virginian, Jubal Early. General Early already has been encountered as one of the front men for the notorious Louisiana Lottery as well as a guardian of Winnie Davis's Confederate chastity. During the war the truculent Early served under Lee at Gettysburg and elsewhere. Early also had been relieved by Lee in the war's last months—in a letter that was a supreme model of tact—for failures in the Shenandoah Valley, but this didn't tarnish his loyalty to his chief.

Connelly points out that it was Early and other Lee comrades who used organizations of Confederate veterans to support the Richmond monument, and who guided the Southern Historical Society after its takeover by Virginians in the 1870s. In writings through the Society's *Papers* and elsewhere, Early and his friends exerted themselves in both controlling the telling of Lee's story and elaborating upon Virginia's role in the war. In its first year, in 1876, the regionally circulated *Papers* published twenty-nine articles on Lee and the Virginia army. It published five on military events elsewhere. The following year, the ratio was forty-four articles to five.

Of much concern, especially to Early, was Gettysburg. It was understandable: the defeat was the dragging anchor on Lee's reputation. Lee had taken the blame as army commander, but his subordinates had also let him down. Jeb Stuart had disappeared. Pete Longstreet had sulked and dawdled. George Pickett had not personally led his division's doomed charge. Corps commander Ambrose Powell Hill may have been distracted by depression or even by a long-simmering venereal disease. Richard Ewell did not press a vital assault on the panicked federal troops in the battle's first day.

Then there was Early, whose work at Gettysburg also was less than spectacular. Under Ewell he had the chance to seize the key high ground of Culp's Hill and Cemetery Hill but fatally hesitated. Then, by dominating his superior Ewell, Early had argued to Lee against renewing his attack, leaving Lee to shift the battle's focus disastrously elsewhere. Some of the first postwar accounts, in fact, had blamed Early and Ewell (and Lee) after these mistakes.

The upshot, writes Connelly, was that Early—from his position of prominence in the Lee resurgence—and his allies looked to deflect blame not only from Lee but from Early. Their scapegoat was Longstreet.

A case could be made against the poky Longstreet but hardly to the extent of having him shoulder the calumny now piled upon him. Longstreet was an easy mark, having become a hated Republican. Moreover, as the villain of Gettysburg he was suddenly responsible for the Cause being Lost—not Lee, not Jeff Davis, not the Confederate Congress which Lee had scathingly criticized as being unable "to do anything except eat peanuts and chew tobacco while my army is starving." Not any of the Yankees. Just poor, non-Virginian Longstreet, who was damned in the *Southern Historical Society Papers* and at various assemblies of old Confederates.

Longstreet never could make a convincing rejoinder to these attacks. He lived with pain from war wounds and died in 1903, stone deaf and nearly blind, of cancer. The United Daughters of the Confederacy in Savannah voted to send no flowers to his funeral.

Lee cultists, Connelly writes, also scolded Stonewall Jackson's biographers, mostly over the sensitive credit for Chancellorsville. Early also challenged a writer who alleged that Lee had ignored Jackson's plea at Fredericksburg to drive the Yankees back into the

Rappahannock River. Fitzhugh Lee, the general's nephew, went on a two-year speaking tour of the South, raising cash for the historical society and further developing Jackson's dependency upon Lee— though it was evident that Lee's fortunes declined after Jackson's death. Also attacked was Joe Johnston for his published aspersions on Lee's handling of McClellan during the Seven Days battles.

An unexpected consequence of Early's labors occurred when secondary blame for Gettysburg was parceled out to the deceased Jeb Stuart. His cavalry ride away from the Confederate advance had cost Lee valuable time and information on the Yankees' whereabouts. In reaction, friends of Stuart were prepared to point out that Early himself had failed to make the expected contact with the cavalry. All they required was proof.

The proof happened to be in Stuart's official battle report. Curiously, that part—where Stuart blamed Early—had been left out when a copy of the report was published in 1876 by the Southern Historical Society. When the omission was discovered (to Early's chagrin), a bargain was struck that would leave Stuart alone. Lee admirers would keep their guns trained on Longstreet.

Regardless that Jackson, Johnston, and Stuart were fellow Virginians, even they (alive or dead) could not stand in the way of Lee's canonization. In Mississippi, Jefferson Davis thought too much of the glory was being given to Lee at the expense of Jackson and Davis's old friend Albert Sidney Johnston. In a letter to a newspaper, Davis groused that Lee "needs no pedestal constructed of the wrecks of his associates' reputations."

These efforts at elevation were abetted by a school of Virginia novelists who extolled the cavalier society from which sprang the well-bred Lee. Among the most prominent of them was John Esten Cooke, who would harken to colonial times, look with romantic fondness on the war in Virginia, and paint plantation life as a world of contented slaves (Nat Turner to the contrary).

Thomas Nelson Page would also charm readers with images of the Old Dominion. His books and stories, which first appeared in magazines in the 1880s, offered comfort to North and South alike. Light-years from Southern Gothic, Page found gratitude from contemporaries such as the New Orleans writer Grace King. "It is hard to explain in simple terms what Thomas Nelson Page meant to us in the South at that time," King would recall. "He was the first Southern writer to appear in print as a Southerner, and his stories, short and simple, written in Negro dialect, and, I may say, Southern pronunciation, showed us with ineffable grace that although we were sore bereft, politically, we had now a chance in literature at least."

The Virginia story was hardly the domain of male writers, however. Women too were cranking out stories (it was the heyday of magazines) and books about the old times. One of the most prominent was Sara Pryor, who had left General Lee his hyacinth and invisible kiss.

To speak of glorious prewar days was not just to recollect those before the Civil War but the Revolution too—indeed, before the French and Indian War and even the War of Jenkins' Ear. Virginia, despite slavery, had been the cradle of civilized behavior, and Virginians didn't really like slavery anyway, and hadn't been keen on secession either. . . .

There is, of course, a little bit of truth in most everything, but there did seem to be occasions when matters got out of hand. Virginia adulation wasn't just to remind crass and materialistic Northerners of their place toward the rear but occasionally fellow Southerners too—even those many who served under Lee. A popular children's magazine, *St. Nicholas*, would inform its young readers about Pickett's Charge that "those on the left faltered and fled. The right behaved gloriously. Each body acted according to its nature, for they were made of different stuff. The one of common earth, the other of finest clay. [Brigadier General J. Johnston] Pettigrew's men [on the left] were North Carolinians. Pickett's were superb Virginians."

In Lee's case, he was probably more help to Virginia's image than Virginia to his. It was, after all, Lee who was proof of the Virginian heritage and thus validated all the kindnesses now heaped upon it. Still, the two would march into the future hand-in-hand, stride-for-stride. Page's biography of Lee, revised and republished in 1912, for instance, would be praised in a *Nation* review for both the detail given to "the greatness of Lee's character" and its linkage to Virginia's environment.

Connelly observes that by the turn of the century Lee was touted as a man who "loved the Union more, hated slavery, disliked secession and seceded out of a sense of honor." Page, in a 1907 magazine article, would praise Lee (as if he had resurrected) as "the leader of the New South." Just as Virginia would seek shelter in Lee's reputation, the South would tag along for a place beneath the ever-extending canopy. For Americans elsewhere who might by now feel a little guilt about the war, Lee would be a beacon.

Thus it was almost inevitable for Lee to be taken up by one of the great embodiments of Yankeedom, a member of the Adams family. Charles Francis Adams, Jr., was Henry's brother. Henry had yet to publish his belittling memories of Lee's son, Rooney. Charles, though, contributed essays and speeches before prominent groups that championed Lee *pere*. His address at Washington and Lee in 1907 (Lee's centennial) was hailed by Northern newspapers.

Lee would be among the first twenty-nine men chosen for the Hall of Fame at New York University. He would be praised by Woodrow Wilson and Theodore Roosevelt for having helped bring the Union back together. Winston Churchill would praise him by playfully speculating on a Lee victory at Gettysburg. The humorist James Thurber would speculate on the consequences had Grant been drunk at Appomattox. Cheers would continue for Lee as national hero and haven't slackened much despite the usual grumps. A great misfortune is not knowing what the modest Lee would have said of all this to his female correspondents.

*

THERE REMAINS a mortal man "always wanting something," who regretted a military education and probably thought of his service as yet another onerous duty laid upon him, for reasons to be explained in the hereafter. While others pulled a curtain over the brutalities of the Civil War, or gloried in them, General Lee did neither. The living and the dead of the Army of Northern Virginia were "my poor boys." They had been his ultimate duty, and he had failed. The love of the South went out to him in his lifetime too, but at Washington College he had "looked as if the sorrow of a whole nation had collected in his countenance, and as if he was bearing the grief of his whole people." And so he was. How many other generals, victorious or not, have been known to lament "my poor boys"?

· 10 ·

THE TURNCOAT

General Sherman had taken his best men, the ones he had trained himself, and left him with "all dismounted cavalry, all sick and wounded, and all encumbrances whatever." Some of the soldiers he was given were at the end of their enlistments. Others were to be allowed to go home to Illinois to vote for President Lincoln in the upcoming election. He was promised veteran reinforcements, but at the moment they were somewhere between Nashville and the Missouri-Kansas border. Then there was Franklin. Despite the slaughter, John Bell Hood had followed John M. Schofield's Union troops the eighteen miles to the outskirts of the Tennessee capital. That was another thing Sherman had neglected to do: take care of Hood before heading off through Georgia to the sea. The job was left to someone else.

George Henry Thomas did his duty, as he always did. For the time being he stayed behind Nashville's hilltop barricades. He strengthened them by putting seven thousand quartermaster employees to work. He ordered the provost marshal to "cause all loafing and unemployed Negroes or white men found on the streets" to be impressed into the labor force. Curious Nashvillians who wandered too close to watch were handed picks and shovels. Thomas's lines of defense paid little heed to the many trees, barns, stables, fences, or gardens.

"From the river to Springside there is not a grove left," lamented a loyalist citizen. Soldiers camped on lawns. Photographs show the denuded countryside.

The reinforcements under General Andrew Jackson Smith finally arrived from the West. The usually dispassionate Thomas gave Smith a big hug. Gunboats prowled the Cumberland River. A hospital boat waited ominously at the docks. But Thomas wasn't about to stay behind his walls forever. His plan was not just to win a battle but to destroy Hood's army.

First, though, he needed cavalry—dismounted infantry with repeater carbines to counter Bedford Forrest and turn Hood's flank and give pursuit. General James Harrison Wilson had returned from Franklin with 6,500 bruised troopers, complaining that Forrest had four times his number. The countryside north of Nashville was scoured for horses. Outraged officials in Louisville, two hundred miles distant, would complain to Secretary of War Edwin Stanton of milk carts and butchers' wagons being left in the streets shorn of their seized animals. Thomas would not budge until Wilson's cavalry was ready.

When Thomas told Washington of his intentions, however, Lincoln grew concerned. George McClellan at last had been vanquished—212 electoral votes to 21—and could be politically put to rest. Military memories of McClellan's foot-dragging died much harder.

Stanton wired Ulysses Grant at City Point, Virginia, with the dreaded words that it all looked like "the McClellan & Rosecranz [General William Rosecrans] strategy of do nothing. . . ." Lincoln, Stanton added darkly, "wishes you to consider the matter."

On December 2, 1864—two days after Franklin—Grant, the general-in-chief, hastily sent the first of a stream of messages urging Thomas to act. He was worried that Hood might go around the city and make for the Ohio River. Four days later Grant was writing Sherman: "I have said all I could to force him to attack without giving the positive order until to-day. To-day however I can stand it no longer and gave the order without any reserve. I think the battle will take place tomorrow." It didn't.

Grant fumed. To General Henry Halleck, the chief of staff in Washington, he floated the possibility of replacing Thomas with Schofield. Halleck, though, replied that the responsibility "will be yours, as no one here, so far as I am concerned, wishes General Thomas removed."

On December 9, Grant drafted an order for Schofield to take over: *"The President orders: I. That Maj. Gen. J. M. Schofield assume command of all troops in the Departments of the Cumberland, the Ohio, and the Tennessee. II. That Maj. Gen. George H. Thomas report to General Schofield for duty and turn over to him all orders and dispatches received by him. . . . By order of the Secretary of War."*

Halleck, however, hung on to the order, though he notified Thomas of Grant's state of mind. Meanwhile an ice storm had struck Nashville, making it impossible to maneuver. This was explained. Grant backed down but mentioned the suspension of the relief order to Thomas and, without naming names, told him: "I hope most sincerely that there will be no necessity of repeating the order. . . ."

Thomas surveyed his corps commanders. Wilson spoke first, in support of Thomas and delay until conditions allowed. The others—except for a silent Schofield—agreed. Thomas quietly thanked them. He soon learned that Schofield had been messaging Grant behind his back, complaining of Thomas's slowness.

The ice storm continued. On December 11, Grant wired Thomas, again worried of Hood—equally frozen in place—marching toward Ohio. "Delay no longer for weather or reinforcements," said Grant. Thomas replied that he would obey the order as promptly as possible, but he wired Halleck the next day that "I believe an attack at this time would only result in a useless sacrifice of life." Grant in the interim had changed his mind about replacing Thomas with Schofield. But then, on December 13, he ordered another general, John A. Logan, to Nashville. Logan was to relieve Thomas if he had not attacked Hood upon Logan's arrival.

Then Grant changed his mind again. He decided to leave for Nashville himself and personally take charge. He arrived in Washington on December 15 and ordered a telegram relieving Thomas. The storm had cut off a direct line to Nashville, but a War Department telegrapher had found a way to reroute. Still, the telegrapher decided to hold the order until he received his nightly report from

Nashville. When he did, the decoded message told of Thomas's attack earlier in the day.

On the 16th, Thomas completed the job and routed Hood. Wilson's rebuilt cavalry, with their rapid-fire weapons, turned the Confederate left flank and began the pursuit of the Rebels through rain, ice, and snow. Nashville would be called the most decisive battle of the Civil War. It would be taught to future U.S. Army officers as an example "as free from faults" as no other during the war. It would be hailed as the victory that won the West for the Union—not Sherman's march through Georgia. Thomas would later say of Grant: "I thought, after what I had done in the war, that I ought to be trusted to decide when the battle should be fought. I thought I knew better when it should be fought than any one could know as far off as City Point."

*

GEORGE THOMAS was a Virginian and U.S. Army officer who, unlike Robert E. Lee and Joseph Johnston, decided to stick with the Union when civil war came. He was a lot like Lee in his military sense and noble dignity. Both men had also worked together at West Point (where Lee was superintendent and Thomas an instructor) and as cavalry officers in Texas. Each was striking in appearance. Cavalry General Wilson was awed by Thomas's "Jovelike figure, impressive countenance and lofty bearing." Wilson thought him closer to George Washington "in appearance, manner and character more than any man I had ever met." The voluble Erasmus Darwin Keyes, Thomas's captain during the 1840s Seminole Wars, would compare the "shape and carriage of his head and the expression of his handsome face . . . with my idea of a patrician of Ancient Rome. . . . All his movements were deliberate, his self-possession was supreme, and he received and gave orders with equal serenity." His veterans would fondly call him "Old Pap."

Lee, of course, would have military renown. Thomas's fame in aftertimes would be far less known except to avid war students. Yet in talent they were probably equal, and a case can be made that Thomas was Lee's superior. They were, however, never to meet in battle.

George Henry Thomas was a Virginian who stayed with the Union. For that, his sisters turned his picture to the wall. Of all the Civil War generals, Thomas was possibly the most capable of leading a modern army, but rivalries and jealousies were blamed for his premature death in 1870. *(Library of Congress)*

Thomas's attention to detail, his perfecting of maps and his thoroughness in gathering military intelligence, his ability to establish and maintain communication and supply lines deep in enemy territory, his creative use of engineers including a railway construction corps that the British would imitate, his concern for the health and training of his men, his careful planning and innovations and overall common sense—all these would stamp him as one of those rare Civil War generals capable of leading a modern army. He was, as well, absolutely fearless.

Still, staying with the Yankees could never endear him to the Virginia school that collected around Lee. Nor did Thomas live long enough to promote himself in memoirs. Like Lee, he died five years after the war and seemed determined *not* to write a book, saying, "my private life is my own, and I will not have it hawked about in print for the amusement of the curious."

Virginia's disdain tragically ran deepest within Thomas's own family, particularly two sisters in his native Southampton County. When Thomas wrote them of his decision to fight for the Union, they turned his picture to the wall and never spoke openly of him again. Other Southerners similarly thought him a traitor and turncoat. Braxton Bragg had been a comrade and benefactor in the old army. At Chattanooga, Tennessee, when Thomas was asked to forward a letter from the North across the lines, and sent a note requesting Bragg, the Confederate commander, to pass it on, Bragg refused. He instead sent back the letter with his own note: "Respectfully returned to Genl. Thomas. Genl. Bragg declines to have any intercourse with a man who has betrayed his state."

Contrarily, Thomas's decision to stay was not that reassuring to the North, though Winfield Scott was delighted. During a ten-day period at the war's beginning, Thomas took the oath of allegiance three times. He said, gamely, "If they want me to take the oath before each meal I am ready to comply." Still, it must have galled him. His determination and quiet intensity may have always contained an element of proving his loyalty and appeasing his personal honor.

Being from a seceded state cost him promotion too. When it came to a choice during the war of giving command of the Army of the Cumberland to Thomas or Rosecrans, who was an Ohioan and a Catholic, Lincoln went with Rosecrans. One reason was votes. Another was that Lincoln had only recently issued the preliminary Proclamation of Emancipation, and the case for the war was subtly shifting from Union to abolition. The Virginian Thomas was a former slaveholder from a slave state, and the political value of Virginians had gone south.

"Let the Virginian wait," Lincoln supposedly said to settle the matter.

Just as supposedly, a disgusted Stanton replied: "Well, you have made your choice of idiots. Now look out for frightful disaster."

When the disaster came a year later, first at Chickamauga and then in the Confederate siege of Rosecrans at Chattanooga, Lincoln still hesitated to make the obvious move. Like Stanton, Lincoln had become a Thomas supporter but also had his own flanks to guard. He had been approached by a "powerful New York delegation," as he put it, to protest favoring a Southerner. In the end the decision was passed to Grant, who had been put over the three Union armies of the West. Grant disliked Rosecrans even more than he disliked Thomas, and so picked the Virginian. It was one of the few favors he ever did for Thomas.

The treatment of Thomas by Grant and others both during and after the war is shameful at the very least and may even be criminal in the sense that it likely contributed to Thomas's death. Years afterward Grant would relish a reference to Thomas as "Slow Trot," a nickname picked up while instructing cavalry classes at West Point. In his *Personal Memoirs*, Grant seldom mentions Thomas except in a disparaging tone. Of his decision to promote Thomas to command the Army of the Cumberland, where an explanation (and perhaps a compliment or two) might be expected, Grant simply writes: "One order left the department commanders as they were, while the other relieved Rosecrans and assigned Thomas to his place. I accepted the latter."

To Grant, Thomas is always slow to act or is indecisive: "I then found that Thomas had not yet started [General Gordon] Granger, thus having lost a full day"; "Thomas made no effort to reinforce Schofield at Franklin, as it seemed to me at the time he should have done"; "Thomas did not get [General George] Stoneman off in time . . ." Even his muted praises come with a veiled threat: "You have the congratulations of the public," Grant wrote six days after the Nashville battle, "for the energy with which you are pushing Hood. I hope you will succeed in reaching his pontoon bridge at Tuscumbia [Alabama] before he gets there."

In his assessment of Thomas, Grant wrote: "Thomas's dispositions were deliberately made, and always good. He could not be driven from a point he was given to hold. He was not as good, however, in pursuit as he was in action. I do not believe that he could ever have conducted Sherman's army from Chattanooga to Atlanta against the defences and the commander [Joseph Johnston] guarding that line in 1864. On the other hand, if it had been given him to hold the line which Johnston tried to hold, neither that general nor Sherman, nor any other officer could have done it better." In other words, good on defense, not so on offense.

It was true that Thomas on the defense saved Rosecrans at Stones River, and later as the "Rock of Chickamauga," holding his ground, he was the bright light in what was otherwise a disaster for Union forces. Yet it was Thomas's men who did the brunt of the fighting for Sherman during the long offensive against Johnston. It was Thomas early in that same campaign who pressed for a quick slash through Snake Creek Gap in Georgia, which would have cut off and doomed the Rebel army but which Sherman botched by giving the task to another. It was the Army of the Cumberland that marched up the slopes of Missionary Ridge at Chattanooga, thus rolling back Bragg, lifting the siege, and rescuing Sherman's muddled flank attack. It was Thomas on the move at Nashville.

Great generals should not have to fight internal enemies too. But they do.

Grant was jealous and held a grudge. Personality likely played a role too. All were part of the same problem. It seems to have begun in 1862, just after Shiloh, when Halleck, then Grant's superior (and the war's slipperiest customer), made Grant his number two to get him out of the way. Halleck also gave Grant's army to Thomas. Thomas, serving under Don Carlos Buell, had arrived too late at Shiloh for anything other than burial detail but had won a notable victory in Kentucky.

"For myself I was little more than an observer," Grant would recall in his memoirs. "Orders were sent direct to the right wing or reserve, ignoring me, and advances were made from one line of intrenchments to another without notifying me. My position was so embarrassing in fact that I made several applications . . . to be relieved."

This arrangement did not last long. Thomas seems to have real-ized that he was being used by Halleck to get at Grant and didn't like it. It has even been suggested that Sherman, the flexible friend of both Thomas and Grant, who was trying to save the latter's career (and possibly his own), played a role in Thomas's decision to ask Halleck for his old job back with Buell.

Grant and Thomas met again in the fall of 1863 when Rose-crans was relieved and Grant had wired Thomas to hold Chatta-nooga "at all hazards" until he could get there. "I will hold the town till we Starve," Thomas had impressively wired back. Their meeting at Thomas's headquarters, however, did not begin well. Grant was found by an aide sitting in a uniform soaked with rain while glumly sharing Thomas's silence. Matters seemed not to lighten up. Thom-as's staff was all business and briskly efficient, the servants unobtru-sive and the meals solemnly formal. Rank, order, and punctuality prevailed. In contrast, Grant's staff, led by his hot-tempered aide John Rawlins, was not the best group to have around when their leader was a sometime drunk.

Grant hastily ordered Thomas to attack Bragg as a way of divert-ing Pete Longstreet, who had been sent to threaten Knoxville, Ten-nessee, to the north. Thomas, though, was expecting reinforcements and believed an attack just then would expose Chattanooga. Grant relented, but he didn't like it. Grant's next scheme gave the hero's role to Sherman, who had finally arrived with Grant's old army after a tardy journey. These soldiers were the ones who got bogged down fighting Bragg on Missionary Ridge. According to Grant's script, Thomas in the center, far below the ridge, was to wait for Bragg's flanks to be turned before launching his own attack.

As the long November day played out, Grant nervously waited on Sherman. He would not order Thomas to advance to the Rebel rifle pits at the base of the ridge and distract Bragg. Grant preferred Thomas to volunteer. Thomas waited for orders. Rawlins began to chafe and to goad Grant. Grant, red-faced, at last gave a direct order, and Thomas obeyed. But instead of marching only to the base, as ordered, the Army of the Cumberland kept on going, up, up, up, to the very top of Missionary Ridge, confounding both Bragg and Grant and winning the battle.

During the attack Grant had angrily asked Thomas, "Who ordered those men up the ridge?" Thomas calmly answered that he didn't know. So Grant turned to one of Thomas's corps commanders, General Granger, to ask if Granger had given the order. "No," said Granger, "they started up without orders." He then pleasantly observed: "When those fellows get started, all hell can't stop them."

Thomas's men, not Grant's old army and Sherman, had won Grant's fight for him. That was especially embarrassing, but within months Grant would get his promotion to the East. Sherman would replace Grant in the West. Both would get credit for the Chattanooga breakout at Thomas's expense, beginning with their battle reports and extending to their memoirs. Grant would not mention his dithering to order Thomas to attack, would suggest that the Confederate center was considerably weakened to fight Sherman, and would say nothing of his surprise but that the Cumberlanders were "effectually carrying out my orders." Given a chance to write of Thomas, he instead gossips about Bragg, Longstreet, and Jeff Davis.

Sherman would reprint Grant's after-battle order that praised Sherman for being the diversion "to make Thomas's part certain of success"—exactly the opposite of what Grant and Sherman had intended. A year later, Nashville would renew the friction. Shortly after that battle, Grant would break up and redistribute chunks of Thomas's army to Sherman and elsewhere.

*

WHY THOMAS CHOSE to stay with the Union rather than Virginia is a cause for speculation. Some, including Fitzhugh Lee, would say years later that Thomas was prepared to go south but Virginia failed to offer him a sufficiently lofty command. Others would blame the influence of Thomas's wife, Frances, who was a Northerner from Troy, New York. Thomas would deny the former claim, and his wife would insist that the general always made up his own mind. Thomas's character and war record—twice he refused promotion because he thought the circumstances improper—support both statements.

Nor did Thomas go to war to abolish slavery. He and his wife had bought a woman to serve as cook while in Texas and had left her in Virginia when they moved north. Thomas was recalled as always kind to the slaves on his family's Virginia farm and even took responsibility to help the woman cook and her family after the war. Moreover he was much more agreeable than Sherman to blacks being Union soldiers. But slavery pro or con appears to have played no important part in his considerations. Union itself is as good a reason to judge Thomas's decision.

Thomas didn't support Lincoln in the 1860 presidential election but favored the faction of John Bell of Tennessee. Bell was a candidate of the Constitutional Union party, a conservative response to the crisis which stood, plain enough, for the Constitution and union while calling for a halt to all the agitation about slavery. It was scarcely a party of abolitionists but of old Whigs and Know-Nothings from the preceding election cycle. Bell in 1860 received more electoral votes than Democrat Stephen Douglas.

Thomas's Unionist politics, then, seem established and of course ran counter to the states' rights advocacy of other Southerners. Thomas's views, in fact, appear to have stiffened in the course of the war. After the Chattanooga battles he ordered the creation of a federal military cemetery for the war dead. Asked by a chaplain if the graves should be grouped by native states, Thomas replied: "No, no. Mix them up. Mix them up. I am tired of states' rights."

Union meant many things to many people, but its defenders in the North, West, and parts of the South often were as vehement in keeping it disconnected from abolition as secessionists sought to keep states' rights and slavery apart. One was not necessarily a cover for the other. The mountain people of East Tennessee, for instance, had been among those strongest for the Unionist Bell. An antisecession argument by such highlanders as the irascible "Parson" Brownlow—eventually the postwar Tennessee governor and Forrest nemesis—was that remaining in the Union was the best way for states to *preserve* slavery, as it would enjoy constitutional protection.

The view of the pro-slavery Brownlow was that slave owners who treated their Negroes well "and instruct them in religion, are better friends to them than those who set them at liberty."

Senator Andrew Johnson, a Union Democrat, arch political enemy of Brownlow, and soon to be Lincoln's man in Tennessee, was not a whit concerned with slaves' souls. "If you liberate the Negro," he asked, "what will be the next step?. . . What will we do with two million Negroes in our midst?. . . Blood, rape and rapine will be our portion. You can't get rid of the Negro except by holding him in slavery."

Abolitionists, in the opinion of Union men such as these, were causing the national breakup for the sake of the Negro and regardless of the consequences to all. Omitting mention of slavery, Brownlow, in an 1858 debate in Philadelphia with an abolitionist minister, summed up with the high-flown oratory of the times a view that was likely then held by most of the country: "Who can estimate the value of the American Union? Proud, happy, thrice happy America! the home of the oppressed! the asylum of the emigrant; where the citizen of every clime, and the child of every creed, roams free and untrammelled as the wild winds of heaven! Baptized at the fount of Liberty, in fire and blood, cold must be the heart that thrills not at the name of the American Union!"

Walt Whitman, of course, put his finger on it too ("We debouch upon a newer, mightier world. . . . Fresh and strong the world we seize"). Union could stand for predestined greatness. If that was too complex, it stood for human freedom—dangerous territory unless one viewed blacks and Indians as less than human. By the time of the Civil War, the nation was still only four score and five years old, the Revolution's glories not yet bereft of living witnesses.

Nearly thirty years before Fort Sumter, Andrew Jackson, who at one time owned 150 human beings, had spoken for the country in writing to a Union man living in the same renegade South Carolina that had started the latest business. "Fear not," he assured him, "*the union will be preserved* and treason and rebellion promptly put down, when and where it may shew its monster head." Winfield Scott was around then too, and Old Hickory rushed him to Charleston to take command of the army garrison there. George Thomas was not yet a West Point plebe, but it's easy to see how Union could get into the national bloodstream of young and old alike and be excited again by the greatest crisis of all.

After the war, Thomas was as warm in his denouncement of secession and as outspoken in defense of the Union as to be worthy of Parson Brownlow. In 1867 several residents of Rome, Georgia, tried to mark the anniversary of their state's rebellion with a display of Confederate flags. Thomas, in charge of Reconstruction in five states as military commander, had them arrested. He also sent a scathing letter to the town's mayor.

"With too many of the people of the South," Thomas said, in part, "the late civil war is called a revolution, rebels are called 'Confederates,' loyalists to the whole country are called d——d Yankees and traitors, and over the whole great crime with its accursed record of slaughtered heroes, patriots murdered because of their true-hearted love of country, widowed wives and orphaned children, and prisoners of war slain amid such horrors as find no parallel in the history of the world, they are trying to throw the gloss of respectability, and are thrusting with contumely and derision from their society the men and women who would not join hands with them in the work of ruining their country. Everywhere in the States lately in rebellion, treason is respectable and loyalty odious. This, the people of the United States, who ended the Rebellion and saved the country, will not permit."

As early as February 1865, Tennessee—with native Unionists in political control and Thomas in Nashville protecting them—had repealed the state laws pertaining to slavery and the Confederacy. Johnson, the vice president-elect, had been succeeded as governor by the bellicose Brownlow, elected by a vote of 23,352 to 35. Although grossly unreflective of state sympathies, the number also served as cover to meet a Lincoln test for readmission. Yet, as Brownlow's biographer would suggest, it "was a strange and dangerous act" to set a man of his record to rule over a million people: "For the promoting of the orderly progress of peace, it would have been impossible to make a worse choice; for carrying out a war of vengeance of a minority against a majority, Brownlow was incomparably the best selection that could have been made throughout the land. As a master in whipping up hate and revenge, he had no peer."

Brownlow still detested blacks but didn't fight passage of the Thirteenth Amendment that freed them. Tennessee's ratification of it and the Fourteenth Amendment—helped by the dragooning of two legislators to compose a quorum—eased the state back into the Union the following year.

Thrown together, Brownlow and Thomas worked together. Gideon Welles, the navy secretary (who also didn't like Grant), called Brownlow a "coarse, vulgar creature" but assessed Thomas as having "intellectually and as a civilian, as well as a military man, no superior in the service. . . ." Thomas may have cooled some of the troubles instigated by Brownlow, but, as in his letter to the citizens of Rome, he could be tough too. Thomas's troops, black and white, were held ready to enforce the shaky peace.

Yet Thomas ultimately wearied of Brownlow's attempts to use the army as a private police force. At the height of the Ku Klux Klan crisis in 1868, amid Brownlow's threats of raising his own army, Thomas moved troops to twenty-one counties to protect the election that Grant would win. Otherwise he was apt to reply that, as Tennessee was now "in the full exercise of all the civil functions of a State," it should try to govern for itself. For better or worse, Thomas found himself at least partly in the camp of the states' righters.

Disowned by Virginians, Thomas was made a citizen of Tennessee by local Unionists in June 1865, and his will would be probated there. They also commissioned a gold medal to be presented in 1866 on the anniversary of the Battle of Nashville. A portrait painting of Thomas was hung in the Tennessee capitol's library; it would provoke Thomas's anger in late 1869 when a Democratic legislator proposed to sell it. Although the motion was easily defeated, Thomas—by then having transferred to California—tried to buy the painting and even vowed to return his medal. He had become increasingly thin-skinned, but not without cause.

A story is told of a more composed Thomas while he and his wife lived in Nashville after the war. They would sit on the front porch of their rented house, just as their neighbors did. For six months one Rebel neighbor especially made a point of snubbing the Thomases. One day the neighbor at last relented and approached Thomas to shake his hand. Thomas declined. "Too late, Sir, too late," he said. "You have sinned away your day of grace."

*

WHEN GRANT received his promotion to lieutenant general of the army and in March 1864 sent a message to Sherman acknowledging his help along the way, Sherman replied in part: "I believe you are as brave, patriotic, and just, as the great prototype Washington; as unselfish, kind-hearted, and honest, as a man should be; but the chief characteristic in your nature is the simple faith in success you have always manifested, which I can liken to nothing else than the faith a Christian has in his Saviour."

The unchurched Sherman, as seen earlier in his views on the Grant presidency, would not always remain so embarrassingly prostrate, and sometime later would sum up the relationship more succinctly: "Grant stood by me when I was crazy, and I stood by him when he was drunk."

They were quite a pair, and one of the engaging aspects of George Thomas was in his being biologically incapable of making either of Sherman's statements. Sherman, though, was wont to go in all sorts of directions. He would complain to Grant of Thomas's slowness in Georgia and the caution of the Cumberlanders. Then, leaving Thomas to face Hood, he would take the cream of Thomas's army to shoot any Scarlett O'Haras who opposed his march to the sea.

On the other hand, in 1887 an annoyed Sherman praised the dead Thomas and took on the Lee cult when a British admirer, Lord Wolseley, wrote that Lee "towered above all men on either side" in the war. Writing in the *North American Review*, Sherman replied that Lee had never transcended Virginia in his conduct of the war. Thomas, he added, "in all the attributes of manhood was the peer of General Lee—as good, if not a better soldier, of equal intelligence, the same kind heart. . . . Nashville was the only battle of our war

234 : AFTER THE WAR

which annihilated an army." He also pointed out that the British and Easterners "still see only the war in Virginia," whereas it "was concluded when Vicksburg, Chattanooga and Atlanta fell." Still, it would have been even more interesting had Sherman made his remarks seventeen years earlier, when both Lee and Thomas were alive.

Grant and Sherman would be at the head of the line when rewards were distributed at war's end. Other than his Tennessee medal and a jeweled badge from his staff, Thomas declined the gifts that were thrust toward him, including a house in Cincinnati and an engraved silver service. When a gift of money was raised, he asked that it be given to war widows and orphans. Thomas explained to an aide that he was "satisfied with his pay"and that whatever "my services were, they were rendered to the country itself." Military rewards, however, were a different matter.

During the war Thomas had resisted promotion when he perceived that he was being used as a tool in the political games of Lincoln, Stanton, and Halleck. He had also been disappointed when he thought promotion deserved. Grant's promotion of Sherman over him at Chattanooga—when Grant moved on to Washington—had Thomas feeling "aggrieved," according to one general, but it's doubtful he was caught off guard. When Andrew Carnegie mentioned to Grant that he supposed Thomas would be his choice, Grant had replied: "No, Sherman is the man for chief command. Thomas would be the first to say so." Andrew Johnson endorsed Thomas to Lincoln but, as in the Rosecrans affair, the decision was Grant's.

Now, in the spring of 1865, Thomas would learn that in the War Department's redistribution of commands he would be the only major general left out. Again he would be made subordinate to Sherman. This time Thomas fought back politically, sending an aide directly to the new president, Johnson. Tell him, Thomas instructed, "that during the war I permitted the national authorities to do what they pleased with me. The life of the Nation was then at stake, and it was not proper to press questions of rank, but now that the war is over . . . I demand a command suited to my rank, or I do not want any."

The aide, Brigadier General John F. Miller, found Johnson in the Treasury Department where he was still awaiting Mrs. Lincoln's drawn-out departure from the White House. Miller carried a map of how the states were to be grouped as military districts, but he hardly had to sell Johnson on intervening. "You know of my appreciation of General Thomas," the president remarked, then drew his pencil along the boundaries of Kentucky, Tennessee, Mississippi, Alabama, and Georgia. "There," he announced, "is his military division." Then he pointed to Nashville. "There are his headquarters." The War Department had to scramble to redraw the districts of Sherman and that of another Grant favorite, Philip Sheridan, the despoiler of the Shenandoah.

Other considerations were also forthcoming. Thomas was honored before Congress where, House Speaker Schuyler Colfax observed, his hand trembled "like an aspen leaf" as he "shrank from the storm of applause." Stanton privately also assured him of his confidence. "Nevertheless," said Thomas, bluntly, "I have not been treated by the authorities as though they had confidence in me." With Johnson he reviewed members of his proud Fourteenth Corps of Cumberlanders as they paraded by as part of Sherman's army. "They made me," he was heard to say through tears.

Washington was always up to something. During the tumult over Stanton's removal from office and with Grant distrusted by Johnson, the president acted to replace Grant with Thomas as general-in-chief. Johnson submitted Thomas's name to the Senate for a brevet promotion to lieutenant general and general. But when Thomas learned of it, he wired the Senate requesting that his name be withdrawn.

In all likelihood, Thomas wanted to avoid the morass that would result in Johnson's impeachment. It was also in his character as a stickler for military propriety. The promotion, Thomas argued, was too late for his war service and not merited by his service afterward. His acceptance also would have been a short-term way of getting back at Grant, but that was not Thomas's style. More cautiously, he could not have been unaware of Grant's political destiny.

Despite his own disdain for politics, Thomas's name was floated for public office. He would have been an interesting choice for president. His administrative skills and decision making in both war and peacetime were superior to Grant's. Even more so, they were superior to Sheridan's, whose harsh rule in postwar Louisiana had aroused suspicions of a Radical-supported White House bid. Thomas, though, was always quick to discourage efforts regarding himself, citing a lack of desire and temperament. While not as hostile to office as Sherman, his views made clear his disgust with politics and politicians. To a would-be advocate in 1867 he wrote, ". . . If there is anything that enrages me more than another, it is to see an obstinate and self willed man oppose what is right morally, & under the law, simply because, under the law, he cannot be compelled to do what is right."

Grant's 1868 election brought another army reshuffling, with Sherman becoming the top general. Sheridan inherited Sherman's star. Thomas had sought a command in the East for the greater convenience of his wife, but it was not to be. When offered a chance to switch places with Halleck, who was being transferred from his postwar command in San Francisco, Thomas refused and chose to stay in Louisville, where he had moved his headquarters from Nashville.

John Schofield, the general at Franklin and Nashville and who had served briefly as Johnson's last secretary of war, was then given the California post. Schofield, however, was Thomas's junior. He was also the sender of damaging telegrams at Nashville. This time Thomas had had enough. He complained hotly to Sherman that his rank "should not be degraded." Sherman tried to get Thomas to go with him to talk to Grant about it. Thomas refused.

The outcome was that Thomas agreed to go to San Francisco. Upon his arrival in 1869, the eastward-bound Halleck gave a dinner. There the two old generals—Thomas worn by battle, Halleck by intrigue—talked of the war and events surrounding the fight at Nashville. Doubtless they shared their grievances regarding Grant, but Thomas did not know the entire story. At some point the opportunity arose for Halleck to divulge the name of the general whom Grant first had in mind to replace Thomas. Perhaps Thomas had heard just enough to inquire. Or perhaps the gossipy Halleck couldn't help himself. Still, the name was surprising only if it surprised. Halleck said it was Schofield. "I knew it, I knew he was the man!" Thomas exclaimed.

*

IF GRANT'S SIN was bullying, Schofield's was his eagerness to hand him the club. Schofield was an intriguer, and a couple of generals on Thomas's staff had warned him. The insecure Grant had been a personality clash who held, as well, a long-festering grievance since Shiloh that Thomas was yet someone else after his job. George Thomas was probably the one man in the Union army whose ambition did *not* threaten Grant. Still, Grant ultimately had retreated from naming Schofield to replace Thomas. His reasons are not known. Perhaps he came to realize the humiliation of replacing Thomas with a junior officer serving under him, one who at Franklin had barely escaped the Rebel Hood; Grant's experience well knew the pain of humiliation. Or perhaps Grant, in reflection, abhorred Schofield's too-familiar politicking. In any event, Grant's sin would not have been betrayal.

No, Schofield shouldn't have been a surprise. Thomas and Schofield had first crossed paths (and swords) in 1852 during Thomas's instructor days at West Point. Schofield found himself dismissed from the academy for a strange business. He had been among cadets assigned to help West Point candidates pass their entrance examinations. Of four who failed entry, three were assigned to Schofield. As it came out, and as delicately described by Thomas's biographer Francis McKinney, "Schofield permitted his class to be turned into a burlesque by making the uses of their procreative and eliminative organs the subject of a blackboard examination."

It was clearly ungentlemanly conduct, and Schofield was booted out. Through the intercession of Senator Stephen Douglas, however, a court of inquiry reconsidered, rescinded the decision, and readmitted Schofield. Thomas, a court member, was one of two to adhere to dismissal.

Although the court vote was secret, Schofield would claim in his 1897 memoirs to have learned of Thomas's vote when, as Andrew Johnson's secretary of war, he gained access to the old hearing records. Schofield would excuse himself as "tolerating some youthful 'deviltry' of my classmates, in which I took no part myself." He also would claim to have repaid Thomas for his "stern denial of clemency to a youth by saving the veteran soldier's army from disaster," and Thomas himself "from the humiliation of dismissal from command on the eve of victory."

It is not impossible that even as a cadet Schofield may have known of Thomas's opposition and already bore a grudge. There is something ludicrous about a war secretary having nothing else to do than sift pages of musty transcripts about "youthful deviltry," and carefully taking names. The self-righteous account, with its air of vindictive triumph, is the stuff of mediocrities, and scheming for another's job is what mediocrities do best. Grudge or not, Schofield during the prelude at Nashville showed no reluctance to humiliate Thomas.

It is like reconstructing the scene of a future murder—or assassination—to revisit Nashville in 1864 amid Grant's threats, Halleck's pestering, ice on the ground, and Hood just outside the city. On December 10, Thomas had gathered his commanders to talk things over. He made known Grant's past orders and his replies.

Wilson, the junior officer present who wrote an account in 1912, spoke at this meeting in support of Thomas and of the importance of delaying an attack until a thaw occurred. Other generals present—T. J. Wood, A. J. Smith, and James B. Steedman—concurred. Smith and Steedman, particularly, Wilson would write, "were equally outspoken and as none present denied or criticised my proposition or the conclusion drawn from it, the meeting was shortly dissolved."

Schofield, wrote Wilson, "upon this notable occasion sat silent."

Wilson would also recall Thomas complaining to him afterward that "the Washington authorities treat me as if I were a boy. . . . I am sure my plan of operations is correct and that we shall lick the enemy if he only stays to receive our attack."

Steedman would record that before December 12, Thomas began to suspect that someone was trying to undercut him with Grant.

Thomas, leery of politicians, wondered if it might be then Governor (and vice president–elect) Andrew Johnson. Steedman was put on the case. A telegram sent to Grant was soon discovered. "Many officers here are of the opinion that General Thomas is certainly too slow in his movements," it said.

When Steedman gave it to Thomas and the handwriting identified it as Schofield's, Thomas asked, incredulously, "Why does he send such telegrams?" Steedman smiled and replied with a question, "General Thomas, who is next in command to you, and would succeed you in case of removal?" Steedman recalled that Thomas sadly shook his head. "Oh, I see," was all he said. Thomas never confronted Schofield or complained to Grant.

In his 1897 memoirs, Schofield's account of the meeting with Thomas and the other generals differs markedly from Wilson's. Schofield writes that Thomas had also mentioned the threat of his own relief, that he had been ordered "to attack Hood at once or surrender his command (not saying to whom), and asked our advice as to what he ought to do."

Schofield continues: "One of the officers present asked General Thomas to show us the order, which he declined to do. This confirmed the belief which I had at first formed that the successor named by General Grant could be no other than myself—a belief formed from the fact that I was, next to General Thomas, the highest officer in rank on the ground where immediate action was demanded, and from my knowledge of General Grant's confidence, which belief has since been fully justified by the record. This, as I conceived, imposed upon me the duty of responding at once to General Thomas's request for advice, without waiting for the junior members of the council, according to the usual military custom. Hence I immediately replied: 'General Thomas, I will sustain you in your determination not to fight until you are fully ready.' All the other commanders then promptly expressed their concurrence." Schofield also suggests that his loyalty to Thomas might have dissuaded Grant from giving him Thomas's army.

Whether Schofield's alleged ringing endorsement of Thomas came before or after sending his discovered telegram to Grant cannot be determined. But it is not the only message to have received attention.

On December 8—one day before Grant's orders for Schofield— a different telegram was sent to Grant from Nashville. It sounded alarms that Rebels were scattered for more than seventy miles down the Cumberland River (the great bulk of them were actually before Nashville), and that Thomas had made no attack. Whether this over-wrought message, and supposedly others too, was sent by Schofield, hard evidence proved skimpy after the war. A former Thomas aide would later cite at least one alleged message of intrigue by Scho-field that could not be found in postwar government files. It leaves the suspicion that Secretary of War Schofield, on behalf of Gen-eral Schofield, did more than ferret out the records of a West Point clemency hearing.

Nashville could not be taken away from Thomas. His plan of turning and smashing the enemy's left flank in force while also gain-ing his rear perhaps drew later notice from Count Alfred von Schlief-fen, chief of the German general staff, whose similarly designed but less successful plan opened World War I against the French. It helped at Nashville that Union combat forces outnumbered Hood's by more than two to one, Forrest was thirty miles away, and Franklin had been a shattering blow. But Hood still had the high ground and two weeks to prepare. In both execution and importance, Nashville was Thomas's shining moment, the battle most closely approach-ing military classroom perfection. Schofield's role, in reserve, was insignificant.

Except on March 12, 1870, an anonymous letter appeared in the *New York Tribune*. Grant's readiness to promote Schofield at Nash-ville had found its way from Halleck into some Western newspapers. In response, the letter elaborated on aspects of the Nashville cam-paign that were favorable to Schofield. Signed by "One who fought at Nashville," it basically contended that the battle there had really been won at Franklin—where Schofield commanded—and "where the enemy had been whipped until there was very little fight in him." It was the sort of letter that Schofield himself might have written (as he claimed much the same), or someone close to him.

Actually the writer was Jacob Cox, Grant's segregationist secretary of the interior, who had been one of Schofield's generals. Cox may have been writing primarily at Schofield's request or attempting damage control for President Grant; the Halleck revelation did Grant no favor among Thomas's old Cumberlanders. In any case, Schofield most likely was the first name to occur to Thomas when he read the letter. On March 28 he sat at his headquarters desk in San Francisco to compose a response.

It had been a long fight. He had turned his back on his state for his country yet had to prove his loyalty and, by extension, his competence, throughout the war—the Virginian kept waiting by Lincoln. He had been handed the rawest, rowdiest greenhorns and shaped them, his steely Cumberlanders, into arguably the most superb army of the Civil War and the closest to a modern force. He had selflessly taken a step back and let others go ahead. He had helped Grant and Sherman gain their inheritances—the presidency, the top generalship—yet found gratitude abysmally wanting. Most of all he had won Nashville and wrecked the one Confederate army that had withstood Grant, Halleck, Buell, Rosecrans, and Sherman. Franklin no doubt had hurt Hood, yet it took Nashville to settle things.

That's what Thomas had done, with his makeshift army after Sherman had taken his cut. Why, Schofield nearly got himself trapped at Franklin, then set himself up on the wrong side of a river! Braver men saved his neck! At Nashville it was Smith and Wilson who carried the day, not Schofield who had to be prodded to join the fight!

Thomas must have seethed as he began to write, just as he had when a politician wanted to sell his portrait, or when the citizenry of Rome, Georgia, refused to make peace, or when Grant favored his friends with promotions and plum assignments after the war—things he no longer could keep to himself. Although he was only fifty-three, Thomas's health had not been good. He may have suffered a mild stroke several years earlier. No longer Jovelike, he had bloated to nearly three hundred pounds. Now he wrote on, to respond to the lies that pass for history.

He had been writing for about three hours when the attack struck. An orderly heard him call out for air. He was helped to a couch in another room. Doctors were sent for and dismissed the attack as indigestion. Thomas soon was complaining of a pain in his right temple.

Frances Thomas arrived, and she and her husband's aide sat with him. Thomas spoke a few words, saying he no longer had pain. He tried to rise but could not. The doctors now called the problem apoplexy. Thomas's pulse grew weaker. His body gave a convulsive spasm, and then he died. His response to the letter about Nashville lay unfinished in the adjoining room.

The funeral was held in Troy, deep in the North, where Thomas was to be buried in his wife's family plot far from strife. President Grant attended. So did General-in-Chief Sherman. John Schofield was among the pallbearers. Twenty-five members of Frances's family attended, but none of Thomas's.

His veterans over the years would rally to the task—the unfinished response, the memoirs never published—on behalf of Old Pap, their own name in preference to Slow Trot. One of them wrote in reply to the Cox/Schofield letter: "No one who knows what that army was and what its failings were will dare dispute the fact that Thomas's removal would have proved a great if not fatal error, and that a very large part of the enthusiasm, vim, and heartiness with which the battle of Nashville was fought was due to the fact that in the current words of the men in the ranks: 'This is Old Pap's fight, and we're going to win it for him.'"

In 1881, Steedman, he of the prebattle conference and finder of incriminating telegrams, emerged to denounce the "intriguer" Schofield's claim of having sustained Thomas, mocked Schofield's courage at Franklin, and took on a further claim of Schofield having suggested a helpful "modification" in the Nashville battle plan. In a signed article in the *Northern Ohio Democrat* of Toledo, reprinted in the *New York Times*, Steedman assailed Schofield in Jubal Early–like fashion: "Robbing a grave of a body is a light crime compared with stealing the honors which rightfully belong to a dead illustrious patriot and soldier. The letter of General J. M. Schofield, claiming that he suggested changes in the battle of Nashville which were adopted by General George H. Thomas, surpasses in cheek and falsehood all the absurd lies about the war we have ever read. Schofield's claim to a part of the laurels that encircled the brow of the grand old 'Rock of Chickamauga' makes the self-lauding fiction written by Gen. Sherman a modest production. . . ."

Thomas's widow would harken back to Grant's treatment of Thomas as contributing to his death, writing, "I will say that it preyed upon and affected his health, which General Schofield's base attack on his military reputation added to, and which was the cause of the fatal attack on March 28, 1870."

There was much more, reminding us once again that former Rebel and Yankee generals got along better with each other than with those who wore the same uniform. In his 1897 memoirs, Schofield reprinted a letter he had written to Grant soon after Steedman's blast, along with Grant's reply. Among other things, Grant assured him that he hadn't received any Schofield telegrams from Nashville, or at least had "no recollection," and that if it did happen "I should now recollect it." Anyway, had it happened "it would have created a prejudice to your disadvantage." Grant *did* change his mind about Schofield, and perhaps this was a small hint of why. But no matter. Schofield's memoirs plunged on, praising Thomas on the one hand, swatting him with the other: "I believe it must now be fully known to all who are qualified to judge and have had by personal association or by study of history full opportunities to learn the truth, that General Thomas did not possess in a high degree the activity of mind necessary to foresee and provide for all the exigencies of military operations, nor the mathematical talent required to estimate 'the relations of time, space, motion, and force' involved in great problems of war."

Life is unfair, and Schofield would have an eventful career. Over time he recommended the building of the U.S. military base at Pearl Harbor (Schofield Barracks is him); became superintendent of the West Point that had once tried to throw him out, then left in 1881 after a scandal involving an attack on the school's only black cadet; and took over as the army's top general when Sheridan (who succeeded Sherman) died in 1888. Before he was through he would acquire a Congressional Medal of Honor for "conspicuous gallantry" at Wilson's Creek, Missouri, a battle that had occurred thirty-one years before.

In Southampton County, Virginia, Thomas's picture remained turned to the wall. Over time and outside Virginia, Thomas occasionally would be seen full frame and frontal. Jovelike in bearing and reputation, but resolutely mute, it has been left to others to speak for the Southern Yankee who exemplifies all that is best in the American soldier.

· 11 ·

LIBBIE'S HUSBAND

In her letters she proudly called him "my boy," "My Dear Boy," and "My darling Boy." He cheerfully reciprocated as "your boy" or "your Bo." Otherwise he was "Autie," a play upon Armstrong which in turn was a family preference to George, his other given name. She was Elizabeth but called "Libbie" throughout her life. Hers would be a very long life, and his would be ruthlessly cut short. They would be married for twelve years, and then she would be a professional widow for fifty-seven more, her eagle's wings spread across the corpse and reputation of her golden boy. They were desperately in love. Although versions of their Civil War letters would be sanitized years later, when made public, the sexual tension still slips through.

Libbie to Autie, from her dull, wartime boardinghouse in Washington: "This morning I have been in the garden, playing with the kitten, smelling the rosebuds, touching the sensitive plant to see it wither, then hearing Miss X complain of the Northerners she has for boarders, and Mr Stires expatiate on the cost of making his new suit. . . ."

Autie to Libbie, from somewhere in Virginia 1864, after losing his belongings in a battle: "I regret the loss of your letters more than all else. I enjoyed every word you wrote, but do not relish the idea of others amusing themselves with them, particularly as some of the expressions employed. . . . Somebody must be more careful hereafter in the use of *double entendu*."

Libbie to Autie: "I suppose some rebel is devouring my epistles, but I am too grateful to feel badly about that. Let me unburden my mind about the matter, since your letter implies chiding, tho the slightest and kindliest. No Southerner could say, if they are *gentlemen* that I lacked refinement. There can be nothing low between man and wife if they love each other. What I wrote was holy and sacred. Only cruel people would not understand the spirit in which I wrote it."

About the same time she wrote to her father and stepmother of a brief but apparently stimulating reunion: "Oh, such a surprise. Genls. [Philip] Sheridan and [Alfred A.] Torbert wanted something done in Washington, and gave Autie 48 hours here in which to accomplish it. I was talking to a lady who was calling on me about Autie when the door burst open. He rushed upstairs so fast the people thought the house was on fire. The lady left immediately."

Later she wrote to a friend of her visit to City Point, Virginia, where Grant had established headquarters: "We arrived here Saturday but Autie had to leave me Sunday. I was so unhappy. But on Wednesday, as I sat here reading, up the stairs came someone with such a bounding step as no one else has, and I had nearly a week I hadn't hoped for with him. But he was far from well when he left. He hadn't taken long enough leave to recruit his strength."

He was pleased when she changed boardinghouses and "glad to hear that there is a soft place upon somebodys carpet because as that lady remarked in reference to piercing ears etc. there are a great many ways of *doing things* some of which I believe are not generally known."

And in the last weeks of the war, she urged him: "Don't expose yourself so much in battle. Just do your duty, and don't rush out so daringly. Oh, Autie, we must die together."

These were the words of a still newlywed. Rumors of jealousy and infidelity would follow within a few years, though Autie would still knowingly write his Libbie: "All the women are but as mere toys compared to you."

They would not have children, though he would be suspected of fathering a "little papoose" after taking a Cheyenne woman captive.

Elizabeth Bacon Custer became a writer and lecturer after the Little Bighorn, and defended her husband for the rest of her life. Many critics respected her and held off to await her death before jumping in. But Libbie lived until age ninety and didn't die until 1933. *(Monroe County [Michigan] Historical Museum Archives)*

Autie would write Libbie from the Kansas frontier in 1868 while she was visiting home in Michigan: "I am delighted and overjoyed that my little darling bride is having an opportunity of really seeing and determining how troublesome and embarrassing babies would be to us. Our pleasure would be continually marred and circumscribed." There was too much fun to be had. For him: hunting Indians and shooting buffalo and agonizing for promotion. For her: basking in his glory when supreme, defending him to the saber hilt when not.

In certain ways George Armstrong Custer was always like a dangerous child while his wife, Elizabeth Bacon Custer, would become like a doting and protective mother.

*

ALTHOUGH Custer's fate at the Little Bighorn River after the Civil War is well known, Libbie's life is less so, and both must be taken together for one is as interesting as the other. Of Custer, most everyone who heard the name had an opinion. Those that were favorable owed very much to Libbie, at least during her lifetime. They were the "next generation." Together the Custers exemplified the triumphant Union's rush of energy after its vicious war with the South and as it turned west to wage yet another with the Indians who now stood in the way.

Custer was born on a farm in eastern Ohio in 1839 but spent much of his youth with a half-sister, Ann, after she married and moved to Monroe, Michigan, on Lake Erie. He was naturally rowdy and liked to chase coons, foxes, and girls, particularly girls. He was sufficiently indiscreet as to brag of his prowess with one in a letter to another. He also discovered that West Point could give him a free college education and somehow got it into his head that a lot of money could be made in the army. Custer's father was an outspoken Democrat. An early example of what came to be called "Custer's luck" was that the youth wangled an appointment from his Republican congressman.

Custer entered the academy in 1857. His time there was inglorious. In his four years he accumulated 726 demerits, just under the bar for dismissal. Many of his demerits were typical of his personality: "Trifling in ranks march'g from parade"; "Calling Corporal in a boisterous tone of voice"; "Throwing bread in M.H. (mess hall) at dinner," and so on. He also tried to steal an exam. His demerits would have been a record for a graduating lieutenant had not Marcus Reno, between 1851 and 1857 as a six-year cadet, run up 1,031. (This same Reno would hover like a death's head years later.)

Yet whenever Custer teetered on the edge he would buckle down and manage, with "Custer's luck," to save himself. He finished last in his class of thirty-four on the eve of First Manassas. None of this would dissuade Custer eight years later—at a low moment in his career—from brazenly applying to General-in-Chief Sherman for a posting as West Point's commandant of cadets.

Custer had a natural talent for self-promotion. During the march to Manassas, Sherman and his men were diverted by a mounted messenger from Winfield Scott. An officer would later write of the rider who "wore long, flowing locks, a hat and plume, a la Murat, and was uniformed in a royal purple silk velvet jacket, brilliant with gold trimmings." This was Custer, whose military trappings would always tend toward the creative. His luck placed him on the staffs of two generals, and by the following spring of 1862 he had caught the attention of George McClellan—another self-promoter—during the Peninsula campaign. McClellan made Custer his aide with the rank of captain. The two men—both ardent Democrats as well—would remain mutual admirers for life.

Custer eagerly took on any mission for McClellan. One of them was a trip aloft in Professor Thaddeus Lowe's experimental reconnaissance balloon, to make notes on Rebel positions near Richmond. Custer would write amusingly of his flight with Lowe's assistant, who urged Custer to stand up in the basket as they soared toward the clouds: ". . . My confidence in balloons at that time was not sufficient, however, to justify such a course, so I remained seated in the bottom of the basket, with a firm hold upon either side. I first turned my attention to the manner in which the basket had been constructed. To me it seemed fragile indeed, and not intended to support a tithe of the weight then imposed upon it. The interstices in the sides and bottom seemed immense, and the further we receded from the earth the larger they seemed to become, until I almost imagined one might tumble through. I interrogated my companion as to whether the basket was actually and certainly safe. He responded affirmatively; at the same time, as if to confirm his assertion, he began jumping up and down. . . ."

Another youthful adventure during the preceding winter had not turned out so well when then Lieutenant Custer returned to Michigan on leave. During his carousing he became so drunk as to have trouble finding his way home to his sister's house. The experience caused him to swear off alcohol forever, a pledge he thereafter kept. After marrying Libbie, he made similar pledges about gambling and profanity but with less success. He was spared a pledge about tobacco, for he never used it. As for other women, there is only Libbie's silence to ponder.

Libbie's father, a stern Monroe judge, had witnessed Custer staggering up the street, and Custer's local female preferences were of a faster lot than Libbie. She was a flirtatious twenty, petite, very pretty and bright, and had plenty of suitors. Nonetheless they seemed a drab lot in wartime while Custer, the next time he returned home, looked splendid in his captain's suit. They met despite the judge. She began to feel a certain unsettling. Custer in his own way was also yielding. He declared to his sister, "There are not more than a dozen girls in Monroe that I like better than Libbie, and that is the truth."

His rising star in battle would help undo the judge. Custer's effusive self-confidence, his zest for danger, and his utter reliability as a staff officer caught the attention of a more aggressive crop of elders. Yet even Custer could be shocked: at age twenty-three he was jumped four grades to brigadier general of volunteers and given a cavalry brigade of Michiganders. Number thirty-four in his class of the same number was suddenly the youngest general in the Union Army. He quickly made good on the promotion. At Gettysburg he led his brigade with saber-waving charges while crying, "Come on, you Wolverines!" Custer and his men, from that point on, were often out in front as the war moved back to Virginia.

His eccentricities also continued to draw notice. A colonel on the staff of General George Meade would write home: "This officer [Custer] is one of the funniest-looking beings you ever saw and looks like a circus rider gone mad! He wears a huzzar jacket and tight trousers, of faded black velvet trimmed with tarnished gold lace. His head is decked with a little gray felt hat; high boots and gilt spurs complete the costume, which is enhanced by the general's coiffure, consisting in short, dry, flaxen ringlets!"

A Custer biographer, Robert M. Utley, has observed that brigade self-promotion was also involved here, an intention by Custer to instill unit identity and esprit. The new general designed a personal flag with crossed white sabers. He organized a band where mounted brass players rode into battle trumpeting "Yankee Doodle." Custer also sported a scarlet necktie, and soon red ties sprouted throughout the brigade. So, to a lesser degree, did flowing locks. "The quick, jerky movement of his sinewy frame," Utley writes of Custer, "together with speech rushing forth in high-pitched bursts bordering on a stutter, betrayed an unceasing and hyperkinetic restlessness."

Northern papers extolled him as the "Boy General."

When Lincoln called Grant east in March 1864, Grant brought Philip Sheridan. The ensuing shakeup mirrored the Grant pattern of favorites in the ascendancy. One cavalry favorite, James H. Wilson—later so helpful to Thomas at Nashville—was jumped in front of Custer as a division commander. The jealous Custer would grouse that Wilson was an inexperienced "imbecile" who "has been engaged in writing a history of Genl. Grant's campaign in the West."

Grant was never a Custer favorite, but Sheridan won him over and would prove something of a guardian angel until the Little Bighorn. By sheer numbers, Union cavalry now dominated the Confederates. At Yellow Tavern, Virginia, one of Custer's men shot and killed the cavalier Jeb Stuart. As with Sherman in Georgia and Grant in eastern Virginia, the war around Custer and Sheridan soon became even more brutalized. Ordered to avenge a lieutenant's death, Yankees seized six members of Mosby's Rangers, shot four of them, and hanged the other two. Mosby won Lee's permission to retaliate. He executed five of his seven Union prisoners (two escaped) and left a note blaming Custer.

Inevitably West Point friends would meet as foes. Custer confronted a former roommate, now Rebel cavalry General Thomas Rosser. Their clashes, where each captured portions of the other's wardrobe, also led to an exchange of jocular messages (Rosser addressed his to "Dear Fanny," Custer's cadet nickname, and signed off as "Tex"). Yet these were only storybook interludes, coming during Sheridan's grim autumn campaign to lay waste both Jubal Early's army and the rich Shenandoah Valley. It was a strategy as much spurred by Grant's standoff with Lee and Lincoln's approaching election. With Custer's considerable help, Early was thrice routed and the luscious valley left a scorched and homeless wasteland. Custer came out as a brevet major general. His brother Tom, a second lieutenant, soon joined him as an aide.

In the spring of 1865, Custer was in the thick of the pursuit of Lee to Appomattox, during which Tom won himself two Medals of Honor. After the surrender, Sheridan bought the writing table on which Grant had written the terms for Lee and sent it to Libbie. "Permit me to say, Madam," Sheridan wrote in an accompanying note, "that there is scarcely an individual in our service who has contributed more to bring about this desirable result than your very gallant husband."

Libbie also journeyed with a congressional group to abandoned Richmond to await Custer. She spent two nights in the emptied bedrooms of Jefferson and Varina Davis.

Libbie and Custer had married in Monroe in 1864, a nighttime affair with hundreds jammed into the Presbyterian church. The bride wore white. Custer wore a "full-dress uniform" of gold braid and epaulets. He also got a haircut; Libbie had the shorn curls made into a ballroom wig.

Left motherless at twelve, Libbie had been stashed in boarding schools. Her education was much like Mary Lincoln's. She was popular, loved books, and kept a diary where she deplored her spiritual shortcomings. She was also thin, which bothered her, as did her "milkmaid" cheeks. She had lots of luscious brown hair and looked on the world with deep-set grey eyes. Her closed-mouth smile expressed a patient sweetness.

In stark contrast to Custer, she had been her class valedictorian, besting a rival Custer had squired about town. Temperamentally they were both adventurous and could calm each other in times of havoc. In their short life together their professions of romantic (or erotic) interest would be well documented. But perhaps as equally consummated was a mutual ambition—he the boy general, she the girl who wanted something more than the parlors of small-town Monroe. In Washington she met Lincoln!

Life could not be better for Libbie, as long as Autie came home alive. When he did, he barely had a scratch—another piece of Custer's luck. Both were ready to take on whatever the world would next throw at them. Back in Monroe, though, it would be alleged that the ultimately amenable judge never entered Custer's name in the family Bible.

*

INDIAN CLASHES with encroaching whites had been going on in the West long before the Civil War. The settlement that preceded the town of Monroe had been attacked during the War of 1812 by Indian allies of the British, who massacred the wounded militiamen, scattered terrified pioneers to Detroit and Toledo, and torched the place. At the time, Michigan was of the West. When the new nation began to look seriously in that direction, naturally the Indians drew much speculation. Before the Lewis and Clark expedition in 1804, Thomas Jefferson and Meriwether Lewis chatted often about the savages. The Mandans were thought to be a tribe of Welshmen. The Sioux, in Jefferson's view, were "very desirous of being on the most friendly terms with us." Seldom has Washington been so out of touch with the heartland.

The quest for buffalo led the Sioux onto other westward lands including, in the 1830s, the Laramie Plain in Wyoming, just southwest of the Black Hills. The Sioux were always the force to be reckoned with. The historian-critic Bernard DeVoto would call them "a populous, arrogant, and bellicose people." Predictably, they were soon quarreling with all around them.

Despite the Civil War, little peace came to the West. The tribes welcomed the war for obvious reasons, but a downside was that more whites than ever were under arms. Along the Minnesota River valley in 1862, hungry Sioux struck in what may be the greatest of the Indian massacres, slaughtering an estimated 644 whites. The uprising inevitably was crushed, and 303 Sioux were sentenced to die for murder, rape, and arson. Lincoln intervened to spare all but 38. They were duly hanged the day after Christmas, and the others were expelled westward.

In 1864 it was the Indians' turn. Some 700 Colorado volunteers and soldiers under Colonel John M. Chivington attacked a village along Sand Creek that contained a similar number of Cheyenne and Arapaho. It happened to be the village of Cheyenne Chief Black Kettle, who had been talking peace with the authorities and from whose lodgepole flew an American flag. Black Kettle waved both it and a white flag, but the attack continued. More than 130 Indians, mostly women and children, were killed. Soldiers also lifted scalps and body parts.

It would be Sioux, Cheyenne, and Arapaho at the Little Bighorn in 1876.

Custer's and Libbie's first taste of the West came shortly after the war, when he was ordered to march six regiments of soldiers to Texas from Louisiana. Custer was a Civil War celebrity, Libbie his socially popular wife. Both were full of themselves, and they stopped in New Orleans to have their portraits painted upon vases. Farther upriver, Custer wrote Libbie's father to advise him to invest in the cheap land expected to attract swarms of carpetbaggers. Libbie complained to the judge that "the advent of the thrifty ingenuous Yankee" was sorely needed.

The soldiers Custer inherited were not trigger-happy Yankees still spoiling to kill Rebels but thousands of war-weary and resentful volunteers who didn't like West Pointers. They wanted to go home, not Texas. Insubordination had become common almost to the point of mass mutiny. So had desertions and plunder of what remained among the hapless populace. Custer tackled the problem head on.

George Armstrong Custer wore no flowing locks at the Little Bighorn in June 1876. News of the massacre did not reach the East until shortly after the July Fourth celebration of the nation's centennial. Four of Custer's relatives died with him. *(Library of Congress)*

He ordered out his entire division to witness a firing squad. At the last moment he spared a popular sergeant accused of being a mutineer, but not a deserter alongside.

He took a different tack to protect the civilians. "Every enlisted man," an order promised, "committing depradations [sic] on the persons or property of citizens will have his head shaved, and, in addition, will receive 25 lashes on his back, well laid on."

Instead of the reverence of the Michiganders, the volunteers from Iowa, Illinois, Indiana, and Wisconsin loathed him. Rumors of assassination ran through camp. Wrote one soldier of Custer: "He did not stop to consider that [volunteers] were citizens, and not soldiers by profession. . . . He had no sympathy in common with the private soldiers, but regarded them simply as machines, created for the special purpose of obeying his imperial will."

Three thousand men were marched west for 240 miles in August heat wearing woolen uniforms and keeping close order. Supplies were short, water was brackish, and meat killed that day was often poorly cooked. Heat stroke and dysentery plagued the column throughout.

Libbie rode in one of the seventeen ambulances. Another hauled Custer's dogs while five more carried headquarters gear. That left ten for the sick. Because of rattlesnakes, Libbie and the general slept in a wagon instead of a tent, and Custer ordered soldiers to wait on her. She was the only woman, but it's unlikely the troops appreciated it. Libbie in turn thought the unruly volunteers had learned discipline. An officer who luckily traveled by boat to reach the Texas destination found the command "in the most destitute situation of any soldiers I had ever seen." Writing years later, Libbie would excuse Custer in part because of his youth but would also truthfully conclude that the volunteer troops "hated us, I suppose."

Some of this enmity reached Washington via complaints from state officials and soldiers' families. Sheridan, however, interceded and assured War Secretary Stanton that Custer had quit flogging enlisted men. Worse from the couple's viewpoint was when breveted Major General Custer reverted, in peacetime, to his regular rank of captain. It dropped his pay from $8,000 a year to under $2,000. So much for getting rich in the army.

Custer shopped unsuccessfully for opportunities during a long leave in Washington and New York while Libbie visited Monroe. He still retained some celebrity (if not notoriety) and was wined and dined by the powerful. He wrote to Libbie in heedless detail of his adventures. One included a night when he and his army pals flirted with New York streetwalkers. He also admired the low-cut gown of a baroness, commenting: "I have not seen such sights since I was weaned." Libbie remained in Monroe, where the judge was dying.

Custer's luck reappeared in the summer of 1866 when Congress enlarged the peacetime army for purposes of Southern Reconstruction and Western expansion. Custer was promoted to lieutenant colonel of one of the new regiments, the Seventh Cavalry. It and Custer would go down in history together. In October he and Libbie were at Fort Riley, Kansas.

*

THE CAVALRY LIFE was scarcely glamorous, nor were its soldiers knights-errant. While the Seventh had its share of hard-bitten war veterans, it also attracted jobless foreigners, drunks, criminals on the run, and would-be gold and silver miners awaiting the first chance to desert. Custer would write Libbie while on one of his Indian hunts of an officer who committed suicide while in a fit of delirium tremens. He also told of desertions so numerous that he feared the loss of his command. Some of the deserters he ordered chased down and shot.

Exhaustion, sickness, bad food—Custer would complain in 1867 of bread packaged before the Civil War—and occasionally a gruesome death were the common lot of the troopers and officers when in the saddle. When not, the regiment's twelve companies were parceled out to remote frontier posts near emigrant trails and future railroad routes. Even a headquarters fort held a dreary and difficult existence. Whenever Libbie tried to follow Custer to his ever-changing postings, she took her life in her hands.

The Seventh also had an infection from within. Colonel Andrew Jackson Smith—another breveted general who had received Thomas's hug at Nashville—was the regiment's commander but soon took on additional responsibilities. In practice and popular perception, then, the Seventh became Custer's. The inevitable result for the regiment was that Custer drew to himself as much hostility as loyalty.

His company commanders didn't lack diversity. Two of them had served in the British army. Another, Irishman Myles Keogh, had been a papal Zouave in Italy. Louis Hamilton was a grandson of Alexander Hamilton. Robert West had been a breveted brigadier general, and Frederick Benteen a breveted colonel. The prickly Benteen, who would have a significant role at the Little Bighorn, from the start had clashed with Custer over Benteen's admiration for, and Custer's disparagement of, Benteen's wartime commander James Wilson (Custer's "imbecile"). West sided with Benteen in a mutual dislike, if not hatred, of Custer.

Around Custer, meanwhile, gathered an assortment of officers and wives, including brother Tom and a brother-in-law, James "Jimmi" Calhoun, in a tight-knit group outsiders called the "royal family." Libbie would note later in her book *Boots and Saddles* of how Custer discouraged gossip and of how constrained she felt in being courteous to those "whom I hated."

While none of this is unusual, men in the Seventh might more easily have pounced on the errors of their fellow officers, and in particular those of their flamboyant leader. The esprit and ultimately the effectiveness of the regiment would seem always at risk. Custer, courageous but dangerously impetuous, was easily open to criticism and even court-martial. Some of his behavior was induced by Libbie.

In late 1866, after Sioux in Wyoming had wiped out a separate force of eighty-one soldiers, an army show was ordered to intimidate or shoot any of the unruly bands wandering the Plains. From the following April into July, Custer and eight cavalry companies chased mostly shadows across Kansas, Nebraska, and Colorado. Libbie waited at Fort Riley in "a perfect whirlwind of anxiety."

Despite the dangers, Custer's letters to her were filled with pleadings to join him. For added measure he composed a guilt-stricken pledge of his eternal faithfulness. While Libbie remained distant, Custer was moody and morose. One of his formerly admiring officers would call him "the most complete example of a petty tyrant that I have ever seen."

Arriving at a place called Fort Wallace near the Colorado border, Custer decided without orders to rush halfway across Kansas to Libbie. He then led seventy-six men on a midsummer's forced march, which took a toll on both horses and riders. At one point Custer noticed that his spare horse was missing and sent a sergeant with six men in search of it. A large party of Indians ambushed the detail and shot two of the soldiers, who were left behind. Custer pressed on. Twenty of his men deserted. At another post he found Colonel Smith, roused him from his bed to inform him that he was going on to Fort Riley, then left his befuddled commander and took a train to Libbie. When Smith shook the cobwebs, he ordered Custer's arrest. A court-martial followed.

Some would later suggest that all of this was more than a case of headstrong homesickness. Captain Benteen would maintain that Custer had received a letter from another officer suggesting he return to Fort Riley and "look after his wife a little closer." A second veteran of those days also would recall an anonymous letter to a newspaper that accused then Lieutenant Thomas Weir of paying too much attention to Mrs. Custer. Weir was Colonel Smith's aide, an alcoholic, and a University of Michigan graduate. For a time he had been left behind with the ladies at Fort Riley.

Libbie's biographer Shirley Leckie raises the possibility that Weir had been used by her to make Custer jealous—that something may have occurred to compel Custer's written pledge (or apology) "never to give you fresh cause for regret by attentions paid to other girls." Perhaps Libbie was still smarting from Custer's letters from New York. On the other hand Libbie, in her own boardinghouse letters to Custer during the war, would protest her virtue, "tho I have a pretty face"; both made use of jealousy. Benteen would also accuse Custer of womanizing and say that Libbie well knew of it, which "rendered her—if she had any heart (?) a broken-hearted woman."

In any case, Benteen would allege that Custer caused Weir to "beg for his life on his knees."

Custer's court-martial considered charges of absence without leave, misuse of government property for private business, and failure to look after the two troopers shot by Indians, one of whom had died. Robert West also brought charges against Custer for having deserters shot without trial and refusing them medical care.

Custer was found guilty and suspended from duty without pay for a year. Grant, still the top general, considered the sentence "lenient." Libbie, however, thought the proceedings "nothing but a plan of persecution for Autie." Indian attacks spurred Sheridan to rescue Custer before his suspension was up.

*

THE GOVERNMENT'S grand strategy for combating the hostiles that would involve the army included the relocation of the Plains tribes in northern Kansas and southern Nebraska. This would then protect settlers already in that corridor as well as travelers on the Santa Fe and Oregon trails, miners headed to Denver and points west, and the Union Pacific and Kansas Pacific railroads. The Sioux would be kept north of the Platte River, and the Southern Cheyenne, Arapaho, Kiowa, and Comanche south of the Arkansas River.

In 1868 a treaty was negotiated with the Sioux establishing a reservation on what was, roughly, all of western, present-day South Dakota. Government negotiators also acquiesced in "unceded territory" of Sioux hunting grounds in much of eastern Wyoming and Montana. In exchange for reservation life, the Indians would receive rations and other provisions—including guns for hunting—but be subject to government controls. In late 1867 something similar had been arranged for the Southern tribes. Here, reservation life for the Cheyenne would still allow them to hunt buffalo south of the Arkansas while receiving government annuities for thirty years.

This looked fine on paper. But buffalo didn't always cooperate, and they, ancient enemies, and unlucky settlers were often summer prey on the land declared off limits by the treaties. Hostiles, in most cases, would then go into winter quarters on the reservations with the rest of their tribe. Even chiefs inclined toward peace couldn't speak for everyone.

A Cheyenne raid on settlers in July 1868, in which fifteen white men were killed and five women raped, eventually brought Sheridan to devise a winter campaign rather than spend all summer pursuing shadows. Custer, as in the Shenandoah, was just the man to chasten the Indians. An officer would write his wife that Custer returned to the Seventh with "his hair cut short, and a perfect menagerie of Scotch fox hounds!" He also began issuing orders immediately.

In late November eleven companies of cavalry set out to the strains of "The Girl I Left Behind Me" and straight into a blizzard. Finding a trail in deep snow made by a hundred warriors going south, Custer followed. At length the cavalry reached a Cheyenne village on the Washita River in western Oklahoma. Coincidentally the village was Chief Black Kettle's of Sand Creek, who was planning on finding Sheridan to restate his desire for peace.

Custer saw only what he took to be hostiles. Eight hundred horsemen charged to the soon-frozen sounds of "Garryowen." They swept through the village from four directions. Fleeing women and children were shot as well as warriors. Also slain were Black Kettle and his wife. Among the few soldier casualties in the charge was Alexander Hamilton's grandson.

Suddenly Custer was surprised by news that hundreds of other tepees had been discovered down river—more villages of Cheyenne, Arapaho, and Kiowa. The occupants were on the way. Unknown to Custer, a detail of twenty men led by Major Joel Elliott had been cut off and killed.

Custer sent skirmishers to hold off attacks, had Black Kettle's village set afire, and ordered men to shoot or slash the throats of nearly nine hundred Indian ponies. Family picture albums found in the village and taken during the July raid fed the fury amid flames and animal screams.

Custer retreated under cover of night without determining Elliott's fate. The detail's chopped-up bodies would be discovered later. Also found would be the corpses of a white woman and child, captives murdered in retaliation.

For retaliation upon Custer, the Cheyenne would have to wait.

*

THE WASHITA ATTACK put Custer back in the public eye, though for the next several years his Indian encounters would subside. A good deal of time was spent hunting buffalo or greeting well-heeled parties from the East and Europe who came for the same sport. Showman P. T. Barnum was among them; his group killed only twenty of the animals to avoid "wanton butchery." Soon enough the slaughter of the buffalo would play as large a part as army muscle in bringing the tribes to heel. By 1878 the once-massive herds were gone from the Southern Plains and would vanish in the North five years later.

Custer also took long leaves from Libbie. One of them, in 1871, was to New York in a futile get-rich scheme to peddle stock in a Colorado mine to the likes of August Belmont and John Jacob Astor. He also couldn't resist boasting to Libbie—stuck in Kansas or Monroe—of New York females supposedly attracted to him. A few years earlier he had begun writing hunting articles for *Turf, Field and Stream* magazine. He now kept his name out front by recounting his Indian adventures for *The Galaxy* magazine. His articles eventually were collected in a book, *My Life on the Plains* (the sour Benteen called it *My Lie on the Plains*).

Also in 1871 the regiment was dispersed to three Southern states for duty against the Klan. Custer and Libbie fought boredom in the backwaters of Kentucky until early 1873. Private John Burkman, hired as an off-duty servant during this time, later recalled that even with all the "laughin' and jokin' and cuttin' up pranks" in the Custer household, "they was times when . . . I seen a kinda unhappy look in his eyes that worried me considerable." When orders came that sent the Seventh to Dakota Territory, an overjoyed Custer celebrated by breaking furniture.

In the early 1870s the Northern Pacific Railroad, pushing northwest from St. Paul, Minnesota, began to lay track in what would become North Dakota. Sherman saw the near future accurately and used an expression that would reappear in Nazi Germany. "The Indians will be hostile in an extreme degree," he wrote to Sheridan in

1872, "yet I think our interest is to favor the undertaking of the Road, as it will help to bring the Indian problem to a final solution."

The immediate problem in the territory consisted of the Sioux and their Cheyenne and Arapaho allies. Like those tribes below the Arkansas, not all were content with reservation life. In the unceded lands to the west, several thousand hunted and roamed, drawn by the magnetism of an unreconciled medicine man named Sitting Bull. Going back and forth between these lands and the Dakota reservation, they made the threat of war always near despite a treaty of peace.

In fact the 1868 treaty had left vague the northern boundary for the Sioux, who quickly saw the railroad as a trespasser. Parties of hostiles began attacks on Northern Pacific surveyors and army escorts as they crossed westward toward Yellowstone country. More cavalry were needed. Again Sheridan summoned Custer.

The Seventh would end up at a new outpost, Fort Abraham Lincoln, across the Missouri River from the town of Bismarck, then the railhead for the Northern Pacific. In the summer of 1873, Custer and ten companies of troopers set out to protect the surveyors going into Montana. Nineteen infantry companies, three hundred supply wagons, two cannon, and a herd of cattle also went along. The entire fifteen-hundred-man force, including Custer, came under the command of Colonel David Stanley.

Stanley, a hero at Franklin and one of John Schofield's critics, was no Custer admirer either. He wrote his wife that "I have seen enough of him to convince me that he is a cold-blooded, untruthful and unprincipled man. He is universally despised by all the officers of his regiment excepting his relatives and one or two sycophants." Stanley, however, was also a drunk, and though he once ordered Custer's arrest (and apologized for it, when sober, two days later), Custer had much his own way on the expedition. Another West Pointer was to pop up as head of the railroad's engineering party: ex-Confederate General Tom Rosser from Shenandoah Valley days. Rosser and Custer, in the ironic way of so many who were enemies during the war, would have a grand time together recounting their battles.

This perceived invasion of the Yellowstone Valley naturally stirred up the Sioux. Near the mouth of the Bighorn River the largest clash of some hundreds of cavalry and Indians brought another Custer victory. It was, however, a tough, three-hour fight which revealed an aggressive foe well armed with repeater rifles from Indian agency traders. Custer would famously return to this area in 1876, but in September 1873 the Yellowstone expedition was hailed as a military triumph. Custer was similarly hailed. Newspapers praised the exploits of what one called the "Glorious Boy." Colonel Stanley went ignored.

The Panic of 1873 had more success than the Sioux in slowing the Northern Pacific's advance. The railroad, controlled by Jay Cooke, went into receivership when Cooke's banking house collapsed about the time Custer came home from the Yellowstone. The Northern Pacific would not run beyond Bismarck for the next six years.

Thus it had to fall back on its greatest asset: an enormous amount of land along the route to sell for settlement and development. When chartered by Congress during the Civil War, the Northern Pacific had been granted up to 47 million acres of public domain to reach its terminus in Oregon. It was a mass one and a half times the size of New York State. As if by Johnny Appleseed, immigrants (many of them German) already had been planted along the way after promises of fecund splendor. More deluded settlers were needed to buy in, and Cooke got busy.

Railroad efforts to promote a Northwest paradise did not pass unchallenged. One dissenter was Colonel William B. Hazen. Hazen, when at West Point, once had his fellow cadet Custer placed under arrest. He also had a lot to do with saving the Union Army at Stones River, but he was a quarrelsome sort. In 1872 he had been banished to a wilderness post where the Yellowstone and Missouri rivers converged. Hazen was unimpressed by Cooke's tropical pretensions and forwarded his own scathing opinions to the *New York Tribune*. This was the same newspaper whose recently deceased editor, Horace Greeley, had once urged young men to "go West and grow up with the country." The paper now bannered Hazen's views: WORTHLESS RAILROAD LAND.

The railroad's Rosser turned to his friend Custer to rebut Hazen. Custer did so in a glowing letter to the *Minneapolis Tribune*. The railroad was grateful. According to biographer Utley, the Northern Pacific provided Custer with a spacious tent to take on his campaigns, free train passes, and occasionally a private railroad car for him and Libbie. Even a special train was once put at their service. Hazen, unbowed, found a new hobby in attacking Custer.

The accelerated quest for land would soon offset any delay of the inevitable posed by railroad bankruptcy. Moreover the Sioux kept the pot boiling with attacks on Nebraska settlers. These assaults turned the army to the Black Hills, which fell within the reservation, as a site to build a more convenient fort. From an Indian viewpoint, the Black Hills really *were* a Northwest paradise, filled with game and firewood. Others thought the army move a violation of the 1868 treaty, but Sherman claimed a military exception. Custer was assigned to explore for a site.

This 1874 expedition, however, was up to more than forts.

Silver and gold found elsewhere in the West had made every inaccessible plot a suspected source of the next great strike. The Black Hills were no different, and rumors of gold had persisted for years. They now fed the desperation of economic hard times. They also stoked the efforts of the railroad and other believers in transcontinental progress to open the territory further to white settlement. Thus the Black Hills expedition that summer took along a thousand soldiers as well as engineers and mapmakers to select the next fort, and two "practical miners" who knew gold when they saw it. A geologist and a paleontologist were also invited to the unexplored country. Custer being Custer, three newspapermen went along too, including one from the *New York Tribune*.

The work was mostly a lark. The Sioux kept their distance, and Custer spent much of his time hunting and enjoying the scenery. "We have discovered a rich and beautiful country," he wrote Libbie. Besides writing letters and drafting reports, he composed a forty-five-page dispatch for the *New York World*. With him this time were not only his brother-in-law Jimmi and his brother Tom but another brother, Boston, age twenty-five and on the books as a "guide."

The miners found gold too. While no bonanza, it did keep the notion of quick riches alive. Although Custer at first was uncharacteristically restrained in his news and urged further examination, the story took off. Territory newspapers especially leaped at the prospect of the next "El Dorado." Would-be miners began packing for the Black Hills.

The result was a quandary, if a temporary one. Sherman, oblivious of contradiction, warned the miners they had no right to invade property that was not theirs. Custer, meanwhile, added to the gold lust with much more encouraging remarks to a reporter. He helpfully observed that Bismarck—still reachable by the Northern Pacific—was the best place to outfit for the Black Hills.

Sherman's views, however, echoed those of the Interior Department, which cited the treaty. President Grant ordered intruders kept out by the army. Sheridan, whose military department oversaw the territory, issued arrest orders. But both Sheridan and Custer were of one mind on the future: that while orders from Washington would be obeyed, they would welcome the "extinguishment" (Custer's word) of the Indians' own claim upon the Black Hills. Both also hinted that Congress could act to do so.

Meanwhile the expedition's geologist questioned the gold find, and newspapers back East branded it as a hoax cooked up by the Northern Pacific. Custer stood by the discovery. The upshot was that another expedition with more scientists was sent to the Black Hills in the summer of 1875 to determine the truth. This time a politically sensitive Sheridan gave the job to his good friend General George Crook. Amazingly, illegal miners were allowed to work with the scientists. Their conclusions favoring large-scale commercial mining kept the flame alive.

The Sioux remained livid throughout. Talks in Washington with reservation leaders about buying the Black Hills went nowhere. Then a government commission journeyed west to discuss the matter before five thousand recalcitrant Sioux from both on and off the reservation. The council gathering broke up angrily.

In early November 1875, Grant, his friend Sheridan, War Secretary William Belknap, and Interior Secretary Zachariah Chandler sat down to review the situation. Miners were frantic to get into the Hills; Grant was reluctant to lift the army's orders to keep them out. On the other hand, Sheridan would later explain, Grant thought "such resistance" only increased the miners' desire "and complicated the troubles." The solution was typically Grantesque: keep the army's orders in place but don't enforce them. And do it quietly.

The Sioux already called the Black Hills path blazed by Custer the "Thieves' Road." They would respond.

*

ONE DAY during the Seventh's initial march to Fort Lincoln in Dakota Territory, the Custers detoured away from the column. When dogs started a deer, Autie gave chase, leaving Libbie behind with an unidentified officer.

"Without the least warning," she writes in her book *Boots and Saddles*, "in the dead stillness of that desolate spot, we suddenly came upon a group of young Indian warriors seated in their motionless way in the underbrush. I became perfectly cold and numb with terror. My danger in connection with the Indians was twofold. I was in peril from death or capture by the savages, and liable to be killed by my own friends to prevent my capture. . . . I had been a subject of conversation among the officers, being the only woman who, as a rule, followed the regiment; and, without discussing it much in my presence, the universal understanding was that anyone having me in charge in an emergency where there was imminent danger of my capture should shoot me instantly. . . .

"If time could have been measured by sensations, a cycle seemed to have passed in those few seconds. The Indians snatched up their guns, leaped upon their ponies, and prepared for attack. The officer with me was perfectly calm, spoke to them coolly without a change of voice, and rode quickly beside me, telling me to advance. My horse reared violently at first sight of the Indians, and started to run. Gladly would I have put him to his mettle then, except for the instinct of obedience, which anyone following a regiment acquires in all that pertains to military directions. The general [Custer] was just visible ascending a bluff beyond. To avoid showing fear when every nerve is strung to its utmost, and your heart leaps into your throat, requires superhuman effort. I managed to check my horse and did not scream. . . ."

If anything is abundantly clear in Mrs. Custer's frontier memoirs, it's that an equal share of courage was demanded of both wives and their soldier husbands. Libbie Custer had grit, and while she constantly refers to her Autie and her dependence on him and need for his approval, it is obvious she was very much a tough cookie. Army life held few comforts and often was just above squalor. Underneath her surface calm was a terror always threatening to break free.

Libbie's march with the regiment into Dakota had also proved harrowing for reasons besides Indians. She tells of being confined to a half-finished cabin during a sudden spring blizzard, her husband sick in bed while snowdrifts piled higher and higher outside. Six frostbitten soldiers soon joined her. From beyond the walls came the haunting cries of animals lost in the storm. Once, a drove of hogs attempted to break into the crowded cabin, and the door had to be held tight.

Libbie had thought of faraway Dakota as Lapland when she first traced their route on a map, and Fort Lincoln was clearly no paradise. Swarms of grasshoppers ruined the Custers' efforts to have a garden. The glare from the sun's reflection off sandy soil proved almost blinding. Across the nearby Missouri River, a stretch of country for eighty miles eastward contained no trees. On their own side, the only significant tree was used by the Indians for their dead. Upon it, seventeen corpses were "lashed to boards and laid across the main branches."

Libbie enjoyed riding with her husband, but even on the east or "safe" side of the Missouri soldiers had discovered the body of a white man who had been tortured. Like other women, she chafed at being confined behind the fort's picket line, yet she well understood and struggled with fear. An old man who would come occasionally to the fort to chat with Custer and who lived alone on his nearby ranch had been found robbed and beaten to death by Indians.

As an army wife, she was quick to rise in its defense. To an aunt who had written her of the denunciations in Eastern newspapers of army severity toward the Indians, Libbie tartly responded: "Surely you do not believe the current rumors that Autie and others are cruel in their treatment of the Indians? Autie and others only do what they are ordered to do. And if those who criticize these orders could only see for themselves. . . . A woman rescued from Indian captivity who has suffered degradation unspeakable; the brutalities of the men, the venom of the squaws. . . . People in civilized conditions cannot imagine it. But we who have seen it know."

At other times she could sympathize with the tribes' plight in dealing with the Interior Department, which oversaw the Indians. Of one unsuccessful attempt to get food to the Sioux, she concluded: "The chiefs were compelled to return to their reservations, where long ago all the game had been shot and many of their famishing tribe were driven to join the hostiles. We were not surprised that the warriors were discouraged and desperate and that the depredations of Sitting Bull on the settlements increased with the new accessions to his numbers."

*

WHEN READING the memoirs it is impossible to ignore the tension building toward the well-known climax. Yet one is reluctant to see the tale turned over to history. It is like a parting aboard the *Titanic*. Whatever the direction of Custer's star, he and Libbie are bound to follow, just as the nation at this time was following its own star to the Pacific. The tribes might even be pitied but needed crushing all the same. And yet, is Custer somehow manipulating the outcome, or is Manifest Destiny manipulating Custer? Perhaps that is unanswerable. Perhaps it is more worthwhile to speculate whether Libbie would have rejected the lifeboat and gone down—had she the chance—with the ship and her soldier.

Custer's journey back to the Yellowstone to subdue the Sioux was almost thwarted by Grant. The issue was the selling of trader licenses for use at the Indian agencies and army forts, a patronage privilege reserved for the secretaries of the Interior and War departments, respectively. The kickbacks for these licenses were notorious and also involved the president's bad penny of a brother, Orvil Grant. In the case of soldiers, the consequences were inflated costs as traders tried to recover their bribe. For Indians, it often meant being cheated. War Secretary Belknap was in the middle of it.

Custer, always cognizant of his New York friends, helped feed information to a reporter sent west by James Gordon Bennett's anti-Grant *New York Herald*. Whether indirectly because of this, or simply because he was in a good position to know what took place at a trading post, Custer was summoned to Washington in March 1876. There he testified before an election-year investigation by the ruling House Democrats into Belknap and War Department corruption. Whatever the value of his testimony, Custer, the staunch Democrat who had worshiped George McClellan, was viewed as unhelpful by the Republicans and Grant.

Meanwhile a campaign had been planned against Sitting Bull's wayward bands who had ignored an ultimatum to return to the reservation. Custer was to lead the Seventh against the Sioux as part of another glorious expedition. Grant, in retaliation, now balked. Only when Custer's unique experience and the political repercussions were pleaded did Grant relent. Still, the mission's leader, General Alfred Terry, was expected to keep Custer on a leash.

The full twelve companies of the Seventh Cavalry marched out of Fort Abraham Lincoln on May 17 of the nation's centennial year. Custer led the column, accompanied by Libbie and his sister Maggie, married to Jimmi Calhoun. Calhoun, of course, went along, as did Tom and Boston Custer. So did a Custer nephew, Harry Armstrong Reed, age eighteen and also called Autie. He was visiting his famous uncle for the summer. The family males would all meet grisly deaths.

Libbie and Maggie rode back to the fort after the first day, but not until Libbie had been given an ominous sign.

"As the sun broke through the mist," she would write, "a mirage appeared, which took up about half of the line of cavalry, and thenceforth for a little distance it marched, equally plain to the sight on the earth and in the sky.

"The future of the heroic band, whose days were even then numbered, seemed to be revealed, and already there seemed a premonition in the supernatural translation as their forms were reflected from the opaque mist of the early dawn."

The battle on the Little Bighorn River has been recounted and dissected more times than there were Indians present, and of these there were thousands. Most were Sioux along with some Cheyenne and a handful of Arapaho. A safe estimate of their village found by Custer is of about two thousand warriors, as well as another six thousand women and children. Eight days earlier the Indians had defeated a column of soldiers sent up from the south by General Crook as part of the army's plan. Custer and Terry knew none of this as they probed for Sioux from the north.

A good guess as to the Indians' whereabouts—if an uncertain one—had been somewhere along the Little Bighorn. Custer was expected to go far enough south where he could swing around and, if there were Indians, to attack and drive them north toward a separate force of infantry to be waiting at the river's mouth.

Setting out and discovering a large trail left by Indians that headed west toward the river, Custer cut short his march south and followed it. He expected to find a village and was confident that the Seventh—as it had done so often before—would prevail. A scout warned that enough Sioux were ahead to keep the regiment fighting two or three days. Custer smiled and replied: "I guess we'll get through them in one day."

To make sure no hostiles would be in his rear when he turned north, he sent Benteen and three companies of 125 men south. Custer took the rest and followed a creek. On one side, Custer kept command of five companies of about 225 troopers. On the other, Major Marcus Reno led three companies of 140. The twelfth guarded a pack train which fell increasingly behind.

Seeing a cloud of dust and believing the Indians were fleeing, Custer ordered Reno forward at a gallop while Custer would follow.

But when Reno came under heavy fire, Custer changed his mind and decided to strike with his five companies from a different direction. The tactic had worked at the Washita. He sent riders to hurry the pack train and its men and to fetch the absent Benteen. Then, without waiting, he rode toward the village to attack.

Custer was overwhelmed. Reno would be blocked, losing about forty men and sent retreating toward nearby bluffs. Benteen—in Utley's words—"dawdled" on the back trail. Benteen would dig in with Reno who outranked him and who couldn't decide what to do. At one point a frustrated Tom Weir—once a target of a jealous Custer—mounted his D Company and rode to the sound of guns. He saw only Indians. The attacks below under chiefs Gall and Crazy Horse killed, from bodies counted later, another 212 men. Most, but not Custer, were found mutilated.

Back at Fort Lincoln, on the same Sunday as the battle, June 25, Libbie would tell of "our little group of saddened women" gathered to sing old hymns. "At that very hour," she writes, "the fears that our tortured minds had portrayed in imagination were realities, and the souls of those we thought upon were ascending to meet their Maker."

*

IN THE AFTERMATH of the Custer disaster, the first casualty for the victors was the Black Hills. That September government commissioners arrived at the Sioux agencies and, threatening to cut off rations, forced the reservation chiefs to sign away all rights to the Hills and the unceded lands. Meanwhile General Terry's military mission was placed in the hands of Colonel Nelson A. Miles, the onetime sadistic jailer of Jefferson Davis and an admirer of Custer. Miles was to be the greatest Indian fighter of them all. He wrapped his infantry in buffalo overcoats and campaigned throughout the harsh winter.

By the following spring, in combination with the efforts of General Crook, most of the hostiles had given up. The rest, with Sitting Bull, escaped to Canada. The decimation of the buffalo herds and starvation brought his surrender five years later. While in Canada he had responded to American charges as lies: "They tell me I murdered Custer. . . . He was a fool and rode to his death." In 1884 the notorious medicine man joined Buffalo Bill Cody's Wild West show but lasted only one season as crowds lustily hissed and booed.

In 1890, Sitting Bull was suspected of being involved in the subversive Ghost Dance movement, which blended Indian and Christian beliefs but also promised bulletproof protection from whites. During an attempt to arrest him, he was shot and killed by Indian reservation police.

Two weeks after Sitting Bull's demise, soldiers of Custer's old Seventh Cavalry attempted to disarm Sioux who had camped overnight at Wounded Knee Creek while on their way to the Pine Ridge reservation in South Dakota. A fight broke out. As the outnumbered Indians tried to flee, artillery fire added to the melee. At least 150 Oglala Sioux died at the scene, including the usual women and children. The Little Bighorn had come full circle, and Indian resistance quickly collapsed.

Other figures prominent in the "Last Stand" would slip from view equally ingloriously.

Thomas Weir, four months after the Bighorn, would write Libbie who was back in Monroe that "I have so much to tell you that I will tell you nothing now." He promised a visit. But Weir died in New York that December, of what a doctor called melancholia but what more likely were the penalties of alcoholism.

Major Reno, who would bear the brunt of the blame for the massacre among those who would not or, like Libbie, could not blame Custer, went steadily downhill. He faced, at various times, accusations of what today is called sexual harassment, as well as drunkenness on duty, threatening a duel, and being a peeping Tom. The last act was directed at the daughter of Colonel Samuel Sturgis, commander of the Seventh Cavalry. Reno's fate was a dishonorable discharge heartily endorsed by President Rutherford Hayes and even more heartily by Mrs. Hayes.

Earlier, in 1879, a court of inquiry had looked into Reno's retreat at the Little Bighorn—that is, why he had not somehow reunited his forces with Custer's or otherwise relieved that fatal pressure. He was exonerated by his fellow officers, though without enthusiasm.

Out of the army and in disgrace, Reno married, but his wife left him after a few months. He died in 1889. Libbie would always hate him. In 1967, however, and at the behest of a Reno descendant and the American Legion, the army corrected the discharge to honorable. Reno was also reburied in Custer Battlefield National Cemetery, established three years after the battle.

Frederick Benteen, who had suffered both Custer and Reno as they had suffered him, also stayed on in the army. Once, when in the same city, he tried to pay his respects to the Widow Custer, but Libbie refused to see him. In 1887, Benteen was court-martialed for drunk and disorderly conduct. He defended himself with customary vigor but was found guilty. Generals Crook and Sheridan interceded to modify his sentence, but upon returning to duty Benteen applied for a medical discharge. He retired to Atlanta and became something of a local character. He was made a brevet brigadier general for the Little Bighorn and another battle, and died in 1898.

John Burkman, the faithful soldier-servant, had ridden with the pack train that fatal day to look after Custer's favorite horse, Dandy. Thus he survived. In 1910, when President Taft helped dedicate a bronze equestrian monument of Custer in Monroe, Burkman borrowed money to travel from Montana for the ceremony and to visit with Libbie, who had traveled from New York. Burkman blamed himself for not sharing in the "Last Stand." In 1925, despondent over his inability to enter an old-age home for veterans, he shot himself.

Dandy was given to Custer's father, who rode him in Monroe parades.

Another horse, Comanche, owned by Myles Keogh, was the sole survivor of the actual massacre. The wounded Comanche was found in a clump of trees and adopted by a trooper, Gustave Korn, who dissuaded another soldier from killing the bleeding horse. Comanche was, of course, a regimental icon who lived a good life until Korn was killed at Wounded Knee. Comanche died soon after but remained a Western favorite through the wonders of taxidermy.

As for Elizabeth Custer, she would build a second life brick by brick—an edifice more formidable than any frontier fort to protect herself and her Autie.

Custer's estate did her no favors. The claims against it amounted to $13,000. These included an $8,500 debt on a loan to cover losses from speculations in railroad stocks. At most Libbie's assets were $8,000, including a meager $30-a-month army pension. A public collection for the widows—among them Custer's sister—helped somewhat, but eventually Custer's debts would be settled at ten cents on the dollar.

Although Libbie returned to Monroe after Custer's death, the following spring she decided to move to New York. Until her pension was raised, she worked part-time as secretary to the Society of Decorative Arts, an organization formed to teach needy women how to make and market household arts and crafts. Through this position she met the wives of such movers and shakers as Belmont, Astor, and others that her husband had earlier cultivated.

The slow climb from genteel poverty was helped by her writings, including newspaper columns. She managed to describe New York's funeral parade for Grant—someone else she didn't like—without mentioning his name (he was "a departed president"). After *Boots and Saddles* in 1885, Libbie wrote two other books of cavalry life and Western lore. One of them, like Grant's memoirs, was published by Mark Twain's company. She also took to the lecture circuit. In both writing and speaking, however, she noticeably avoided the Little Bighorn.

Libbie traveled around the world three times, marveling at Mount Fuji and, in her seventies, riding horseback through the Khyber Pass. Andrew Carnegie and his wife befriended her, and she spent time as their guest in Scotland. She had visitors of her own when in New York. Another columnist and famous widow, Varina Davis, and daughter Winnie called on her. While it is not known whether Libbie's wartime slumber in Jeff's bed was brought up, she later told a reporter she thought Winnie was spoiled.

Mrs. Custer seldom returned to Monroe. She preferred a summer cabin at a Catskills artists' colony or another in the piney woods of Thomasville, Georgia. She also kept a tent to sleep in as in the old days when roughing it with the cavalry on the Plains.

All of this flowed from or was in the service of her second life's purpose of protecting and burnishing the name of Lieutenant Colonel George Armstrong Custer, brevet major general. She gave her blessing and encouragement—and often her suggestion—to all works favorable to his life, and used her increasing influence as public widow and popular writer-lecturer to thwart or rebuke the legend's doubters. Their writings had to pass the Libbie standard, and critics—or witnesses who might assist the critics—were constrained by an admitted fondness or respect for little Mrs. Custer. Most awaited her death before jumping in. Instead, Libbie outlived them.

Public works on behalf of Autie also had to gain the widow's approval. This was learned in a big way when a monument was commissioned at West Point to mark Custer's new grave site, where his remains had been transferred from the battlefield in 1877. Libbie played a key part in the transfer, having had the burial rescheduled from summer to autumn (at Superintendent John Schofield's suggestion) so that the full corps of cadets could be present to pay the proper tribute.

But she wasn't consulted on the monument project. The work, when unveiled in 1879, was of an unmounted, long-haired Custer clenching a saber and pistol. No matter. Libbie was already sworn to hate it sight unseen. She considered it "a cross for me to bear" and got busy to have the monument undone. She went to Sherman, who passed the buck to the secretary of war. He was the unlucky Robert Lincoln, already well versed in the grievances of prominent widows. He passed it to West Point, which had Libbie going back to Sherman.

At length Libbie found an old friend of Lincoln *pere* who urged the son to act, in 1884, with only a few months left in office. The profane monument was quietly shuffled off to storage. It was replaced by an obelisk, near which Libbie was buried when she died in 1933 at age ninety.

Elizabeth Custer would be blamed for keeping the truth about her husband and the Little Bighorn hidden or obscured during her lengthy lifetime. But what was the truth?

It was evident that Custer took on too many well-armed Indians and had added to the risk by splitting up his smaller command. Moreover he had crossed to the Little Bighorn without going farther south before making his turn, which would have delayed events long enough for the northern force of infantry to have marched closer to the scene of battle. Typical glory-hunting and rashness led to the Last Stand, his critics would eventually contend.

On the other hand, said Custer's friends, General Terry's strategy already had divided his forces, Custer had discretion to choose his opportunity to cross to the river, and his rashness was courage. Besides, they said, the quaking Reno could have done more. So could have the others who survived.

Most of the country got the news of the massacre shortly after the nation's huge centennial celebration in Philadelphia. Grant, whose scandalized administration needed no further disasters, was quick to respond. "I regard Custer's Massacre," said the president, "as a sacrifice of troops brought on by Custer himself, that was wholly unnecessary—wholly unnecessary."

What was the Widow Custer to do? A case could be made for love and devotion, or for a wife's pretended blindness. But Libbie Custer also faced poverty as well as hometown stares and whispers and triumphant pity. Guilt by association—the wife of the man who led so many others to awful death—was not beyond her reasonable fears. Someone of that sort, a reminder of unpleasantness or possibly of crime, has no seat in even the most sequestered sewing circles.

It helped for her to believe it, or at least to tell herself she believed it, but her husband as hero and martyr to Western expansion and national glory was also essential to her own survival. Why, she would say in 1927, it was all done to protect the Northern Pacific, for "whose right of way my husband and his men had died"! She would not go quietly, for she could not. When West Point ignored her to create the infamous monument to her Autie, she made her own stand against insignificance in an uncaring world. She would fight them all. She had to. If strangers wished to call it wifely devotion or love, that too was a weapon.

Pretty Libbie Custer possessed a will of iron. And for the better part of a century her husband accepted the applause and took his bows upon bronzed horseflesh back in Michigan. Except for that terrible afternoon, Custer's luck still held by having Libbie to carry the Seventh's guidon. On the whole, his adventure lasted longer than most myths in a nation always so eager to believe before it so eagerly destroys.

NOTES

Chapter 1: The Daughter of the Confederacy

page

4 "I must have . . ." William Davis, *Jefferson Davis: The Man and His Hour* (New York, 1991), 553.

4 "As I sat . . ." Mary Chesnut diary entry for May 1864. C. Vann Woodward, *Mary Chesnut's Civil War* (New Haven, Conn., 1981), 601–602. The Woodward version of the diaries is the personal preference to earlier versions, including Ben Ames Williams's *A Diary from Dixie*, and is used throughout.

4 "Mr. Davis's hope and greatest joy in life." From Varina Davis 1890 memoir, vol. II, 496–497, cited by William Davis, *JDMHH*, 552.

4 Varina Anne was first "Piecake" to the family, then came to be called "Winnie." Elisabeth Muhlenfeld, *Mary Boykin Chesnut* (Baton Rouge, La., 1981), 121.

4 "an Indian name meaning bright, or sunny." Jefferson Davis papers, 8:169, Rice University, http://jeffersondavis.rice.edu/resources.cfm?doc_id=1556, attributed to Varina.

5 Pen name Filia and Varina's reaction are cited by Hudson Strode, *Jefferson Davis Tragic Hero* (New York, 1964), 422–427, whose sources for his three-volume Davis biographies are many, including interviews with witnesses, but are not always specific. Joan E. Cashin, in her *First Lady of the Confederacy: Varina Davis's Civil War* (Cambridge, Mass., 2006), 220–221, confirms Varina's discomfort from letters and other sources. Cashin, 393, far less sympathetic to Jefferson Davis than the admiring Strode, alleges that Strode altered manuscripts. Strode, in *Jefferson Davis: Private Letters, 1823–1889* (New York, 1966), xix, says he made numerous deletions in the letters he presents for reasons of irrelevance, including "gossipy paragraphs," and that he "eschewed the marks of ellipsis" for the reader's convenience. While this may have served convenience, it also arouses curiosity.

5 Attribution for the sleeping-car episode is from *New York Times*, July 17, 1871; Tom Carney's *Portraits in Time: Stories of Huntsville and Madison County* (Huntsville, Ala., 1998), 75–78; and from Cashin, *FLC*, 200–201, who cites several newspapers, primarily Northern, that printed variations of the report. Upon returning to the Huntsville area after the war, Virginia Clay seems to have lived as little as

she could with her husband, who was poor, sick, and alcoholic, and she often visited friends in Memphis. Whether the train story was true, she did not mention it in her 1905 memoir, *A Belle of the Fifties.*

6 Strode's account is in *JDTH*, 429–443. He maintains that Davis was surprised, when Mrs. Dorsey's will was read, that she had left him Beauvoir. Cashin, 226–229, says Davis had a general idea of the will's contents and notes that Dorsey relations appealed the gift all the way to the U.S. Supreme Court.

6 The Davis dog story—"President Davis and His Dog, Traveler," by L.H.L.—was splendidly set forth in the April 1909 issue of *Confederate Veteran*, 173. Had Traveler been with Davis on the flight from Richmond, Davis might well have eluded capture.

7 "My darling Baby . . ." Strode, *JDPL*, 451–452.

8 "The new girls . . ." Ibid., 497.

10 "Large, intellectual, bright eyes" and "gracefully arched insteps" are among the descriptions of Winnie in her obituary in *New York Times*, September 19, 1898.

10 "My darling Father" was Winnie's sometime address; darlings were fairly frequent in letters to and from Winnie and her parents.

10 Details on Winnie and her father together are from William Davis, *JDMHH*, 684–686, who attributes several sources.

10 "I would . . . break squares." Ibid., 686.

10 "Is there not . . ." Ibid., 684.

10 Mention of visitors to Beauvoir and of Winnie's participation in New Orleans' Mardi Gras is drawn here from the *Times* obituary of 1898 and from an account by the Associated Press, printed in *Augusta* [Ga.] *Chronicle* of August 4, 1999. The latter concerns the opening in New Orleans of "The Lost Princess of the South" exhibit at the Memorial Hall Confederate Museum in 1999. The Oscar Wilde visit to Beauvoir is humorously presented by Strode, *JDTH*, 459–461. Wilde, on tour, professed to be a Jefferson Davis admirer, but the Beauvoir ladies were more impressed than the chilly Davis, who told Varina afterward, "I did not like the man."

11 Strode, *JDTH*, 484, infers that *Atlanta Constitution* managing editor Henry W. Grady pinned the name on Winnie, but other accounts credit General Gordon. So did General Gordon. The source relied upon here is the account of the United Daughters of the Confederacy, Winnie Davis Chapter 442, of Greenville, S.C.

11 Cashin, *FLC*, 247–248, citing Winnie's scrapbook, letters.

12 Strode, *JDTH*, 492; again, a more sympathetic look at the aging Jeff Davis and Winnie.

12 W. H. Payne letter to Jubal Early, December 6, 1889: "The Yankees are posing over Mr. Davis's death-bed, and propose to pardon him—Can't you prevent him or any who speak for him, asking for it—I would not have him disgraced by it for the world. . . ." Jubal A. Early Papers, Library of Congress. Payne had taken the oath of allegiance. Strode, *JDTH*, 411–414, says James G. Blaine was behind the amnesty exclusion of Davis.

12 ". . .The faces I see." From Strode, *JDTH*, 495, and an admiring pamphlet by Herman Frey, *Jefferson Davis* (Nashville, Tenn.,1977), 44, citing archival sources.

13 Both Cashin, 249–263, and Strode, 498–499, are drawn upon here on the beginnings of the Winnie-Wilkinson romance. Cashin is more thorough and relies in part not only on Davis family letters and papers but on reports in the *Syracuse* [N.Y.] *Standard* of the era and accounts of the Onondaga (County, N.Y.) Historical Association. Cashin includes Davis's "Death would be preferable" remark; the AP/Chronicle article of 1999 also cites it; Strode does not, but considering Davis's opposition at the time it is hardly out of character.

14 Strode makes several references to Davis's love for Sarah Knox Taylor and his lengthy grief at her death. Cashin, 38, citing a conversation with a descendant of Varina, says the second Mrs. Davis tired of being compared to the "sainted Sarah."

14 Strode, 499, cites a 1957 interview with a Davis neighbor who recalled Winnie excitedly divulging the news of Davis's approval but noting that the engagement was to be kept secret for a while. Although undated, this suggests the possibility of a leak and a reaction before Winnie's trip abroad with the Pulitzers in October 1889. Cashin, 270, cites the April 1890 date, and the *New York Times* carried a report on April 27, 1890, while Winnie was in Europe. Still, the news circulated some weeks before the latter date. In his biography of Jubal Early, *Old Jube* (Boyce, Va., 1955), Millard K. Bushong cites a letter to Early dated April 3, 1890, from another ex-general, L. L. Lomax, president of a Virginia college, urging Early to use his influence with the Davises to break off the engagement because the prospective groom was a Yankee (the letter is also part of the Early papers, vol. XIV, in the Library of Congress). Varina wrote Early on April 20, 1890, defending Wilkinson, which suggests she was replying to an Early letter following up on that of Lomax and possibly others. The brief account in the *Times* of April 27, dateline New Orleans, begins: "Inquiry among the relatives of the lady fully confirms the report of the approaching marriage of Miss Winnie Davis to Mr. Wilkinson of Syracuse. . . ." The "relatives" is most likely Varina, answering queries and hearing fire bells.

15 "My dearest . . ." Strode, *Letters*, 562–563. Strode says that Davis refused to let either of his daughters be apprised of the seriousness of his last illness.

15 Cashin, 271–272, is more specific than Strode, *JDTH*, 499–503, but both make clear what the reaction was. So does Early biographer Bushong, 303. Strode, however, says that Winnie felt a sense of guilt at bringing new trouble on her father, and that the reaction and his concerns over Winnie's health had made Davis ill. This again infers that the engagement leaked before her trip to Europe while Davis was alive. Varina's letters to Early, April 20 and 27, 1890, are in the Early Library of Congress collection.

16 "The South will secede . . ." remark is recalled by Mary Chesnut in May 1865, after the war has been lost, *MCCW*, 800.

16 "If—is the best you could do . . ." Ibid., 24.

16 Details on Robert Emmet are from the ever helpful *Funk & Wagnalls New Encyclopedia* (New York, 1975), vol. IX, 10–11. Information about Winnie's monograph regarding title and means of publication derives from the *Times* obituary and Cashin, 252.

17 Information is from Cashin, 274, and Strode, *JDTH*, 527–528, on Varina and Winnie at Beauvoir and in New York. Cashin puts Varina's pay at $1,200 a year;

Strode says $1,500. Generally, newspaper salary truth is on the side of a lower figure.

17 "a clear style . . ." *New York Times* obituary.

17 Winnie's name as an author—Varina Anne Jefferson Davis—is found in a biographical sketch on the Davis papers/Rice Website previously cited; Varina seemed to use the Jefferson Davis part of her name with and without a hyphen, according to Cashin, 276.

17 Winnie's letters to the Marquis de Ruvigny, November 3 and December 1, 1892, are from the collection at the Museum of the Confederacy, Richmond, Va.

17 "Miss Davis's health . . ." and "prominent gentleman of Mississippi" are from a report datelined Syracuse in *New York Times*, October 14, 1890. The reference to "Miss Winnie having severed . . ." is from a *Times* article of October 12, datelined Biloxi, Miss. Both articles followed an earlier *Times* story of October 7, from Syracuse, interviewing friends and relatives of Fred Wilkinson in an attempt to gain confirmation of a report from New Orleans of the broken engagement. Cashin, 271–273, also has an account that cites the same *Times* sources as well as those of the Onondaga Historical Association and others. Cashin also raises the suggestion of Rebel arson.

17 Cashin, 172, bears this startling news of Maggie Howell, citing letters of Varina and other documents, including the child's death certificate in 1942 at age seventy-five. Varina's other family, the Howells, appears to have been something of a burden.

18 Details of Winnie's death come from the *Times* obituary of September 19, 1898, and Cashin, 290–291. Of Varina's death, Cashin, 305–308, is also relied on. As this is written, Beauvoir is gradually recovering from Hurricane Katrina.

19 William Davis's *JDMHH*, 669–673, is the source for Jeff Jr.'s expulsion and later death—among thousands—during the 1878 yellow fever epidemic that swept the Mississippi Valley. Strode, *JDTH*, 435–437, has more detail. Life had begun to look up for young Jeff. He had a job at a bank and had fallen in love.

20 General Gordon's response is recorded in *New York Times*, October 1, 1898. Gordon at the time was also commander-in-chief of United Confederate Veterans and was replying to an inquiry after a Miss Lucy Hill alleged that her Southern friends had conferred the title upon her. Gordon based his case on the fact that Davis was the only Confederate president and that Winnie was his only daughter born in the Richmond White House. Even a Robert E. Lee daughter wouldn't qualify, Gordon determined. Confederate veterans in Virginia quickly agreed and adopted a resolution that retired the title with Winnie (*Times*, October 7, 1898). Details of the UDC's monument unveiling ceremony are thoroughly provided by the correspondent for the December 1899 *Confederate Veteran*, 532–533. Praises are sung for the Winnie monument, but with a bronze figure of Davis also unveiled the correspondent was not at all impressed.

20 Dr. Clarkson's contribution is also mentioned in the same *Confederate Veteran* article, but the ode is excerpted from a Civil War poetry website. The entire ode may be viewed at http://civilwarpoetry.org/confederate/postwar/winnie.html.

20 "The Lost Princess of the South" exhibit source is noted above. Queen of Comus is mentioned by Bell Wiley in *Confederate Women* (Westport, Conn., 1975), 136.

Chapter 2: The Conqueror's Son

22 "The city was full of . . . " William T. Sherman, *Memoirs of General W. T. Sherman* (New York, 1875/1885/1990), 214–215.

23 Sherman, ibid., 216–220. The numbers are Sherman's. Johnston, according to Thomas L. Connelly, in *Army of the Heartland* (Baton Rouge, La., 1967), 63, had an army of only 27,000 scattered between East Tennessee and Memphis when he took command in September 1861. John F. Marszalek, in *Sherman: A Soldier's Passion for Order* (New York, 1993), 158–159, notes that on September 27, 1861, Sherman was reporting that he had 4,000 men to hold off Buckner's 15,000, while Buckner was complaining of having only 6,000 to Sherman's 13,000 to 14,000.

23 *Sherman*, Memoirs, 221–223.

24 "Rumors and Reports . . ." Stanley P. Hirshson, *The White Tecumseh: A Biography of General William T. Sherman* (New York, 1997), 100, citing a Sherman letter of November 1, 1861, to Ellen Sherman.

24 Thomas's aborted East Tennessee invasion is succinctly summed up in Thomas B. Buell's *The Warrior Generals: Combat Leadership in the Civil War* (New York, 1997), 142–143. Sherman has other things on his mind in his *Memoirs*.

24 "Send Mrs. Sherman . . ." Letter of Captain Frederick Prime to Thomas Ewing, November 8, 1861, and cited by Hirshson, *TWT*, 101. Hirshson's frequent use of letters and quotes makes his biography of Sherman one of the most readable, as well as useful, in detailing the give-and-take between Sherman and his wife and children.

24 "Knowing insanity in the . . ." Ibid., 101, citing letter of November 10, 1861.

26 Ibid., 103–106, regarding the nefarious headline and reaction. It would not be the last time the *Cincinnati Commercial* stirred up trouble (see Chapters 6 and 7). James M. Merrill, in *William Tecumseh Sherman* (Chicago/New York, 1971), 191, notes that Ellen Sherman also accompanied her father on a visit to the White House, writing her husband: "The President is very friendly to you. . . . A little time will wear away this slander and then you stand higher than ever."

26 Hirshson, ibid., ix–x, 2, 72, 342, 389, documents letters within the Sherman family mentioning mental illness through the Hoyt connection.

27 "absolutely more Catholic than . . ." Ibid., 366. Sherman would make this observation about Ellen in a letter to John Cardinal McCloskey of New York, in trying to solicit the cardinal's help and convince Tom not to take holy orders.

27 "that I am sure . . ." Ibid., 5, and Lloyd Lewis, *Sherman: Fighting Prophet* (New York, 1932), 34. A Ewing brother-in-law of Sherman's would marry a Presbyterian minister's daughter and convert.

27 Lewis, *SFP*, 34. The baptism story is almost as essential to a Sherman biography as the march through Georgia.

28 "an eloquent Priest . . . " Hirshson, 56.

28 "I am anxious . . ." Ibid., 269, Ellen to Sherman, January 4, 1865.

28 "I will risk . . ." Ibid., 269, Sherman reply, January 15, 1865.

28 "I dont want you . . ." Ibid., 269, Sherman to Tom, January 21, 1865.

28 "Why can you . . ." Ibid., 268, Ellen to Sherman, December 30, 1864.

29 "She is too sweet . . ." Ibid., 129, Ellen to Sherman, June 12, 1862.

30 "Poor Dan McCook . . ." Ibid., 224, Ellen to Sherman, July 20, 1864.

30 The burning of the Catholic church in Jackson is from Hirshson, 154. Sherman blamed "mischievous soldiers." Hirshson goes to some lengths to defend Sherman in the burning of the Columbia convent, 284–286, whose mother superior—who had once taught Sherman's daughter Minnie in Ohio—had been given assurances of protection. The nun would later praise Sherman. Burke Davis, in *Sherman's March* (New York, 1980), 170, cites witnesses to the taunting behavior of drunken soldiers as the convent went up in flames. Davis, 166–167, and John G. Barrett, *Sherman's March Through the Carolinas* (Chapel Hill, N.C., 1956), 85, write of the assaults on women, citing witnesses including the novelist William Gilmore Simms. The drinking of whiskey from the chalice and more on the convent's burning is told by James Everett Kibler in *Our Father's Fields: A Southern Story* (Columbia, S.C., 1998), 310. Kibler's book is an excellent recounting of an upcountry plantation and the family that farmed it for two centuries, and parallels much of what occurred elsewhere in the South. The expulsion of families, including children, from their Georgia homes, as well as female workers from fabric mills, and the sending of them hundreds of miles north in boxcars is described by Hirshson, 212–226.

30 "The Christian soldier business . . ." Hirshson, 175–176.

31 "I proposed to come . . ." Ibid., 46, Sherman to Ellen, July 14, 1855.

31 Sherman, *Memoirs*, 370–375.

32 "You are now . . ." Hirshson, 166, undated.

33 "Mother's superstitions . . ." Ibid., 267–268, Ellen Sherman to an aunt, December 11, 1864.

33 "with Willy died . . ." Ibid., 268, Ellen to John Sherman, December 26, 1864.

33 "Oh, that Willy . . ." Ibid., 302, Sherman to Ellen, April 5, 1865. Merrill, *WTS*, 274, quotes a Sherman letter to Ellen where he says of Tom: "I may be mistaken but I don't think Tommy so entirely identifies himself with my fortunes. He is a fine manly boy and it may be as he doubtless will realize our fondest expectations, but I cannot but think that he takes less interest in me than Willy showed from the time of his birth. It may be I gave the latter more of my personal attention at the time when the mind began to develop."

33 "Poor Cump . . ." Hirshson, ibid., 323–324, Ellen to a cousin, December 16, 1865.

33 "It was Vicksburg . . ." Ibid., 330, Sherman to General Edward O. C. Ord, April 23, 1867.

33 The family dinner clash is related by Lloyd Lewis, 627.

34 Hirshson, 321. Merrill, 211, says Tom's corporal stripes were part of a uniform devised for the boy when he and Ellen visited Sherman in Memphis in late 1862. Six-year-old Tom would take his blanket over to the army camp every few nights and sleep in a tent with the soldiers.

35 Hirshson, 352–353. Sherman's move back to St. Louis in 1874 stemmed from army cuts promulgated by Congressman John A. Logan, one of the war's many political generals. Sherman felt it was beneath his dignity to stay in Washington. Noting that the cuts would reduce an army company to only forty-six men—the ideal strength was one hundred—Sherman complained to another congressman-general: "Make the usual allowance for 'sick,' 'in confinement,' 'extra duty,' &c,

and I ask any man how he would like to be posted in the Indian country with such a company."

35 "not satisfied that . . ." Ibid., 349, Sherman to Tom, March 29, 1872.

35 "I am sure . . ." Ibid., 362, letter of March 3, 1877.

36 "That Tom will remember . . ." Ibid., 363, letter of September 19, 1877. Sherman was usually unequivocal about Indians. In one of his "total war" statements to General Philip Sheridan, whose military district covered much of the area of hostile outbreaks, Sherman said: "Go ahead in your own way and I will back you with my whole authority. If it results in the utter annihilation of these Indians, it is but the result of what they have been warned again and again." The citation is Robert M. Utley's *Cavalier in Buckskin: George Armstrong Custer and the Western Military Frontier* (Norman, Okla., 1988), 61.

36 "the readiest and . . ." Lewis, 632.

36 "it is all hell . . .," "to be killed . . .," and "War is usually made . . ." Ibid., 635–636. Sherman's famed "war is hell" quote stems from a speech given in Columbus, Ohio, August 11, 1880, to five thousand Union veterans: "There is many a boy here today who looks on war as all glory, but, boys, it is all hell. You can bear this warning voice to generations yet to come. I look upon war with horror, but if it has to come I am here." Shortened, it soon spread, though Lewis writes that years later Sherman could not remember having said it at all.

37 "In justice to myself . . ." Hirshson, 364, Tom to Sherman, May 20, 1878.

37 "I have not dared . . ." Ibid., 364–365, Ellen to Sherman, May 25, 1878.

37 "I have warned . . ." Ibid., 365–366, Sherman to General Schofield, May 28, 1878.

37 "I tried coaxing . . ." Ibid., 366, Sherman to a friend, Samuel H. M. Byers, June 30, 1878.

38 "My father, as you know . . ." Lewis, 627–628. Marszalek, *SSPO*, 409, points out that Sherman—who frequently preached economies—had also come to view Tom as one day being the financial pillar of the family: "With Tom in financial command," Marszalek writes, "there would be no groveling for government pensions; there would be no breakup of the family and no children forced to accept the charity of neighbors and relatives, as Cump had been forced to do as a nine year old."

38 "I am forced . . ." Hirshson, 367, Sherman to a friend, Henry S. Turner, June 28, 1878.

38 "because Tom, dear fellow . . ." Merrill, 372–374, who also mentions Sherman's new will and that Ellen Sherman used her husband's spite toward Tom as another reason to live in Baltimore and not Washington, which she disliked.

38 "he was not in love . . ." Hirshson, 368, Samuel Bowman to Sherman, July 4, 1878.

38 Hirshson, 368–373, writes of the thawing of relations between father and son, but that Sherman would continue to brood.

38 "The General was seated . . ." Lewis, 645. Ellen was buried in St. Louis, beside Willy and the infant Charles.

39 "I can't get over . . ." Ibid., 628. Hirshson, 386, mentions Sherman avoiding Tom's ordination as a Jesuit priest.

40 Both the Hirshson, 387, and Lewis, 650–651, accounts provide details on Sherman's death and funeral. Although Tom sobbed when he saw Sherman in his casket, he read the funeral and graveside services clearly. Marszalek, 498, writes that when General Oliver Howard later asked Father Tom how he had avoided tears, the priest smiled and replied, "General, do you know what it is to obey orders?"

40 Edmund Wilson, *Patriotic Gore* (New York, 1962), 210.

40 "You know me . . ." Hirshson, 313, Ellen to Sherman, April 26, 1865. As Ellen had with her husband, Sherman had his marital crosses to bear.

42 "looked like nothing . . ." Wilson, *PG*, 212, citing the Reverend Durkin's *Father Tom* (New York, 1959). Several biographies of Sherman say little or nothing regarding Tom's struggle with mental illness during his priesthood. Hirshson's is by far the most forthright about the illness in the Sherman family.

42 "Socialism asks . . ." A review of Father Durkin's book by *Time* magazine, May 18, 1959, is the source.

42 "The man who shoots . . ." Ibid.; also Wilson, 212.

42 Wilson, 213–214, again from Durkin.

42 Ibid., 214–215, reprints some of the uproar regarding Tom's "march." See also *New York Times*, May 2, 1906.

42 "If Father Sherman . . ." Ibid., *NYT*. The same article carries the War Department explanation that the episode was actually a study trip.

43 "My connection with . . ." Ibid., May 7, 1906.

43 "Repeated confessions . . ." *Time*, May 18, 1959 (citing Durkin).

43 Wilson's vivid account of Tom Sherman's ordeal, from Durkin, is in *Patriotic Gore*, 211–218. Father Tom Clancy, S.J., in an article on a website, "Tale of a Jesuit Cemetery," www.companysj.com, records the priest's last years and burial.

Chapter 3: The General's Last Battle

45 "There was a Mr. Ralston . . ." Ulysses S. Grant, *Personal Memoirs of U.S. Grant* (New York, 1885/1990), 26–27. Among the *Memoirs'* literary admirers was Edmund Wilson, who would write that perhaps "never has a book so objective in form seemed so personal in every line, and though the tempo is never increased, the narrative, once we get into the war, seems to move with the increasing momentum that the soldier must have felt in the field." (*Patriotic Gore*, 143–144.)

45 Jack Hurst, *Men of Fire* (New York, 2007), 23, cites Grant's West Point jump record that stood for a quarter-century. Richard Goldhurst, *Many Are the Hearts* (New York, 1975), 36–43, provides other details, including the Sherman and Butler remarks. William S. McFeely, *Grant: A Biography* (New York, 1981), 16–17, discusses Grant's literary tastes and habits. Charles Lever, for instance, wrote of "exuberant young men traveling in Europe," and Grant liked the books so much he ordered more. He seems to have preferred to read books rather than talk about them.

46 Julia Dent's slave ownership and her possession of the maid Julia on her trips to visit her husband at his headquarters are mentioned by McFeely, *GAB*, 62.

46 "One of my superstitions . . ." Grant, *Memoirs*, 38.

46 Besides Longstreet, writes Goldhurst, *MAH*, 54–59, Grant's other groomsmen were Cadmus Marcellus Wilcox and Bernard Pratt, both of whom would also fight for the Confederacy. Goldhurst also records Grant's time with the Sons of Temperance as well as other prewar misadventures. Both the Goldhurst and McFeely books are eminently readable, Goldhurst on Grant's last days and McFeely as a thorough overview of Grant's life. Both, particularly McFeely's, make good use of the wealth of Grant material. This includes not only Grant's *Personal Memoirs* but, in McFeely's case, those of Julia, which weren't published until seventy-three years after her death. While the latter publication was not in time for Goldhurst's book, he draws from a variety of sources about the relationship between General Grant and Mark Twain that is most helpful here.

47 "the Vicar of . . ." McFeely, 48. Moses, in the Oliver Goldsmith novel, is the vicar's son who sells the family's colt at a fair and is cheated out of the money when sold a pair of worthless green spectacles.

47 Simon Bolivar Buckner, a true friend of Grant, still didn't trust him enough to give Grant the money outright but accompanied him back to his hotel to guarantee payment, writes Goldhurst, 59–60. McFeely, 48 and 56–66, writes further of these low points in Grant's life. Understandably, such events are given short shrift—if any at all—in the memoirs.

48 The Fort Donelson surrender account is from Hurst, *MOF*, 304–317. Grant's reply is from *Memoirs*, 208. Goldhurst, 148, mentions the cigars but says that Grant's doctors would later ascribe the cancer to a variety of causes, including the failure of Grant & Ward. The surrender figures of between 12,000 and 15,000 are based on what Buckner estimated to Grant (*Memoirs*, 212), and these numbers are what Grant passed along to Henry Halleck. Hurst puts the number at 16,500 to 17,500. Hurst writes that the disgruntled Buckner thought Grant "ungenerous and unchivalrous" in his response, but later—shortly before Buckner was put aboard a boat to a Northern prison—Grant took him aside and offered him money to while away his time. Buckner declined. Hurst, 389, also notes that Buckner would go on to a more satisfactory military career and, after the war, be governor of Kentucky, a vice-presidential nominee in 1896 for the National Democratic party ("Gold Democrats"), and editor of a Louisville newspaper where he thrashed his enemies with biting prose. Buckner would be the last surviving Confederate officer above the rank of brigadier general, dying in 1914. Buckner's son, by the same name, at Okinawa would be the highest-ranking American to be killed by enemy fire during World War II. He would become a full U.S. Army general posthumously. Of the Fort Donelson battle, a case could be made that the loss was the Confederacy's greatest setback.

49 "Full of only this idea . . ." Hirshson, *TWT*, 120.

49 The estimate of one in four soldiers at Shiloh being a casualty comes from Shelby Foote, *The Civil War: A Narrative* (New York, 1986), vol. I, 350, who also says it was the same at Waterloo.

50 McFeely, 232 and 236, and Goldhurst, 10, mention the gift houses. The Washington house came from a subscription drive led by the merchant king A. T. Stewart, later nominated by Grant for treasury secretary and quickly foiled by Senator Sumner.

50 Hirshson, *TWT*, 306–307, is the source for the Sherman-Johnston surrender controversy, as mentioned in Chapter 2 (see also Chapter 8), while McFeely, 228–229, notes Grant's adroitness in dealing with his friend Sherman and the vindictive Edwin Stanton. McFeely, 264–274, also provides details for the Grant–Andrew Johnson–Stanton tenure-of-office debacle.

51 "he evidently felt . . ." Richard S. West, Jr., *Gideon Welles* (New York, 1943), 332–333, citing *The Diary of Gideon Welles* (New York, 1911), vol. III, 261. A less flattering view of Johnson is presented by Brooks D. Simpson in *The Reconstruction Presidents* (Lawrence, Kans., 1998), 121–122, who writes that "Johnson duped several of his Cabinet officers and a good number of historians into believing that Grant had betrayed the president." Simpson maintains that Johnson was out to discredit Grant as a rival in the 1868 election.

51 Grant's sole vote cast for president—for James Buchanan in 1856—before his own election is pieced together from Calvin D. Linton, *The Bicentennial Almanac* (Nashville, Tenn., 1975), 198, who says that Grant had voted only once, and from McFeely, 64–69, who mentions the Buchanan vote. McFeely also writes of Grant being chided by brother Orvil in 1860 for voting for the Democrat Buchanan, but Grant explained it as having voted *against* Buchanan's opponent, the Republican John Charles Fremont.

51 McFeely, 224, writes of the Ford's Theatre invitation. For more, see Chapter 7. McFeely, 287, cites a *New York Times* report that Johnson did not attend Grant's swearing in because he thought Grant had snubbed him.

52 "I shall have no policy . . ." and "Let us have peace" Ibid., 277.

52 "The office has . . ." Linton, *TBA*, 198.

52 "the original occupants . . ." McFeely, 289.

52 "Whatever amount Congress . . ." The revealing nonrequest is taken from a sketch on the Credit Mobilier scandal written by Brian Trumbore and found on the website www.buyandhold.com. Grant's speech, in which it appears, delivered December 6, 1869, is no more tedious than similar presidential reports. It is more a list of suggestions for Congress and happily speaks of millions of dollars rather than trillions. The entire address is part of the presidential speech archive of the Miller Center of Public Affairs at the University of Virginia. It can be read at millercenter.org.

53 Grant's problem cabinet is discussed in McFeely, 291–294. The count of twenty-four changes in seven cabinet posts is Goldhurst's, 99.

53 Information to summarize the four major scandals denoted is mostly from Goldhurst, 94–99. McFeely, 329 and 415, raises questions of whether Julia Grant was a beneficiary of the gold and whiskey scandals but says no firm proof exists.

54 Linton, 209, cites the huge Republican loss of eighty-nine seats in the U.S. House of Representatives in 1874.

54 "All this time . . ." Hirshson, 358, citing Sherman letter to Admiral David D. Porter, March 15, 1876.

54 "Lee massed heavily . . ." Grant, 554–555.

55 Hurst, 392, makes the point of Grant not abandoning the freed slaves and that less racist times have shown more appreciation.

55 McFeeley, 300, writes of Cox's racism. On 375–379 he discusses James Webster Smith of South Carolina, a black youth who would be the first to integrate West

Point. McFeely faults Grant for not using the promotions list to force academy officers to better protect Smith from the conduct of other cadets.

55 Ibid., 367–373, regarding Amos Akerman. More on the Klan is in Chapter 6.

55 Information on the Santo Domingo annexation attempt is from McFeely, 300 and 337–352, and Grant, 778. Used as well is Brooks Simpson's contention, *TRP*, 145, that Grant saw the island as a place where blacks could retreat, and by their absence raise their value as workers in their former home.

56 C. Vann Woodward, *The Burden of Southern History* (Baton Rouge, La., 1960; New York, 1969), 71–78, notes abolitionist apprehensions and is used to summarize Republican election plans. A numerical comparison is that Alabama's voting age population in 1860 was 113,871 whites and 92,404 (nonvoting) blacks. Looking at numbers in 1867 and 1868, however, Woodward cites 61,295 registered whites to 104,518 blacks. Woodward adds that the number of disfranchised whites is unknowable. Eric Foner, in *Reconstruction: America's Unfinished Revolution 1863–1877* (New York, 1988), 291–324, contends that many Republicans couldn't reconcile disfranchisement of Rebel whites with their party's "democratic rhetoric" (for black voters), and that denials of the vote to certain whites was slight or nonexistent in Georgia, Florida, Texas, and the Carolinas. The standard was, however, recognized in more severe degrees in Alabama, Arkansas, Louisiana, Mississippi, and Virginia. While black turnout approached even 90 percent in these early elections to rewrite antebellum constitutions, apathy and protest by non-Republican whites would also contribute to the racial disparity in election numbers.

56 McFeely, 278–279, discusses the contradiction of black voter exclusion in the majority of states. Although blacks were registered to vote in Mississippi, Texas, and Virginia, the electoral vote of the three states was not counted because they had not yet been readmitted to the Union. William Gillette, *Retreat from Reconstruction, 1869–1879* (Baton Rouge, La., 1979), 22–38, writes of various ways recalcitrant states and towns discouraged black voting. Frankfort, Kentucky, for instance, made blacks wait all day and then closed the polls before they could vote.

57 "the most important . . ." Gillette, *RFR*, 22.

57 "He says he opposed . . ." Woodward, *BSH*, 82, citing Hamilton Fish diary entry of January 17, 1877.

57 "You take the Darkies . . ." McFeely, 358.

57 "was tired of the autumnal . . ." Ibid., 422. Gillette, 42, notes only a 34 percent conviction rate in election law violation cases between 1870 and 1877 in the South.

57 Grant's Indian policy is detailed by McFeely, 305–318. The Black Hills decision, 437–438, is further discussed in Chapter 11.

58 "inarticulate, uncertain . . ." Henry Adams, *The Education of Henry Adams* (Boston, 1918/New York, 1931), 297.

58 "the progress of evolution . . ." Ibid., 266.

58 "Of a nature kindly . . ." Richard Taylor, *Destruction and Reconstruction* (1879/Nashville, 1998), 274.

58 "ignorant of civil government . . ." Ibid., 264.

58 "Grant did not rise . . ." and the account of Theodore Bowers's death are in McFeely, 244–245, citing James Garfield's published diary and *New York Times* accounts.

58 "His imperturbability . . ." Ibid., 434.

59 McFeely, 413–435, has much to say about Orville Babcock and Orvil Grant. Babcock's job as a lighthouse inspector, unfortunately, caused his death by drowning off Florida in 1884. Probably no one was sorrier to see Grant leave the presidency than brother Orvil. George Armstrong Custer's congressional testimony in 1876 regarding War Secretary William Belknap and Orvil aroused presidential ire to the extent that Grant, as punishment, almost kept Custer from leading the fatal cavalry expedition to the Little Bighorn a few weeks later. See Chapter 11.

59 "so sacredly intimate . . ." Ibid., 299.

59 "is the millstone . . ." Ibid., 406.

59 "Grant's whole character . . ." Ibid., 495.

60 "I do not feel . . ." Hurst, 28. Goldhurst, 65, has a slightly different version.

60 Grant's encounter with a stranger in a rainstorm is told by Goldhurst, 202–203.

60 Grant also would write his father in the fall of 1861 that "My inclination is to whip the rebellion into submission, preserving all constitutional rights. If it cannot be whipped in any other way than through a war against slavery, let it come to that legitimately." (McFeely, 96.) On his world tour after his presidency, Grant would correct Germany's Prince Bismarck that the war was fought "Not only [to] save the Union, but destroy slavery." When Bismarck supposed that Union was still the "dominant sentiment," Grant expanded: "In the beginning, yes, but as soon as slavery fired upon the flag it was felt, we all felt, even those who did not object to slaves, that slavery must be destroyed." (McFeely, 470.) Of this exchange, Edmund Wilson, *PG*, 171, would observe that Grant is "quite unaware that, by putting the thing in this way, he has indicated that slavery, on the part of the Unionists, has at the last moment been recruited to justify their action in the struggle for power."

60 McFeely, 285, mentions an incident when Grant impressed a reporter by his calm and insightful solution regarding Mississippi River levees, but adds: "Frequently, as president, Grant demonstrated this same immediate firmness and good sense on confronting a situation, only to vacillate later and fail to uphold his own good first judgment." Richard Taylor writes of his similar experience in *D&R*, 269–270.

60 "History shows . . ." McFeely, 442. Of the intractable problems of Reconstruction, Brooks Simpson, 232, asks, "Who else could have done a better job, and how?"

61 Grant's travels are a summary of McFeely, 464–473, but should be read in full. Victor Hugo's complaint was that Grant had congratulated the Prussians in their recent and victorious war with France.

61 "How would it . . ." Ibid., 265.

61 The Grant cartoons, along with commentary, are from a collection of political art from 1879 to 1898 in Mary and Gordon Campbell's *The Pen, Not the Sword* (Nashville/London, 1970), 55–57. The era's cartoons were no less savage to nearly everyone else.

61 "General Grant was . . ." McFeely, 488.

61 Goldhurst, 4, 11–13 and 108, writes of the gifts to Grant and remarks by W. H. Vanderbilt and Jay Gould.

62 The summary of the Ferdinand Ward swindle is from Goldhurst, 8–20, and McFeely, 489–492. Ward served six and a half years in Sing Sing. Between December 19, 1909, and January 16, 1910, his five-installment recollection of Grant appeared in *New York Herald Magazine* and is available on www .granthomepage.com.

62 The peach incident is cited by Goldhurst, 141.

62 "I said I had . . ." Grant, 1111. The Library of America edition of the *Memoirs* also reprints Grant's notes to his doctor and provides much other useful information.

63 "For rich men . . ." McFeely, 492.

63 Goldhurst, 22–25, writes of the back-and-forth between Grant and Vanderbilt, and of Grant's dismissive attitude toward the dryness in his throat, 141–142. Goldhurst's account of Grant's last days is particularly compelling.

64 Grant's literary undertakings with *The Century* and Adam Badeau are taken from Goldhurst, 110–112. Later Badeau would sue over money he believed owed for work on the *Memoirs* and in 1888 would settle with Fred Grant for $11,253 (Goldhurst, 251). McFeely, 494, mentions Sherman's book.

64 The discussions of Grant's medical condition at this stage are from Goldhurst, 142–146, including the quote of Dr. G. F. Shrady that "General Grant is doomed."

65 Goldhurst writes, 127–131, of the literary discussions between Grant and Mark Twain that led to publication of the *Personal Memoirs*, as does Wilson, 131–132. Samuel Clemens's pen name Twain is the preferred reference here.

65 "My family is American . . ." Grant, 17.

65 The effects of the illness and Grant's method of writing the *Personal Memoirs* are from Goldhurst, 149–154. Fred Grant's presence during the Vicksburg campaign is mentioned by Grant in the *Memoirs*, 325. The irritable and envious Badeau, writes McFeely, 499, soon proved dispensible.

66 "At this stage . . ." Grant, 285–286.

66 The newspaper death watch, the appearance of the Reverend John Philip Newman, and Grant's baptism are related by Goldhurst, 180–192, as is the account of the challenge to the book's authorship, 194–196. Among those commenting on the dying Grant to newspapers was William Rosecrans, fired by Grant at Chattanooga during the war (see Chapter 10). "No man," said Rosecrans, a congressman after the war, "can think of General Grant's deathbed without feeling that the country is losing a great man—and a soldier, a gentleman with a heart."

68 "When I left camp . . ." Grant, *Memoirs*, 735.

69 "I fear the worst . . ." Goldhurst, 226.

69 Twain, says Wilson, 132, believed Grant's book might well rank as "the most remarkable work of its kind" since Caesar's *Commentaries*. Julia Grant's payment on Grant & Ward debts is mentioned by Goldhurst, 250. Goldhurst, 249, writes that Twain's printing company went under in 1894 after Twain sank all his money into a newfangled typesetting machine that never took off. Goldhurst observes that the machine's inventor took Twain much as Ferdinand Ward had taken Grant.

69 Grant's Tomb was dedicated April 27, 1897, the seventy-fifth anniversary of his birth.

69 Buckner, says Goldhurst, 225, told reporters afterward of Grant that when "I was poor, he borrowed $50 of me; when I was rich, he borrowed 15,000 men."

70 "General Grant is dying . . ." Ibid., 179–180.

Chapter 4: The Diarist

72 "the guess that . . ." W. J. Cash, *The Mind of the South* (New York, 1941), 14.

72 "by the recurrence . . ." Wilson, *Patriotic Gore*, 278.

72 "Of course, there are . . ." Cash, *MOS*, 19–20, citing Frederick Olmsted, whose newspaper articles on the South were gathered into a book, *The Cotton Kingdom*. Cash, 12–13, also quotes an 1853 book, *The Flush Times*, on the adaptation problems of the Virginia aristocrat to the cotton frontier. The antebellum South was hardly a rich-poor society, though. Another view of its class structure was given by Frank L. Owsley. In *Plain Folk of the Old South* (Baton Rouge, La., 1949), 7–8, he writes that "the core of the social structure was a massive body of plain folk who were neither rich nor very poor. These were employed in numerous occupations; but the great majority secured their food, clothing and shelter from some rural pursuit, chiefly farming and livestock grazing. It is the plain country folk . . . that great mass of several millions who were not part of the plantation economy. The group included the small slaveholding farmers; the nonslaveholders who owned the land which they cultivated; the numerous herdsmen on the frontier, pine barrens, and mountains; and those tenant farmers whose agricultural production, as recorded in the census, indicated thrift, energy, and self-respect."

74 "Tall, largely built . . ." Henry Adams, *The Education of Henry Adams*, 57–59.

74 Sarah Morgan, *The Civil War Diary of Sarah Morgan*, edited by Charles East (Athens, Ga., 1991; also *A Confederate Girl's Diary*, printed 1913), 5 and 43–47.

75 Muhlenfeld, *Mary Boykin Chesnut*, 12–42, provides details of these early years. The biography uses descendant sources and archival collections for its portrait of Mrs. Chesnut beyond her diaries, and is invaluable to any recounting of her life. William W. Freehling, *The Road to Disunion: Secessionists at Bay, 1776–1854* (New York, 1990), 220–221, offers an interesting look at the plantation society and economy in prewar South Carolina. Mark Urban's *Fusiliers: The Saga of a British Redcoat Regiment in the American Revolution* (New York, 2007) has an absorbing account of the Battle of Camden from the British point of view.

75 "Ah, dear girl . . ." Wiley, *Confederate Women*, 8, quoting Chesnut's letter of May 9, 1839.

76 C. Vann Woodward, *Mary Chesnut's Civil War*, xxxvi, provides details on Colonel Chesnut's property, human and otherwise. Also Muhlenfeld, *MBC*, 110.

76 "absolute a tyrant . . ." Woodward, *MCCW*, xxxv, quoting from the diaries.

76 Muhlenfeld, 43–63 and 129, on details of Mary's relations and prewar life at Mulberry.

76 "These people . . ." Woodward, *MCCW*, xxxv, diaries.

77 Further prewar details are found in Muhlenfeld, 59–73.

77 "very plain but nice . . ." Muhlenfeld, 69–70. The Buchanan story is on 68.
78 "I dare not . . ." Woodward, *MCCW*, 226.
78 Woodward, *MCCW*, xv–xxix, gives the definitive explanation of how the diary/journal was originally composed, and his own approach to the material. His revelations of how Mary Chesnut worked on her account of the war as late as twenty years afterward, attempting to write several novels in the interval, provoked criticism that the "diaries" were more fiction than fact. She did, however, keep diaries during the war—personal and frank diaries which she later cleaned up or fleshed out from the original account. These diaries, which cover the war's first year and its last months, were brought out by Woodward and Muhlenfeld in 1984 as *The Private Mary Chesnut: The Unpublished Civil War Diaries* (New York) and certainly legitimize the fuller insights composed later. While her works are popularly known as "diaries," being partly published in 1905 and reorganized in 1949, both under the title *A Diary from Dixie*, it was a designation that did not involve Mary Chesnut—she having died in 1886. It is more accurate to call her assembled efforts a memoir or autobiography written, if unconventionally, in diary form. It is also literature. She therefore should be suspected no more than anyone else of straying from the truth, and though that truth may be softened in parts, it remains sufficiently stark and agreeable with known fact as to maintain her memories as a valuable historical tool. An interesting essay that examines Woodward's and Muhlenfeld's work is "In Search of Mary Chesnut," by Drew Gilpin Faust in her *Southern Stories Slaveholders in Peace and War* (Columbia, Mo., 1992), 141–147.
79 "At first Mrs. Joe Johnston . . ." Woodward, *MCCW*, 136
79 "Like the patriarchs . . ." Ibid., 29.
79 "My wildest imagination . . ." Ibid., 170.
79 "I do not believe . . ." Ibid., 581.
79 "Halcott Green came . . ." Ibid., 413. Some historians, such as Peter Cozzens, *No Better Place to Die: The Battle of Stones River* (Urbana, Ill., 1990), 4, say this incident has been exaggerated. That many believed it hardly helps Bragg's reputation.
80 "General Lee had . . ." Ibid., 589.
81 "Mrs. Bartow . . ." Ibid., 802–803. The earlier, February raid on Camden is described by John G. Barrett, *Sherman's March Through the Carolinas*, 101–102. Of that short raid, "one local inhabitant observed, hair turned gray and bodies aged."
81 Details on Colonel Chesnut's fortunes—or misfortunes—are from Muhlenfeld, *MBC*, 128–132.
82 "We live miles . . ." Ibid., 132–133, from a letter of April 1866.
82 Details of upcountry life elsewhere are provided by James Everett Kibler, *Our Father's Fields A Southern Story*, 311–316. The Hardy Plantation in the Tyger Valley, of which Kibler is most interested, saw its cash value fall from $40,700 in 1860 to $6,300 in 1869, which did not include the value of the loss of its slaves. Its livestock numbers had also plunged, particularly swine which went from the hundreds to twenty and mostly were too small to butcher. Still, says Kibler, the Hardys were better off than most Carolina planters.
82 "Dear Sir. I will be . . ." Kibler, *OFF*, 316.

82 Stephen Budiansky, *The Bloody Shirt: Terror After Appomattox* (New York, 2008), 110–145, writes extensively of Klan terror in York County and the efforts of Seventh Cavalry Major Lewis Merrill—who would later escape the Custer massacre—to bring the Klan to heel. Francis Butler Simkins and Robert Hilliard Woody, *South Carolina During Reconstruction* (Chapel Hill, N.C., 1932/1966), 458–464, mention James Chesnut's testimony and provide further details on the Klan crackdown. Some five hundred people would be indicted. Of these, five would be convicted (by mostly black juries) and another fifty would plead guilty.

83 Information on James Chesnut's life after the war are summaries from Muhlenfeld, 119–196. Simkins and Woody, *SCDR*, 423, credit Chesnut with also supporting black schools, having "established one on his estate and that what he did was not an unusual occurrence"—though the practice may have been as much to keep the hired black laborers satisfied.

83 "Oh! Peace . . ." Muhlenfeld, 196, and Woodward, *MCCW*, 335.

83 Muhlenfeld, 138–141, regarding household details and Sarsfield.

83 Woodward, *MCCW*, xlii, regarding the sale and relocation of Stuart's Washington portrait.

83 Muhlenfeld, 114–221, has details of Chesnut finances, Mary's health and family deaths, and sightings in Camden.

84 Thomas Dabney's heroic labors were recalled in *Memorials of a Southern Planter* (1887) written by his daughter, Susan Dabney Smedes, and excerpted in *The American Scene: 1860 to the Present*, edited by William J. Chute (New York, 1966), 27–33.

85 "I feel lonely . . ." Wiley, *CW*, 76–77.

85 Don H. Doyle's article "Leadership and Decline in Postwar Charleston, 1865–1910," looks at the Old Guard's grip on the city and such things as the importance of an invitation to the ultra-exclusive ball given by the locally ancient St. Cecilia Society. Among U.S. cities, he writes, Charleston had slipped from sixth in 1830 to twenty-sixth in 1870, on its way to ninety-first by 1910. The article is in *From the Old South to the New: Essays on the Transitional South*, edited by Walter J. Fraser, Jr., and Winfred B. Moore, Jr. (Westport, Conn., 1981), 93–106. Sarah Morgan's postwar life is recounted in the introduction of her diary, previously cited, xxxiv–xli.

85 Much on Mary Chesnut's novels and the preparation of her journal is found in Muhlenfeld's "textual introduction" to *Two Novels by Mary Chesnut* (Charlottesville, Va., 2002), one in the series of publications of the Southern Texts Society, xxi–xxxv, and in Woodward's introduction, *MCCW*, xv–xxix.

87 "How I wish . . ." Woodward, *MCCW*, xxiv.

87 "if published just now . . ." Ibid., xxii.

87 "If so, it . . ." Muhlenfeld, *MBC*, 159.

88 "The sanest . . ." Woodward, *MCCW*, 61.

88 "I have been interrupted . . ." Muhlenfeld, *MBC*, 195.

88 Ibid., 205–207, on the publication of "The Arrest of a Spy."

89 "I have been so ill . . ." Ibid., 217, citing a February 2, 1886, letter to a nephew's wife.

89 Details on James Chesnut's estate left to Mary and her own financial condition are from Muhlenfeld, 210–212.

89 "one by one . . ." Ibid., 212.
90 "I am awfully . . ." Ibid., 213.
90 Muhlenfeld, 223, quotes from Louly's memoir, *A Southern Girl in '61.*
90 "Childless, property-less . . ." *A Belle of the Fifties: Memoirs of Mrs. Clay of Alabama,*
   Put into Narrative Form by Ada Sterling (New York 1905/1969), 50.

Chapter 5: The Crippled Knight

92 John Bell Hood's plan is generalized here, and some scholars hardly credit it
   as a plan at all. Richard M. McMurry, *John Bell Hood and the War for South-*
   ern Independence (Lexington, Ky., 1982), 167, notes the post-Atlanta campaign's
   "poor preparation, lack of attention to logistics, and poor reconnaissance. . . .
   Hood was confused and bewildered. He was led on by the unrealistic dream of
   reaching Kentucky. Equally saddening was his desire to go back to Virginia—to
   return to Lee." Details of the war council are drawn from Thomas Connelly,
   Autumn of Glory: The Army of Tennessee, 1862–1865 (Baton Rouge, La., 1971),
   503; Wiley Sword, *The Confederacy's Last Hurrah: Spring Hill, Franklin, & Nash-*
   ville (Lawrence, Kans., 1992), 179; and Craig L. Symonds, *Stonewall of the West:*
   Patrick Cleburne and the Civil War (Lawrence, Kans., 1997), 255. Sword, 269, says
   approximately 22,000 federal infantry actually engaged in the battle.
93 Connelly, *AOG*, 506–507, provides the numbers for Hood's army at Franklin and
   how its 1,750 battle deaths exceeded Union losses in some of the war's bloodiest battles. He also writes of Hood congratulating the army on its "victory." An
   Internet search for the death toll among the several Confederate divisions in
   "Pickett's Charge" finds a range from a little more than 1,100 to 1,500. McMurry,
   JBH, 176, writes of the dead piled seven deep at Franklin. Carnton, restored, is
   open for tourists. Bloodstains from the amputations are still visible on its floor.
93 "if we are . . ." Symonds, *SOW*, 255. Cleburne's famous response was made to
   General Daniel Govan, who had remarked, "Well, General, there will not be
   many of us that get back to Arkansas."
93 "sickening, blood-curdling . . ." Winston Groom, *Shrouds of Glory from Atlanta to*
   Nashville: The Last Great Campaign of the Civil War (New York, 1995), 220, quot-
   . ing Captain Robert Banks.
93 Besides Hood, Lee, and Joseph Johnston, the other full generals were P. G. T.
   Beauregard, Braxton Bragg, Samuel Cooper, Albert Sidney Johnston (killed at
   Shiloh), and Kirby Smith.
93 John P. Dyer, *The Gallant Hood* (New York, 1950), 20, 23–25, and McMurry,
   6–11, give details of Hood's early life and West Point days. While cadet lives'
   were regimented and harried, some still managed to slip off campus for a drink
   or to steal chickens for a feast in their rooms; sometimes prostitutes were also
   smuggled into the barracks.
94 Mary Chesnut's "transparent" remark is from Sword, *CLH*, 434. Her remark
   on flattery is in Woodward, *Mary Chesnut's Civil War*, 519, i.e., that whoever
   Hood told his compliment to could then pass it on. "Man and wife are too
   much one person to receive a compliment straight in the face that way—that is,
   gracefully."

94 Private Sam R. Watkins, *'Co. Aytch': A Side Show of the Big Show* (Nashville, 1882), 169, noted the reaction of the Army of Tennessee to Hood's ascension, saying that upon hearing the news five men who were pickets along the Chattahoochee River threw down their guns and in "ten minutes they were across the river, and no doubt had taken the oath of allegiance to the United States government."

96 McMurry, 191, cites 1864 newspaper references to Hood as having "knightly virtues" and being a "chivalrous soldier." Upon Hood's death in 1879, a Kentucky newspaper would call him a "man born and bred to be a soldier" and nothing else, and that in the "days of chivalry he would have made as courageous, gallant a knight as ever couched a lance."

96 "A braver man . . ." Harold B. Simpson, in a profile of Hood in *Ten Texans in Gray* (Hillsboro, Tex., 1968), 66–67, and attributed to Louly Wigfall's book, *A Southern Girl in '61*.

97 "But then, there seemed . . ." Woodward, *MCCW*, 430–431. The diary account is drawn on heavily between 430–825 for details of this actual thwarted romance.

97 Emory M. Thomas, *The Confederate State of Richmond: A Biography of the Capital* (Austin, Tex., 1971), 152, quotes from the *Whig*.

98 "Now, Buck! . . ." Woodward, *MCCW*, 555.

98 "Heavens, what a . . ." Ibid., 561–562.

98 "Look here . . ." Ibid., 562.

98 "Parents' ways . . ." Ibid., 567.

99 "Maggie said . . ." Ibid., 568.

99 Ibid., 579, regarding Hood's thirty-page letter to Buck, entry dated March 5, 1864.

99 "Things are so bad . . . " Ibid., 622. The convent Buck mentions probably was that of the Ursuline sisters in Columbia, which Sherman's soldiers would later burn along with its school. Burke Davis, *Sherman's March* (New York, 1980), 177, writes that after the fire nuns and schoolgirls would find sanctuary in the Prestons' vacated house. Used as headquarters by General John Logan, the nuns' arrival interrupted soldiers as they prepared to torch the house. The stately home, he writes, "was little worse for wear—though Sherman's soldiers had mutilated some fine paintings and statuary, adding mustaches to portraits and clothing to nude figures." A bust of Buck, shown in a photo in *MCCW*, also suffered mutilation.

99 McMurry, 183, says Hood's immediate superior, P. G. T. Beauregard, secured authorization in January 1865 to remove Hood and replace him with Richard Taylor.

100 "that agony in . . ." Woodward, *MCCW*, 708.

100 "The Hood melodrama . . ." Ibid., 769.

100 "I think it began . . ." Ibid., 804–805.

101 Mary, 588, mentions the Lowndes-Hood tailor incident. Muhlenfeld, *MBC*, 135, is the source for the Prestons in Paris and John Preston's seeking repayment from James Chesnut.

101 "with calm, sad eyes . . ." McMurry, 192.

101 "Buck, my poor . . ." Woodward, *MCCW*, 813.

102 Wilson, *Patriotic Gore*, 446.

102 Dyer, *TGH*, writes of the Rawlins Lowndes' challenge, 279; Groom, *SOG*, 289, mentions the Lowndes family money in England at the beginning of the war.

102 Details of James Morgan's postwar life are from Robert Carse's *Blockade: The Civil War at Sea* (New York, 1958), 245–246.

103 Dyer, 309–310, and McMurry, 192–193, on Hood's return to Texas and departure.

103 Dyer, 311–312, on the Kentucky loan, move to New Orleans and the cotton business, and the Texas fund-raiser for Hood.

104 ". . . as commission . . ." McMurry, 194.

104 *New York Times*, May 19, 21, and 26, 1866, on floods and the year's Southern cotton crop. McMurry, 194, also comments on the treacheries of the cotton business during this period.

104 McMurry, 194, says that by 1870 the New Orleans *City Directory* listed Hood as head of his insurance company as well as a commission merchant, but there was no such listing for the cotton firm.

105 Dyer, 313–314, writes of the reaction to Longstreet's stance on Reconstruction. He also mentions, 158, that after the battle at Fredericksburg, Virginia, Longstreet almost censured Hood for failing to act but thought better of it because Hood was "high in favor with the authorities." Budiansky, *The Bloody Shirt*, 152–155, has a fuller version, and quotes are also excerpted from that account. Budiansky is also the source for Longstreet's job from his old friend Grant. McFeely, *Grant*, 363 and 417, mentions the Port of New Orleans family connection.

106 McMurry, 117–122, writes of Jefferson Davis's decision to replace General Joseph Johnston, whose army had retreated across the Chattahoochee River outside Atlanta in July 1864. Davis had sent Braxton Bragg, his military adviser and former army commander, to size up the situation, and during this visit Hood had given Bragg a letter. McMurry writes: "No motive other than ambition can be ascribed to the writing of this letter. While Hood accurately depicted the results of the [Georgia] campaign and the number of casualties, he was lying when he wrote that he had constantly urged battle and that his views . . . were 'so directly opposite' those of 'officers high in rank' in the army." The letter by Hood also falsely implicates William Hardee. Keith S. Bohannon, writing on Hood in Gary Gallagher and Joseph Glatthaar's *Leaders of the Lost Cause: New Perspectives on the Confederate High Command* (Mechanicsville, Pa., 2004), 268, adds that "most recent historians of the Atlanta campaign agree that Hood's July 14 letter was a bid to replace Johnston as commander of the Army of Tennessee."

106 Hood's efforts for the disabled and his appearances before veterans' groups is from McMurry, 197.

107 "Thomas is a grand . . ." Benson Bobrick, *Master of War: The Life of General George H. Thomas* (New York, 2009), 321.

107 Symonds, *SOW*, 262, writes of Sue Tarleton's short life. Sword, 440, relates Frank Cheatham's aversion to the Franklin battlefield. Watkins's assessment is in *Co. Aytch*, 226.

108 "The war is over . . ." McMurry, 196.

108 Ibid., 196, on the additional Stephen Lee–Hood exchange.

108 Details on Hood and Anna Marie Hennen are from Dyer, 314–315 and 363 (who refers to her as Anna Maria); McMurry, 195 (who calls her Anna on second reference); *Confederate Veteran*, March 1912, which bemoans that Hood and his wife have only a small stone to mark their New Orleans graves (and where her name is inscribed as Marie Hennon Hood); and *New York Times*, August 31, 1879, Hood obituary, which seems to settle the matter of the Hennen family name spelling but unfortunately sheds no light on what Mrs. Hood's friends and relatives called her. I have avoided the safety of "Mrs. Hood" and presume that someone dictated the preferred names (if not the spellings) to the gravestone chiseler.

108 Muhlenfeld, *MBC*, 186, mentions the daybook entry on Hood's death. Sword, *CLH*, 437, provides the wedding date for Buck. A Lowndes family website lists Buck's death date as December 15, 1880.

109 Dyer, 315, mentions the Hood children "brigade."

110 The Sherman visits are recounted by Hirshson in *The White Tecumseh*, 355 and 448*n*.

110 Dyer, 316–317 and 364, and John Steele Gordon, "Born in Iniquity," *American Heritage Magazine*, February/March 1994, write entertainingly of the Louisiana Lottery. Gordon estimates that presiding Generals Early and Beauregard made $10,000 a year each to show up; Dyer takes the estimate up to $30,000 each. In his essay on Beauregard in *Leaders of the Lost Cause*, 66, Charles P. Roland says the lottery was also instrumental in the overthrow of Louisiana's Reconstruction government in 1877 by helping to buy off Republicans. Wade Hampton, he writes, was first choice over Early, but then was elected South Carolina governor and so declined. Charles C. Osborne, *Jubal: The Life and Times of General Jubal A. Early, C.S.A.* (Chapel Hill, N.C., 1992), 424–425, also writes of the lottery and notes how "the white-maned Beauregard, regal in black, put one witness [to the drawing] in mind of a French generalissimo in the manner of Napoleon, reviewing his battalions on some Gallic plain."

110 Hood's speech before the annual meeting of South Carolina's Survivors Association, December 12, 1875, is reproduced on a website, www.johnbellhood. org. Symonds, *SOW*, has details on Cleburne's proposal to emancipate slaves in exchange for military service, 182–195. Symonds also notes that Bragg, now Davis's military adviser, called Cleburne and a handful of officers who supported him "agitators, and should be watched." Cleburne was one of the host of Confederate officers who had run afoul of the inept Bragg during his own tenure as an army commander.

111 McMurry, 197–201, writes of the Johnston and Sherman books and Hood's response.

111 "About that time . . ." Cleburne's alleged statement is from Hood's posthumously published *Advance and Retreat* (Secaucus, N.J., 1985), 293–294.

112 "The American Experience," PBS, has an internet account of the yellow fever outbreak at www.pbs.org, from which general information on its spread and toll is used. Nathaniel Cheairs Hughes and Roy P. Stonesifer, Jr., *The Life and Wars of Gideon J. Pillow* (Chapel Hill, N.C., 1993), 321, provide details on Pillow's inglorious end. William C. Davis, *JDMHH*, 673, mentions Jeff Jr.'s death.

113 Dyer, 317–318, writes of the impact on Hood's fortunes and the fatal summer of 1879. McMurry, 201–202, discusses Hood's attempted sale of his papers, which even Sherman was helpless to bring about, and quotes from Hood's speech before

Louisiana veterans. A consideration is that, as most of the Louisiana units in the Army of Tennessee were in Stephen Lee's trailing corps, which missed most of the bloodbath at Franklin and the final Union assault at Nashville, Hood may have felt more comfortable before his audience than had they been from those states and units with higher casualties.

114 *New York Times* obituary, ibid.; Dyer 318–319 and 211; and W. C. Nunn, *Ten Texans in Gray*, 71, provide information on Hood's last months. According to Hood's memoirs, 65, Dr. Richardson was also president of the Medical Association of the United States during this period, 1878–1879. Still, Hood didn't take his advice.

114 Dyer, 319, 364–368; Dyer lists the children as well as their adoptive parents.

115 "With maidenly modesty . . ." *Confederate Veteran*, October 1898.

115 "To mere slander . . ." *Southern Historical Society Papers*, vol. XXXII, 151–156.

116 McMurry, 199, comments on the quality of Hood's reportage. The Lowndes Family Genealogy website provides further details on Buck and Rawlins. Muhlenfeld, 186, provides the year of death for Dr. Darby.

Chapter 6: That Devil Forrest

117 "A man I've never . . ." Brian Steel Wills, *A Battle from the Start: The Life of Nathan Bedford Forrest* (New York, 1992), 1. Jack Hurst, *Nathan Bedford Forrest: A Biography* (New York, 1993), 383, mentions Joseph Johnston.

117 Hurst, 360, has the Forrest-Sherman exchange.

117 James R. Chalmers, *Southern Historical Society Papers*, vol. VII, October 1879, refers to "winged infantry."

118 "That devil Forrest was down about Johnsonville [Tennessee], making havoc among the gunboats," complained a frustrated Sherman to Grant in 1864, after Forrest's land-based cavalry captured a gunboat and later shelled the town. Andrew Nelson Lytle, *Bedford Forrest and His Critter Company* (copyright 1931, 1984/Nashville 1992), 351, has an exciting account.

118 Hurst, 262, cites Forrest's claim of dead horses and enemy, which came in an interview with a Northern writer just after Forrest's surrender.

118 "a battle from . . ." Wills, *BFS*, 377, is Forrest's own description of his life shortly before his death.

118 Wills, 13–14, and Hurst, 21, write of the panther incident. Wills, 22, also writes of the young Forrest's gunfight and, 25–26, of his courting and marriage. Wills, 42, cites Forrest's testimony to Congress in 1871 that before the war he had been worth "a million and a half dollars." Other early biographical details are from Robert Selph Henry, *First with the Most—Gen. Nathan Bedford Forrest* (Indianapolis, 1944/New York, 1991), 22–27.

118 "I doubt if any man . . ." Taylor, *Destruction and Reconstruction*, 205.

118 Hirshson, *The White Tecumseh*, 123, quotes Sherman: "I am sure that had he [Forrest] not emptied his pistols as he passed the skirmish line, my career would have ended right there."

118 "He was restrained by no . . ." Chalmers, *SHSP*, October 1879.

119 "General Forrest, as a . . ." and "Whenever I met . . ." Robert Selph Henry, ed., *As They Saw Forrest* (Jackson, Tenn., 1956), 271–272.

119 "Git thar fustest . . ." Wills, 1.

119 "Charge them both . . ." Ibid., 95.

119 "I never see a . . ." Hurst, *NBF*, 27.

119 "I told you twist . . ." Henry, *ATSF*, 286n.

119 "I had a small brush . . ." Ibid., 287–288.

120 "If you're a better . . ." Wills, 290.

120 "You have threatened . . ." Lytle, *BFCC*, 238, and Hurst, 140, are among the accounts of Forrest's dressing down of Bragg, as recollected by J. B. Cowan, a military surgeon and Forrest relation who may have been taken along as a witness.

120 Wills, 122–127, writes of the stabbing incident. Hurst, 7, has Forrest's physical specifications, calling him "almost gigantic by the standards of the times."

120 Chalmers, *SHSP*, October 1879.

120 Lytle, 164–165, has the unfortunate scout story.

121 "The dog's dead . . ." Wills, 145. Wills, 170–171, writes that even Chalmers ran afoul of Forrest in March 1864, after complaining that Forrest "took my only tent from me and gave it to his brother"—several of whom served with Forrest. Forrest relieved Chalmers, but Richmond quickly reinstated him. Wills suggests that the more veteran Chalmers resented being placed under Forrest after he and Forrest had previously cooperated as equals.

122 Hurst, 26 and 33–65, has a thorough account of Forrest's slave dealings and adventures in Memphis politics.

122 "kind to his . . ." Ibid., 38.

122 Wills, 33, writes that contrary to the myth of the slave trader as a pariah, many were "citizens of standing, like almost any other successful businessman. . . ."

122 The account here of Fort Pillow is drawn from those in Henry, *FWM*, 248–268; Wills, 172–196; and Hurst, 158–196. "The poor deluded negroes" quotation is from a letter by Sergeant Achilles V. Clark to his sisters and cited by Wills, 193. Wills, 334 and 339, mentions Forrest's offer to Andrew Johnson to waive immunity, and Hurst, 283–284, reprints a large part of the 1866 letter in which Forrest defends himself and promises to promote "a spirit of moderation and accommodation." Shelby Foote, *The Civil War: A Narrative*, vol. III, 111, notes the high Union death toll of 40 percent. Wills, 196, cites a study that places garrison deaths even higher, at 47 to 49 percent.

125 Hurst, 180, writes of the politics behind the congressional investigation. Henry, 248, brings up the labeling of Fort Pillow as the "atrocity" of the war and cites Laura A. White's "Atrocity Charges of the Civil War" from *The World Tomorrow* in 1929.

125 Hurst, 262, quotes from Forrest's interview by Northern writer Bryan McAlister, four days after Forrest's surrender, where Fort Pillow was discussed.

125 "promiscuous shooting . . ." Nathaniel Cheairs Hughes, Jr., with Connie Walton Moretti and James Michael Browne, *Brigadier General Tyree H. Bell, C.S.A.: Forrest's Fighting Lieutenant* (Knoxville, Tenn., 2004), 126.

126 "drunken condition . . ." Hughes, *BGTB*, 129, which also quotes General James Chalmers, who would serve two terms in Congress from Mississippi, as boasting that the Rebels "taught the mongrel garrison of blacks and renegades a lesson long to be remembered."

126 "the hero of the . . ." Hurst, 302.

126 "Where's that damned . . ." Ibid., 300.

126 "Yes, madam . . ." Ibid., 302.

127 Lawrence, Kansas, was sacked by Quantrill's band, who killed 150 of the inhabitants. Foote, *TCW*, vol. I, 563, writes of the sacking and rape of Athens, Alabama, as a reward to his men by Colonel John Basil Turchin—formerly Ivan Vasilevich Turchininov. A marker on the city's courthouse square keeps memory alive but is silent about rape. An account of a "Northern correspondent" who called Athens "an everlasting disgrace, that can never be wiped from the pages of history," is mentioned in *Southern Historical Society Papers*, vol. XIV, 1886, 210. Turchin, afterward, was cashiered by a court-martial but almost as quickly was promoted to brigadier general by Lincoln. Hurst, 414*n*, and *Confederate Veteran*, vol. XXIII, October 1915, mention the killing of surrendering whites by black soldiers at Fort Blakely, Alabama, though it was nothing on the scale of Fort Pillow. Hurst writes of an 1864 letter by black chaplain Henry M. Turner to the editor of the *Christian Recorder*, "complaining about black atrocities, which were understandably numerous in the face of the official Confederate policy of refusing to treat black soldiers as prisoners of war." Hurst, 382, also offers the view that Fort Pillow "was neither the Civil War's first nor its last large-scale racial atrocity; but it was the only one studied by Congress. . . ." James I. Robertson, Jr., *Tenting Tonight: The Soldier's Life* (Alexandria, Va., 1984), 135, has numbers on deaths among prisoners of war of both sides. Watkins, *Co. Aytch*, 223, relates the harrowing story of escaping with his life when Union soldiers shot two surrendering Rebels at Nashville late in the war. More information is found in Stephen V. Ash's *Middle Tennessee Society Transformed, 1860–1870: War and Peace in the Upper South* (Baton Rouge, La., 1988), 150–156, which details guerrilla activities in mostly occupied Middle Tennessee and the worsening conditions and growing civil resistance as the war continued. Guerrilla families and neighborhood aristocracy were often the retaliatory targets of Union forces. According to Hughes, 85, the pre–Fort Pillow atmosphere in West Tennessee was further poisoned when "the guerrillas and desperados [were] joined by a number of paroled soldiers, angry, despondent human wreckage from the Vicksburg debacle. It was a time of revenge and reprisal."

127 "I went into the . . ." Hurst, 342.

127 Wills, 320–323, and Hurst, 265, write of this period of Forrest's return home.

127 "I carried seven Federal . . ." Wills, 321.

128 "I have Setled . . ." Ibid., 323.

128 Ibid., 325–330, on the killing of Thomas Edwards and Forrest's arrest and trial.

128 Ibid., 339–343, on Forrest's business dealings in 1867.

128 Henry, 452–453, tells of Forrest's plan to conquer Mexico.

129 Details of Forrest's railroad career are from Hurst, 323 and 348–356.

129 Hurst, 360 and 368, says that the last house for Forrest and his wife was "'a small but comfortable old-fashioned double log house, improvised from two cabins.' Thus they finally came to occupy a house reminiscent of the one in which they set up housekeeping in Hernando in 1845, except that this one evidently had no clapboards covering the logs." *Southern Historical Society Papers* (attributing the 1894 *Brooklyn Eagle* and Richmond, Va., *Times*), vol. XXII, 65, mentions other

Confederates of high standing who were impoverished by and after the war, including Admiral Raphael Semmes and Inspector and Adjutant General Samuel Cooper. General Thomas Benton Smith, with whom Forrest discussed his Mexican adventure, had suffered brain damage from being struck by a Union officer's sword after surrendering at Nashville in 1864, and would die insane many years later.

129 Dates vary for the Klan's beginnings, though the site's plaque gave December 24, 1865. Information from Henry, *FWM*, 443, and Hurst, 278, is used.

130 "four years of measuring . . ." Cash, *The Mind of the South*, 104.

131 "I had twice been . . ." George F. Kennan, *Memoirs, 1925–1950* (Boston, 1967), 428–429.

131 Wills, 331, writes of the various racial clashes. Hurst, 277, describes Brownlow's actions. Henry, *FWM*, 443, is one of several sources for the Klan's big meeting and the likelihood of Forrest becoming Grand Wizard. Henry, 444, also says that while Forrest never publicly admitted his role, Major James R. Crowe of Sheffield, Alabama, who was one of the original six Klan members in Pulaski, would say in a letter published posthumously in 1914: "After the order grew to large numbers we found it necessary to have someone of large experience to command. We chose General N. B. Forrest." Doubts seem to be few that he wasn't Grand Wizard, even if years later, according to Wills, 336, the widow of another Tennessee Confederate general, George W. Gordon, would claim the dubious honor for her own spouse.

132 "The man and . . ." William C. Davis, *Jefferson Davis*, 307.

132 "entrusted with proper . . ." Hurst, 361.

133 Wills, 365, notes the extent of Congress's investigation of the Klan by 1871.

133 Henry, *FWM*, 441, is the source for the Francis Blair quote. Hurst, 280–281, has more on Forrest and Blair. Wills, 347, writes of the 1868 Democratic party convention and of the belated arrival, in July 1868, of Forrest's presidential pardon from Johnson.

134 Hurst, 302–312, has a compelling account of the Klan, particularly in Tennessee, during these times.

134 Ibid., 312–315, on Forrest's newspaper interview. Also relied on is that copy contained in *Fortieth Congress–House of Representatives, Executive Document No. 1, Report of the Secretary of War*, chapter X, 193.

135 Henry, *FWM*, 444–448, and Hurst, 339–344, have interesting accounts of Forrest before the congressional committee. McFeely, *Grant*, 368, relates some of the background leading up to the congressional investigation.

136 Hurst, 324–327, writes of this post-1868 election period in Tennessee and the gradual decline of the Klan, for which there was no need after Democrats regained state power. Hurst cites several Klansmen recalling years later that disbandment in Tennessee was ordered during this time, but that it might have come as late as 1870. Disbandment would presume Forrest's resignation. Gillette, *Retreat from Reconstruction, 1869–1879*, 41, discusses some of the steps taken by states to control or negate black voter gains.

137 "the white race . . ." Hurst, 327.

137 Hurst, 329, also comments that after 1868 the Klan's operations tended to be more scattered but more savage.

Notes for pages 138–144 : *303*

138 Hurst, 359, cites a Memphis woman, Mrs. J. M. Farrington, as recalling how Forrest would help his wife set the table and pitch in with the family washing, and that his "spoken English was very correct—not at all like his written English."

138 Ibid., 330–333, on Forrest's efforts for his railroad. At the Alabama barbecue, near Gadsden in 1869, Forrest told the Yankees it was "the proudest hour in my life, when I can stand here and extend the right hand of fellowship to these men from the North."

138 "striven as hard . . ." Ibid., 331.

138 "was just as ungovernable . . ." Wills, 370.

138 Hurst, 346–347, mentions Forrest's two narrowly averted duels. Perhaps not surprisingly, Forrest's last warhorse, King Phillip, was equally irascible. According to Hurst, 266–267, when a party of Union soldiers rode up to Forrest's plantation shortly after the war, the horse took offense at their blue uniforms and tried to bite them. Lytle, 387–388, adds that on another occasion, when hitched to a buggy in Memphis, King Phillip charged a squad of blue-clad police.

139 "Sir, your sermon . . ." Hurst, 370.

139 "Why, General . . ." Wills, 371.

139 "I came here . . ." Hurst, 366–367, quoting from an account in the Memphis *Appeal*, July 6, 1875. Hurst, 366, also writes of Forrest's precautions with black barbers.

139 Forrest's postwar health problems are discussed by Wills, 372–377.

140 "pale, thin face . . ." Hurst, 377.

140 "My life has been . . ." Wills, 377–378. Hurst, 387, has death dates for Forrest's wife and son, and other details on descendants.

141 Lytle, 389–390, relates this belated admission by Jefferson Davis. Hurst, 381–382, categorizes the *Times* obituary as "understatedly scathing."

141 Author's communication with William and Nedra Trebing of Pulaski, Tenn., 2008, on the status of the Klan birthplace and commemorative plaque.

Chapter 7: The Mad Woman

142 McFeely, *Grant*, 211–212, 224; Jean H. Baker, *Mary Todd Lincoln: A Biography* (New York, 1987), 238–240; David Herbert Donald, *Lincoln* (New York, 1995), 572–573; and Jason Emerson, *The Madness of Mary Lincoln* (Carbondale, Ill., 2007), 18, all draw on Adam Badeau's 1887 *Grant in Peace: From Appomattox to Mount McGregor* as well as other accounts. Julia Grant's own posthumously published memoirs, Emerson has noted, did not go nearly as far as Badeau's. The account by Badeau is included in full in a more recent look at the Lincolns by C. A. Tripp, *The Intimate World of Abraham Lincoln* (New York, 2005), 172–177. Badeau speculated that Mrs. Edwin Stanton's similar aversion to Mary Lincoln may have saved her husband's life as it did Julia Grant's.

143 Baker, *MTL*, 3–44, on details of Mary Todd's early family life and education.

144 "clear blue eyes . . ." and other details. Ibid., 51.

144 Ibid., 60 and 79, on politics and the move to Illinois.

144 Baker, 83–129, is the primary source for the courtship and early years of the Lincolns' marriage. Irving Stone, *Love Is Eternal* (Pleasantville, N.Y., Autumn 1954), 202, entitled his popular novel after the wedding-band inscription. Donald,

Lincoln, 85–108 and 163–164, also provides details of their courtship and domestic life, including their quarrels. William Herndon's reference to Lincoln's children as "brats" is in Baker, 120; Donald, 160, has him further saying, "I have felt many and many a time that I wanted to wring their little necks and yet out of respect for Lincoln I kept my mouth shut."

145 "she was destined . . ." Emerson, *MML*, 9.

145 "Mr. Lincoln may not . . ." Donald, 108.

146 Baker, 136–162. Donald, 235, says Lincoln's expressed doubts about being president went so far that he wrote one newspaper editor, "I must, in candor, say I do not think myself fit for the Presidency."

146 "Mary, Mary . . ." Baker, 162.

146 Wilson, *Patriotic Gore*, 117–119, quotes Herndon and John Hay.

147 Baker, 180–202, writes of Mary Lincoln's turn as first lady, drawing from no lack of sources, including seamstress Elizabeth Keckley's 1868 *Behind the Scenes: Thirty Years a Slave and Four Years in the White House*. Tripp, *IWAL*, 163, writes of Mrs. Lincoln's "embezzlements." One instance is of a dinner given for Napoleon III's visiting nephew, Prince Napoleon, where afterward Mrs. Lincoln apparently padded the caterer's bill. When refused payment of $900 by a suspicious interior secretary, she then—according to a source—"made her gardener make out a bill for plants, pots., etc. of the required amount, certified it herself and drew the money." Donald, 476, reports that "Satanic Majesty" originated with Lincoln's private secretary John Nicolay. Marguerite Merington, editor, *The Custer Story: The Life and Intimate Letters of General Custer and His Wife Elizabeth* (New York 1950), 91, includes newlywed Libbie Custer's remarks in an 1864 letter to her father.

147 Samuel A. Schreiner, Jr., *The Trials of Mrs. Lincoln* (New York, 1987), 182, mentions Lincoln's favors. Richard Goldhurst, *Many Are the Hearts*, 107, mentions Long Branch. Among those who also regularly enjoyed the resort was Edwin Booth, actor-brother of John Wilkes.

147 Baker, 208–209, and Donald, 336–337, on Willie's death. Lincoln, Donald also points out, "did not become a member of any Christian denomination, nor did he abandon his fundamental fatalism. He continued to quote *Hamlet*: 'There's a divinity that shapes our ends, / Rough-hew them how we will.'"

148 Baker, 217–222; also Donald, 427. David S. Reynolds, *Waking Giant* (New York, 2008), 374, puts the number of professional mediums by the late 1850s at twenty thousand, with more than two million U.S. believers.

150 Baker, 222–225, writes of the stormy relationship between the Lincolns and the Todds during the war. Donald, 324, quotes the *Cincinnati Commercial*.

150 Donald, 594–595, writes of the Lincolns' difficulties finding theater companions.

150 Schreiner, *TML*, 8, tells of the finding of the "MTL Insanity File" in a closet at Hildene. Also, Emerson, *MML*, draws on information found in his own discovery in 2005 of lost letters between Mary Lincoln and the Bradwells.

151 "an educated man . . ." Baker, 225.

151 "My notions of duty . . ." Emerson, 22.

151 Information on Robert Lincoln and Grant is from McFeely, *Grant*, 211, and Schreiner, 285.

152 "a butcher who . . ." Donald, 515, and Schreiner, 153, who attributes Keckley.

152 "one of her paroxysms . . ." Emerson, 13.

152 Baker, 246–253, writes of the weeks following the assassination.

152 "I wish to heaven . . ." Emerson, 24.

152 Baker, 253–263, and Emerson, 25, on Mary Lincoln's return to Chicago.

153 "in view of . . ." Schreiner, 102.

153 "What a future . . ." Ibid., 105.

153 Baker, 272–278, on the clothes-selling trip and its reaction.

154 "The simple truth . . ." Emerson, 28.

154 Schreiner, 108, cites the *Springfield* [Ill.] *Journal* for the report on the Lincoln estate distribution; Baker, 294, mentions the bonds.

154 Baker, 280–285, writes of the treatment of Keckley, her response, and of Mary Lincoln's decision to live abroad.

154 Ibid., 287–293.

155 "Do not allow the . . ." Ibid., 288.

155 Baker, 296–301, and Emerson, 30–31, write of the quest for a larger pension.

155 "Thad Stevens is gone . . ." Schreiner, 117.

156 Schreiner, 272, and Baker, 254–255 and 303, write of young Tad Lincoln.

156 Baker, 305, and Ishbel Ross, *The President's Wife: Mary Todd Lincoln* (New York, 1973), 292.

156 Baker, 307–308, writes of Tad's death.

156 Emerson, 34–35, and Baker, 310, mention the difficulties between the Marys. Baker, though, saying evidence is circumstantial (*n.*, 405), alleges that Robert's wife was an alcoholic, which led to some of the difficulties with her mother-in-law.

157 Baker, 310, writes of Mary's finances; Emerson, 36, writes of Mumler.

157 "My dearly beloved . . ." Emerson, 43.

157 "Start for Chicago . . ." Ibid.

158 Baker, 320–324, discusses some of the possible influences on Mrs. Lincoln's behavior, including the effects of chloral hydrate. Baker writes that she mixed the drug with a potent laudanum compound of opium, saffron, cinnamon, and wine. The kick alone of chloral hydrate when mixed with alcohol, according to the drug information website http://drugs.uta.edu/chloral.html, was the basis for a "Mickey Finn"—knockout drops—during the Victorian era.

158 Emerson, 55–56, discusses the events that brought changes in Illinois law to provide jury trials for all in mental illness cases. The woman whose case brought her to crusade for the changes by the Illinois legislature—Elizabeth Packard—was avidly supported by Myra Bradwell.

159 Baker, 316–320, writes of how Mrs. Lincoln was brought to court. Emerson, 44–46, describes the testimony of hotel employees and store merchants regarding her behavior. Schreiner, 76, relates Dr. Danforth's testimony about "table taps" from the dead president.

159 Robert Lincoln's testimony, the verdict, and reaction is taken from Schreiner, 85–87 and 129, and Baker, 320–325. Emerson, 68–69, writes of Mary Lincoln's attempt to kill herself.

159 "I have no doubt . . ." Baker, 321.

160 "O Robert . . ." Emerson, 59–60.

161 "And you are not . . ." Ibid., 67. Emerson, 70, mentions the carpetbags filled with footstools.

161 Descriptions of Bellevue Place Sanitarium and Dr. Patterson's approach are from Baker, 332–333.

161 Baker, 330, discusses Patterson's diagnosis of monomania; Emerson, 62, mentions bipolar disorder. Emerson, 73, also notes the visits of Robert and Mamie.

162 The efforts to release Mary Lincoln are in Emerson, 77–101.

163 Emerson, 105, writes of Robert Lincoln's financial liability as conservator.

163 "She says she . . ." Ibid., 109.

164 "trust to the chances . . ." Schreiner, 241.

164 Emerson, 112–114 and 169, writes of the hearing and its immediate aftermath.

164 "I go an exile . . ." Emerson, 122–123.

164 Baker, 355–361, on Mary Lincoln in Pau, France.

164 "I live, very much . . ." Ibid., 357.

164 Ibid., 360–362, on the Grants, Eugenie, and Robert. Schreiner, 277, reproduces a June 22, 1879, letter from Mrs. Lincoln where she refers to R. T. Lincoln and mentions the death of Eugenie's son—"Cut to pieces after receiving the fatal shot, in so unnecessary a cause." Emerson, 129, writes of Mrs. Lincoln's injuries from a fall off a stool in December 1879 and down a flight of stairs six months later, as well as her return voyage with Sarah Bernhardt. He quotes the actress's recollection from her memoirs.

165 "he'll be shot . . ." Emerson, 130.

165 Ibid., 130–132, writes of Mary Lincoln's return and of her last years.

165 Ibid., 132, on death and cause. Baker, 368, writes of the widow's successful attempts to increase her pension but says she died before collecting a cent of it.

166 Schreiner, 305–306, discusses Robert's efforts to control the Lincoln story, and that he was, from afar, able to persuade Scribner's not to publish a version of Herndon's biography. Another onetime Abraham Lincoln associate published a book carrying the charge that Lincoln had been an illegitimate child, and though (writes Schreiner) publication could not be stopped, Robert was able ten years later to prevent the author's appointment as Denver postmaster. Schreiner, 307–310, provides details on Jack Lincoln's death, Hildene, Robert's career, and Mary Harlan Lincoln's steps to keep her own family together and not in Springfield. Schreiner, 308, also reprints an assessment of Robert by journalist Ida Tarbell who interviewed him: "To be drinking tea with the son of Abraham Lincoln was . . . unbelievable to me. I searched his face and manners for resemblances. There was nothing. He was all Todd, a big plump man perhaps fifty years old, perfectly groomed, with that freshness which makes men of his type look as if they were just out of the barber's chair, the admirable poise of the man who has seen the world's greatest and has come to be sure of himself; and this in spite of such buffeting as few men had had—the assassination of his father when he was twenty-four [Robert was twenty-one], the humiliation of Mary Lincoln's half-crazed public exhibition of herself and her needs, the death of his brother Tad, the heart-breaking necessity of having his mother committed for medical care, and more recently the loss of his only son. Robert Lincoln had had enough to crush him, but he was not crushed. At the moment he looked and felt, I think, that he had arrived where he belonged." Emerson, 141–145, writes of the emergence of the Mary biography by the Bradwell descendant and the subsequent effort to suppress it. The settlement cost Robert's widow $22,500, but the writer was so restricted, said one observer, that "if she is apprehended reading a book about Lincoln, or mentioning his name or the name of his lady, she is likely to subject herself thereby to imprisonment for life, if indeed not summary execution." An armchair tour of Hildene as well as Mamie's house a half-mile away was made available via *Colonial Homes* magazine, May–June 1985.

Chapter 8: The Good Hater

168 "J.C. said he told . . ." and "No man exposes . . ." C. Vann Woodward, *Mary Chesnut's Civil War*, 482–484.

169 Much about General Johnston for this chapter is drawn from Craig L. Symonds's absorbing study *Joseph E. Johnston: A Civil War Biography* (New York, 1992). The writer, on 4–6, observes that before his book there had been only three biographies of Johnston, and all were flawed though admiring. Johnston's own account of the war, *Narrative of Military Operations*, is dismissed as "turgid." Symonds also notes a dearth of Johnston statues—just one, in Dalton, Georgia, where he is fatally bareheaded. Since then, a second statue has sprung up in North Carolina, dedicated in March 2010 through a private effort and in connection with the 1865 Battle of Bentonville, his last.

170 William C. Davis, *Jefferson Davis*, 37, brings up the West Point fistfight rumor between Johnston and Jeff Davis, purportedly over the daughter of Benny Havens, who ran an off-campus grog shop. Davis got the worst of it, according to the rumor impossible to leave unmentioned.

170 Symonds, *JEJ*, 20, mentions "The Colonel"; an 1897 biography by Robert M. Hughes is cited.

170 "Tell Lizzie . . ." Symonds, 48, from a November 19, 1840, letter.

170 "Good night my love . . ." Ibid., 52.

171 Ibid., 72, on the "castles in the air" lament, from a December 3, 1860, Johnston letter to George McClellan.

171 Johnston's slow march toward promotion until Secretary Floyd came along is recounted by Symonds, 76, 88–91; Robert K. Krick in *Leaders of the Lost Cause*, 169–171; and Davis, *JD*, 359. Johnston's heroism while a civilian, says Krick, occurred when he was working in Florida with a detachment of soldiers and sailors. Having come under fire from Seminoles, Johnston led a successful retreat. Robert E. Lee's attitude is additionally set forth by Krick, 173, and by Clifford Dowdey in *Lee* (New York, 1965), 122. Lee said Johnston epitomized "the system of favoritism," according to Thomas L. Connelly, *The Marble Man: Robert E. Lee and His Image in American Society* (Baton Rouge, La., 1978), 9.

171 Mary Chesnut, 187, has a touching account of Scott appealing to Lydia Johnston to talk her husband into staying in—or at least not fighting against—the Union Army.

172 On the promotion dispute, much reliance is placed on the interpretation of Steven H. Newton, *Joseph E. Johnston and the Defense of Richmond* (Lawrence, Kans., 1998), 6–7, who cites the consideration of line or staff service. Symonds, 126–129, is also valuable on the reactions of Johnston and Davis after the fact.

William C. Davis, 359–361, makes the case for Jefferson Davis acting for friendship's sake.

172 Symonds, 130–131, 141–159, and 166–172, and Newton, *JEJ*, are sources on the Peninsula war between Johnston and McClellan, and Johnston's subsequent wounding. Davis, Symonds correctly observes, was "probably the last person on Earth" that Johnston wanted to see just at that moment at Seven Pines.

173 Symonds, 177–181, writes entertainingly on the Wigfalls.

173 "Mr. Yancey . . ." Ibid., 179.

174 Ibid., 187–201, and Connelly, *Autumn of Glory*, 38, 74–80. Both sources have very good accounts of Johnston's first encounter with the Army of Tennessee, while Braxton Bragg was commander, before and after the Battle of Stones River. Connelly says that another disagreement between Johnston and Davis was that Davis did not consider "the seizure of Tennessee to be a major Federal aim"— a contention that events would refute. Both note that War Secretary James A. Seddon suggested to Johnston that he take over the army and keep Bragg on as a sort of chief of staff. The bishop-general Leonidas Polk also charitably suggested to Davis that Bragg be made inspector general to get him out of the way for Johnston. In brief, there was no shortage of ideas for manipulating a change in command.

174 Foote, *The Civil War*, vol. II, 368–379, has a thorough account of events preceding the siege of Vicksburg, including a failed linkup between Johnston and General John Pemberton.

174 "Dogs howled . . ." Richard Wheeler, *The Siege of Vicksburg* (New York, 1978/1991), 223.

174 Foote, 613, says that besides 2,872 Confederate casualties during the siege (about 2,000 fewer than Union losses), Grant bagged 2,166 Rebel officers, 27,230 enlisted men, and 115 civilian employees. All were paroled except for one officer and 708 soldiers who preferred prison camp in the North rather than risk being exchanged and put back into a future battle.

174 "Yes, from want of provisions . . ." Symonds, 217.

175 Connelly, *AOG*, 281–283, sheds light on Davis's dilemma and Lee's reluctance on grounds he (Lee) would not find "cordial co-operation" in the Army of Tennessee and a suitable replacement for himself in Virginia couldn't be found. William Davis, 529, says Lee "respectfully declined" the president's offer. Dowdey, *Lee*, 410, mentions Lee's health problems as well as close identification with the Virginia army.

175 "Boys, this is . . ." Symonds, 252.

175 Symonds, 262, discusses the winter offensive strategy. Bragg also suggested that if Johnston were to take the army north toward Knoxville, he could turn west toward Nashville and "capture the place before the enemy can fall back." Johnston, however, would first have to leapfrog the Cumberland Mountains while the railroad lines between Nashville and North Georgia could easily bring up Sherman's army in time to meet the threat.

175 Symonds, 356–357, describes the surrender negotiations between Johnston and Sherman. Davis, 625–626, writes of this final wartime clash between Johnston and Jefferson Davis.

176 Both Symonds and Richard McMurry's *Atlanta 1864: Last Chance for the Confederacy* (Lincoln, Nebr., 2000), are excellent studies of the war in Georgia.

176 "'Now,' says Mr. Hamilton Boykin, . . . " Woodward, *MCCW*, 268.

177 "I can see where . . ." Watkins, *Co. Aytch*, 168.

177 William C. Davis, 399, says Jeff Davis never liked John B. Floyd.

178 Symonds, 360, and Gilbert E. Govan and James W. Livingood, *A Different Valor: The Story of General Joseph E. Johnston C.S.A.* (Indianapolis, 1956), 380–381, write of Johnston's insurance career.

178 "with equal virulence . . ." Woodward, *MCCW*, 623, and Krick, 192. Krick's essay is pointedly titled, "'Snarl and Sneer and Quarrel': General Joseph E. Johnston and an Obsession with Rank."

180 Symonds, 343, writes of Wigfall's revelation to Johnston about Lee's support.

180 "In youth and early manhood . . ." Ibid., 344.

180 Marshall W. Fishwick, *Lee After the War* (New York, 1963), 193, speculates on the impact on Lee of seeing the rank poverty of Georgia five years after the war, as compared to Virginia.

180 Wilson, *Patriotic Gore*, 383–388. Wilson's account of Davis's imprisonment is contained within an essay about Alexander Stephens. An assessment of Nelson Miles as the army's most successful Indian fighter comes from Utley, *Cavalier in Buckskin*, 205.

181 "Widely as I differed . . ." Wilson, 383.

181 "I feel sure . . ." Symonds, 361.

182 "I wish very much . . ." Govan and Livingood, *ADV*, 380, letter to a Dr. Pendleton.

182 Symonds, 360–364, writes of Johnston's grievance-filled war memoir which managed to be "at once matter-of-fact and stuffy."

182 William C. Davis, 445, writes of the Wigfall-Davis falling out. Senator Wigfall's public outbursts during bouts with the bottle kept the quarrel hot. Wiley, *Confederate Women*, 16–17, mentions that Davis rode off to First Manassas without telling Wigfall, his aide, subsequently leaving Wigfall and his Texas battalion out of the first big fight. Wiley, 100, also repeats Charlotte Wigfall's remark about Varina Davis. Richard McMurry, *Two Great Rebel Armies: An Essay in Confederate Military History* (Chapel Hill, N.C., 1989), 136, mentions how Lee kept his distance from the anti-Davis cliques, unlike Johnston and Beauregard, and cites the Richard Taylor quotation.

183 "Johnston has more effectively . . ." Symonds, 364.

183 Govan and Livingood, 387, record Wigfall's death.

183 Johnston's excursions into political campaigning are related in Symonds, 374–377.

183 Govan and Livingood, 388, on Hayes's consideration of Johnston in his Cabinet. Merrill, in *William Tecumseh Sherman*, 364, says Sherman made his views to Hayes known through a letter to his brother, John Sherman.

184 "It's shameful a . . ." Symonds, 376.

184 Govan and Livingood, 389–390, on the dilemma of Johnston's campaign funds.

184 "Of all the men . . ." Dabney Maury's reminiscences about Johnston appeared in the Richmond *Dispatch*, April 26, 1891, and were republished in the *Southern Historical Society Papers*.

184 Terry L. Seip, *The South Returns to Congress* (Baton Rouge, 1983), 10–14 and 289–290, offers a wealth of statistical information on the regeneration of the Democratic party in the South. The omission of Tennessee in the figures is due to that state's earlier 1866 readmission to the Union, though its elected members encountered initial difficulties in taking their seats. Seip's survey begins midway (1868) of the following session of Congress. *The American People: A History* (Princeton, N.J., 1962), vol. II, 8–9, compiled by Rembert W. Patrick, Frank L. Owsley, Oliver P. Chitwood, and H. C. Nixon, is the chosen source for the Hayes-Tilden election.

185 Seip, *SRC*, 39, 42, has the congressional statistics on soldiers and scalawags as well as the number of old Rebel generals who served. Govan and Livingood, 390, also list Johnston's Confederate colleagues. Symonds, 377, characterizes the short career of Congressman Johnston as having "initiated no legislation, seldom spoke in floor debates, and voted the straight Democratic Party line."

185 Davis, 676, writes of Jefferson Davis's memoirs.

185 "Mr. Davis has never . . ." Symonds, 367. The writer has other details, 366–367. The *Memphis Appeal's* "mean and dastardly assault" charge comes from Connelly, *TMM*, 80.

186 "The pestilent interviewer . . ." Strode, *Jefferson Davis: Tragic Hero*, 452.

186 "no man ought . . ." Strode, 453.

186 "I am sorry . . ." Ibid., 453.

186 Lewis, *Sherman: Fighting Prophet*, 618, mentions the favor for Braxton Bragg.

187 "But young man . . ." Govan and Livingood, 393–394.

187 "This death has . . ." Ibid., 395.

187 Goldhurst, *Many Are the Hearts*, 166–167. Other unsuccessful attempts would be made to put Grant on the army retired list and thus secure a pension for him. An effort in 1885 failed in part because of the opposition of Congressman William Rosecrans.

187 "I was as happy . . ." Cited by Maury, ibid., *SHSP*, 180. Goldhurst, *MAH*, 242 and 250, points out that Johnston was an honorary pallbearer at the funeral of Grant as well as at Sherman's.

187 Hirshson, *The White Tecumseh*, 308–309, is the source relied upon for the Sherman-Johnston surrender discussions and Stanton's role. According to *Confederate Veteran*, May 1920, the Confederate courier between Johnston and Sherman—when Johnston surrendered what was left of Hood's old army—was Colonel Rawlins Lowndes, who, of course, would marry Buck Preston.

188 "Now that the . . ." Lewis, *SFP*, 556.

188 "The enlarged . . ." Ibid., 556. Lewis also notes Sherman's generosity of rations and "enough farm animals to insure a crop." Grant restored Sherman's name so that it came first.

188 Symonds, 370, makes the point about Sherman's kinder memoirs. Lewis, 618, tells of some of the kindnesses Sherman performed for Johnston and other old foes.

188 "Well, General . . ." Hirshson, *TWT*, 369.

188 Information on Johnston's railroad commissioner appointment and Sherman's help was taken from a eulogy by Josiah Patterson at a Johnston memorial service in Memphis on March 31, 1891, published in the *Southern Historical Society Papers*.

188 "Did you succeed . . ." Hirshson, 385.

188 Symonds, 367–370, writes of Johnston's response to Davis's book and his dealings with *The Century*.

189 The mutual skipping of the Lee memorial ceremony by Johnston and Davis was acknowledged in the occasion's introductory remarks by General Jubal Early, found in *Southern Historical Society Papers*, vol. XI, nos. 8–9, August–September 1883.

189 "If Genl. Johnston had never. . ." General Dabney Maury in an 1891 letter to General Richard Ewell, cited by Symonds, 358.

189 Both Symonds, 372, and an article, "Terminology and Meanings of Early Illnesses & Diseases," in *The Volunteer*, Journal of the Lincoln County (Tennessee) Historical Society, Fall 2005, are in agreement on the broad application of "neuralgia."

189 Recollections of Johnston and Lydia are in Maury's *Dispatch* newspaper article.

190 Symonds, 379–380, writes of Johnston's last days.

190 "General, please put on . . ." Lewis, 652, who also provides the account of the Sherman funeral, though he misstates Johnston's age as eighty-two. He was eighty-four.

Chapter 9: The Legend

192 Marshall W. Fishwick, *Lee After the War* (New York, 1963), 1–4, 36–39; Dowdey, *Lee*, 633–636; Charles B. Flood, *Lee: The Last Years* (Boston, 1981), 36–44. Fishwick, 3, notes that the Richmond home's owner, John Stewart, told the Lees—who insisted on paying rent—that he would accept only Confederate currency, which by this point was worthless.

192 "I've come to see . . ." Fishwick, *LAW*, 45.

193 Douglas Southall Freeman, *R. E. Lee: A Biography* (New York, 1935), vol. IV, 241, mentions Lee's reply to the spiritualist. Fishwick, 104, writes of having met octogenarians who as children had ridden on Traveller at Lee's request. Elizabeth Brown Pryor, *Reading the Man: A Portrait of Robert E. Lee Through His Private Letters* (New York, 2007), 200, writes that Lee "loved to flirt."

193 "The great mistake . . ." Fishwick, 145.

193 "I . . . find too late . . ." Connelly, *The Marble Man*, 218.

194 "How can I sit . . ." Connelly, *TMM*, 188.

194 Ibid., 5–6, and Dowdey, *Lee*, 11–49, provide information on Lee's early years and family. "Black-Horse Harry" would flee to Tennessee and be given a job by Andrew Jackson. He would die in Paris in 1837.

194 "How can I live . . ." Connelly, 169.

195 Pryor, *RTM*, 60, writes of the remarkable Cadet Mason. While Lee received 299½ points on his multiple courses, Mason consistently achieved a perfect 300.

196 Dowdey, 53–62; Pryor, 78–81; and Connelly, 166–167, discuss Mary Custis. Connelly says doctors diagnosed her illness as "rheumatic diathesis."

196 The very accurate description of Mrs. Roger Pryor as a beautiful *brune* is Virginia Clay-Clopton's in her *A Belle of the Fifties*, 44.

196 "Last night . . ." Fishwick, 103.

196 "You must endeavor . . ." Connelly, 178–179, who also discusses Lee's "obsessive concern for training his children."

197 "always wanting . . ." Fishwick, 94.

197 "When I speak of . . ." Reynolds, *Waking Giant*, 31.

197 Economic comparisons of Virginia with the rest of the Confederacy, and the latter with the North, are from McMurry, *Two Great Rebel Armies*, 20–26.

198 Freehling, *The Road to Disunion*, 178–195, discusses the Nat Turner uprising and the ensuing debate over slavery in Virginia. Some opponents of legislative action to end slavery saw it dying of "natural causes" as demand for Deep South cotton depleted Virginia's slave supply. William Hague, in *William Wilberforce* (London, 2007), 393, notes that Virginians were already breeding slaves for these markets and Cuba in the early 1800s.

198 ("nothing but . . .") Dowdey, 120.

198 "a Union that can . . ." and "I shall return . . ." Ibid., 120–121. Freeman, *REL*, vol. I, 439–441, notes that Lee's "great model" Washington had also embraced "a revolutionary cause" and that the Lee family's older allegiance (pre-Revolution) had been to Virginia. Connelly, 147–148, who accuses Freeman of also giving Lee psychic powers against his Yankee enemies, has some sport in summing up what he calls the traditional "Virginia argument": "Virginia (and Lee) loved the Union more than other Southerners, disliked secession, and hated slavery. Virginians had little use for the cotton South, and Lee 'had no regard at the time for the South as a section. . . . His mind was for the Union.' But Lee's sense of duty had determined from the outset that he would adopt the course of his beloved Virginia. And like other Virginians, 'he could not bring himself to fight against the states that regarded secession as a right.'"

198 Dowdey, 129–134, writes of Lee's dilemma, Winfield Scott's efforts to keep him, and the secession debate in Virginia.

199 "Lee, you have made . . ." and "No one should . . ." Ibid., 133.

199 "My husband has wept . . ." Ibid., 134.

199 Fishwick, 162, recounts the 1868 Senate debate on Lee's resignation and Simon Cameron's accusation.

200 "I prefer Lee to . . ." McMurry, *TGRA*, 37, and Foote, *The Civil War*, vol. I, 465, are sources. McMurry also quotes McClellan on Lincoln: ". . . an old stick, and of pretty poor timber at that."

200 "I am looking for . . ." Dowdey, 639.

200 "My dear, I would . . ." Connelly, 35.

200 Dowdey, 646–651, describes Lee's brief months in the country and his plans to write a history of the Virginia campaigns. A New York publisher already had contacted Lee and had visited.

201 "what my poor boys . . ." Ibid., 649–650.

201 "The Southern people . . ." Fishwick, 48.

201 Fishwick, 48–58, and Dowdey, 653–658, write of Washington College's offer to Lee.

201 Dowdey, 641–644, discusses Lee's efforts to gain a pardon, further complicated by a Radical judge's procurement of an indictment for treason against Lee and others. The case never came to trial.

202 "I think it is . . ." Fishwick, 59.

202 "It is supposed . . ." Ibid., 83.

202 Details from Lee's early days at the college are from Fishwick, 83–87; Dowdey, 661; Pryor, 438; and Freeman, vol. IV, 232–299. Fishwick, 85, also writes of the struggle of many Southern colleges to stay open or reopen, with some having to shut down for lengthy periods, including the state universities of North and South Carolina and Alabama. Lee's role, if just by personal prestige alone, no doubt helped save smaller Washington College from a similar fate.

203 "We must look . . ." Fishwick, 136–137.

203 "The great object . . ." Pryor, 438.

203 "to take to themselves . . ." Fishwick, 150.

203 "Never marry unless . . ." Ibid., 151.

203 "don't seem to like . . ." Ibid., 156.

204 "She rules her brother . . ." Ibid., 151.

204 "His army demanded . . ." Ibid., 208, quoting Colonel Walter Taylor.

204 "Life is waning away . . ." Ibid., 154.

204 Pryor, 446–447, on the Arlington visit. Connelly, 126, writes of the Supreme Court restoring Arlington to Custis Lee. Flood, *TLY*, 250, says the federal government offered $150,000 and Custis, not wanting to move into a cemetery, accepted.

204 Pryor, 203–205, and Connelly, 174–175, write of Lee and Markie Williams. Their letters and Markie's diary, writes Pryor, were often filled with "sentiments that surpassed the bounds of close cousinly affection." They were still corresponding up to a couple of months before Lee's death.

204 "But oh, what . . ." Connelly, 175–176.

205 "there is nothing . . ." Ibid., 219.

205 "I fear the . . ." Freeman, vol. IV, 236.

205 "I would suggest . . ." Ibid., 237. Freeman, 237, also mentions the British visitor, Herbert C. Saunders.

205 Connelly, 18–20, writes on the South's wartime adoration of, and grief for, Thomas "Stonewall" Jackson. Mary Chesnut's remark is on 616 of *MCCW*.

206 Connelly, 80–82, writes of Lee's reaction to the Stonewall biography by Robert Dabney. Connelly says this set a precedent for the revision of Jackson's image, which Jubal Early and others eagerly took on later, particularly in giving Lee credit for the Battle of Chancellorsville. Freeman, vol. IV, 241, politely writes "that in his zeal for the fame of his chief, Major Dabney had unintentionally made some claims that were at variance with Lee's knowledge or his recollection of the facts." Fishwick, 181, writes of the Volck lithograph that "no visits by Lee to Jackson's grave are mentioned in local newspapers or diaries. Here again, only Lee knew Lee's thoughts."

206 Both Fishwick, 108–116, and Freeman, vol. IV, 251–256, write of Lee's appearance before Congress, each citing the Reconstruction Committee's official report as source. The testimony is taken from Fishwick, 115–116, which differs slightly from that of Freeman but is more directly stated. There is no significant difference in content.

207 Lytle, *Bedford Forrest and His Critter Company*, 383, and Hurst, *Nathan Bedford Forrest*, 286–287, write on the Klan. Lee's alleged compliments to Forrest are quoted from Lytle. Hurst does note Lee's views that the Radical Republicans were subverting the Constitution—a view shared in the Klan—and observes that Lee's "opinions imparted privately to friends don't appear to have been nearly as scrupulously apolitical and submissive as he tried to make his public ones. . . ."

208 Dowdey, 687, cites the Klan-denied Virginia girl. Pryor, 455, introduces the prospect of a Klan chapter at Lee's college and faults Lee for not exercising "the near imperial control he had at the school, as he did for more trivial matters. . . ." Other Lee biographers consulted for this period in his life are silent on any Klan connection, except to note that Lee was no advocate of violence.

208 "General, I have always . . ." Freeman, vol. IV, 250.

209 "My dear sir . . ." Ibid., 250–251.

209 Foote, *TCW*, vol. III, 930, writes of Lee's reaction to seeing Pickett after Five Forks. At that battle Pickett had left his men to attend a "shad bake," and the subsequent fight was about as disastrous as Gettysburg's charge. Fishwick, 186, and Freeman, vol. IV, 445–446, write of the Lee-Pickett encounter, taken from Mosby's memoirs. Flood, 232, mentions Mosby's rejoinder to Pickett: "Well, it made you immortal." Carol Reardon, in Gary Gallagher's *The Third Day at Gettysburg and Beyond* (Chapel Hill, N.C., 1994), 68, says Pickett was a pallbearer.

209 "I am easily . . ." Freeman, vol. IV, 319.

210 Lee's disciplinary approach and the tobacco-chewing expulsion are from Fishwick, 140.

210 "I don't know . . ." Fishwick, 141.

210 "I wished he . . ." Pryor, 439.

210 "you will fail . . ." Fishwick, 178.

210 Pryor, 438–440, cites Lee's temper and Mildred's spiked cobbler. Fishwick, 139, speaks of "General Lee's boys."

210 "I never saw . . ." Fishwick, 168.

210 Ibid., 128–129, on Lee's aspirations for a college chapel.

211 "the best news . . ." Ibid., 214.

211 Pryor, 228–232, writes of Lee's Episcopal confirmation and the example set by his mother-in-law. Pryor says that several months after Mrs. Custis's death, visiting her grave with Lee, Markie Williams "was startled to see him sobbing uncontrollably."

211 "We do not . . ." Thomas L. Connelly and Barbara L. Bellows, *God and General Longstreet: The Lost Cause and the Southern Mind* (Baton Rouge, La., 1982), 14.

211 Fishwick, 210, also writes of Lee's religiosity during the war. Pryor, 236, mentions the army's fervor after Gettysburg, and says some analysts "believe that the nearly superhuman efforts of Lee's men during the Wilderness campaign were sustained by the charismatic belief in God's protection."

211 "How thankless and . . ." Connelly, *TMM*, 182.

211 "Don't be discouraged . . ." Dowdey, 389.

211 "God's will . . ." Connelly, 191.

211 "I know affliction . . ." Ibid., 193.

211 "It has been . . ." Fishwick, 90–91.

212 Ibid., 161–162 and 217, discusses Lee's heart problems.

212 "Doctors do not . . ." Ibid., 185.

212 "You had best . . ." Ibid., 201.

212 The account of Lee's death is in Connelly, 11–12. The description of the chapel and burial scene today is based on my visit on October 20, 2009.

213 Connelly, 12, 42–47, discusses the Lee memorial rivalries. The Lee grave (still at Washington and Lee) sparked other controversy shortly after World War I when the college's president proposed to replace the chapel Lee had built with a huge new building that would serve as both mausoleum and auditorium. The Lexington United Daughters of the Confederacy considered the original chapel inviolate and fought the plan, often alone, until the college dropped the proposal five years later. The site is certainly worth a visit. Flood, 276*n*, mentions the 1975 restoration of Lee's rights.

213 Connelly, 51–54 and 73–74, profiles Jubal Early's career and the Virginia take-over of the Southern Historical Society by Early and his friends. Freeman, vol. IV, 508–509, has Lee's letter relieving Early, where Lee says, in part, "While my own confidence in your ability, zeal, and devotion to the cause is unimpaired, I have nevertheless felt that I could not oppose what seems to be the current of opinion, without injustice to your reputation and injury to the service."

213 Connelly, 54–56, on Early's underachiever performance at Gettysburg. McMurry, *TGRA*, 30–32, sums up the blame game played by a small army of writers over the years against a half-dozen or more of the Confederate leaders at Gettysburg.

214 Connelly and Bellows, *GGL*, 32–37, relate Longstreet's unfortunate journey.

214 "to do anything . . ." Fishwick, 99.

214 Connelly, *TMM*, 69–89, writes of the Lee cult's attacks on Jackson, Joseph Johnston, and Stuart, as well as Davis's reaction. Davis was placated somewhat by being fed material critical of Beauregard and Johnston.

215 "needs no pedestal . . ." Ibid., 77.

215 Connelly and Bellows, *GGL*, 54–58, and Connelly, *TMM*, 103–104, write of John Esten Cooke and Thomas Nelson Page.

216 "It is hard to explain . . ." Wilson, *Patriotic Gore*, 605.

216 Connelly, 104, lists besides Mrs. Pryor other Southern women writers such as Mary McClelland, Amelie Rives, Jennie Woodville, Molly Seawell, Lucy Thompson, and Phoebe Yates Pember—all of whom "wrote of the glories of a destroyed past."

216 Reardon's essay, "Pickett's Charge," in *TDG*, 69, records the treatment of the famous event with its particular Virginia twist.

217 "the greatness of . . ." Connelly and Bellows, 84.

217 "loved the Union . . ." Connelly, 107.

217 "the leader of . . ." Ibid., 110.

217 Ibid., 116–117, on the interest of Charles Francis Adams.

217 Ibid., 121, on Wilson, Theodore Roosevelt, and the Hall of Fame.

217 Winston Churchill's clever what-if article proposed that Lee had lost at Gettysburg, with all the defeat and repercussions of Reconstruction that followed, while in reality Lee had *won* the battle, marched on Washington, abolished slavery single-handedly, and procured Southern recognition by England and France—thus achieving independence. It appeared in *Scribner's Magazine*, December 1930, and the essay has been more recently reprinted in *The Collected Essays of Sir Winston Churchill* (London, 1976), vol. IV. James Thurber's satire, inspired in part by Churchill's what-if, proposed "If Grant Had Been Drinking at Appomattox," and is found, among other places, in *The Thurber Carnival* (New York, 1957), 140–142.

Chapter 10: The Turncoat

219 "all dismounted cavalry . . ." Buell, *The Warrior Generals,* 380.

219 Buell, 380, observes that when Sherman parceled the troops, if Thomas felt he was left holding the bag it was the time to speak up. That he didn't may suggest he was too eager to have an independent command. Francis F. McKinney, *Education in Violence: The Life of George H. Thomas and the History of the Army of the Cumberland* (Chicago, 1991, reprint; original, 1961), 373–381, also points out that John Schofield's "army" or corps was assigned to Thomas but that its numbers had been exaggerated by Sherman to Grant, and that James Wilson's cavalry assigned to Thomas had been "dismounted and stripped" to supply Sherman's march to the sea. A. J. Smith's promised troops, of course, were on the Kansas border at the time. McKinney also mentions Thomas being ordered to furlough Illinois troops for the election.

219 Walter T. Durham, *Reluctant Partners: Nashville and the Union* (Nashville, Tenn., 1987), 202–220; Freeman Cleaves, *Rock of Chickamauga: The Life of General George H. Thomas* (Norman, Okla., 1948), 246–262; Benson Bobrick, *Master of War: The Life of General George H. Thomas* (New York, 2009), 279–286; Stanley F. Horn, *The Decisive Battle of Nashville* (Baton Rouge, La., 1956), 50–72, and Buell, 397–399, contribute to the account of events before the Battle of Nashville. Horn, a Nashvillian, is the most thorough.

219 "cause all loafing . . ." and "From the river . . ." are from Durham, *RP,* 219–220. The latter quotes Maggie Lindsley, a Unionist and daughter of A. V. S. Lindsley who had a farm in then fashionable Edgefield, across the Cumberland River from Nashville.

220 *The World Almanac and Book of Facts* (New York, 2008), 544, records the 1864 presidential electoral vote.

220 "the McClellan & Rosecranz . . ." Buell, 398.

220 "I have said . . ." Ibid., 399.

220 "will be yours . . ." Bobrick, *MOW,* 281.

221 *"The President orders: . . ."* Sword, *The Confederacy's Last Hurrah,* 292–293.

221 "I hope most . . ." Grant, *Personal Memoirs,* 1074.

221 "Delay no longer . . ." Grant, *PM,* 659.

221 "I believe an . . ." Bobrick, 285.

221 McKinney, *EIV,* 401–403, writes of efforts by T. T. Eckert, the War Department's chief telegrapher, to get news from Nashville, and of Schofield's intrigues. Also, McKinney, 423–424, writes of the Nashville battle: "Nearly half a century after the event, selected officers of the United States army were taught that 'of all the attacks made by the Union forces in the course of the [Civil] war none other was as free from faults as this one.'" Horn, *DBN,* xii, calls attention to General J. F. C. Fuller in 1942, whose book *Decisive Battles of the U.S.A.* included Nashville and his view that it was Thomas's victory and not Sherman's march that decided the war in the West and thereby its end.

222 "I thought . . ." Bobrick, 286.

222 "Jovelike figure . . ." Cleaves, *ROC,* 185.

222 "shape and carriage . . ." Cleaves, 20.

223 Buell, 188–193 and 388, is among those particularly admiring of Thomas's modern skills. Buell, who taught military history at both West Point and the

Naval War College, calls Thomas's work at Nashville so "modern in concept, so sweeping in scope, it would become a model for strategic maneuver in twentieth-century warfare."

224 "My private life . . ." Bobrick, 332.

224 McKinney, 3–7, mentions Thomas's sisters, who seemed more eager to talk of their experience regarding the Nat Turner slave uprising, which had occurred in their native Southampton County and which they and their mother had fled in terror.

224 "Respectfully returned . . ." Cleaves, 192, quotes from Lewis, *Sherman*, 316, regarding the Bragg-Thomas exchange as related by Sherman, who in turn noted that Thomas—apparently some days afterward—was still seething from Bragg's refusal: "'Damn him [Bragg],' growled Thomas. 'I'll be even with him yet.'" Perhaps he got there. Stephen Berry, *House of Abraham: Lincoln and the Todds, a Family Divided by War* (New York, 2007), 149, writes that when Confederate Brigadier General Benjamin Hardin Helm, Lincoln's brother-in-law, was killed at Chickamauga, his widow Emilie—then in Georgia—asked Bragg's assistance to return to her mother in Kentucky. Bragg wrote a pass for Emilie and her three children to cross the army lines, and sent a request for permission to Thomas for "Mrs. Helm, widow of Gen'l B. H. Helm of our service and sister of Mrs. Lincoln" to return to "her friends" in the North. Thomas refused; no reason given. Grant, though, the Union commander, acceded, but the military situation in Chattanooga by then was such that no one could pass. The Confederate *Macon* [Ga.] *Telegraph* reported the Thomas refusal in its paper of November 4, 1863.

224 "If they want me . . ." Cleaves, 69.

225 "Let the Virginian . . ." McKinney, 167.

225 McKinney, 166–169, writes of William Rosecrans and Thomas's reaction to being passed over. It is possible that Thomas did not learn until later, after he had agreed to serve under Rosecrans, that Lincoln had backdated Rosecrans's commission from August 21 to March 31. Buell, 186, says Rosecrans jumped thirty-nine other major generals. Cozzens, *No Better Place to Die*, 22–23, notes the cabinet clash, with Salmon Chase favoring Rosecrans. Rosecrans would also recall for his staff how, at West Point, he had compared Thomas with George Washington. Cozzens, *The Darkest Days of the War: The Battles of Iuka and Corinth* (Chapel Hill, N.C., 1997), 301–303, writes that the mutual dislike of Rosecrans and Grant stemmed from Grant's orders for Rosecrans to end the pursuit of Rebel forces in North Mississippi in October 1862. Rosecrans hotly maintained that his men were on the verge of a great victory; Grant believed that the fleeing Confederates were out of reach and headed for cover, and that Rosecrans was insubordinate. Rosecrans would later claim that, with reinforcements, "If Grant had not stopped us, we could have gone to Vicksburg."

225 Cleaves, 180–183, has the decision to replace Rosecrans with Thomas. Lincoln had remarked of Rosecrans that ever since Chickamauga the general had been "confused and stunned like a duck hit on the head."

225 Cleaves, 49, brings up "Old Slow Trot"; McKinney, 53–54, also writes of Grant mentioning it during his world trip. McKinney says the pace ordered by Thomas for the cadets might have been a precautionary one as West Point's horses at the time were sorry nags.

225 "One order left . . ." Grant, 403–404.

225 "I then found . . ." Ibid., 453.

225 "Thomas made no . . ." Ibid., 655.

225 "Thomas did not . . ." Ibid., 681.

225 "You have the . . ." Ibid., 1075.

226 "Thomas's dispositions . . ." Ibid., 762.

226 Cleaves, 125–129, is useful as a battle summary of the first day of Stones River. Although not as nearly invisible as the Franklin battlefield, that of Stones River today is hemmed in and broken up by urban encroachment, despite the guardianship of the U.S. Park Service. Any of the Thomas biographies mentioned here has details on his other battles while under Rosecrans and Sherman.

226 "For myself . . ." Grant, 251.

227 McKinney, 140–141, raises the suggestion of Sherman's role in Thomas stepping aside for Grant's return and adds as a possible explanation of Grant's attitude toward Thomas that "it proved the truism that one way to make an enemy is to put him in your debt."

227 "I will hold . . ." Buell, 276.

227 Buell, 278–293, offers the contrasts between the camps of Grant and Thomas as well as the flaws in Grant's initial plans of attack on Missionary Ridge and details of the eventual attack. McKinney, 274–297, goes into more detail on the Missionary Ridge attack. McKinney also mentions a rivalry between the Army of the Cumberland and the Army of the Tennessee, dating to the Cumberlanders' timely arrival at Shiloh in 1862, which could also have influenced the Cumberlanders' aggressiveness. Grant, 448, goes to great pains to state there "was no jealousy—hardly rivalry" between any of the four Union armies represented at the battle.

228 "No, they started . . ." Buell, 292.

228 McKinney, 303–304, says Thomas was considered for commander of the Army of the Potomac to replace George Meade, but that Thomas vehemently opposed the transfer. "The pressure always brought to bear against the commander of the Army of the Potomac would destroy me in a week," Thomas wrote the politically connected James Garfield.

228 Grant's claims are in his memoirs, 443–451. Besides Sherman, Grant also tosses a bouquet to his friend Philip Sheridan. Sherman, *Memoirs*, 390, reprints Grant's letter of praise.

228 Buell, 34–35, and McKinney, 89–91, write of Thomas during the time between Texas and Fort Sumter. McKinney says Thomas seemed to believe that most Virginians supported the Union and were misled into war by the state's politicians. Buell also mentions Fitzhugh Lee's assertion that Virginia had not offered Thomas a position of suitable rank. McKinney, 82, notes that Fitzhugh Lee thought Thomas's feelings during this time were "Southern to an almost bellicose degree." McKinney, 89, says Frances Thomas wrote in 1884 that "never a word passed between myself or *any one* of our family upon the subject of his remaining loyal to the United States government," and that "no one could persuade him to do what he felt was not right." Thomas had stood with Don Carlos Buell when Washington wanted Buell removed in 1862 before the imminent Battle of Perryville in Kentucky (Cleaves, 112–113), and had stood by Rosecrans after

Chickamauga (Buell, 274–276), yielding only to Grant's order. In both instances Thomas likely saw politics involved.

229 Cleaves, 3–4, writes of Thomas's attitude toward the family's slaves, and that "he seemed to love the Negro quarters more than his own house." McKinney, 82–83, writes of Thomas's treatment of the servant woman purchased in Texas and his continued responsibility for her. McKinney, 320, and Buell, 351, write of the difference in attitude of Thomas and Sherman toward black soldiers.

229 Cleaves, 64, on Thomas's preference for John Bell in the 1860 presidential election.

229 "No, no. Mix . . ." Buell, 294.

229 E. Merton Coulter's *William G. Brownlow: Fighting Parson of the Southern Highlands* (Chapel Hill, N.C., 1937/Knoxville, Tenn., 1971), 94–109, and 130–138, amply sets forth Brownlow's positions on slavery.

230 "and instruct them . . ." Coulter, *WGB*, 138.

230 "If you liberate . . ." Ibid., 109.

230 "Who can estimate . . ." Ibid., 106.

230 "We debouch upon . . ." Walt Whitman, "Pioneers! O Pioneers!" in *Leaves of Grass*, (New York, 1944), 262.

230 "Fear not . . ." Robert Remini, *Andrew Jackson* (New York, 1969), 133. Remini, 45, also says Jackson on the whole "treated his slaves decently, but when he felt punishment was needed, he had them whipped and, on occasion, chained."

231 "With too many people . . ." Cleaves, 293.

231 Coulter, 261, writes on Brownlow's election.

231 "For the promoting . . ." Ibid., 262.

232 Ibid., 313–314. Brownlow was so anxious to have a legislative quorum to ratify the Fourteenth Amendment that he asked Thomas for troops to round up some of the members in hiding. President Johnson, no friend of Brownlow, told Thomas to take no part.

232 Cleaves, 288, on Gideon Welles's opinions of Brownlow and Thomas.

232 Coulter, 324 and 357–364, on Tennessee's state of excitement that Brownlow and the Klan induced, and on the honors for Thomas. McKinney, 460, also writes of Tennessee honors for Thomas. Cleaves, 304, writes of Thomas's anger when a legislator proposed to sell his portrait.

232 "in the full . . ." Coulter, 357.

233 "Too late, Sir . . ." McKinney, 454.

233 "I believe you are . . ." Bobrick, 226.

233 "Grant stood by . . ." Ibid., 227.

233 "in all the attributes . . ." Lewis, *Sherman*, 643–644.

234 Bobrick, 322, relates Thomas's refusal of more lavish gifts for war service.

234 "No, Sherman is the . . ." McKinney, 313–314, who also mentions Johnson's support of Thomas to succeed Grant, telling Lincoln: "He will, in my opinion, if permitted, be one of the great generals of the war, if not the greatest. . . ." Hirshson, *The White Tecumseh*, 187, says General James Rushing believed Thomas was "aggrieved."

234 "that during the war . . ." Cleaves, 285.

235 "You know of my . . ." McKinney, 451.

235 "like an aspen . . ." Cleaves, 288.

235 "Nevertheless, I have . . ." McKinney, 452.

235 "They made me . . ." Ibid., 453.

235 Ibid., 466, relates the political issues with Johnson and Grant.

236 Cleaves, 291, mentions the suspicions of Sheridan's presidential ambitions.

236 "If there is anything . . ." Ibid., 297. Cleaves says Thomas refused one entreaty to run for office by describing himself as "being but a mere tyro in the science of government."

236 McKinney, 467, writes of the command changes following Grant's election.

236 Ibid., 468–469, regarding Thomas's reaction to a Schofield appointment and his meeting with Halleck.

236 "should not be . . ." Cleaves, 302.

237 "I knew it . . ." McKinney, 469.

237 Bobrick, 288, says both Generals David S. Stanley and Thomas Wood warned Thomas of Schofield, and that Stanley later would write that Schofield's "fear of politicians made him play a very low, mean part in many things."

237 McKinney, 54–55, cites 1852 correspondence between West Point and the army's chief engineer and writes of the inquiry as well as of Schofield's admitted look through the files. Groom, *SOG*, 235, cites some of Schofield's remarks, which are contained fully in his memoirs, *Forty-Six Years in the Army* (Norman, Okla., 1998), 241–242. Schofield, whose family had moved to Illinois, cites Douglas, 12.

238 "were equally outspoken . . ." Cleaves, 258.

238 "upon this notable . . ." Groom, 234.

238 "the Washington . . ." Cleaves, 259.

239 "Many officers here . . ." Ibid.

239 Cleaves, 257–260, offers a clear account of events at Nashville, using James Wilson's memoirs, T. B. Van Horne's biography, *Major General George H. Thomas* (New York, 1882), and General Steedman's revelations to Thomas, citing newspaper clippings from the *Cincinnati Enquirer*. A more detailed account is Stanley Horn's, 43–62. McKinney, 403, adds that Schofield felt insufficiently congratulated by Thomas after returning from Franklin, in contrast to the hug given A. J. Smith upon his arrival from Missouri. Schofield, *FSY*, 226, also mentions Thomas's "undemonstrative" nature. Groom, 234, points out that while urging on Thomas, Grant with 100,000 men had been sitting outside Petersburg, Virginia, for six months "mostly looking" at Lee's 50,000 troops inside the city.

239 "Why does he . . ." Cleaves, 260.

239 "to attack Hood . . ." Schofield, 237–238.

240 Horn, 49–50, mentions the river warning message, which Grant cited in telling Halleck on December 9 to order Thomas's relief. But Horn says there was no record of such a message in the official archives while there is a record of the order for Thomas's relief. Sword, *CLH*, 292, writes of the alleged message of intrigue that could not be found in postwar files. He says the Thomas aide so mentioned was Captain Sanford Kellogg, a Thomas nephew by marriage (McKinney, 492), who spoke of the missing message in an 1881 letter. The unflattering telegrams of Grant to Thomas, however, survived to reappear in Grant's memoirs, 656–660.

240 Barbara W. Tuchman, *The Guns of August* (New York, 1962), 20–27, writes of Schlieffen's plan in detail, which derived from Hannibal's double-flanking plan at Cannae. Whether Schlieffen studied Thomas and Thomas studied Hannibal, nothing was particularly original about it even in Hannibal's day. It's just that Thomas's smaller attack—unlike that of the Germans—overwhelmingly succeeded. Schlieffen's last words in 1913, writes Tuchman, were: "It must come to a fight. Only make the right wing strong."

240 Groom, 258, writes of Thomas's impatience with Schofield's reluctance to go forward at Nashville, where Thomas said to him, after others had begun launching a final attack, "General Smith is attacking without waiting for you. Please advance your entire line."

240 Cleaves, 304–305, discusses the 1870 letter claiming Franklin had settled the Battle of Nashville (see also Schofield, 185). So does Bobrick, 329–330, saying the author was Jacob Cox. Hirshson, *TWT*, 343, writes of the letter and mentions another factor in Schofield's disfavor: that he had been offered the chance by Sherman to join the march to the sea but instead chose to aid Thomas in Tennessee as it offered greater opportunity for glory.

241 Cleaves, 252, writes that General Stanley, wounded at Franklin, would excoriate Schofield for having stationed himself to the rear with a reserve unit and safely out of the way during the battle. But Groom, 280–281, says that in his memoirs Stanley excoriated nearly all his fellow generals at Franklin.

241 Cleaves, 305–306, McKinney, 466–474, and Bobrick, 330–332, write of the circumstances of Thomas's death. His wife, says McKinney, 472, stayed on in San Francisco to settle affairs and did not arrive in New York until six days after the military funeral. Not said is whether she also wished to avoid certain generals past and present. Frances Thomas died in 1889.

242 "No one who . . ." Cleaves, 305.

242 "Robbing a grave . . ." Steedman's remarks are from the June 22, 1881, *New York Times*. Schofield, 290–292, explains his battle suggestions, which involved shifting the position of his Twenty-third Corps. Schofield, in reserve, suffered light casualties in the two-day battle and wasn't a factor. What induced Steedman's remarks exactly at this time is not known, unless the 1870 letter somehow resurfaced or Schofield made his claims publicly elsewhere. Schofield, though, was in Europe when Steedman's letter appeared. Steedman, says Groom, became Toledo's police chief.

243 "I will say . . ." Bobrick, 332.

243 Schofield, 293–295, reprints his letter to Grant and Grant's reply.

243 "I believe it must . . ." Ibid., 242.

243 Groom, 279, has a brief postwar biography of Schofield. So does Schofield, not brief.

Chapter 11: Libbie's Husband

245 Utley, *Cavalier in Buckskin*; Shirley A. Leckie, *Elizabeth Bacon Custer and the Making of a Myth* (Norman, Okla.,1993); and Merington, *The Custer Story*, are primary sources used in this account. Evan S. Connell, *Son of the Morning Star*

(New York, 1984), and, of course, Elizabeth B. Custer's *Boots and Saddles, or Life in Dakota with General Custer* (Norman, Okla., 1961) also were helpful. Merington, from whom many excerpts of Custer letters are drawn, was Libbie's friend and literary executrix. Both Utley and Leckie warn that Custer researchers have found that Merington altered and expurgated letters, but to what extent is unknown. She seems actually to have purged them of certain intimacies—that is, cleaned them up. Still, the versions selected and reprinted here carry both the flavor of Libbie's voice from her own books and that of Custer's from other public sources, and may suffer only from slightly more subtlety.

245 "This morning I . . ." Merington, *TCS*, 89.

245 "I regret the . . ." Ibid., 105.

246 "I suppose some . . ." Ibid., 105–106.

246 "Oh, such a . . ." Ibid., 94.

246 "We arrived here . . ." Ibid., 114.

246 "glad to hear . . ." Leckie, *EBC*, 65.

246 "Don't expose yourself . . ." Merington, 144.

246 "All the women . . ." Utley, *CIB*, 110, who also mentions, on 107, Custer's "little papoose" remark.

248 "I am delighted . . ." Utley, 108.

248 Utley, 13–17, writes of Custer's misspent youth both before and during his time at West Point. Connell, *SMS*, 40, writes of Marcus Reno's record at West Point, though Reno did finish better than Custer: twentieth in a class of thirty-eight. Connell, 107–108, also lists some of the rules infractions committed by Cadet Custer.

249 Utley, 105, mentions Custer's frustrated attempt to return to the Academy in 1869 as commandant.

249 "wore long flowing . . ." Hirshson, *The White Tecumseh*, 90.

249 Utley, 18–19, writes of Custer and McClellan.

249 "My confidence in balloons . . ." Connell, 109–110.

250 Utley, 18, mentions Custer's "protracted revel" and his pledge to go dry. Merington, 114 and 231, records Custer's letters to Libbie forsaking oaths (1864) and gambling (1869). Leckie, 36, says he never kept the gambling promise.

250 Merington, 48–51, and Utley, 19, write of Custer, Libbie, and the obstacle judge. In telling her father, says Merington, 51, that she will not cause him any more trouble about Custer, Libbie wrote in 1862: "You have never been a girl, Father, and you cannot tell how hard a trial this was for me."

250 "There are not . . ." Utley, 20.

250 Utley, 21–24, writes of Custer's promotion and his conduct at Gettysburg, which thwarted an attack by Jeb Stuart.

251 "This officer . . ." Foote, *The Civil War*, vol. II, 910.

251 Utley, 24–25.

251 Merington, 60, notes newspapers' adulation of "The Boy General."

251 Merington, 110–111, writes of Custer's jealousy of James Wilson, quoting from a letter from Custer to Libbie, July 1, 1864.

251 Connell, 117, writes of the exchange of prisoner executions. Foote, *TCW*, vol. III, 563–572 and 629, has a good account of the war in the Shenandoah Valley. Utley, 28–29, writes of Stuart's death and, with Connell, 118, of Custer and Thomas Rosser.

252 Utley, 28–33, further discusses the campaign to Appomattox and Tom Custer's valor. Leckie, 67–68, also writes of Appomattox and of Libbie's nights in the Davis's beds.

252 "Permit me to say . . ." Leckie, 67.

252 Leckie, 10–37, writes of Libbie's pre-Custer girlhood and of her wedding. Connell, 114–115, also describes Custer's wedding suit as having "lightning-rod pants."

253 Merington, 91, reprints Libbie's April 1864 letter about meeting Lincoln, which includes her remark of Mary Lincoln being "short, squatty, and plain."

253 Utley, 33–34, writes of "Custer's luck" regarding personal war wounds. Leckie, 37, mentions the judge and the Bible.

253 Leckie, 4, describes the River Raisin massacre of 1813. Stephen E. Ambrose, *Undaunted Courage: Meriwether Lewis, Thomas Jefferson, and the Opening of the American West* (New York, 1996), 154, notes Jefferson's direct order to Lewis regarding the Sioux that he might encounter: "On that nation we wish most particularly to make a favorable impression."

253 Bernard DeVoto, *Across the Wide Missouri* (Boston, 1947), 224. Francis Parkman's *The Oregon Trail* (Garden City, N.Y., 1946), originally published in 1849, is a classic study of the West and the Sioux during this prewar period. The 1946 Doubleday edition has the advantage of illustrations by Thomas Hart Benton.

254 Foote, vol. III, 725–726, writes of both Minnesota and Sand Creek. Connell, 252, has the death figure in Minnesota of 644 whites.

254 Leckie, 70–72, and Utley, 37, write of Custer's problems with his new charges in Louisiana. Merington, 168–169, reprints some of the advice and complaints of Custer and Libbie forwarded to Father Bacon in Michigan.

255 "Every enlisted man . . ." Merington, 172.

256 "He did not stop . . ." Utley, 38.

256 Leckie, 73–78, writing of the nineteen-day march from Alexandria, Louisiana, to Hempstead, Texas, says that Libbie was shocked to look in a mirror to find that the sun "had tanned her face and streaked her hair"—an affliction millions of American women would dauntlessly invite in the following century.

256 "in the most . . ." Ibid., 77.

256 "hated us . . ." Ibid., 78.

256 Ibid., 80–86, on Custer's pay and journey east.

257 "I have not seen . . ." Utley, 39.

257 Ibid., 40–43, on the creation of the U.S. Seventh Cavalry and Fort Riley posting.

257 Ibid., 44–47, about the makeup of the Seventh.

258 Merington, 204–208, reprints Custer's 1867 notes from his daybook on his meandering pursuit of Indians, where he writes of the gory suicide of "Col. Cooper" (actually Major Wyckliffe Cooper) as "another of rum's victims," as well as of troop desertions and of bread baked in 1860. Leckie, 91, writes of Benteen and Wilson.

258 Utley, 115, mentions the "royal family."

258 Leckie, 93–105, writes of the massacre that launched the Custer mission; Custer and his renewed pledge of faithfulness; the perception of Custer as a "petty tyrant"; Custer's unauthorized return; and Custer's encounter with the unfortunate Lieutenant Weir. Utley, 47–53, has a more concise account of Custer's 1867 march.

258 "the most complete . . ." Utley, 50.

259 Utley, 107–108, quotes Benteen and discusses the likelihood of mutual adulteries. Utley concludes: "Whatever dalliances had occurred, or still occurred, the two had worked out an accommodation that preserved one of history's most intimate and glowing love matches." Leckie, 102–103, speculates on jealousy. Merington, 101, has Libbie's full quote from a June 1864 letter: "I know, my dear, that tho I have a pretty face it is my husband's reputation brings me so much attention."

259 "rendered her . . ." Utley, 107.

259 "beg for his . . ." Ibid., 108.

259 Ibid., 53–54, and Leckie, 106–107, write of the court-martial. Leckie adds that Lieutenant Weir assisted the Custers by giving favorable testimony.

260 "nothing but a . . ." Leckie, 107.

260 Utley, 58–59 and 112–113, and Leckie, 107–108, write of the efforts to move the Indians out of the path of Manifest Destiny and of the 1868 raid.

261 "his hair cut . . ." Utley, 61, quoting Captain Albert Barnitz.

261 I rely on Utley's vigorous account, 59–71, for details of Custer's attack on the Washita River village and events leading to it. Leckie, 113, says that Custer described the finding of the bodies of Elliott and his men, as well as that of the two white captives, in a letter to Libbie.

262 Leckie, 121–136, describes buffalo, Custer's time in the East, relations with Libbie, and the regiment's transfer to duties in the South. Utley, 54, passes on Benteen's disparaging description of Custer's memoirs.

262 "laughin' and jokin' . . ." Leckie, 133.

262 Utley, 112–115, describes the emergence of the Northern Pacific and the impact upon the Sioux and Cheyenne as well as the attraction of Sitting Bull to the discontented tribes. Both Utley and Leckie, 154, observe that Generals Sherman and Sheridan supported the Northern Pacific request for army protection, as the completion of a transcontinental railroad through Sioux territory was the fastest way to resolve the "Indian problem" on the Northern Plains by bringing white settlements and destruction of the buffalo.

262 "The Indians will be . . ." Utley, 112.

263 Ibid., 115–123, on the account of Custer's 1873 expedition along the Yellowstone.

263 "I have seen enough . . ." Connell, 234. David Stanley's view of General Schofield is mentioned in Chapter 10 footnotes.

264 Leckie, 162–163, writes of the Northern Pacific's promotional tracts, which described the arid countryside in glowing terms (skeptics called the land "Jay Cooke's Banana Belt"), and of William Hazen's disputations. Hazen believed that Dakota territory land along the railroad would never "in our day and generation, sell for one penny an acre, except through fraud and ignorance."

264 Utley, 124–126, also covers the railroad's claims as well as the Custer-Hazen clash and the Northern Pacific's gratitude to Custer. Cozzens, *No Better Place to Die*, writes of Hazen's courage at Stones River. Patrick, Owsley, Chitwood, and Nixon, *The American People*, vol. II, 28–29, give further background on the Northern Pacific's land grant, its reach, and its up-and-down fortunes. The railroad would resume its westward march under Frederick Billings, but he would be deposed by Henry Villard, owner of the Oregon Railroad and Navigation Company. When completed in 1883, the Northern Pacific was the third transcontinental system with more than 2,500 miles of main lines.

265 Utley, 132–140, writes of the Black Hills expedition of 1874. Both Utley and Leckie, 165, mention that the Sioux had wrested the Black Hills from the Kiowa almost a century earlier.

265 "We have discovered . . ." Utley, 136.

266 Ibid., 140–147, on the return survey to the Black Hills and events surrounding it, and negotiations with the Sioux. McFeely, *Grant*, 437–438, discusses Sherman's views and the Grant-Sheridan meeting. Sheridan, in an 1875 letter to General Alfred Terry, would advise that Grant "decided that while the orders heretofore issued forbidding the occupation of the Black Hills country, by miners, should not be rescinded, still no further resistance by the military should be made to the miners going in. . . ."

267 "Without the least warning . . ." Elizabeth Custer, *BAS*, 56–57.

268 Ibid., 10–14. Libbie writes of the snowstorm and of having opened the door to the "neigh of a distressed horse, almost human in its appeal." The sight of "the strange, wild eyes of the horse, peering in for help, haunted me long afterwards."

268 Ibid., 5–6, on Dakota as Lapland and anxieties over living there.

268 Ibid., 126–129 and 137–142, on bleak conditions at Fort Lincoln, the Indian burial tree, and the depredations of grasshoppers and Indians.

268 Ibid., 128-129, on the settler's murder.

269 "Surely you do not . . ." Merington, 284.

269 "The chiefs were . . ." Libbie, 188–189.

269 Utley, 152–163, discusses the Indian trading post scandal as well as Custer's troubles with Grant. McFeely, *Grant*, 428, looks at William Belknap and kickbacks from a trading post at Fort Sill, Oklahoma. Belknap, he writes, "won the raging hatred of General George A. Custer, who, in a manner not untypical of many army officers, saw nothing incongruous in being at once ruthlessly lethal in fighting the Indians and outspokenly critical of those who swindled them." Merington, 286, says the trading-post scandal did work to the advantage of Indians, as the "War Department was selling the traderships to men who sold weapons— the newest and best—to the hostiles, weapons that would be turned against the servicemen legitimately employed by the War Department." In this she reflects Libbie, 220, who comments on seeing "on a steamer touching at our landing its freight of Springfield rifles piled up on the decks en route for the Indians up the river. There was unquestionable proof that they came into the trading posts far above us and bought them. . . ."

270 "As the sun broke . . ." Libbie, 218.

271 Utley, 165–193, concisely provides the details of Custer's Last Stand.

271 "I guess we'll get . . ." Utley, 181.

272 Leckie, 198, says 263 officers and men were killed. Connell, 383, pointing out various estimates, says the total number is usually fixed at about 265, adding that 212 bodies were counted among those with Custer, including Custer, at interment, but several troopers were missing. Also, some who survived the immediate battle died later from their wounds. Utley, 4, mentions the figure of 210 in the five companies under Custer, including Custer. Utley, 188, also gives the number for Reno's battlefield dead.

272 "At that very hour . . ." Libbie, 222.

272 Leckie, 246–247, writes of Sitting Bull and Buffalo Bill—the latter winning Libbie's sanction of his Wild West Show's performance of the "last stand." Leckie, 259–260, also writes of the death of Sitting Bull—as does Connell, 392—and the clash at Wounded Knee. Utley, 203–205, writes of the demands for the Sioux to turn over the Black Hills and of Nelson Miles's winter campaign. Utley, citing how alike Custer and Miles were, speculates that—had he lived—Custer might also have been as successful.

273 "They tell me . . ." Connell, 232.

273 Leckie, 210–211, writes of the unfortunate Thomas Weir.

273 Connell, 42–48, and Leckie, 221–230 and 310, track the post-Custer misadventures of Marcus Reno.

274 Connell, 33–40, writes of Benteen. Among the captain's afflictions were four children who died of spinal meningitis. Leckie, 230, mentions Libbie's refusal to see Benteen.

274 Leckie, 283 and 298, on John Burkman; and 224 on Dandy.

274 Connell, 296–298, writes of the noble Comanche.

275 Leckie, 176, 207–219, and 236–306, recounts Elizabeth Custer's financial problems as well as the rest of her full life, detailed herein.

275 Cashin, *First Lady of the Confederacy*, 270, on Libbie's opinion of Winnie. Winnie Davis could never catch a break.

276 "a cross for me . . ." Leckie, 226.

277 "I regard Custer's Massacre . . ." Utley, 6.

277 "whose right of way . . ." Connell, 325.

BIBLIOGRAPHY

Adams, Henry, *The Education of Henry Adams* (Modern Library/Random House, New York, 1931)

Ambrose, Stephen E., *Undaunted Courage: Meriwether Lewis, Thomas Jefferson, and the Opening of the American West* (Simon & Schuster, New York, 1996)

Ash, Stephen V., *Middle Tennessee Society Transformed, 1860–1870: War and Peace in the Upper South* (Louisiana State University Press, Baton Rouge, 1988)

Baker, Jean H., *Mary Todd Lincoln: A Biography* (W. W. Norton, New York, 1987)

Barrett, John G., *Sherman's March Through the Carolinas* (University of North Carolina Press, Chapel Hill, 1956)

Berry, Stephen, *House of Abraham: Lincoln and the Todds, a Family Divided by War* (Houghton Mifflin, Boston/New York, 2007)

Bobrick, Benson, *Master of War: The Life of General George H. Thomas* (Simon & Schuster, New York, 2009)

Budiansky, Stephen, *The Bloody Shirt: Terror After Appomattox* (Viking, New York, 2008)

Buell, Thomas B., *The Warrior Generals: Combat Leadership in the Civil War* (Crown, New York, 1997)

Bushong, Millard K., *Old Jube* (Carr Publishing, Boyce, Va., 1955)

Campbell, Mary and Gordon, *The Pen, Not the Sword* (Aurora Publishers, Nashville, Tenn., and London, 1970)

Carney, Tom, *Portraits in Time: Stories of Huntsville and Madison County* (Old Huntsville, Huntsville, Ala., 1998)

Carse, Robert, *Blockade: The Civil War at Sea* (Rinehart & Co., New York, 1958)

Cash, W. J., *The Mind of the South* (Alfred A. Knopf, New York, 1941)

Cashin, Joan, *First Lady of the Confederacy: Varina Davis's Civil War* (Belknap Press of Harvard University Press, Cambridge, Mass., 2006)

Chesnut, Mary Boykin, *Two Novels by Mary Chesnut* (University Press of Virginia, Charlottesville, 2002), Elisabeth Muhlenfeld, editor

Chute, William J., *The American Scene: 1860 to the Present* (Bantam Books, New York, 1966)

Clay-Clopton, Virginia, *A Belle of the Fifties: Memoirs of Mrs. Clay of Alabama* (Doubleday, Page, New York, ed. Ada Sterling, 1905/Da Capo Press, New York, 1969)

Cleaves, Freeman, *Rock of Chickamauga: The Life of General George H. Thomas* (University of Oklahoma Press, Norman, 1948)

Connell, Evan S., *Son of the Morning Star* (Promontory Press, New York, 1984)

Connelly, Thomas Lawrence, *Army of the Heartland: The Army of Tennessee, 1861–1862* (Louisiana State University Press, Baton Rouge, 1967)

Connelly, Thomas Lawrence, *Autumn of Glory: The Army of Tennessee, 1862–1865* (Louisiana State University Press, Baton Rouge, 1971)

Connelly, Thomas Lawrence, *The Marble Man: Robert E. Lee and His Image in American Society* (Alfred A. Knopf, New York, 1978)

Connelly, Thomas L., and Barbara L. Bellows, *God and General Longstreet: The Lost Cause and the Southern Mind* (Louisiana State University Press, Baton Rouge, 1982)

Coulter, E. Merton, *William G. Brownlow: Fighting Parson of the Southern Highlands* (University of North Carolina Press, Chapel Hill, 1937/University of Tennessee Press, Knoxville, 1971)

Cozzens, Peter, *No Better Place to Die: The Battle of Stones River* (University of Illinois Press, Urbana, 1990)

Cozzens, Peter, *The Darkest Days of the War: The Battles of Iuka and Corinth* (University of North Carolina Press, Chapel Hill, 1997)

Custer, Elizabeth B., *Boots and Saddles, or Life in Dakota with General Custer* (University of Oklahoma Press, Norman, 1961)

Davis, Burke, *Sherman's March* (Random House, New York, 1980)

Davis, William, *Jefferson Davis: The Man and His Hour* (HarperCollins, New York, 1991)

Donald, David Herbert, *Lincoln* (Simon & Schuster, New York, 1995)

Dowdey, Clifford, *Lee* (Crown, New York, 1965)

DeVoto, Bernard, *Across the Wide Missouri* (Houghton Mifflin, Boston, 1947)

Durham, Walter T., *Reluctant Partners: Nashville and the Union* (Tennessee Historical Society/Williams Printing Co., Nashville, Tenn., 1987)

Durkin, Rev. Joseph T., S.J., *Father Tom* (Farrar, Straus & Cudahy, New York, 1959)

Dyer, John P., *The Gallant Hood* (Konecky & Konecky, New York, 1993/Bobbs-Merrill, Indianapolis, 1950)

Emerson, Jason, *The Madness of Mary Lincoln* (Southern Illinois University Press, Carbondale, 2007)

Faust, Drew Gilpin, *Southern Stories: Slaveholders in Peace and War* (University of Missouri Press, Columbia, 1992)

Fishwick, Marshall W., *Lee After the War* (Dodd, Mead, New York, 1963)

Flood, Charles Bracelen, *Lee: The Last Years* (Houghton Mifflin, Boston, 1981)

Foner, Eric, *Reconstruction: America's Unfinished Revolution, 1863–1877* (Harper & Row, New York, 1988)

Foote, Shelby, *The Civil War: A Narrative* (Vintage Books, New York, 1986)

Fraser, Walter J., Jr., and Winfred B. Moore, Jr., editors, *From the Old South to the New: Essays on the Transitional South* (Greenwood Press, Westport, Conn., 1981)

Freehling, William W., *The Road to Disunion: Secessionists at Bay, 1776–1854* (Oxford University Press, New York, 1990)

Freeman, Douglas Southall, *R. E. Lee: A Biography* (Charles Scribner's Sons, New York, 1935)

Gallagher, Gary W., editor, *The Third Day at Gettysburg and Beyond* (University of North Carolina Press, Chapel Hill, 1994)

Gallagher, Gary W., and Joseph T. Glatthaar, *Leaders of the Lost Cause: New Perspectives on the Confederate High Command* (Stackpole Books, Mechanicsburg, Pa., 2004)

Gillette, William, *Retreat from Reconstruction, 1869–1879* (Louisiana State University Press, Baton Rouge, 1979)

Goldhurst, Richard, *Many Are the Hearts* (Reader's Digest Press, New York, 1975)

Govan, Gilbert G., and James W. Livingood, *A Different Valor: The Story of General Joseph E. Johnston, C.S.A.* (Bobbs-Merrill, Indianapolis, 1956)

Grant, Ulysses S., *Personal Memoirs of U.S. Grant* (Library of America, New York, 1990)

Groom, Winston, *Shrouds of Glory: From Atlanta to Nashville: The Last Great Campaign of the Civil War* (Atlantic Monthly Press, New York, 1995)

Hague, William, *William Wilberforce: The Life of the Great Anti-slave Campaigner* (Harcourt, Orlando, Fla., 2007)

Henry, Robert Selph, editor, *As They Saw Forrest* (McCowat-Mercer Press, Jackson, Tenn., 1956)

Henry, Robert Selph, *First with the Most—Gen. Nathan Bedford Forrest* (Bobbs-Merrill, Indianapolis, 1944 / Mallard Press, New York, 1991)

Hirshson, Stanley P., *The White Tecumseh: A Biography of General William T. Sherman* (John Wiley & Sons, New York, 1997)

Hood, John Bell, *Advance and Retreat: Personal Experiences in the United States and Confederate States Armies* (Indiana University Press, Bloomington, 1959)

Horn, Stanley F., *The Decisive Battle of Nashville* (Louisiana State University Press, Baton Rouge, 1956)

Hughes, Nathaniel Cheairs, Jr., and Roy Stonesifer, Jr., *The Life and Wars of Gideon J. Pillow* (University of North Carolina Press, Chapel Hill, 1993)

Hughes, Nathaniel Cheairs, Jr., with Connie Walton Moretti and James Michael Browne, *Brigadier General Tyree H. Bell, C.S.A.: Forrest's Fighting Lieutenant* (University of Tennessee Press, Knoxville, 2004)

Hurst, Jack, *Nathan Bedford Forrest: A Biography* (Alfred A. Knopf, New York, 1993)

Hurst, Jack, *Men of Fire* (Basic Books, New York, 2007)

Kennan, George F., *Memoirs, 1925–1950* (Atlantic Monthly Press / Little, Brown, Boston, 1967)

Kibler, James Everett, *Our Father's Fields: A Southern Story* (University of South Carolina Press, Columbia, 1998)

Leckie, Shirley A., *Elizabeth Bacon Custer and the Making of a Myth* (University of Oklahoma Press, Norman, 1993)

Lewis, Lloyd, *Sherman: Fighting Prophet* (Harcourt, Brace, New York, 1932)

Linton, Calvin D., *The Bicentennial Almanac* (Thomas Nelson, Nashville, Tenn., 1975)

Lytle, Andrew Nelson, *Bedford Forrest and His Critter Company* (J. S. Sanders, Nashville, Tenn., 1992)

Marszalek, John F., *Sherman: A Soldier's Passion for Order* (Free Press, New York, 1993)

McFeely, William S., *Grant: A Biography* (W. W. Norton, New York, 1981)

McKinney, Francis F., *Education in Violence: The Life of George H. Thomas and the History of the Army of the Cumberland* (Francis F. McKinney, 1961/Americana House, Chicago, 1991)

McMurry, Richard M., *John Bell Hood and the War for Southern Independence* (University Press of Kentucky, Lexington, 1982)

McMurry, Richard M., *Two Great Rebel Armies: An Essay in Confederate Military History* (University of North Carolina Press, Chapel Hill, 1989)

McMurry, Richard M., *Atlanta 1864: Last Chance for the Confederacy* (University of Nebraska Press, Lincoln, 2000)

Merington, Marguerite, editor, *The Custer Story: The Life and Intimate Letters of General Custer and His Wife Elizabeth* (Devin-Adair, New York, 1950)

Merrill, James M., *William Tecumseh Sherman* (Rand McNally, Chicago, 1971)

Morgan, Sarah, *The Civil War Diary of Sarah Morgan*, edited by Charles East (University of Georgia Press, Athens, 1991; originally *A Confederate Girl's Diary*, printed 1913)

Muhlenfeld, Elisabeth, *Mary Boykin Chesnut* (Louisiana State University Press, Baton Rouge, 1981)

Newton, Stephen H., *Joseph E. Johnston and the Defense of Richmond* (University Press of Kansas, Lawrence, 1998)

Nunn, W. C., editor, *Ten Texans in Gray* (Hill Junior College Press, Hillsboro, Tex., 1968)

Osborne, Charles C., *Jubal: The Life and Times of Jubal A. Early, CSA* (Algonquin Books, Chapel Hill, N.C., 1992)

Owsley, Frank L., *Plain Folk of the Old South* (Louisiana State University Press, Baton Rouge, 1949/1977)

Parkman, Francis, *The Oregon Trail* (Doubleday, Garden City, N.Y., 1946)

Patrick, Rembert W., Frank L. Owsley, Oliver P. Chitwood, and H. C. Nixon, *The American People: A History, Volume II* (D. Van Nostrand, Princeton, N.J., 1962)

Pryor, Elizabeth Brown, *Reading the Man: A Portrait of Robert E. Lee Through His Private Letters* (Viking Penguin, New York, 2007)

Remini, Robert, *Andrew Jackson* (Twayne Publishers, New York, 1966/Harper & Row, New York, 1969)

Reynolds, David S., *Waking Giant* (HarperCollins Publishers, New York, 2008)

Robertson, James I., Jr., *Tenting Tonight: The Soldier's Life* (Time Life Education, Alexandria, Va., 1984).

Ross, Ishbel, *The President's Wife: Mary Todd Lincoln* (G. P. Putnam's Sons, New York, 1973)

Schofield, John M., *Forty-six Years in the Army* (University of Oklahoma Press, Norman, 1998)

Schreiner, Samuel A., Jr., *The Trials of Mrs. Lincoln* (Donald I. Fine, New York, 1987)

Seip, Terry L., *The South Returns to Congress* (Louisiana State University Press, Baton Rouge, 1983)

Sherman, William T., *Memoirs of General W. T. Sherman* (Library of America, New York, 1990)

Simkins, Francis Butler, and Robert Hilliard Woody, *South Carolina During Reconstruction* (University of North Carolina Press, Chapel Hill, 1932/1966)

Simpson, Brooks, *The Reconstruction Presidents* (University Press of Kansas, Lawrence, 1998)

Stone, Irving, *Love Is Eternal* (Doubleday, New York /Reader Digest Association, Pleasantville, N.Y., Autumn 1954)

Strode, Hudson, *Jefferson Davis: Tragic Hero* (Harcourt, Brace & World, New York, 1964)

Strode, Hudson, *Jefferson Davis: Private Letters, 1823–1899* (Harcourt, Brace & World, New York, 1966)

Sword, Wiley, *The Confederacy's Last Hurrah: Spring Hill, Franklin, and Nashville* (University Press of Kansas, Lawrence/HarperCollins, New York, 1992)

Symonds, Craig L., *Joseph E. Johnston: A Civil War Biography* (W. W. Norton, New York, 1992)

Symonds, Craig L., *Stonewall of the West: Patrick Cleburne and the Civil War* (University Press of Kansas, Lawrence, 1997)

Taylor, Richard, *Destruction and Reconstruction* (J. S. Sanders, Nashville, Tenn., 1998; D. Appleton & Co., 1879)

Thomas, Emory M., *The Confederate State of Richmond: A Biography of the Capital* (University of Texas Press, Austin, 1971)

Thurber, James, *The Thurber Carnival* (Modern Library/Random House, New-York, 1957)

Tripp, C. A., *The Intimate World of Abraham Lincoln* (Free Press, New York, 2005)

Tuchman, Barbara W., *The Guns of August* (Macmillan, New York, 1962)

Twain, Mark, *Life on the Mississippi* (Bantam Books, New York, 1963).

Urban, Mark, *Fusiliers: The Saga of a British Redcoat Regiment in the American Revolution* (Walker & Co., New York, 2007)

Utley, Robert M., *Cavalier in Buckskin: George Armstrong Custer and the Western Military Frontier* (University of Oklahoma Press, Norman, 1988)

Watkins, Sam R., *'Co. Aytch': A Side Show of the Big Show* (original edition Nashville, Tenn., 1882/Broadfoot Publishing Co., Wilmington, N.C., 1994)

West, Richard S., Jr., *Gideon Welles* (Bobbs-Merrill, New York, 1943)

Wheeler, Richard, *The Siege of Vicksburg* (Thomas Y. Crowell, 1978/HarperCollins, New York, 1991)

Whitman, Walt, *Leaves of Grass* (Random House, New York, 1944)

Wiley, Bell Irvin, *Confederate Women* (Greenwood Press, Westport, Conn., 1975)

Wills, Brian Steel, *A Battle from the Start: The Life of Nathan Bedford Forrest* (HarperCollins, New York, 1992)

Wilson, Edmund, *Patriotic Gore* (Oxford University Press, New York, 1962)

Woodward, C. Vann, *The Burden of Southern History* (Louisiana State University Press, 1960)

Woodward, C. Vann, *Mary Chesnut's Civil War* (Yale University Press, New Haven, 1981)

Woodward, C. Vann, and Elisabeth Muhlenfeld, *The Private Mary Chesnut: The Unpublished Civil War Diaries* (Oxford University Press, New York, 1984)

INDEX

A NOTE ON THE AUTHOR

David Hardin is a veteran newspaperman who grew up on the battlefield of Nashville, Tennessee. He has been a writer and editor at newspapers across the South, including those in Nashville; Raleigh; Savannah; Miami; Tampa; Jackson, Mississippi; and Huntsville, Alabama. Among his national journalism awards is a Pulitzer Prize. He is married with two daughters and lives in the Huntsville area.